MURDER WITHOUT BORDERS

TERRY GOULD

MURDER WITHOUT BORDERS

**DYING FOR THE STORY
IN THE WORLD'S
MOST DANGEROUS PLACES**

RANDOM HOUSE CANADA

www.randomhouse.ca

Random House Canada and colophon are trademarks.

LIBRARY AND ARCHIVES CANADA CATALOGUING IN PUBLICATION

Gould, Terry, 1949–

Murder without borders : dying for the story in the world's most dangerous places / Terry Gould.

ISBN 978-0-679-31470-7

1. Journalists — Biography. 2. Journalists — Crimes against. I. Title.

PN4820.G69 2008   070.92'2   C2006-905867-9

Design by CS Richardson

Printed and bound in the United States of America

2   4   6   8   9   7   5   3   1

To my daughter, Elisha

CONTENTS

"I am not interested in why man commits evil;
I want to know why he does good."

VACLAV HAVEL

THE PSYCHOLOGY OF SACRIFICE

EFRAÍN VARELA KNEW HE WOULD BE MURDERED. He even knew the options his assassins would consider. "If they kill me in the town, they are going to shoot me," he told his fellow journalists two weeks before his death. "If they take me in the rural area, I am going to be tortured first." Varela specialized in exposing paramilitary atrocities and corrupt politicians in Arauca, a remote town on Colombia's lawless plains. Over the years he'd refused bribes and survived other assassination attempts. Then, in June 2002, a hair's-breadth escape from kidnappers convinced him his moment was near. Against the advice of his colleagues, he continued his exposés, until, as he'd predicted, he was seized in the countryside, tortured and shot.

When most people think of journalists dying for a story, they picture war correspondents caught in a cross fire, but Varela's death is a more typical case. Almost three-quarters of the more than 720 journalists who have died in the line of duty since 1992 have been targeted and murdered. The majority of the fallen—more than 85 percent—have been local journalists. Almost all the masterminds of these murders—95 percent—have escaped punishment.

I first encountered this plague of murder-with-impunity while researching a book in the Philippines between 2000 and 2003. Fourteen journalists were assassinated outside Manila during that period and not one of their killers was brought to justice. Philippine press freedom advocates complained to the nation's president that many of the slain had been publicly threatened by politicians and businessmen. The Philippine Center for Investigative Journalism predicted worse to come if the perpetrators were not prosecuted. None were, and in 2004 another eight journalists were murdered after being warned to stay silent.

The international organizations that attempted to bring world-wide attention to these unpunished killings were the New York–based Committee to Protect Journalists and the Paris-based Reporters sans frontières. To government leaders and the general public they made the case that while the murder of any person was reprehensible, the murder of a journalist for his or her reporting had consequences that went far beyond the individual's death. Journalists stood for the public's right to know what public figures were doing; they exposed criminality when the police refused to pursue it (or were part of it); and they enlightened communities to the activities of illegal armed groups and terrorists in their area. If journalists could be murdered in retaliation for their work and the killers suffered no consequences, then the societies in which these murders occurred would be at the mercy of sociopaths.

In May 2005, the Committee to Protect Journalists issued a bulletin called "Marked for Death," reporting that the top five countries where journalists had been assassinated since 2000 were, in order of most killed, the Philippines, Iraq, Colombia, Bangladesh and Russia. These nations were weighted with problems specific to their regions and cultures, but they bore striking similarities in the systematic way criminality was licensed and protected. The journalists, too, bore striking similarities. Most worked low-paying jobs in remote areas controlled by corrupt officials. In their districts, bribery of journalists was the norm, but a lot of those assassinated were famous for being clean. Many had predicted they would be murdered if they kept at their reporting, but they persisted until the bloody end.

Though both the Committee to Protect Journalists and Reporters sans frontières were scrupulous in their analyses of hundreds of "kill cases," their summaries of the lives of these journalists were necessarily short, rarely more than an account of their last stories and a paragraph or two of professional résumé. Neither organization attempted to guess at what made these individuals tick. Reading the brief descriptions of the victims left me wondering at the source of their bravery. They had dogged the lives of people who were immune to prosecution but hadn't lived in the kinds of secure hotels used by foreign correspondents. Often they went home to bungalows with nothing between them and murder but a quarter-inch plywood door. Indeed, a lot of them had publicly announced their intention of pursuing stories in the face of an ethic of impunity that guaranteed retribution. Were they idealists? Egotists? Devout believers in God? Were they motivated by a macho defiance of thugs? A revolutionary's zeal to help the masses? Perhaps they had become so obsessed with a great story that they were blind to its consequences? Or were their lives so personally buffeted by bandits and death squads that they felt that sacrificing themselves was the price that had to be paid to get the story out?

In the fall of 2005, I chose representative cases in the five most murderous countries and set out to visit their hometowns, interview their families, friends and colleagues, and try to understand their personal motivations. I had two questions in mind:

What makes a poor, small-town reporter stay on a story even though he has been threatened with certain death and offered handsome rewards if he looks the other way?

What is it that allows entire societies to function like criminal enterprises, where truth tellers are publicly killed and no charges are brought against the public figures who ordered the killings?

When journalists are murdered, their lives and work explode, the shards driving deep into the bodies of those closest to them. The people who bore the pieces of these abbreviated lives shared with me the journalists' private and public sides, noble and flawed.

The tales they told revealed that while each risked being murdered according to his or her own unique psychology, these journalists' professional goals were the same. They believed passionately in the principle that the powerful should be prevented from oppressing the weak. While fallible themselves, they went to work each morning with the conviction that the calling of journalism was to defend the defenseless.

The criminals they faced believed in the opposite principle: that the weak offered opportunities for the enrichment of the powerful. Political and religious predators who organize governments permit no investigation into their ultimate motives, and they react violently when journalists reveal that they serve themselves. In one form or another, all of the slain journalists in this book attempted to expose the organized criminal structure that ruled their nations, and came fatally close to its true workings and affiliations.

At its most fundamental level, organized crime is a licensing system. A gangster maneuvers or murders his way to the top and, to ensure he stays there, awards the right to engage in illegal activities in his territory, expecting tribute in return and providing protection from the law. That single mechanism governs all the nations where journalists are being murdered in greatest numbers. It follows the universal modus operandi: the rise to power is always accompanied by the return of favors—but with a twist. In nations run according to the principle of organized crime, favors are returned in the currency of impunity. Thus, political or religious rulers act like gang bosses, appointing their subordinates to bureaucracies with the understanding that while their salaries will be low, their incomes will be high. Corruption, an ad hoc arrangement in some countries, becomes a formal structure in these places. Lawlessness occurs within the law, and the system of organized crime is locked into the business of the nation. In this manner, the people are robbed and the rulers get rich, and anyone who attempts to defy the rulers finds out very quickly how "organized" organized crime can be.

Across borders and across time, this national licensing system is uniform. Understanding that system, and how governments use it to rule billions of people over millions of square miles, is crucial to understanding how much of the world works. It is also crucial to understanding why journalists are murdered with impunity when they attempt to expose it. In societies where everyone knows the truth but is afraid to speak it, laying out the facts can be an invitation to death. Yet for journalists who are motivated to expose destructive forces, publishing the truth is often the only option—an unavoidable step on the road to societal change, and, in some cases, personal redemption.

During my travels for this book, I tried to discover if there was one moment in the lives of these men and women when they realized they were willing to die for their stories. I am still not certain if all of them deliberately chose martyrdom, or merely used the acceptance of death as a psychological tool that was necessary to do their work. Some were so outraged by the criminality of their nations that they pushed their reporting into the realm of contemptuous editorializing, and were murdered shortly thereafter. Many of their colleagues were equally outraged but survived, and they offered me insights into what journalists had to do to increase their longevity when covering very dangerous territory. In one case, I was scheduled to interview a journalist who had defied the odds and, under constant threat of assassination, was still producing work even more defiant than that of her murdered colleagues. Her name was Anna Politkovskaya, and when I landed in Moscow I learned she had been shot to death while I had been in the air on my way to meet her. Politkovskaya is the subject of one of the chapters in this book.

Her murder, and other unexpected events in the countries I visited, turned what I thought would be a one-year project into one that has lasted four years. At all times I followed the advice of local journalists, pursuing the research slowly. At no time did I put myself in the crosshairs of the danger the victims had faced. I did not go into their towns announcing that I was there to incriminate evil-doers, as the murdered journalists had done. I did not conduct a series of murder investigations, but life investigations.

My greatest fear is that I have fallen short of doing justice to my subjects' work. When murdered, all of them were in the midst of exposés that went a long way to explaining the problems of their countries. In turn, the problems of their countries went a long way to explaining the problems of their regions: Latin America, the Pacific Rim, South Asia, Eastern Europe and the Middle East. When put together, the historical and emotional contexts of the journalists' exposés amounted to a compendium of the social and political forces at play in the world today. The *way* the journalists died underscored the power of these forces. I can only hope that I have conveyed at least part of what they taught me.

There is little doubt that in many countries murder works. It is the ultimate form of press censorship, eliminating the immediate problem and often intimidating others into silence. It works best when it occurs with impunity; and in the most murderous places for journalists, impunity reigns. Impunity scars the lives of innocent people, and it scarred the lives of the journalists in this book. And yet they kept at their work, with the full knowledge that their countries were ruled by murderous thugs who lived by the principle of organized crime. I have tried to honor them by bringing their lives and the stories they worked on to light, telling truth to those who would murder truth tellers.

ONE

SMALL TOWN, BIG HELL

Guillermo Bravo Vega, Colombia

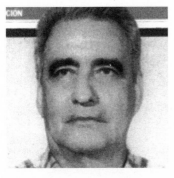

I SAW GUILLERMO BRAVO VEGA for the first time in a photograph his colleagues showed me in a newsroom in Neiva, the Colombian town where he'd declared war on corruption. Under the headline "Journalist Assassinated" was a large-boned handsome man with rugged features, heavy brows and a full head of salt and pepper hair. Everything about him looked rough-cut, from his logger's-sized hands gripping a microphone to his towering height against the backdrop of a cheering crowd. He was standing in a local union hall, announcing his latest exposé, a doubly defiant act in a country where three thousand trade unionists and three dozen journalists had been murdered. Bravo himself had narrowly escaped several assassination attempts, ignored countless death threats and been ordered to leave Neiva six times. Then, on April 28, 2003, after refusing to obey the seventh order, Bravo was murdered in his home. He was sixty-four years old.

Neiva is a heavily garrisoned coffee town in the Upper Magdalena Valley, about 150 miles southeast of Bogotá. Two ranges of the Andes flank the valley, with the eastern slope dropping to a jungle plain. In Bravo's last years, the region from the valley to the plain was the main battleground of Colombia's forty-year civil war, earning Neiva the sobriquet *Pueblo chico, infierno grande*—"Small Town, Big Hell." Marxist guerrillas launched daily raids from a Switzerland-sized territory they controlled in the jungle, and right-wing paramilitaries roamed the valley, assassinating anyone whose left-wing politics offended them.

Bravo, an avowed leftist, blamed the unending conflict on what he called Colombia's feudal injustices. The state of Huila and its capital Neiva, he wrote, were "shrouded by conquistadorean darkness." Land, industry and government were in the grip of a tiny group of families, known as the Opitas Mafia, who were descended from the original Spanish colonizers and who had maintained their overlord status for three hundred years. Putting an end to their crony capitalism and criminal impunity was Bravo's burning mission in life.

For most of his career that mission had been a lonely one. Bravo had quit or been fired from every newspaper he'd worked at, usually leaving in a rage after being forbidden to investigate the paper's advertisers. He eventually began self-publishing a little magazine called *Eco Impacto* and then privately produced a half-hour TV show called *Facts and Figures* (*Hechos y cifras*). Over the years his independent journalism had sent ten people to jail and wreathed him in laurels, including a Simón Bolívar Award—the nation's equivalent of the Pulitzer Prize. Despite his renown, Bravo's journalism had never earned him more than a few hundred dollars a month.

"Guillermo never cared about money, he was obsessed with corruption," a reporter named Diógenes Cadena told me as we sat in the lineup room of *La Nación*, one of the newspapers that had considered Bravo *irrefrenable* (uncontrollable). Cadena had worked for two years on the set of *Facts and Figures*, and said it felt as if he were inside a tornado that was willfully trying to turn the town upside down—or right side up. "Man, he had a temper. If he found out someone was up to something and covering it up, he'd come to the studio, he'd bang the table, he'd scream, 'I'll get that guy!'"

"Self-censoring was not one of his traits," added Carlos Mora, the legal affairs reporter for the paper. "Even if it would save his life, he would not change a word."

Neither man knew precisely when Bravo had become obsessed with exposing corruption, only that he'd been born poor in a nearby rural area and hadn't even become a journalist until he was forty. He'd left Neiva as a relatively young man and been away for a long time, returning in 1981 with his Bolívar Award and an advanced degree in economics. He almost immediately accused the town's reporters of selling flattering coverage to businessmen, which did not endear him to the local press corps. As a result, Bravo was wary of being too frank about himself with other journalists. Then, during his last decade, he'd become part of the news himself: he feuded on television with top officials, took on a multinational oil company and ran for mayor. He also gained a reputation as a lady's man, juggling one legal wife, two common-law wives and a string of glamorous mistresses, along with the needs of five sons. His union allies called him "*Viejo loco y enamorado*"—an old lunatic in love with life—and Mora and Cadena had punnishly nicknamed him *Loco Bravo*.

Bravo received his last death threat on March 8, 2003, when a *sicario*—a hired assassin—paid a visit to the bungalow he shared with his most recent common-law wife. The *sicario* told him to leave town or be killed. Bravo checked the veracity of the threat with his own sources and then told Mora and Cadena, "This time they'll get me." For the first time in his life, he fled to the capital. But after only two weeks in Bogotá, he came home.

A few weeks later he was working alone at night in his bungalow when an intruder surprised him at his desk and shot him dead. The killer simply walked in from the street. Earlier that evening his wife had gone out to work, locking the door behind her, but after she had left the house Bravo got up and opened the door. She'd found him alone at his desk with the door open every night since he'd come back from Bogotá, and had screamed at him for recklessly ignoring the threat. His excuse for such blatant courting of death was always the same: "I wanted the breeze."

In 1998, five years before he was murdered, Bravo celebrated a land-mark issue of *Eco Impacto*. "After 13 years we have reached edition No. 50," he wrote in the lead article. "Many times we have had to confront being kidnapped, assassinated or driven into exile by dark masterminds whom everyone knows but no one will denounce."

In honor of his milestone edition, Bravo offered a summary of the exposés he'd published over the years. Most concerned the theft of public assets by Huila's Opitas Mafia, the members of which, he said, were part of the national fabric. At the time, brazen deals between Colombia's highest public officials and its wealthiest businessmen and criminals were commonplace, the level of cor-ruption profound. In its 1998 Corruption Index, Transparency International gave the nation a dismal rating of 2.2 out of a possi-ble 10, making it the seventh most corrupt country in the world, below Russia and just above Nigeria.

As an economist, Bravo took the long view in explaining his country's bottom-ranked status, tracing Colombia's systemic prob-lems to the sixteenth-century Spanish conquistadors who had crossed the sea in search of El Dorado and seeded the land with their greed and criminality. Bravo used a slang term to describe the economics the conquistadors had practiced: *regalame*. Loosely translated, *regalame* means "give it to me for nothing." The con-querors had slaughtered their way up the Magdalena Valley with *regalame* in their hearts, and their descendants in the Opitas Mafia had been raised on it.

Over the centuries, *regalame* had tainted every strata of Colombian society. In Neiva, for instance, it was acceptable to ask for a meal at a restaurant by saying *"Regalame"*—half-hoping the waiter would take the tip and forget the bill. Judges and bureau-crats offered positive treatment in exchange for some *regalias* ("gifts to the deserving"). Paramilitaries and guerrillas said *"Regalame"* when they shook down politicians or landowners. Narcotraffickers uttered *"Regalame"* when they bid goodbye to a ton of cocaine headed north. And speculators on the coffee market mentioned *regalame* in their prayers for a bonanza (another Spanish word).

"Bravo was a fanatic about *regalame,*" his best friend, Juan Carlos Cirdenas, an oil union official, told me in his Neiva office. "We'd be sitting in a cantina, somebody would ask for a *doble anis* and say, *'Regalame.'* Everyone says it here as a joke, to pretend you're a boss, but Bravo would shout, 'Shut up! Don't use that word around me. You want a drink, say, *'Please!'*"

In his 1978 economics thesis, *Bonanza Capitalism and the Culture of Exploitation,* Bravo stated that the lust for something-for-nothing "leaves no room for honest enterprise, less for social fraternity and ethical behavior. . . . Neither law nor morality can co-exist with the pathological quest for El Dorado." When the conquistadors failed to discover their fantastical City of Gold, they "turned cruelly on the natives to make themselves as wealthy as they believed they had a royal right to be." They all but enslaved the local population and set them to work. Immediately, two economic classes were born, with no in-between: the high-living few and the low-living many. In the early development of Colombia, the two classes became both economically and geographically distinct, and Bravo blamed the grasping upper classes for keeping them that way.

Flying into western Colombia from the north you follow the same route the conquistador Jiménez de Quesada took in 1536 in his search for El Dorado. Between the green Andean ranges of the Cordillera Oriental and the Cordillera Central lies the thousand-mile-long Magdalena Valley, its patchwork of yellow-green pastures melding into dark green coffee plantations on the slopes. To the west a third range, the Cordillera Occidental, enfolds the narrower but equally fertile Cauca River Valley. To escape the equatorial heat and diseases of the lowlands, the royal officials who followed the conquistadors built their regional capitals on plateaus high in these ranges, where they could live in eternal springtime. Bogotá sat at 8,500 feet in the Oriental Range, Medellín almost a mile high in the Central Range, and Popayán overlooked the Cauca Valley from an altitude of 5,700 feet. The Spaniards in these cities forcibly recruited the local Indians to cultivate the mountain flanks around them, while in the lowlands and vast Llanos plains to the east, they established huge cattle ranches and plantations worked by thousands of indentured peons and African slaves. This arrangement left the literally high-living rulers of the three cities insulated from the laboring Colombians beneath them.

Throughout Colombia's modern history, the Spanish upper-class minority, the Criollos, ruled the vast majority of blacks, mestizos and mulattos mainly from their mountaintop capitals, sharing ownership of the lowlands only with fellow Criollos such as the Opitas Mafia. In Bravo's day, 61 percent of Colombian land—the best farmland in the country—was owned by 4 percent of the population. The top echelons of the two political parties, the Liberals and the Conservatives, came from that same 4 percent. Ten percent of the population controlled more than half of the total wealth, and they were almost all white Spanish. Meanwhile, half the country's population of forty million lived in poverty, 15 percent were illiterate, a quarter had no running water or electricity, and there was an acute lack of schools and hospitals to handle the needs of the rural population.

All this inequality and regional separation had combined with the ethos of *regalame* to produce unending internal conflict. Since the founding of modern Colombia in 1831, there have been eleven civil wars and sixty violent insurrections. Between 1948 and 1958, 300,000 people were killed in the aptly named *La Violencia,* a civil war fought between Liberals and Conservatives. Between 1964 and Bravo's murder in 2003, a quarter million died in a civil war that was simply called "the armed conflict." In Bravo's last decade, the fighting between guerrillas, paramilitaries and government forces had cost the country almost US$50 billion, at least two million people had been displaced from their homes, and over thirty thousand had been kidnapped.

The guerrillas traced their lineage to the extreme left wing of *La Violencia*, and had never accepted the peace settlement worked out between Liberals and Conservatives in 1958. Led by a Castro-inspired group of Marxists seeking to violently overthrow the Criollo-run government, they launched their revolution when Bravo was in his twenties and Neiva was still recovering from *La Violencia*. The largest faction of the guerrillas to survive the decades was called the Revolutionary Armed Forces of Colombia—the FARC. Its commanders decreed two methods of terror as legitimate: *Plan Pistola* and *Pesca Milagrosa*. The first tactic meant that every government official, and every journalist "allied" with the government, was an acceptable target for assassination. The second, "Miracle Fishing," meant that the guerrillas had the right to troll the country and kidnap anyone they could squeeze for tribute. To additionally finance their attacks on Colombia's infrastructure, the FARC commanders decreed that because most of the country's cocaine ended up in the hated United States, it was acceptable for the FARC to take part in the drug trade.

In the summer of 1998, the FARC persuaded the recently inaugurated president, Andrés Pastrana, to call a truce and allot them a sixteen-thousand-square-mile "safety zone"—essentially a state within a state—on the jungle plain just east of Neiva. The sanctuary was immediately and sarcastically labeled FARClandia by opposition politicians, who doubted the wisdom of the truce. The FARC, in fact, used the ensuing peace talks to build up its forces while continuing its attacks, making Pastrana look like a fool. In May 2002 Pastrana's successor, Álvaro Uribe, reversed course and declared all-out war. The FARC went underground in towns near Neiva and hung on in camps in its erstwhile safety zone, its ambushes, kidnappings and targeted murders conducted by the Teófila Forero, a battalion of shock troops named after a dead rebel. The Teófila Forero had violated the truce in 2001 by invading Neiva Centro and kidnapping fifteen civilians, including the wife and children of the former governor, Jaime Lozada. In 2003 they set off a bomb in Bogotá's Club El Nogal on a crowded Friday night, killing thirty-six people. When I arrived in Neiva, they were still on the attack, blowing up a downtown electronics store, ostensibly because the proprietor had refused to pay them *vacunas* — the "vaccination" fee they charged businesses to inoculate them against mishaps.

Bravo's reaction to the atrocities committed by the guerrillas was to condemn the perpetrators, but with an excuse. He believed the guerrillas were the result of the country's problems, not the cause. In Huila, the *causa última* was the corrupt Opitas Mafia, and it did not surprise Bravo when they allied themselves with the paramilitaries, whose atrocities, Bravo felt, greatly exceeded those committed by the FARC.

The paramilitaries, who went by the righteous-sounding name United Self-Defense Forces of Colombia, or AUC, had originated in the early 1980s as bands of mercenaries hired by land barons in the north to fight the guerrillas. While the Colombian army looked the other way, the AUC massacred trade unionists and human rights workers, wiped out an entire left-wing political party — the Patriotic Union — and was by far the greatest killer of journalists. By the end of the 1990s, it had become a big player in the $7-billion-a-year cocaine trade and had accrued enormous political influence up and down the Magdalena Valley.

The death threats that Bravo received came mainly from the paramilitaries who served the Opitas Mafia. In theory, he could seek the protection of an FBI-like arm of the government called the Administrative Department of Security, or DAS. Under the direct control of the president, DAS was responsible for gathering

intelligence on all illegal sides in the armed conflict and for guarding public figures. Bravo, however, never thought of DAS as anything
more than another arm of the corrupt government in league with
the AUC. When I arrived in Neiva, paramilitaries were being exposed
in the press as working within DAS—some as fully sworn agents. In
regions where they weren't actual DAS agents, they still had access to
classified DAS files, and cases were coming to light in which DAS had
conducted intelligence operations on behalf of the AUC. In 2006,
President Uribe's highest DAS commanders and sixty of his closest
allies in the legislature were criminally charged for collaborating
with paramilitary death squads.

All of this left Bravo facing certain murder if he ignored the
warning of the *sicario* and returned to his journalism career in
Neiva. And yet that is exactly what he did.

To gain an insight into the character and childhood of Guillermo
Bravo, I took a taxi to the edge of town to meet the people who
loved him most. Army trucks patrolled the ring road and sandbag
emplacements were manned by soldiers pointing heavy-caliber
machine guns at the farm fields. Bravo's second eldest son, Juan
Carlos, lived in hiding in the district with his mother, his wife, and
his children. They had retreated here after Juan Carlos had published an article with the Inter American Press Association in early
2005. Entitled "A Crime of Hate," it detailed the conflicts Bravo
had had with various public figures before his murder and complained that there had been no police investigation of the possible
masterminds of the crime.

"My father had a very complicated upbringing that caused him
to have a harsh and angry personality," thirty-five-year-old Juan
Carlos told me in his tiny apartment. "The circumstances of his
youth were very bad."

Bravo, he said, was born in the rural town of Gigante, about fifty
miles south of Neiva, on September 2, 1938. His mother was a

teenage coffee picker who went home to a hovel in an alley, but his father was Antonio Vega Lara, one of the most wealthy and powerful men in the state. Vega owned coffee plantations and businesses and often made overtures and promises to the poor and illiterate women in his employ. "He had a lot of very young mistresses, many of whom bore his children out of wedlock," Juan Carlos said of his paternal grandfather. "My grandmother was one of them."

Juan Carlos only knew the barest details of his grandmother's life. The first was that she herself was the child of a young woman who bore her out of wedlock to a wealthy man. A more disturbing detail was that Bravo's mother was murdered when she was twenty-five—poisoned to death, like her own mother before her, who had been murdered at seventeen. "The wealthy in Huila have always been able to do what they want," Juan Carlos said, painting a picture of disposable women.

Juan Carlos's mother, and Bravo's legal wife of forty years, Angela Ortiz Pulido, said that Bravo, who was twelve when his mother died, never directly accused Antonio Vega of killing her, but it seemed likely she had either demanded support from him or had sought support from another man, making Vega jealous. "Whatever the reason for her murder, I know Guillermo was scarred by the episode terribly," she said.

Antonio Vega had been a rare visitor to his mistress's dirt-floored hovel, and Bravo had never even seen the Vega hacienda. Left on his own after his mother's poisoning, the boy believed he'd been orphaned. But his circumstances were about to change.

The year was 1950, and the bodies of men were filling the streets of Gigante, casualties of civil war. Two years previously, in April 1948, a popular leader of the Liberal left, Jorge Gaitán, had been assassinated in Bogotá, which had touched off street rioting between Liberals and Conservatives that had killed two thousand people—the opening battle of *La Violencia*. After an election that the Liberals boycotted, an ultra-rightist president named Laureano Gómez had been installed. An admirer of Hitler and Franco,

Gómez ruled as a fascist dictator, unleashing his army and police against his opposition. The fighting spread to the countryside and soon the cruelty and mass slaughter of *La Violencia* arrived in Gigante. As a backer of Gómez and a member of what would soon be known as the Opitas Mafia, Antonio Vega helped organize the Conservative forces. When they caught a Liberal leader, they gave him "a red necklace," slitting his neck and esophagus just enough that the victim was forced to try to hold his throat together until he suffocated or bled to death.

This was no time for a motherless boy to be making his way in the streets of Gigante—waifs such as he were being recruited to fight for the Liberals. That would have been an unappealing prospect for Antonio Vega, who decided it was time to provide for his son and give him a proper Criollo education. He paid for him to move into Gigante's exclusive Elias Seminary to begin Catholic studies. No one knows how Bravo felt about this sudden paternal interest, but as Juan Carlos says, "he was so young and for him it was obvious in which direction his safety lay. He knew Antonio Vega was well positioned. It would have been best not to let his mind be seized by thoughts that alienated him from that protection."

In 1951, Vega sent Bravo away to Conservative-controlled Bogotá to attend the exclusive La Salle Academy, where it seems Bravo began to accept himself as part of the establishment. At sixteen he announced an ambition to become an airline pilot, and wrote Antonio Vega for financial support to attend flight-training school. Vega wrote back that "a man with wings cannot help but find success in service to our nation," and enclosed a check. But Bravo never became a pilot: he loaned the tuition money to a friend at La Salle, who never paid him back.

At eighteen, Bravo decided instead that after he graduated La Salle he wanted to become an actor. It was 1956, and the Liberals and Conservatives were working toward a truce, negotiating a deal to alternately rule Colombia in four-year terms, with the Liberals to be given the presidency in 1958. There was still political violence in the countryside, and rural banditry had become endemic, so Vega thought Bogotá would be a safe place for a Conservative-leaning young man to establish himself as a thespian. He paid to enroll Bravo in Bogotá's Colón Theater School.

Bravo graduated in 1960, but instead of pursuing a life on the stage or in film, he decided that what he really wanted to be was a singer. Again Vega paid, this time to enroll his son in Mexico's Monterrey Academy of Music, where Bravo spent a year learning to sing *rancheros*, modeling his style on the famous balladeer José Alfredo Jiménez. When Bravo couldn't make a living in the crowded field of Mexican *ranchero* singers, his father enrolled him in the Cabral Academy to train as a professional radio announcer. After the six-month course, however, Bravo, now twenty-three, couldn't find work, and his father's patience at last ran out. Vega suggested Bravo return to Huila, where this time Vega would find something for him to do.

Despite his artistic cravings, Bravo had always received his highest marks in mathematics. Vega used his contacts in Neiva to get his son a job as an accounts manager and bookkeeper at Neiva's police headquarters. At this job Bravo very likely ran across some of the odd financial transactions endemic to policing in Huila but, his son says, "he was not political at that time and he got along well with the policemen at his station. He was courting my mother and so needed the work."

Bravo had first met the upper-class Angela at a church dinner held to introduce marriageable men and women of the region. Antonio Vega approved of the relationship, and, in early 1962, the couple were married in a ceremony at Neiva's grand Campo Nuñez church. Angela soon became pregnant with Juan Carlos's older brother, Guillermo, and, over the next several months, Bravo compliantly served the police. Had he given them any trouble, he would have endangered himself and his young family

The tensions of *La Violencia* were still unsettled in regions like

Huila, and were exacerbated that spring because the Liberals were set to yield the presidency to the Conservatives. The police in Neiva were on the side of the Conservatives, and so, from all accounts, was Bravo. Then, as Juan Carlos said, "something happened that changed his entire life."

It was during the San Pedro carnival, held in Neiva Centro each year at the end of June. As usual, a *baubuco* band played the music of Huila, filling the square with the fiesta yelps of vocalists accompanied by drums, guitars and sour brass. There was a lot of *aguardiente* drinking, the townsmen whooping it up and young women dancing the *sanjuanero* in peasant costume. At the corners of the square, platoons of police stood ready to deal with any fights that might break out between Liberal and Conservative factions. Bravo and his brother-in-law were standing around with policemen friends, the two as drunk as anyone else on the square. A couple of the police officers walked into a crowded cantina to use the toilet and Bravo and his brother-in-law followed them. "Evidently some of the patrons in the bar were opposed to the police," Juan Carlos said, "because when my uncle and the police-men went to use the toilet, one officer left his gun on top of the bar so my father could protect himself." At one of the tables a heated political discussion was in progress. "My father might have said some-thing cutting, but he was very drunk and never remembered," Juan Carlos said. "In any case, it turned into a confrontation, and one of the working men at the table made a pun on his name: 'If you're so brave, man, kill me.' So my father picked up the gun and shot him dead."

The policemen rushed back from the toilet to find a man shot between the eyes, and Bravo standing with the gun in his hand. They hustled Bravo to the station, and when he sobered up, they advised him to insist that he was so drunk when he pulled the trigger that he was in a state of what they termed "mental unconsciousness" — which would absolve him of any intention or guilt in the murder. Bravo went along with this defense at first, telling an investigator that he couldn't remember killing the man and that he was aiming at the jukebox behind him. But then he admitted that if he couldn't remember killing the man, how could he remember he was aiming at the jukebox? The police witnessing his statement told him if he couldn't stick to a story he should run away, or perhaps get Antonio Vega to fix things. "In the end, my father made no excuses and asked no favors," Juan Carlos said. "He was soon to be a father, but he resisted the urging of others. He told everyone he should be punished and pled guilty to murder."

When Bravo went to prison, he also turned his back on Antonio Vega and everything that Vega represented. All at once he seems to have realized that ever since his mother had been killed, he himself had been practicing the art of getting something for nothing.

The Neiva jail was filled with feuding Liberals and Conservatives incarcerated during *La Violencia*, but instead of crossing to the Liberals, Bravo walked farther left, to a group of trade unionists and socialists jailed by the Conservatives for "syndicalism." They were running a literacy program for their fellow prisoners, and Bravo spent his days in jail as an arithmetic teacher and his nights discussing trade unionism and socialism with his new friends. During conjugal visits with Angela, he talked about land distribution and bank reform, topics she'd never heard him mention before.

In 1968, after he'd served more than five years, the newly installed Liberals reviewed the file of the now left-wing Bravo and pardoned him, expunging his record—which was soon forgotten by all but Bravo himself, his family, and the family of the victim. Out of jail, Bravo became one of the local leaders of the leftist National Popular Alliance Party (ANAPO), and for a brief period served in the state legislature as an ANAPO representative. At the same time he began outlining a novel, which he eventually published as *Morir de Pie* (*Die Standing*). It was a political (and polemical) tale involving the left's bloody fight against the fascist Gómez after the assassination of Jorge Gaitán. In the book, Bravo clearly tries to identify the cause of the anger that had plagued him since the death of his mother, and that finally drove him to commit a mindless murder. "The Conservatives passed their sins to the sons," he wrote. "One day, the sons gave birth to everlasting consequence."

A few months after Bravo's release from jail, the son of the man he had killed tracked him down; he followed Bravo down a side street and confronted him with a gun. Juan Carlos related what happened next: "My father said, 'Yes, you can kill me, but if you let me live, I will make up for my crime, I promise you. For my beliefs, I am ready to die standing.'"

The man let him live, and Guillermo Bravo Vega was as good as his promise. He committed the rest of his life to a quest for redemption.

In 1971, Bravo set himself a grand goal to expiate his sin: change Colombia, and perhaps the world.

That year he won a scholarship in economics to a university in Bogotá, and for his thesis he chose to examine the coffee industry — coffee being the most heavily traded commodity in the world after petroleum. Bravo believed that if he could explain the business of coffee, which accounted for the livelihood of 15 percent of Colombia's population and was controlled in Huila by the Opitas Mafia, he could get at the mechanism of injustice that kept the rich in their haciendas and the poor in their hovels.

For producing nations, coffee had always been the quintessential boom-and-bust commodity, fueling inflation when world prices were high (usually for brief periods) and crushing economies when world prices were low (for much longer periods). During high-price cycles, speculators on the coffee futures market bought up beans and held them until increased scarcity sent prices even higher; at the first hint that the market was about to turn, they dumped their beans, creating oversupply and driving prices to the bottom.

Reaping none of the profits of the boom years and suffering the effects of the bust years were millions of people whose lives

resembled that of Bravo's mother. Coffee is a labor-intensive industry, particularly in Colombia, where coffee trees do not ripen all at
once and workers must search individual branches repeatedly for
ripened beans. Plantation owners like Antonio Vega had always used
the cost of production as an excuse to pay bean pickers starvation
wages, even during inflationary boom years. Workers thus earned a
living "according to two wage scales," Bravo wrote, "low and zero."

In Bravo's view, the coffee market was ruled by the immorality of
regalame and the lust for El Dorado. He thought there was a logical
alternative, which he presented in his thesis. After offering a
hundred pages of history and social economic theory, he used
graphs, tables and structural charts to lay out a blueprint for an international coffee agreement between producing nations that would
set up export quotas to create price stability. Floating quotas would
be governed by an export board; coffee pickers would be guaranteed a minimum wage commensurate with a stabilized market; and
exporters would establish a fund that would direct a portion of their
profits to social welfare programs in the coffee zones.

In 1978 Bravo successfully defended his thesis then used his background and further research to write an article called "Bonanza:
The Boom and Bust of the Economy," which he published in the
liberal newspaper *La República* the next year. Overnight, the article
made him famous in the halls of academe and in journalism. It even
garnered praise from right-wing nationalists, who were deeply resentful that big American coffee buyers seemed always to be searching for
ways to collapse the local market. Bravo was hailed as one of South
America's most brilliant economists, won the Simón Bolívar Award
and was invited into the parlors of the wealthy to discuss his findings.
Job offers poured in from universities and the mainstream media,
and multimillionaire coffee magnate Jorge Cárdenas Gutiérrez
offered Bravo an executive position in his international company.

But converting his prize-winning article into his own bonanza
was not Bravo's goal. "I wanted a free voice in the midst of all the
political deal-making and cronyism of Bogotá," Bravo recollected

twenty years later. "I chose journalism to give me the opportunity for that free voice."

He accepted a job at *La República*, but the voice they gave him turned out to be less free than he'd anticipated. He soon ran into problems with other Bogotá journalists and then with his editors. This was in part because in Colombia many journalists supplemented their meager income by soliciting advertisements for their papers, a practice that appalled Bravo because, of course, the advertisers then expected (and received) positive coverage.

"He said, right to his colleagues' faces, 'You have sold out for a plate of beans,'" the Neiva journalist Diógenes Cadena told me. "That was why he never lasted long at any job. He fought with every editor. Every time they tried to tone down his work, he thought they were giving in to corruption. He thought corruption the worst· cancer of society."

Bravo left *La República* and freelanced articles while he lobbied for his reforms. In 1981, inspired in part by his thesis, Latin American coffee growers drew up a plan that became known as the International Coffee Agreement, and that eventually implemented much of the regulation Bravo had called for. In addition, Jorge Cárdenas established a social welfare fund to build schools, hospitals and housing for Colombian pickers.

After that success, Bravo decided to move back to his home province to see if he could turn Neiva on its head the way he had the national coffee industry.

Bravo's homecoming in 1981 was a little complicated on the personal front. He moved back with Angela and their two sons, but he also set up house in the city with a beautiful Bogotá schoolteacher named Ismery Gómez, who happened to be pregnant with the first of three children they were to have together in the space of four years. He divided his domestic time between his two families, and did so completely openly.

When I met with Angela, she told me, "We were never divorced, we were married to the end!"—but from the way she stared at the floor after she said this, her thin lips set, I suspected that Bravo's sexual betrayals had not been as easy for her to live with as for him. I asked her if Bravo, who had denounced his father's ways, was uncomfortable about following in Antonio Vega's womanizing footsteps. Angela had no comment, but her son, Juan Carlos, argued that there was a crucial difference between the two men. "My father was not exploitative," he said. "He always had a loyal relationship with his wives and his five sons, loving all equally and with devotion. He was a caring, supportive man, an open and honorable man." That explanation sounded a little too forbearing to my ears, and as I dug further into Bravo's work and life, I came to learn how inextricably intertwined his wide-open affairs were with his dangerous crusades, and how complex his motivations for philandering were.

Bravo got his first job in Neiva with *Diario del Huila,* then the town's only newspaper. He did a "lifestyle check" of the town councilors and discovered that they were living in split-level homes and driving big American cars on salaries of a hundred dollars a month. He pursued the councilors' business relationships with the paper's main advertisers, and when the story he handed in about the councilors' conflicts of interest was spiked, he exploded at the entire newsroom, accusing his fellow journalists of *"hablar con sus bocas llenas"*—talking with their mouths full. That was the end of his short tenure at *Diario.* For an income he turned to doing part-time accounting for a construction union, which led him down another avenue of investigation that brought him back to his first, setting him on an independent path of publishing he would follow for the rest of his life. Years later, he would advise journalists who were just starting out: "Call the unions. They know everything."

At the beginning of 1983 a group of wealthy businessmen proposed a shopping center—Neiva's first—on Calle 21, south of Centro. The site of the development, eventually called the

Confamiliar, was on land owned by the city. The directors of the Confamiliar Corporation sought the support of two city officials, who quickly persuaded the mayor and councilmen to hand over the land to the developers and support the project with tax dollars. The project was announced at a council meeting as a lucrative public–private partnership that would eventually pay for big capital projects and enhanced security measures against the guerrillas.

Bravo knew the support of city politicians was usually procured through the payment of *regalias*, and at the council meeting he called for an independent board of auditors to oversee the development. The council considered his proposal and ruled that the auditing currently in place would be adequate.

Construction began in 1984, and Bravo worked with the union to monitor the huge cost overruns the city soon began paying out. He hounded the municipal officials who were approving most of the payments to Confamiliar. When the city auditor did attempt to block a payment, he was overruled by the officials, who explained to Bravo that it wasn't in the public interest to jeopardize a project in which so much had already been invested.

In 1985, Bravo wrote a ten-thousand-word forensic investigation of the shopping center, although he had no idea where he would publish it. The big Bogotá dailies were then showing some interest in Huila because of its burgeoning oil industry, but Bravo didn't trust them not to cut the heart out of his story. His union friend, Juan Carlos Cirdenas, told me that Neiva's big businessmen and officials were thought to be untouchable. "Journalists were very afraid of being jailed for criminal defamation by a judgment in Neiva's corrupt court system," Cirdenas said. "Bravo, though, wasn't afraid to call those guys Opitas Mafiosos."

The word *Opitas* itself was not a pejorative in Neiva; it was how Colombians referred to people from Huila, harkening back to the indigenous tribe of the Upper Magdalena Valley, which had long since disappeared through conquest and interbreeding.

The city's flag, in fact, sported a distinctive arrow with five vanes at the base that was once used by the Opitas aboriginals. But linking the word *Mafia* to Opitas was another matter. In his article, Bravo defined the Opitas Mafia as "a brotherhood of Huilanese bandits who rule us like tribal chiefs." The members of that brotherhood thought they were entitled to receive government contracts in closed or rigged bidding, the economic wheels always lubricated "with bribes and kickbacks that are ultimately borne by the taxpayer." If he could get it published, Bravo's article would mark the first time anyone had sought in print to accuse the rulers of Huila of being a mafia.

This was when Bravo came up with his idea for an independent magazine. He called it *Eco Impacto*—a pun on the echoing impact of the economy. Bravo himself would do all the writing for the magazine, and the union would take out ads to help defer printing costs. To keep the issue under wraps, the union secured a printing press in another town and swore the printers to secrecy—if copies of the article leaked out before the issue was printed and distributed, Bravo could expect an injunction preventing publication. Or worse. Big landowners had been hiring paramilitary guards to protect themselves against guerrillas, and it was no secret that the guards could be hired for other purposes.

The article, which he titled "Proceso Confamiliar," arrived in the city "like an avenging angel," Cirdenas told me. "Bravo gave an accountant's analysis of where all the money disappeared." Bravo alleged that the officials and their partners in Confamiliar had received kickbacks from subcontractors, forged receipts for work that was never done, issued fraudulent pay stubs for laborers who were never hired, paid themselves bonuses and, all in all, gouged the taxpayer for funds that could, in fact, have been used for capital projects and to increase security measures—the original justifications for Confamiliar.

———

"Retract your document. Silver if you do. Lead if you don't."

Bravo received the crayoned note—his first death threat as a journalist—a month after the publication of his big article. *Plata o plomo* notes, offering the choice between a bribe and a bullet, were as common in Colombia as cocaine, and Bravo told both his wives he didn't take this one seriously. "If they kill me, who will retract the article?" he said with a laugh. Two months later, the General Prosecutor's Office, known as the *Fiscalia*, opened an investigation into the Confamiliar affair. Ten businessmen and municipal officials were eventually charged with corruption—something of a miracle in Neiva.

In the midst of the official investigation, Bravo was crossing the street in Neiva Centro when he saw a motorcycle with two people on it bank steeply around the corner and accelerate toward him. Bravo focused his eyes on the hands of the back-rider, an instinctive reaction for a Colombian, since motorcycle back-riders had a local name that had become synonymous with assassin: *parillero*. So many murders had been committed by *parilleros* in Bogotá that the capital had banned them. As the screaming motorcycle approached Bravo, the *parillero* drew a machine pistol. Bravo dove through the door of a cantina, landing on the wooden floor as bullets sprayed above him.

In the wake of the shooting, Bravo redoubled his attacks in *Eco Impacto* against the men charged in the Confamiliar scandal. As the group went to trial, a local government official named Jamie Lozada Perdomo accused Bravo of being a "moral *sicario*." Lozada was destined to be the future governor of Huila, a man whom Bravo would one day characterize as the "*autore intellettuale*" of the state's corruption. The mastermind.

I interviewed Lozada in his luxury suite atop the Mira Flores condo tower in Neiva, just south of where Bravo had escaped the *parillero* twenty years earlier. He did not seem to mourn the journalist's death. "You cannot imagine the chaos in our country in the 1980s," Lozada told me. "At the same time as Bravo came out with

his articles, twelve of our Supreme Court justices were killed by
guerrillas in Bogotá. Maybe thousands of politicians and businessmen suffered the same fate. Kidnapping and bombings were
common. Bravo had an inclination to declare people guilty before
they were even tried, and that caused the guerrillas to target them.
We had a mayor some years later whom Bravo accused of crimes.
Not accused—declared guilty." That mayor, Gustavo Penagos, was
murdered, a deed for which Lozada felt Bravo bore some moral
responsibility. "It is unreasonable to stir up such emotion against
those who have not yet seen their day in court, but that is what
Bravo did."

Lozada was an obese, silver-haired man in his late sixties,
wearing a green golf shirt that barely covered his belly and loose
gray trousers that left room for his thighs. In the spacious living
room with us were an assembly of important-looking men talking
quietly. Beyond them, the view from Lozada's balcony looked
across the Upper Magdalena Valley to the eastern mountains,
glowing orange in the sunset. Somewhere on the other side of the
mountains, Lozada's wife, Gloria Polanco, was being held captive
by the Teófila Forero. In 2001, at the height of Bravo's attacks against
Lozada, she had been kidnapped from this very apartment.

Like Bravo, Lozada had received an advanced degree in economics; but unlike Bravo, he had used his education to procure an
executive position at the Chemical Bank in New York, and then
the First National Bank in Milwaukee. He moved back to Neiva
in the late 1970s and was serving as Huila's finance secretary in the
Conservative administration when Bravo returned in 1981. Because
of their common profession, the two men were on respectful terms
until Bravo "mounted a high horse," as Lozada put it, over the
Confamiliar affair.

I reminded Lozada that the trial of the Confamiliar Ten eventually ended in convictions and jail terms.

"I don't say his investigation was incorrect," Lozada said. "The
judges agreed that in Confamiliar, Guillermo had uncovered bad

deeds committed by several private and official persons. But you cannot declare a person guilty before trial. His crusades afterwards became even more ideological and less journalistically sound."

"Was he a communist?" I asked.

"More or less. He was definitely leftist. He became an official adviser to the unions. He put himself in opposition to legitimate free enterprise in the department. I am the head of the Conservative Party in Huila and am pro–free enterprise. After Confamiliar, he worked with the unions to socialize our oil industry—a very bad mistake for the state of Huila."

Bravo began investigating the oil industry in the early 1990s, when a conglomerate of foreign oil companies, known as Hocol, applied to renew its thirty-five-year lease in Huila, due to expire November 18, 1994. Having mortified the city government for its graft-ridden partnership with private enterprise, Bravo took a hard look at how Huila's most profitable resource was being exploited by the federal government and a big multinational. Hocol was then paying 13.5 percent royalties to the state on oil extracted on its 49,000 acres, and the ever-suspicious Bravo wrote an article in *Eco Impacto* that questioned whether the royalties being paid reflected the actual amount of oil being pumped. In early 1993, the oil workers' union asked the Liberal government of President César Gaviria to increase the royalties to 20 percent in the new lease agreement and provide more government oversight at the wellheads. If Hocol refused, they said, the rights to the oil fields, plus all the infrastructure, should be "reverted" to the state-owned oil company, Ecopetrol.

"Bravo always said, 'Oil is the new El Dorado,'" Juan Carlos Cirdenas told me in his oil-union office. He was a bull of a man, now in charge of interunion affairs, and his friendship with Bravo, which began during the Confamiliar affair, was cemented during the dangerous period when they joined forces to battle Hocol. "There was terrible poverty in the region," Cirdenas said. "Many of the small towns within the leases had no electricity or running water, and yet the Hocol rigs and trailers all had generators and wells. We wanted that extra revenue for the workers in the towns."

Because of guerrilla activity in the area, the drilling rigs were protected by security guards—men the union alleged were paramilitaries. Hocol, like many other multinational companies working in Colombia at the time, never acknowledged that the guards at its operations might be connected to a network responsible for some of the worst human rights violations in Latin America. Nor did Hocol acknowledge that, in the words of Cirdenas, "every union member is a target of paramilitaries." The day after Cirdenas filed his petition with President Gaviria, Hocol fired him and nine other union organizers, who were then informed that henceforth they were banned from the rigs. Roadblocks were set up on the routes to the Hocol leases. The union organized a protest near the rigs, and a few days later two union members were shot on the road back to their pueblo.

In the next eighteen months, eleven journalists were murdered in Colombia, many by suspected paramilitaries. Between the launch of the union protest and the expiration of the lease, Bravo was ordered to get out of town two times and survived another assassination attempt. Nevertheless, at least once a week Bravo drove to the oil fields. He checked the research the union accumulated and went to Bogotá to examine the books of the state-owned Ecopetrol. He interviewed government officials involved in the lease negotiations, and put together a dossier of Hocol's pressure tactics in the capital, its activities in Huila and the company's long-running relations with some officials at Ecopetrol—which led Bravo to believe the officials were not unbiased stewards of the nation's petroleum reserves.

He published his findings in *Eco Impacto*, and when the articles did not sway the government, he launched another magazine in early 1994, *Café Petrolio*, which he distributed in Bogotá and which was devoted exclusively to the oil and coffee industries. At the same time he launched a local radio show, *Radio Café Petrolio*, its *baubuco* music and his own *ranchero* singing interspersed with editorials he read from his magazine in his deep actor's voice. All this media combined to give one-man blanket coverage to the oil story in the run-up to the government's decision on the extension of the Hocol lease.

Hocol reached into its bottomless pockets to pay for a counter-campaign. The company offered politicians free vacations in lakeside cabins. It staged rock concerts at which sexy PR women gave away thousands of T-shirts emblazoned with the words *Hocol le pone el hombro al Huila* ("Hocol cares for the people of Huila"). It backed pro-oil candidates leading up to the state and federal elections, to be held in May. In the midst of the campaign, Bravo revealed on *Radio Café Petrolio* that Hocol had hired two lobbyists. One was the daughter of the general prosecutor of Huila. The other was a candidate for the Colombian senate.

The federal election installed a gruff Liberal president named Ernesto Samper, who had bragged during his campaign that he bore eleven bullet wounds from his crusade against the Medellín cocaine cartel. Shortly before his inauguration in August, however, tape-recorded phone conversations between Samper and members of the Cali cartel were leaked to the Bogotá press; they seemed to imply that Samper had fought his crusade against the Medellín traffickers on behalf of the Cali traffickers, who had given his presidential campaign $6 million. Caught in a scandal at the very start of his administration, Samper turned for political salvation to the uproar Bravo was making over the Hocol lease and ordered Ecopetrol to terminate the lease and return the underground reserves to the government. Just after the announcement, at a Sunday victory celebration held by the oil union, Bravo recited the poetry of Cuban revolutionaries and acted in a play depicting the lives of *"los campañeros del lucha"* — the word *lucha* ("struggle") being used in its old Castroite fashion as code for revolution.

As I sat with Cirdenas and a couple of equally burly union organ-izers in their dimly lit, paint-chipped office — adorned with a mural of Che and protected by armed guards outside the front door — I posed the question I'd put to Jaime Lozada. "Was Bravo ever one of the guerrillas?" I asked. "Was he a communist in league with them?"

Absolutely not, they replied in chorus. Bravo did join the far-left Patriotic Union party (UP), which got its start in the 1980s as the polit-ical arm of FARC; but by the time he became a member, the UP had renounced violence and the FARC had renounced the UP. "He was a nationalist, and many of Neiva's small-businessmen supported his economic programs," said Cirdenas. "He wanted to radically change things, but not so radically as the guerrillas wanted, and by peaceful means. Maybe some of them saw him as a voice in their struggle, but so did we." He laughed heartily and called Bravo "*Viejo loco y enam-orado,*" then parsed the expression to explain what he meant: "'Crazy old man' because he was maximally energetic and passion-ate for his age. 'In love' because he was in love with everything about life: women, nature, politics, art, journalism, truth, his wives — "

When I interrupted Cirdenas to joke that he had just mentioned a lot of *mujeres* there, he smiled and said, "'In love' describes him well."

Males in Huila are not inclined to make an issue over the sex lives of men whom they deeply admire (or whom they don't admire, for that matter). From my conversations around Neiva, it seemed to be culturally acceptable for husbands to openly cheat when oppor-tunities arose, even though their wives suffered emotionally and sometimes financially. Men with a lot of money, of course, had more opportunities to cheat than poor men. Bravo had almost no money — but he had as many affairs as the richest of men. Since his Confamiliar exposé, he'd not only split his time between two wives but had engaged in a train of affairs with beautiful women he met at union rallies. Then, in the midst of his Hocol exposés, he began yet another affair that would lead to his third household, which he maintained to the end of his life. Were all these women an important part of Bravo's motivations for risk taking, or just an added benefit? Did he use his reputation as a fearless crusader to draw women to him? Did he, at least in part, take those risks in order to get that reputation?

Bravo's third wife, Ana Cristina Suárez, came walking up the block to the Peter Pan ice cream parlor in Neiva Centro, her high heels clicking on the cement. She was forty-five, statuesque and tanned, with dyed blonde hair and wearing a blue peasant blouse off the shoulders that matched her electric blue eye shadow and set off her hot pink headband and hot pink earrings.

"It was right around this corner," she said, pointing to Parque Central. "The eve of the festival of San Pedro, June 24, 1993. There was a beauty queen pageant and Guillermo was videoing it. He approached me carrying his camera. 'Can I sit with you?' he asked. I was with my sister, a neighbor and her child. My sister is much older than me and I thought he was actually interested in her, because I was only thirty-three then and he was twenty years older. I wasn't attracted to him at all because of the age difference."

"How did he make it clear you were the one he was attracted to?" I asked.

"He said he was looking through his video camera and saw these two beautiful eyes jump out of the crowd and he had to come up to film them. He introduced himself as Guillermo Bravo Vega, the publisher of *Eco Impacto*. He asked if I'd heard of him, but I hadn't, because in those days I had nothing to do with politics, I was just involved with being a mother, a schoolteacher and a housewife."

"You were married?"

"Yes, but my husband and I were not getting along so well. Guillermo said he was an investigator of economic corruption, he had a radio show, too—he exposed the corruption of the dangerous Opitas Mafia. He explained to us the power structure of Huila, the tentacles of power. All of it concerned topics I'd never heard before or cared about. I was raised by nuns, I never questioned anything socially and I grew up always having everything I needed. But I can say from that moment on, my life started changing. From that night, he began to raise my consciousness to the dark forces he fought, and we soon became lovers. Four months later I told my husband, 'I'm in love with another man.' Then Guillermo and I moved to a rented place together with my daughter."

"Did you get divorced?" I asked.

"Yes, of course, but Guillermo was very loyal to his legal wife, Angela Ortiz Pulido. They were married in the church when they were young, thirty years before, and he didn't want to hurt her with divorce. He was a very loyal man that way."

That definition of "loyalty" still sounded strange to my ears, so I sought out another woman who knew quite a bit about Bravo's private life and motivations, meeting her at her home near the airport. Her name was Irma Castaneda, and she worked as a litigator on behalf of people who said they'd been unfairly dismissed from municipal positions because of their politics. For fifteen years, in exchange for being mentored by the master investigator, Castaneda had served as Bravo's researcher and assistant. Although she said her own relationship with Bravo was platonic, she'd had a bird's-eye view of the romantic comings and goings in his life from 1988 until his murder.

"There were many women," Castaneda admitted, laughing. "He was a very flirtatious person and women loved him. They were aware of his work, the dangers he bravely faced, his ideals, and found his attentions irresistible. If they hadn't heard of his work, he would let them know about it. He was not a shy man with women, although at the end, of course, he was slowing down."

On a podium in her living room sat a book, displayed like a Bible, whose cover featured the Statue of Liberty holding an M16. The title was *United States: Intervention of the Imperial Power in 40 Countries of the World.* Beside it was a primitive painting done by a co-worker of Castaneda's: Jesus Christ reached down from the cross to a female guerrilla, over the inscription "I was also perse-cuted. They called me a guerrilla." Castaneda said this was Bravo's favorite painting and that he would often stand before it when he was seeking inspiration for his writing.

Bravo's incongruities and paradoxes seemed legion to me. He wrote that he did not believe in violence, but he had a soft spot in his heart for guerrillas who were ravaging the country in ways that were not much better than the paramilitaries he hated. He was scarred by what privileged men had done to his mother and grand-mother, but he flagrantly hurt the women who loved him most, and possibly many other women who were only permitted to love him at his convenience.

What, then, were the true forces that drove him to take the risks that would eventually lead to his murder? There were his ideals—ending corruption and stopping the powerful from exploiting the weak—and I'd found out when those had been born. There was his relationship to women: he had clearly used his reputation as a risk-taking investigator to impress them. The payoff in sex is quite often a motivation for male accomplishment, and, God knows, a lot of women are attracted to men who accomplish great things by living dangerously—just read any biography of Che Guevara. Finally, Bravo was attracted to martyrdom, if his favorite painting was anything to go by. Here was a liberation-theology Jesus bless-ing a guerrilla who would, in all likelihood, soon share His suffering death.

Before I'd traveled to Neiva, I'd read that martyrdom was a Big Idea among leftists in Catholic Colombia, where, since the days of the Great Liberator Simón Bolívar, hundreds of thousands had been slain for their beliefs. I'd come across this quotation from the diary of the president of the Patriotic Union, Bernardo Jaramillo, written before he was assassinated in 1990: "When the things that we fight for and believe in—what we've always believed in—dissolve into the reality of the world, men seem to find, almost happily, death."

Bravo fought heroically for his ideals, but for profoundly complex reasons. He had become filled with anger after his mother's murder, then filled with self-loathing when that anger had driven him to an act of drunken homicide. He had then redirected the anger at its cause: the wealthy and authoritarian Opitas Mafia, who were responsible for his own misery and the misery of Huila. That anger drove him to fight the corrupt brotherhood in a social cause that also expiated his sin. But it additionally drew him to the kind of heroic martyrdom suffered by the men he admired most, causing him to take at least some risks that could have been avoided. And all the while, the wound he had borne at such a tender age remained with him. Perhaps to salve the pain of his motherless childhood, he sought the comfort of numerous women, paradoxically imitating the father he'd set out to defeat. He was then driven to take even greater risks to fight the injustice of the oppressors, using the hazards he faced as sexual selling points to attract more women.

But even if becoming a martyr for a cause was the Colombian way, the idea of martyrdom is one thing and the reality another. Why, nine years after his victory over Hocol, had he left his door open to his killers?

Jaime Lozada was elected governor of Huila in the spring of 1995. At the time, the three most profitable (legal) industries in the region were oil, coffee and liquor. Thanks in part to Bravo's efforts, oil profits were now being shared with the remote regions and coffee prices were regulated to prevent the boom-and-bust cycle. The liquor industry, meanwhile, was in the control of a government corporation called Industria Licorera del Huila, whose ups and downs Bravo had been monitoring for some time.

Three months after Lozada moved into the governor's mansion, Bravo conducted his usual quarterly examination of the corporation's books and discovered that it was losing a lot of money. He checked

with the liquor union, whose members told him that Licorera's production of its most popular products—Doble Anis, Cocosol and
Kanoh—was actually up. Further investigation revealed that the
company was engaged in a campaign of "product enhancement,"
allotting a higher number of free samples to distributors, which
seemed to account for increased production costs and commensurate loss of revenue. As the corporation's revenue continued to
decline, Lozada proposed a bill to the State Assembly: the company
should be leased to a private investor for ten years, relieving the taxpayer of the burden of subsidizing an enterprise that was sinking
further and further into the red. Lozada blamed the reversal in the
company's fortunes on the shenanigans of out-of-control union
members, who were "turning it into their own gold mine."

Bravo reached the opposite conclusion: he believed Lozada's
administration was making the company look unprofitable as an
excuse to privatize it. He made the charge in an article in *Eco
Impacto* called "The Big Hit," which eventually won Huila's top
journalism prize, the Reynaldo Matiz Award. Nevertheless, at the
beginning of 1997, the State Assembly passed Lozada's bill and
Licorera was "opened up" for bidding. The government kept the
bidding open for only one day, and just two companies had time
to make offers: one was a Miami-based firm whose owners Bravo
couldn't track down and which he called "a ghost company"; the
other was a newly formed company called Licorsa (Industria de
Licores Global S.A.), which, after some investigation, Bravo discovered was owned by a man he alleged was Lozada's friend and
business partner, Orlando Rojas Bustos. A frequent commuter
between his homes in Colombia and Miami, Rojas owned large
tracts of real estate in downtown Neiva and a Chevy SUV dealership, and was about to become the largest shareholder of Huila's
soccer team, of which Lozada was the president.

Licorera del Huila was soon awarded to Rojas, with almost no
oversight from the government auditor and no criticism in the
mainstream press. "A day after the announcement, Bravo looks

around and he sees key people in the decision-making process driving Chevy SUVs," Juan Carlos Bravo told me. The inside deal was so glaring to Bravo that in "The Last Drink," his summary of the affair (also awarded a Matiz prize), he demanded an investigation by the *Fiscalia*—the main prosecutor's office. The liquor contract, he said, violated Colombia's Federal Law 80, which states that government companies must be open to public bids for a reasonable period of time. Bravo had other questions about the deal as well. He alleged that in return for taking on the money-losing company, Rojas was given the inventory of free samples for minimum charge, along with a tax exemption on a portion of the profits for a number of years. Bravo calculated that if his allegations were true, over the course of the ten-year lease Rojas would garner revenues of $50 million. He alleged that Governor Lozada would share in those revenues.

Spurred by Bravo's exposés, the *Fiscalia* launched an investigation into Licorsa for illegal profits, false documentation and nonpayment of taxes. The investigation dragged on for years and eventually found no wrongdoing.

After he published "The Big Hit," Bravo received another *plata o plomo* note in an envelope that also contained a squashed spider. Ana Cristina Suárez suggested that perhaps they should quietly move out of their rented flat in the center of town. Since Bravo had no money, she used her savings to make a down payment on a stuccoed bungalow in the suburban district of Virgilio Barco, north of the city. They made the move on April 13, 1997.

Carrera 5 was immaculately clean and tree-lined, and Bravo was delighted with the neighborhood. Their bungalow was just up the street from a forested cul de sac and a couple of blocks from a basketball court where he could shoot hoops with the local boys at the end of his workday. There was so little traffic that every motor scooter and car that entered the lane drew the attention of neighbors.

Bravo set up his office behind a curtained and barred window that faced the street, a position he chose so he could observe anyone who knocked at the door. The door itself was hardwood and reinforced with a dead bolt, above which Bravo added a slide bolt. A cooling breeze blew into the bungalow from its walled backyard, in the middle of which the couple planted an organ pipe cactus that reminded them of their vacations to the Guajiran Desert in the north.

"Immediately, neighbors started talking about seeing strange people around the house," Suárez remembered. "Everybody thought there would be retribution from his denouncements of the governor, but he said, 'If self-censorship is what they demand, self-censorship is not what they will get.'"

Bravo kept up his broadsides against Lozada and Rojas, to the point where the subject was featured in almost every edition of the now bimonthly *Eco Impacto*. Many workers were being laid off in the privatized liquor company and Bravo emblazoned the cover of issue 47 with the words "The Night of the Hate." He was alluding to the title of a metaphorical novel he'd just published, which takes place during *La Violencia* and centers on a plane crash in the jungle east of Huila. The chances for the survival of the passengers on the plane are torpedoed by a group of thieving Conservatives who bear a strong resemblance to the Opitas Mafia of modern Huila. Reflecting the book's theme of corruption, he titled the magazine's lead article about the liquor industry "From the Patrimony of the Huilanese to the Patrimony of 'The Family.'"

After Lozada left the governor's mansion in 1998, Bravo included in his repertoire of targets Neiva's mayor, Gustavo Penagos, whom he accused of pocketing funds meant for road building. Penagos was murdered shortly after Bravo's exposé was published; his assassins were suspected to be Teófila Forero guerrillas. Bravo's critics, such as Jamie Lozada, blamed the personal tone of the journalist's attacks for inciting the guerrillas.

Bravo was accumulating so many enemies during this period that it was impossible for him to tell who was responsible for the barrage of death threats he was receiving. He dealt with the threats by publicizing every one of them on his radio show, a poor tactic according to Neiva's most prominent radio journalist, Roberto Castaño, who had received his own share of death threats from both the FARC and paramilitaries. "It gives license to a murderer," he told me. "If there are so many publicized threats to this one person, then a mastermind might be tempted to act. He will think, 'They will not know whom to arrest among the crowd of people with a motive.'"

On April 16, 1998, a thirty-seven-year-old colleague of Bravo's named Nelson Carvajal was murdered in Pitalito, just south of Gigante, where Bravo had grown up. Carvajal had worked as an investigative journalist and news editor at a radio program called *Momento Regional*. Like Bravo, Carvajal had specialized in exposing political corruption, and he had been a thorn in the side of a former mayor of Pitalito, Fernando Bermúdez. Carvajal was leaving a school where he moonlighted as a teacher when he was shot ten times by a *parillero* on a motorcycle. Shortly after the murder, a local DAS investigator claimed that the FARC had been behind the assassination.

Along with several other journalists, Bravo drove to Pitalito, where he learned from Carvajal's colleagues and family that the radio journalist was going to accuse Bermúdez of being an arms trafficker in his next broadcast. Bravo also discovered an eyewitness to the shooting, a prostitute named Carmen Raigoza, who identified by name the two paramilitary hitmen.

Bravo gave his information to the *Fiscalia*'s investigative team, and on January 5, 1999, Bermúdez and the paramilitaries were arrested. A succession of four separate prosecutors came and went on the case over the next several months. As the wheels of justice ground slowly, another journalist, Pablo Medina Motta, was killed in Gigante, this time verifiably by FARC guerillas who machine-gunned him as they attacked the town, killing six other civilians and wounding twenty. When the FARC apologized to Medina's boss for the killing, Bravo called them "mindless fools" for launching the attack to begin with. "You don't save the country by mowing down its innocent sons," he said on the radio. A couple of days later he received a note from Gigante: "We know your heart, but don't like your mouth." Bravo read the note aloud on air, retorting, "Pablo knew your hearts but didn't like your bullets."

In December 2000, the three men accused in the murder of Carvajal were acquitted, based on the finding by the court that their motives were not proven and that the testimony of the eyewitness was not credible because she was a prostitute. Carlos Mora, the *La Nación* legal affairs reporter who covered the trial, was threatened with death for questioning the verdict, but neither Mora nor anyone else I spoke to remembers Bravo publicly commenting on it. By then he'd become fully engaged in a battle with Rojas and Lozada that every journalist in Neiva thought would cause him the biggest trouble of his life.

The battle had begun in early 2000, when Orlando Rojas announced he was running for mayor against a veteran politician named Javier Osorio. Bravo, having exposed Mayor Penagos, could not bear the thought that the city might now be handed over to the clutches of the Rojas/Lozada clique. He decided to run for mayor himself, and on February 4, 2000, he called a press conference.

"I am campaigning against impunity, corruption and the assault of the public by the powerful," Bravo declared. He described Huila as "a feudal society run for the illicit enrichment of hereditary lords, pirates, thieves and criminal liars." The problem with the rulers was that they were psychologically incapable of feeling the pain they caused. "They do not see the suffering of the motherland in the tears of its hungry and abandoned children. On the contrary, they promote the selfish injustices that cause the tears." In place of the organized theft practiced by the city administration, Bravo offered "an ethical belief system. . . .

We are a tightly structured social organization, a pole upon which the flag of human dignity shall fly. We will be the fulcrum of personal, economic and political development."

When a reporter asked him how he would implement this lofty ideal of development, Bravo replied, "By applying the law to everyone, without exception! Is this not common sense? We have the law! Simply by applying it we will eliminate the historical privileges and corrupt and disreputable influence of the hereditary class. . . . Businessmen, workers, professionals, laborers and farmers; blacks and whites, religious people and atheists alike are tired of the yoke around their necks, tired of their impotence. They have been treated like domesticated beasts in a backward land dominated by impunity and run for the benefit of the political master class."

He concluded with a rousing peroration: "Get up, look at the new morning! It is filled with life and strength! Breathe the light of the sunrise! You have the strength of your own energy! Wake up! Walk, fight, come with me! Make the decision and, with love and faith in life, you will triumph with me!"

It turned out to be an election filled more with anger and curses than with love and faith, according to a *Diario del Huila* reporter named Germán Hernández. "Most of the anger was between Rojas and Bravo," Hernández told me in his office. "They called each other all kinds of names—you can imagine."

Until Bravo decided to run for mayor, Hernández had thought his journalism was accurate and groundbreaking, and he'd agreed with much of Bravo's criticism of the local press corps. (Indeed, when Hernández became editor of *Diario* in 2005, one of his first edicts was to ban the solicitation of ads by reporters.) But he thought the three-month campaign marked a dividing line in Bravo's career. "Bravo erased the border between his politics and his journalism," he said, referring to the fact that the liquor, oil and construction unions financed Bravo's campaign and helped him to launch his half-hour afternoon TV show, *Facts and Figures*. Bravo used the show to reiterate the findings in all of the articles he had published in *Eco Impacto*, but with quite a bit of editorializing that ignored the show's title.

In the middle of the campaign, a *mano a mano* TV debate took place between Bravo and Rojas. A moderator who looked like Groucho Marx sat between them. "I am for the patrimony of the people!" Bravo shouted, throwing his arms around. "He is for the patrimony of his family and cronies." Rojas, about twenty years younger than Bravo, half his size and with coal black hair to Bravo's speckled gray, took this broadside slumped in his chair. In the clip I saw, his most cutting riposte was that "the citizens of Neiva understand Señor Bravo has affiliations he needs to deflect attention from."

Osorio won the election, Rojas placed second, and Bravo third. He took it hard. "After his years of trying to reverse the Licorera deal and losing the fight, he now lost the election he hoped would change the city," Germán Hernández told me. "He also permanently lost his journalistic objectivity."

After he'd been defeated, Bravo submitted a blistering editorial column to *La Nación*. The paper rejected it as libelous, defamatory and malicious. Still, *La Nación* couldn't resist publishing it when Bravo resubmitted it as a paid ad. The column dropped the jaws of every Huilan between Neiva and Pitalito. It recapped the entire history of the partnership between Lozada and Rojas, alleging in unusually direct ways (even for Bravo) how their relationship had benefited both men to the detriment of Huilans. To describe the exact relationship Rojas had to Lozada, Bravo called Rojas a *testaferro*. Colombian Spanish offers no worse epithet for a public figure than this.

"Rojas sued," Hernández said, "and Bravo was charged with criminal defamation. He showed up for the judgment expecting to go to jail; he brought flip-flops with him. But for one reason or another, the judge gave him a last chance. He wouldn't send him to jail if he retracted his column."

To the surprise of everyone (including me as I listened to the story), Bravo accepted the deal. But he executed it on his own ornery terms, publishing another ad in *La Nación* that summarized his original charges and concluded with the news that the judge was forcing him to retract the column and so, under duress, he was doing so. Rojas could have demanded more contrition but, announcing that he was the bigger man, decided not to go back to court to jail the journalist. Bravo then returned to railing against Rojas and Lozada in his magazine and on his TV show.

Jaime Lozada had by then become a senator, and Bravo attacked his voting record as being perfectly congruent with a *politquero* — a lying politician who serves his own interests. Bravo also attacked Lozada's wife, Gloria Polanco, a candidate for the Colombian House of Representatives. He attacked Lozada's lavish lifestyle on the top floors of the Edificio Mira Flores, demanding to know where he got the money to live in such splendor. On July 26, 2001, the guerrillas launched their own attack — Teófila Forero–style. At 11 p.m., twenty gunmen raided the tower and went straight to Lozada's eleventh-floor suite, broke down the door and grabbed Lozada's wife and their two teenage boys, then began breaking into other luxury suites, kidnapping a total of fifteen people and hustling them off in vehicles to the jungle. They missed Lozada by one day. He was in Bogotá.

Lozada eventually negotiated a ransom of $300,000 that would free his sons, but during the negotiations the guerrillas insisted on holding onto his wife. Lozada told the media that, according to his intermediaries, money wouldn't help: the guerrillas would release her only in a prisoner exchange. Indeed, after the boys were finally let go, on July 14, 2004, the guerrillas included Polanco on a list of fifty-nine hostages — politicians, soldiers and three Americans — whom they were willing to exchange for five hundred jailed guerrillas. Long before then, however, in an off-the-cuff remark on his TV show, Bravo infuriated Lozada by cracking that Lozada most likely was too cheap to pay for the release of his wife.

In November 2002, Bravo published one more lead story in *Eco*

Impacto, titled "The Selling of Neiva: The Concealments of Licorsa and Its Double Dealing," attacking Lozada's and Rojas's reputations. But his colleague, Diógenes Cadena, says that his heart wasn't in it: "After so many years of laying out how these two were getting richer and richer off what he said should have been going to the people, he became very discouraged, very depressed. He said it was like 'planting in the desert.'" It was the last edition of *Eco Impacto* that Bravo published.*

Two weeks later, on December 1, 2002, another radio journalist, Gimbler Perdomo, was shot to death in Gigante. Bravo, in a eulogy on his TV show, incriminated "the whole structure of this lost department, corrupt from top to bottom. Nothing ever changes because those who raise their voices above a whisper are silenced, either by fear or by murder." He then launched into a rambling monologue about his long struggle to defeat the liquor deal and then to expose its principal beneficiaries. "Confronting this latest act of slaughter," he said, "I personally feel no fear. My face is half in shadow, but the other half remains a mirror to events past and present."

"There's a man who enters the picture now," Germán Hernández told me in his office at *Diario del Huila.* That man was Yesid Guzmán Guitiérrez, an official with an elite federal forensics unit called the CTI. "He was known around town as 'The Fiscal,'" Hernández said, "but Guzmán's rank was nowhere near the rank of a chief prosecutor." Guzmán received his nickname, Hernández explained, because of his reputation for arbitrarily wielding the power of the state, as if he *were* a chief prosecutor. "Guzmán was either a paramilitary himself or served them closely," Hernández said.

---

*Bravo honored the magazine by renaming his TV program *Eco Impacto* TV.

Around this time, Guzmán was approached by a person or persons in his circle and informed that Bravo needed to be liquidated. "We have a general picture of what happened next," Hernández said, "from people lower down the ladder, but the masterminds are still a matter of some conjecture." Guzmán assigned subordinates to take care of the murder, and they contacted a paramilitary *sicario* who went by the nom de guerre Carlos Humberto. Arrangements were made for an agreed-upon amount to be paid to Humberto, who was left with the impression that his payment would be a fair portion of the thirty million pesos (about $15,000) he was told the mastermind had paid to Guzmán to organize the assassination. Humberto surveilled Bravo's neighborhood and studied his habits. However, on the day the deed was to be done, March 8, 2003, Guzmán's agents informed Humberto that their client had only given them two million pesos for the job, or about a thousand dollars, part of which they would keep. This proved to be a counterproductive move.

Bravo wasn't home when Humberto rolled up to the bungalow on a big motorcycle. Ana Cristina Suárez heard the rumble and went nervously to the door. The stranger standing on her doorstep gave her his name and said that he had to speak to Guillermo Bravo. "I immediately knew that this guy was there to kill my husband," she told me. "He wore boots and had a *paraco*"—the haircut worn by paramilitaries, shaved on the side and with a brush cut on top. "'Señora, I need to tell your husband something very important. I came to warn him that he is going to get killed.' I asked, 'Who are you!?' He said, 'I am an agent of the AUC.'" Suárez recalled her despair: only hours before, eating breakfast with Bravo, she'd felt a glimmer of hope that the threats might soon end. "Guillermo was getting very tired of the whole thing in Neiva," she recollected. "He said people deserved their own destiny. And now, here was his destiny."

Ten minutes later, Bravo came around the corner on Ana Cristina's scooter. "The man just stood there," she said. "I went to

Guillermo. I told him, 'The man there says they are going to kill you. He says he's here to warn you.'

"Guillermo walked right up to him and said, 'Are you armed?' Guillermo lifted his shirt right up over his belt. And when he saw he wasn't armed, he said, 'Well, come in and tell me your story.'"

"He wasn't frightened?" I asked.

"He was just very tired," Ana Cristina replied. "Very weary that now, here, there was another threat. And we sat down at the table, me, Guillermo and my daughter, and Guillermo just looked at this young man, without saying anything. And the *sicario* looked back at him. So I asked the *sicario*, 'Why are you warning us?' and he said to Guillermo, but not to me, 'Because I also have a family.' I asked, 'Who sent you?' He said, 'They told us it is someone from Cali, but usually they tell us lies.' I asked, 'Why is he going to get killed?' He said, 'I don't know, I think it is a debt thing.' I said, 'A debt? You don't know who this man is!? He's a journalist, and if they are going to kill him, it's because he exposes them! I know who sent you! He exposed the last governor, who's a thief!' Guillermo said, 'Shut up, dear,' but not to me—he was still looking at the *sicario*, and the *sicario* was looking back at him. The *sicario* said to him, 'The guy who is after you is an expert killer, studying you. You were playing basketball last week when the guy drove around and studied you. He was going to try today. But for one reason or another, the guy has changed his mind.' Guillermo said to him, 'I am lucky.' And the *sicario* said, 'My advice is that you keep your windows and door shut and that you get out of town. You should stop your work immediately.' Guillermo said, 'Then I suppose they will leave me alone.' He said, 'Señor Bravo, I've done this before. I'm a businessman, but I also have a father. It will do you no good to ask for protection from DAS, because over there are the same people who are against you.' Guillermo said, 'If it's money, I don't have anything; the only thing I have is my computer and this.' Guillermo took out a twenty-thousand-peso bill, and the guy took it! Guillermo said—

he laughed—he said, 'Don't they give you money for gas?' When they said goodbye at the door, they shook hands and Guillermo asked, 'Well, will we see each other again?' and the guy said, 'Probably. Until then, heed what I say. Because it will not be me who comes here next.'"

It's likely that Bravo could thank the greed of the middleman Guzmán for being given this warning, Hernández told me. Guzmán had held back so much of the actual payment "that the shooter became resentful. But because of the way the shooter portrayed himself to Bravo, he became publicly known as a man with a conscience." The press called him *Sicario arrepentido*—the Regretful Shooter.

Bravo verified what the Regretful Shooter had told him through his sources among the left, who had a double agent on pay in the AUC. When he heard what they had to say, he told his friend Carlos Mora at *La Nación*, "This time they'll get me." The next day, Sunday, March 9, he took the bus to Bogotá.

In the capital, he looked up some old friends from his university days who had influential contacts in the government who might be able to help him. All of them advised him to stay in Bogotá and start his career over. President Uribe was then on the offensive throughout the country against the guerrillas, with considerable backing from the public, and the current anti-left climate did not look good for journalists of Bravo's reputation outside the city. Indeed, nine days after his arrival, the papers carried headlines that yet another crusading journalist, Luis Alfonso Parada, had been murdered in Arauca, a remote town on the eastern plains. The details of the killing were both sad and horrifying, a testimony to the sadism of the paramilitaries who were thought to have been behind the murder. The thirty-three-year-old Alfonso was just five feet tall, weighed 250 pounds and had legs so abnormally bowed that he rocked and swayed on the outside of his soles when he walked. Defying death threats, he had returned to radio reporting after paramilitaries had kidnapped his co-host Efraín Varela, tortured and shot him. Now, nine months later, the AUC had caught up with the malformed Alfonso, shooting him as he begged for his life outside his radio station.

Neither these gruesome killings nor the urgings of Bravo's friends could convince him to remain in Bogotá. Five days later, on March 23, he wrote a last note to an old friend—"See you soon, if the killers allow it"—and took the bus back to Neiva.

Given that he had fled Neiva for his life, Bravo returned as if *sicarios* were not on his mind. Instead of going home and staying there, he made the rounds of all the spots in Neiva Centro that were being watched by paramilitaries, including the downtown headquarters of the oil and liquor unions. From the liquor union he phoned his son, Juan Carlos, and a nephew, both of whom had worked with him for over a decade. He told them to report at his home office as usual the next morning. Then he visited Carlos Mora at *La Nación* and announced that he had come home to continue his investigations. He explained that his situation was "extremely grave," but he used an ironic tone, as if he wasn't afraid. "Truly, he joked about the death threat," his nephew Eduard Ortiz told me. "When we went to work at the computer the next morning, he said, 'Move over so they shoot you and not me.'"

Privately, however, he was deeply depressed. "He went back to work, but not with his heart," Ana Cristina told me. "When something about corruption came on the TV, he shouted, 'Turn it off! I can't live with this anymore! It's useless to struggle against it. In six years I will be seventy and still struggling!'"

The first TV program he chose to produce after he got back had nothing to do with municipal corruption. It was a global feature on the dangers posed by the herbicides that military helicopters were using to spray Colombia's coca plants—an important topic, but not the subject he'd been dealing with before the visit of the Regretful Shooter.

That evening, Ana Cristina made Bravo swear he would keep the door locked when she went to her job teaching night school in the town of Sena, forty minutes away. He promised, but when she got back at eleven that night, she found the door wide open. The next night, the same thing happened. And the next. "Ai! I got tired of telling him to close that door!" she told me. "Guillermo *knew* that closing the door was sacred to me! He sat in his office with the door to the house open! I always told him as I left, 'Keep the door locked!' When I got back he always said, 'Nothing is going to happen to me, I wanted the breeze.' But he *knew* something would happen to him. The Regretful Shooter *told* him something would happen!"

"And you kept the door shut when you were in the house?"

"Always! Shut, locked, and I was always going to the window when I heard a motorcycle. He left it to me to be his guard. But when I was not there, he had no guard."

During the week of April 26, Bravo and Eduard Ortiz worked on a program they were putting together as a memorial to the thousands of Colombians murdered by paramilitaries. Bravo taped the introduction to the show on April 27. It is the last video clip of him alive. Watching it in Juan Carlos's apartment, I was struck by how haggard he appeared compared with the vigorous fellow I had seen in the mayoralty debate with Rojas. Everything he had been through in those last three years showed: his failure to reverse the liquor deal between Rojas and Lozada; the moral blow he had sustained when the citizens of Neiva gave more votes to Rojas than to him; his loss in the criminal defamation suit; and the public humiliation he'd had to endure by saying no to jail and retracting his article. With those burdens written all over him, the women of Bogotá could not have paid him the kind of attention he'd been used to for most of his life.

At 5 p.m., April 28, 2003, Ana Cristina left for her teaching job in Sena. She pulled the door shut and locked it. As she was getting on her scooter, Bravo got up from his desk, went into the foyer, unlocked the door and pulled it open. Ana Cristina was so furious that as she made a U-turn on Carrera 5, she didn't wave goodbye.

"Do you think he opened the door because he wanted the breeze?" I asked her.

She didn't answer at first, just gazed at her hands that were gripping a napkin tightly. Two tears welled onto her cheeks and then she began to weep, without lifting the napkin to wipe the tears away.

"He knew the closed door was sacred to me!" she said when she could finally speak. "Guillermo violated my trust every night by leaving that door open!"

The sun sets in Neiva at 6 p.m. year round. By 6:30, the sky is black. Walking home from the market, Bravo's neighbor across the street, Dianna La Rotta, saw him sitting at his desk in his office, lit and framed like a picture through the open doorway — an old, gray-haired writer hunched at his computer, finishing a script about murder. Over the next hour she prepared dinner in her kitchen, which faced the street, but she does not remember hearing an engine. The motorcyclist on the big Yamaha must have cut the power half a block away and coasted to Bravo's door. As the bike came to a halt, La Rotta did not look up to see the *parillero* who got off the back. She did not notice his silhouette as he entered Bravo's home.

"Bravo would have known then that this was his moment," Germán Hernández said. "The shooter must have held the gun on him as he walked through the doorway, because Bravo swiveled in his chair as the killer came around the divide into his office. He was shot with his back to the computer, spraying his keyboard with blood. I have written that it seems he was shot with some forethought." Guillermo Bravo was shot near his heart, in the jaw and in his forehead, as if, Hernández wrote, "to erase his thoughts, his feelings and his voice."

Hearing the three shots, Dianna La Rotta looked up from her sink to see a man leaping onto the back of the Yamaha. The bike roared to life and then headed fast up the block. Witnesses later told police they saw Yesid "The Fiscal" Guzmán rendezvous with two men on a Yamaha at the basketball court a couple of blocks away. "One assumes that Guzmán believed in his impunity to such an extent that he felt bold enough to pay them for the deed right then," Hernández said.

La Rotta ran across the street and found Bravo sprawled in his chair, his head lolling back. She raced back to her house to call for help. Ana Cristina was laughing with her students over a slide show she was presenting when La Rotta reached her by phone. She arrived at the hospital to find a crowd of reporters and police in front of it. Inside, talking with doctors, were Bravo's legal wife, Angela Ortiz, his son Juan Carlos and his nephew Eduard Ortiz. Eduard took Ana Christina aside and told her Bravo was dead; his body was being transferred to the morgue to be autopsied by the CTI—the forensics unit for which Guzmán worked.

The next morning, Eduard edited the memorial to the victims of paramilitary murder on Bravo's bloodstained computer. There was a hole in the desk's drawer from which detectives had extracted the bullet that had passed through Bravo's mouth. "I never thought I would have to include Guillermo on that night's show," Eduard told me. "We made him the main subject, but we included the others, as he would have wanted."

Watching the video of Bravo, and of the many murdered trade unionists and journalists, I tried to imagine what was going through his mind as he wrote his last words, "The martyrs of our land say, 'Don't be a Judas, don't. . . . '" For a lot of intricate reasons, he'd wanted to transform Neiva, and when it looked like he would enter old age without seeing the city change, he'd simply waited for the killers to enter his house—"almost welcomed by the door he left open to let the breeze in," as the Bogotá press phrased it.

———

The funeral was held April 30, at Neiva's Cathedral of the Immaculate Conception, attended by hundreds of union members, journalists and small-businessmen from Neiva Centro. "They murdered the man, but not his ideas," Juan Carlos said in his eulogy beside his father's flower-bedecked coffin. "We demand that there be no impunity. We will find and prosecute these rats who are infesting Neiva!"

As the mourners filed by the coffin and paid their condolences to the family, three men pulled Eduard Ortiz and Juan Carlos Bravo aside. "They informed us they were Teófila Forero," Ortiz told me. "One said, 'We have come to pay our respects to a brave man and to tell you we did not kill him. We inform you that we will take vengeance for the murder of Guillermo Bravo Vega.'"

"Aside from using them as sources," I asked them, "did Guillermo ever have anything to do with the Teófila Forero?"

"No, he didn't," Juan Carlos said. "During the time of FARC-landia, they invited him to come to their main camp and lecture on economic theory, but he refused. After his violent act as a young man, he was opposed to all violence. The only act of violence he was connected to was the violence done to him."

Bravo was buried in the nearby Gardens of Paradise Cemetery, after which Ana Cristina gave an emotional interview to Germán Hernández of Diario del Huila. "Guillermo Bravo was killed by people who saw they were at risk of losing the goose who laid the golden egg," she said. "And when I say 'goose' and 'golden egg,' a lot of people in Huila know which goose and which egg."

In its subsequent coverage of the murder, the respected Bogotá news magazine Semana gave considerable space to Bravo's dogged investigation of Governor Lozada's transfer of Licorera del Huila to Orlando Rojas. "All of this made Bravo believe—and tell his family after the visit of the Regretful Shooter—that the threats against him could be related to his exposure of the liquor industry case," Semana stated. "Addressing this issue, Rojas said, 'No one can say, or even imply, that I've ever been involved in any public quarrel, or that I've committed a violent act. The differences I had with Guillermo Bravo were solved through legal means.' Lozada agrees with Rojas, saying that Bravo's murder was not related to the articles that he published, but to the fact that 'he had gained a lot of enemies and that he had a leftist ideology.'"

Germán Hernández co-authored the *Semana* article, even though he had been warned off the case by an anonymous murder threat. "At every turn, Yesid Guzmán frustrated the police investigation," Hernández told me. "He had the power to do it. They found the motorcycle, but were there fingerprints? We don't know: that is the CTI's responsibility. The suspects who were identified as being on the motorcycle that night were shortly found, and shortly released." After the release of the suspects, the Regretful Shooter, who had betrayed his mission to kill Bravo, was hunted down, shot in the face and left for dead. He survived, however, and showed up wounded at DAS to offer his testimony against both the shooters and Guzmán.

"Yet Guzmán only became 'a preliminary suspect,'" Hernández went on. "He was fired from his post—officially for other reasons, his connections to paramilitaries and possible drug dealing—but he was never arrested. With so much evidence, how can an investigation stay in its preliminary stages? But it did. Then they moved the investigation to Bogotá, and it has been there ever since, with no progress. It is still in its 'preliminary stages'"—where it remains at this writing.

"What happened to Guzmán after he was fired?" I asked Hernández.

"About eight months later, January 14, 2004, two farmers found his body near Algeciras, about fifty kilometers south of here, Teófila Forero territory. He was tortured before he was shot in the head and chest. They found another corpse with him, also tortured, Jesús Alexander Rojas. It is possible Jesús Alexander was the shooter of Bravo. A third person was also later found murdered, possibly the driver of the motorcycle. The Regretful Shooter was ultimately hunted down too."

"So the Teófila Forero took revenge for a journalist they thought was on their side?" I asked.

"I suspect the Regretful Shooter was shot by his own side," Hernández said. "As for the others, they were probably tortured to find out who was the mastermind of the crime."

"I have two dreams in my life," Jaime Lozada told me. "One dream is to get the championship for my soccer team, Atlético Huila. And the other dream, to get the freedom of my wife. Two dreams."

I wrote the dreams down, in the order he listed them.

"Where exactly did they take your wife and boys?" I asked.

"Somewhere to the FARC territory, fifty miles from here, no more. It was easy for them. They knew where to come. It was like a movie. They were dressed as soldiers, they blew open the door, took everybody and ran to their territory. They asked for money for my children, but not for my wife. The only possibility that she could return to us, they said, was a prisoner exchange."

He called one of his freed sons into the room and introduced him. Then he led me across the living room into his home office, paneled in dark teak and illuminated by antique electric lamps with green glass shades. "These are my military decorations," he said, opening his palm in the green glow to indicate a large display case filled with ribbons, citations and sunburst medals. "The army gives me honors. And you can see here, my friends in Colombia." He pointed to two trophy walls of photos, Lozada arm in arm with the presidents of Colombia for the last fifty years, from a teenage Lozada with Mariano Ospina Perez to a mature and hefty Lozada with Álvaro Uribe. "When I was the governor of Huila State, Uribe was the governor of Antioquia; and when I was in London as the general consul for Colombia, Uribe was in Oxford studying.

So we are acquainted, you could say. The governor of Huila is a very good friend of mine, too. He's a Liberal. But he got the job thanks to me, because of my work for him. I met Bill Clinton, too. I love America."

Above these photos was an old, ornate diploma—his economics degree, from the same university Bravo had attended.

"You got along with Bravo once," I said.

"I did, a long time ago," he agreed. "Because we were both economists. Then we became neutral to one another, and then we became opponents, because Bravo was with the unions. When I became governor, he declared himself my enemy. But you see, politicians, we don't hold rancor at each other." He hunched his big shoulders, squinched his face and gave me an old-boy look of mutual understanding. "It's a game, you know that."

"But for journalists it's not a game," I said.

"No, but for us—" This time he physically nudged me. "It's a game."

"Yes, politicians pretend," I said, then asked if I could take a picture of him on the balcony.

As we strolled out to the view, I asked Lozada if he was worried for his safety.

"I don't need to protect myself," he replied. "The people protect me. And God. Many people—excuse me for saying it myself—but many people *love* me in this state. Of course, I have competitors, because I am a public man. Right? But many people, they love me."

Six weeks later, on December 3, 2005, the Teófila Forero finally caught up with Jaime Lozada. He was en route from Gigante to Neiva after a well-publicized celebration for his eldest son, who had just been elected an executive of the Huila Conservative Party. The guerrillas ambushed Lozada, his son and their bodyguards with hand grenades and machine-gun fire. Lozada was shot four times and killed. The son was wounded by the two grenades but survived. The car was destroyed, but when it rolled to a halt, the guerrillas stopped long enough to check inside, then sped away, letting the others live. They'd got the man they wanted.

TWO

I GREW UP ON BULLETS

Marlene Garcia-Esperat, Philippines

IN THE GRIMY HEART OF MANILA stands a wedding-cake palace called Malacañang, a reminder, as one tour guide puts it, "that many rulers of poor countries live in more luxury than those of rich countries." Built in 1802 by a Spanish colonial lord, the palace's name derives from the casual way Filipinos first referred to it: *May lakan iyan*— some nobleman lives there. Rococo arcades, crested parapets and pink-roofed balconies were added by succeeding lords, the last of whom surrendered the extravagant abode to the United States after the Spanish-American War. The Japanese, in turn, evicted the Americans during the Second World War, and when the battle-ravaged and poverty-stricken Philippines achieved independence in 1946, Malacañang became the residence of the nation's first elected president. From the outset, Manuel Roxas took the name of the palace to heart, living like a nobleman off the proceeds of graft and setting an example for future presidents. Four decades on, after numerous riots in front of the palace gates, outraged Filipinos invented a novel way to interrupt the terms of their thieving rulers. They called it "People Power."

Because they occur periodically, People Power revolutions in the Philippines are given numbers, like movie sequels. In each revolt, a million or so demonstrators gather round the fifty-foot statue of the Holy Virgin at Manila's EDSA Shrine, out of tear-gas range of Malacañang. They stand in the tropical heat for days, praying, waving posters and vowing not to leave until one or another president vacates the palace. When the generals of the country decide the forces opposing their chief are too powerful to crush, they switch sides and the revolution is successful. That was the case when the archbishop of the mostly Catholic Philippines backed People Power 1 in 1986, dethroning the mega-larcenist dictator Ferdinand Marcos, and again in January 2001, when People Power II overthrew the plundering playboy Joseph Estrada. Four months later, however, People Power III ran into difficulty when a million anticlerical slum dwellers tried to oust Estrada's erstwhile vice president and autocratic successor, Gloria Macapagal-Arroyo. Raised in the splendor of Malacañang as the daughter of an earlier president, the fifty-three-year-old Arroyo kept the church and army onside, declared a state of rebellion and bloodily smashed the uprising.

Arroyo ran an administration that was as scandal-plagued as any that came before it, but over the next three years she maintained the support of the two institutions crucial to power in the Philippines. Pleasing the church, she blocked the distribution of contraceptives in the massively overpopulated country; buying the loyalty of the army, she bloated its top ranks with promotions and gave its generals grandiose perks at public expense. On May 10, 2004, defying her low standing in the opinion polls, Arroyo won a national election, her narrow margin of victory lopsidedly accrued on the insurgency plagued island of Mindanao, six hundred miles south of Manila.

Nine months after the election, on February 15, 2005, Arroyo received an angry letter from a journalist who lived on Mindanao. At forty-five, Marlene Garcia-Esperat was relatively new to the profession: an agricultural chemist by training and a mother of four, she had turned to writing investigative columns for a rural newspaper just four years earlier. Yet while her name was unknown to average Filipinos, her fiery articles, raven-haired beauty and penchant for dressing in miniskirts and plunging necklines had inspired veteran reporters at Manila's Center for Investigative Journalism to dub her "the Erin Brockovitch of the Philippines" — a reference to the sexy and unstoppable legal crusader made famous by the Hollywood film.

Esperat began her letter to Arroyo by summarizing her investigations of "high-profile scams" that had taken place on Mindanao prior to the 2004 election. She'd discovered that millions of dollars meant for poor farmers had been secretly diverted by the federal Department of Agriculture to pay off mayors, governors and congressmen — all of whom had the power to pad and shave votes on her tormented island. "Lately, reports reveal that military intelligence operatives are allegedly out and tasked to liquidate the undersigned," she stated, adding that Arroyo's top cabinet secretaries were "suspects of threats to my life due to my series of exposés." Esperat, who had survived several previous assassination attempts, concluded her letter by flinging down a righteous gauntlet: "I am ready to *die for this cause but you can never stop the will of the Lord.*"

Five weeks later, on March 24, 2005, Esperat was shot dead in her home in front of her children. She was the twentieth journalist murdered on Arroyo's watch, but none of the other killings stirred the nation's heart so dramatically. Within days, almost everyone in the family-oriented Philippines knew Esperat's name and work. By the summer, in good part because of that work, Arroyo found herself battling congressional investigations, impeachment hearings and the growing threat of People Power IV. When I stepped off the plane in Manila a few months later, it looked as if Esperat's "will of the Lord" was about to be accomplished.

Perennial convulsions calling for a president's head had not been the promise for a sunny future made by Gloria Macapagal-Arroyo's father. In the early 1960s, when Esperat was a child, President Diosdado Macapagal told the nation that the Philippines was on its way to becoming Asia's leading economy. "We are building materially and spiritually for our destiny," he told his countrymen from his palace home. Supported by seven thousand coral-fringed islands spread out over the rich fishing grounds of the South China Sea, a growing tourism industry, vast natural resources and a bountiful agricultural sector, the prospects for the Philippines did indeed seem bright. On closer inspection, however, there was one worrying problem that made the lives of ordinary Filipinos miserable. From Luzon in the north to Mindanao in the south, laws and regulations were worth no more than the price of a bribe to avoid them.

At the time of Esperat's murder forty years later, Transparency International listed the country as more corrupt than war-torn Afghanistan; the Philippine Center for Investigative Journalism reported that as much as half the country's taxes were lost to corrupt officials; and the disparity between rich and poor was among the most glaring in the world. In Manila, on the island of Luzon, oligarchs and politicians lived in high-walled enclaves while over a million families squatted in slums and garbage dumps. Thirty percent of the nation's 85 million citizens survived on less than a dollar a day, 15 million reported being hungry and 29 million thought their lives were getting worse year by year. Aside from a thriving sex trade that drew thousands of Western men to the smog-choked capital, tourism had been on the decline for years: rivers and beaches were polluted, coral reefs had been ravaged by dynamite and cyanide fishing, and 97 percent of the country's primary forests had been logged. Indeed, the most reliable source of foreign exchange for the Philippines came from the people who'd left it. Each day twenty-five hundred Filipinos joined 12 million of their countrymen who were guest workers in faraway places such as the United Arab Emirates, where they were often treated like slaves, or Iraq, where they faced kidnapping and beheading. They'd gone overseas to uncertain fates because their mayors, governors, police and presidents had ignored their needs, skimmed their salaries, stolen their taxes and robbed their votes. One in nine Filipinos had arrived at a desperate solution: get out of the country and wire money directly to relatives, which would at least keep their earnings out of the clutches of a national conspiracy of organized theft.

Filipinos had a saying that encapsulated their fatalistic attitude toward government thievery: *Baka maagawan*. The Tagalog words mean "Don't worry, they'll ask," which sums up the expectation of the country's citizenry that they'll be extorted by the authorities or heavily leaned on for bribes. Coupled with the national philosophy, *Bahala na*, or "That's the way it is," the leaders of the Philippines have always been confident that while their constituents occasionally take to the streets to protest their grossest displays of corruption, for the most part they put up with their leaders' antics because they expect little better of them. The leaders themselves live by the saying *Baka makalusot*, which essentially means "Everybody does it, nobody gets caught, so I'll do it too."

The nation's "metastatic corruption," as it is called by the Philippine Institute for Popular Democracy, has its roots in pre-colonial history, when Philippine tribal leaders attained their power in small *barangays*, or communities, based on a system known as *pasalubong-pabaon*—the giving of gifts in anticipation of receiving gifts. Aspiring chiefs distributed wealth in order to gain power and then accepted even more wealth for slanting their exercise of power, to the great benefit of themselves, their extended family and their circle of allies. While on the village level the needs of the chief and the group were often congruent, that balance was destroyed when the Spanish conquered the islands in the sixteenth century. Spanish overseers informed the chiefs that they could continue running their barangays, but only if they agreed to hand most of their tribute to Spain and her civil servants. Three centuries later, after the United States wrested the Philippines from Spain in 1898, the Americans continued that machinery of governance, but with a twist. In the 1930s the U.S. colonial administrators helped

Filipinos to draw up an American-style constitution, which was to prove but a veneer of democracy over the time-honored tradition of *pasalubong-pabaon*. After independence, Filipino politicians who had served U.S. mining and sugar interests entrenched themselves in power by harvesting vast amounts of government money to finance their election campaigns, flagrantly buying votes at *barangay* fiestas and bribing the officials who tabulated the ballots. The 1961 election that brought Gloria Arroyo's father to power used up 13 percent of the national budget. By the time of Marcos's election in 1965, it was up to about 20 percent, and Marcos's re-election in 1969 harnessed 25 percent. Marcos did away with the need for buying elections by declaring martial law in 1972, but the practice continued even after his overthrow, which installed the supposedly reformist Cory Aquino in 1986. The revered wife of the assassinated opposition leader Ninoy Aquino managed to sidestep her own reform legislation, earning her administration the derisive name "Relatives Incorporated" because of its rampant patronage and simony. In 1992, her successor, Fidel Ramos, Marcos's former chief of the army, siphoned millions from the passport office to elect himself and his chosen candidates.

Marcos and his wife, Imelda, were human vacuum cleaners when it came to theft of the Philippine treasury, stealing over $12 billion, and one would think any president would look good by comparison—except in the Philippines. Midway through his term, Ramos became embroiled in what Filipinos call "the Grandmother of All Scams": the sale of $600 million worth of public land in Manila Bay at a 95 percent reduced price so that Ramos cronies could collect the real value in payoffs. All of this larceny would, in turn, be mirrored by the corruption of Ramos's vice president and eventual successor in 1998, Joseph Estrada, who openly entertained gangsters at Malacañang and purchased palatial mansions for his numerous girlfriends with millions in government funds.

While the poor in the ostensibly democratic Philippines had the numbers to elect people who would not steal from them, they were robbed of that right too. They were simply powerless against an entrenched oligarchy that kept stealing elections and then stealing the funds that would address their needs. Year after year the politicians allotted hundreds of millions of dollars to national development, but very little of it got where it was supposed to go. A May 2002 opposition-party Senate study of national development funds estimated that as much as 60 percent was lost to corrupt politicians and their appointed officials. An August 2003 review of the personal wealth of officials conducted by the Philippine Transparency Group revealed that though the top civil servant salary in the Philippines was less than seven hundred dollars a month, "more than 80 percent of officials in the Bureau of Internal Revenue, Bureau of Customs, and Department of Public Works are millionaires." Indeed, nearly *all* members of the Senate and House of Representatives were millionaires, according to a survey by the Philippine Center for Investigative Journalism (PCIJ). Most were "also part of political families whose members have held public office for two or more generations." The theoretically opposing parties under which these families ran for office all had short life spans, being little more than temporary alliances between rival clans who dreamed up new names for new parties every election cycle as they realigned themselves in their endless quest for power and spoils. "There is simply no lasting check on the unbridled theft practiced by our nation's elite," according to Dante Jimenez, the founding chairman of the organization Volunteers Against Crime and Corruption. Again and again party leaders and their cronies were charged with monumental corruption only to successfully fight their cases in an equally corrupt judicial system and return to haunt the country in the next election.

A state of perpetual unrest was the result, with the Philippines plagued by frequent coup attempts and never-ending insurgencies. In addition to the three People Power revolts, between 1986 and 2003 there were ten attempts by lower-ranking military officers to overthrow the government, all unsuccessful and many ending in bloodshed. In that same period, two guerrilla insurgencies raged across the length and breadth of the country, one in the central and northern islands, led by communist rebels whose ranks were filled by twenty thousand unemployed young men, the other on Mindanao, led by a Muslim separatist army whose ranks of twelve thousand were similarly filled by unemployed young men.

The thousands of dead on all sides and the chronic atmosphere of crisis that caused one financial panic after another seemed to teach the Philippine government nothing. "People Power events come and go in our country, but the modus vivendi of our politicians never changes," Leonard de Vera, a former spokesman for the Philippine Bar Association, told me in Manila. "The goal of most of our politicians is not to govern the country but to divert its treasure to their pockets and collect bribes from gangsters who run *jueteng*"—the nationwide, multibillion-dollar illegal numbers racket, of which almost every politician got a cut. The People Power II coup that overthrew Estrada in 2001 had been sparked by revelations that in the two and a half years since his election, he had collected at least $60 million in bribes from *jueteng* gangsters, the money funneled to him by governors and senior policemen who took their share before passing the money up the line. Promising "honesty, transparency and unswerving dedication to upholding the laws of our nation," his replacement, Gloria Arroyo, promptly became godmother to the son of the Philippines' biggest illegal gambling lord, Rodolfo "Bong" Pineda, claiming the Catholic Church had told her that because Pineda had asked for the blessing, it was her "Christian duty" to give it.

Unsurprisingly, exposing corruption in the Philippines was not only a feckless exercise but a dangerous one. Since the fall of Marcos, the Philippines has had a wildly free press, but the impunity of the powerful has meant that journalists who offend them can be murdered without consequence. In the twenty years between Marcos's overthrow in 1986 and my visit to Mindanao in February 2006, sixty journalists had been targeted and murdered for their work—twenty-four of them on Mindanao and six of those in Marlene Esperat's region of the island. In a rare couple of cases the triggermen were caught and tried; in no cases were the officials who ordered the killings tried. Two eyewitnesses to the 2002 murder of Mindanao journalist Edgar Damalerio—a fellow journalist and a soldier—were themselves murdered before the trial of the accused police sergeant finally began in 2005. The sergeant was convicted, but the two politicians whom Damalerio had repeatedly exposed in print and on radio were never investigated by the police.

Shortly after Marlene Esperat's death, a veteran *Manila Standard* reporter named Joel Egco, himself the survivor of assassination attempts, took the desperate step of founding an organization called ARMED (Association of Responsible Media), advocating that journalists carry guns for self-protection. On the firing range at which he trained his colleagues in the use of 9mm pistols, Egco told me he had the despairing feeling that his country was almost beyond reform. Virtually all transactions in the Philippines, he said, were still based on *pasalubong-pabaon*. "Our interactions are viewed as investments for our extended family," he related. "I give you this now, you give me that later. Filipinos expect that kind of exchange in their relationships, even at the national political level." Hence the cultural logic behind why an incorruptible journalist in the Philippines was sometimes considered a legitimate target by politicians. "If they refuse gifts and give bad press, they violate *pasalubong-pabaon*. You can't run a society like that! You have to die!"

Journalists themselves were not immune to the system of *pasalubong-pabaon*, and members of the press were the source of almost as many corruption scandals as politicians. Most cases involved bribery or blackmail and were referred to as "ATM journalism," "envelope journalism" and "AC/DC journalism" (for "attack collect/defend collect"). A PCIJ study of journalists during the 1998 presidential election revealed that one-third openly admitted to taking money from their sources. In 2001 a senator and former national police chief, Panfilo Lacson—himself facing corruption charges—told me that when he took the job of top cop in 1998, he discovered his predecessor had been paying $40,000 a month to journalists.

And yet, surrounded by this sea of graft, bribery and extortion, Marlene Esperat somehow kept her integrity. Just before she was murdered in her hometown of Tacurong, she'd told her lawyer, Nena Santos, and her sister, Valmie Mariveles, that she had been offered a hundred-thousand-dollar bribe in return for ending her investigations of the Department of Agriculture. Esperat had never earned more than a hundred dollars a month as a journalist, but she refused the bribe.

Tacurong is a mid-size town of seventy thousand in Mindanao's predominantly Muslim province of Sultan Kudarat. When I arrived it seemed like a peaceable southeast Asian trade center, with a never-ending roar of rickshaws and farm trucks circling a stupa-like Muslim monument called a *salakof* in the central plaza. The nearby streets were lined with an exotic mix of peasant markets, fast-food outlets, a mosque and Internet cafés. On the edge of town, bougainvillea- and palm-lined neighborhoods melded into an agri-cultural valley of pineapple fields and rice paddies, walled to the east and west by green volcanic mountains. It was a paradisiacal-looking locale, well placed between ocean ports and international airports just an hour or two away. Eighty miles north, at the mouth of the Mindanao River, was Cotabato City, where the island's Department of Agriculture had its headquarters; forty miles south was the island's main port and largest city, General Santos.

During the day it was almost possible to forget that things changed in the Mindanao River Valley after sunset, the buzz of insects broken by rifle fire, explosions and drive-by assassinations. For three decades the Moro Islamic Liberation Front had been violently pressing their demand for independence from the Catholic-run Philippines, using Cotabato City as their political headquarters and the mountains as redoubts from which to attack army posts and government buildings. In recent years their nationalist rebellion had been complicated by psychotic attacks on civilians by the Muslim fundamentalist group Abu Sayyaf, whose insurgents had been linked to al-Qaeda and to the Indonesian-based Jemaah Islamiyah. Overall, the death toll from these insurgencies had made the life expectancy on Mindanao twelve years lower than in the rest of the Philippines. Yet, according to Marlene Esperat's father, Luis Garcia, when people in the province were polled in 2005 about their most pressing problem, they listed the guerrillas second, ranking government corruption as their first concern. One of the richest agricultural valleys in the Philippines was chronically underproducing because it was starved of the seeds, fertilizer and irrigation equipment that were allotted to it by government development programs, whose funds to buy those "farm inputs" were stolen by federal officials in the Department of Agriculture in Cotabato City.

When Marlene Garcia was born, on August 29, 1959, her father was fully engaged in the fight against corruption as a crusading city councilman. Indeed, Luis Garcia had been risking his life in the service of causes since he was a twenty-year-old farmer in the province of Iloilo (pronounced Yo-lo), in the central Visayan Islands. After the surrender of American forces to the Japanese in 1942, he joined a guerrilla band to fight the invaders, was wounded three times, and earned a wall full of U.S. military honors that, lifting his cane, he pointed out to me proudly. After the war he moved south, buying fifty hectares of rice fields outside Tacurong. In 1948 he was elected the town's police chief, and quickly uncovered a rat's nest of official corruption. Because those he arrested reaped the benefits of having *pares* (friends) on the bench, in 1956 he decided to enter politics, and won a city councilor's seat. "They were all corrupt on that council—that was why I ran for office, as a reformer," he told me. "The people of the town agreed with me. In each of the terms I ran, I got the most votes of all the candidates— even with their cheating."

There were three attempts on his life, in 1967, 1968 and 1969, the last of which took place inside the main church. The targets were Garcia and the chief judge of the area, Carlos Valdez, who had rendered decisions unfavorable to councilmen. Judge Valdez was shot dead in the communion booth, and as the assassins fled down the aisle they fired at Garcia, sitting in the pew beside Marlene. Father and daughter were sprayed with blood when the bullets missed Garcia and hit a civilian. The civilian was struck in the chest and head, fell to the floor and died at their feet.

"I had seen much violence of this sort in my life, but for a ten-year-old girl the horror of such a scene went deep into Marlene's being," Garcia told me. "She wept in my arms on many nights to come, 'Father, they will kill you, they will kill all of us!' 'They will not,' I said. 'Good is greater then evil. That is why there are many, *many* more good people than there are evil ones.' I told her, 'Marlene, by this code I live! The good people will defeat the evil people! This is the order of the world. God has declared it so with His will by making so many good people.'"

Garcia may have had the good people of Tacurong on his side, but the threats against him became so severe that when Marlene was thirteen he sent her to the island of Panay to live with his sister in his home province, three hundred miles to the north. In Passi High School, Marlene flowered into a brilliant student, with A-plus grades in math, science and physics. She won a science fair—a rarity for a female in the Philippines at the time—and graduated with honors at the age of fifteen. She was quite a beauty, as well: a studio portrait she sent home at the end of her first year at the University of San Agustin on Panay caused her father to think she was losing her Catholic modesty. Braless in a tight, spaghetti-strap shirt emblazoned with the words "The Spirit of Spring," she holds up an apple, her lips parted, her black hair teased a little wild, her eyes wide—a teenage Eve. After seeing the photo, her father asked her to quit school and return to Tacurong.

Marlene refused, and her dad's premonition that she was headed off in her own unleashed direction proved correct. She was, after all, the daughter of a man who'd defied death and the status quo for most of his life. In her second year of college, at the age of seventeen, needing money for lab supplies as she worked toward a bachelor of science degree, she entered a singing contest sponsored by a local radio station. At the contest she met a man eight years her senior, Severino "Rino" Arcones, a hard-hitting broadcaster at DYFM, Bombo Radio, a nickname that derived from the drum Arcones beat to introduce his searing exposés of politicians.

Marlene won the singing contest and became intimate with the ruggedly handsome Arcones that evening. Giving another indication that she would live her life a little bit differently, she teamed up with Arcones on ensuing weekends to make the rounds of cash-prize talent shows, entering a new category each time and winning first-place prizes for folk, rock and traditional Filipino singing. Marlene and Arcones soon moved in together, and she left school in her last year to have her first child, Janice, out of wedlock.

That was too much for her father. This time he didn't ask but ordered Marlene home. She refused again, returned to school, and graduated with an honors degree in chemistry, the only woman to do so that year. It was 1981, Ferdinand Marcos had ruled as a dictator for almost a decade, the mostly Catholic Philippines was not free in any respect—not socially and not politically—yet Marlene ignored the conventions. Choosing to be a chemist—not a nurse or teacher or pharmacist, as most Philippine women embarking on professional careers were doing at the time—was also out of the ordinary. A colleague she met years later, Fermin Diaz, recollected that she told him she'd always had a burning curiosity about the hidden workings of the world, the beautiful organization of things on the molecular level and how that organization could be deduced through equations that proved correct when tested against reality. "She believed in God's will underlying the truth and order of the physical world," Diaz told me. "I think even then, looking at the repression of the Marcos regime, she began to wonder why she could find little evidence of truth and order in the political and social sphere."

After she graduated, she took a part-time job as a technical assistant for the Department of Agriculture in the province of Iloilo, bore another child, Rynche, and, while she was home with both children, studied for the government's chemist license exam. When she passed the exam in 1984, and was able to make a living as a full-time chemist, she met opposition from Arcones, radical in politics but, like so many Filipino men, conservative in his attitude toward women. Refusing to bow to his order that she be a stay-at-home mom, Marlene took the children and moved to Manila, where she got a job as a lab technician. A year later the couple reconciled and she moved back to Iloilo and took a seasonal job that would have a lasting affect on her: for six months she became a staff assistant to the prosecutor of the Municipal Trial Court. Here she encountered laws set out according to principles of jurisprudence that were as logical as those that governed molecules; here was a court that seemed, at its best, a laboratory for determining the facts. The law, if followed, would ensure that the Philippines functioned fairly and honestly, for the benefit of good people, as her father had taught her it should.

Except that was not what she observed during her six months in the court. The law was not being followed; rather, the tradition of *pasalubong-pabaon* was being followed—the giving of gifts in anticipation of receiving gifts. The scientific beauty of the system was in large measure ignored, depending for results on who you knew or paid. "Marlene felt the system was good," Nena Santos, the lawyer she retained years later, told me, "but the people who ran it were bad. She said she didn't need to reform the system, just— well, the entire country!"

Politically, that was the goal of Arcones, too. On air, banging his drum, he loudly criticized the mayor, the local police chief and bureaucrats who made life for people in Iloilo a through-the-looking-glass experience that was subject not to law but to whim or payoffs. Death threats came his way and he became even more intolerant of what was, to him, Marlene's incomprehensible insistence that she continue working instead of staying home as a watchful housekeeper and mother. Domestic tensions rose to the point where, according to their daughter Rynche, their relationship became a battle of wills. Despite Marlene's love for Arcones and sympathy for his mission, in December 1985 she left him again and moved back to Mindanao to take a job as a chemist in the town of Koronadal, just south of Tacurong. The couple remained in tortured contact, however, and were pondering a reunion when, on October 17, 1989, Arcones was assassinated. As was usual in the lawless Philippines, no one was ever charged with the killing.

"The murder changed her life—she was never the same," her sister Valmie Mariveles told me. "She became a hard woman."

Four months after Arcones's death, in February 1990, Marlene Garcia became the chief of the Department of Agriculture's Central Mindanao Chemical Analysis Laboratory, based in Cotabato City. Soon after she arrived, she learned that an employee had been murdered ten months earlier. The victim, gunned down in his home, was Geronimo Provido, the seed coordinator for Central Mindanao. The local police had attributed the killing to an interrupted robbery, but Provido's widow, Victorina, said her husband had been submitting reports about corruption in the Cotabato office and she had asked the agriculture secretary to reinvestigate the killing for possible motives. Now, in March 1990, the Department of Agriculture's Board of Personnel Inquiry recommended that, because of verified information supplied by Provido regarding overpriced seeds, the region's chief finance officer, Osmeña Montañer, should be charged with "dishonesty and conduct prejudicial to the best interest of service." Marlene realized there was something amiss in the department when, based on an assessment in Manila that Provido was deceased, the board's recommendation was shelved two weeks after it was issued, and no one was pursuing the charges.

Marlene confided to her family that there were other dark stories about Osmeña Montañer swirling around the office. These concerned the attempted murder in 1982 of another employee, Estelita Jardino, then the department's newly appointed accountant. Jardino had begun auditing Montañer after she discovered that funds had been disbursed to buy "planting materials" that had been used to purchase either cheaper, substandard products or sometimes nothing at all. Jardino interviewed the suppliers, who complained that Montañer was demanding 50 percent kickbacks on what they were paid. The suppliers maintained they had never reported the kickbacks because they were afraid of Montañer. Jardino would later testify in court that, after she imposed strict reporting rules on Montañer, he tried to bribe her, and, when she refused the bribe, told her to leave the city. When she refused again, she began receiving anonymous death threats by phone and mail. In September 1982, she was shot in the left temple as she was walking to work though the compound. She survived, although she was in a coma for weeks, restricted to her bed for two years and blinded in her left eye. When she returned to work in 1985, she filed graft and attempted murder charges against Montañer. As she would later tell the Philippine Center for Investigative Journalism for an article published in 2000, "Montañer cornered me. He said, 'Lita, sign this document. It's a statement of desistance. Sign it or you will not get out of Cotabato alive.'" Jardino signed, took up a position in Manila and never returned to Cotabato City again.

It was in this environment that Marlene Esperat ran into the kind of malfeasance and corruption that Provido and Jardino had tried to expose. She was assigned to test livestock and feed for harmful chemicals in a laboratory that was in total disrepair: it was pest-ridden (including with poisonous snakes and rodents), dust-covered, and had no air-conditioning or running water. This was the facility that was in part meant to ensure that mercury, arsenic and lead did not get into the food chain. Marlene began lobbying for new equipment and a new building. When her requests for better facilities yielded a yearly grant of less than half of what she needed to maintain the existing facilities, she approached an accountant in the auditor's office to show her the department's recent regional financial statements.

The accountant was George Esperat, a rail-thin man with thick round glasses who worked for the federal Commission of Audit, assigned to oversee the books of the Central Mindanao Department of Agriculture. A Muslim widower with two children, George needed a wife, and suddenly here was Marlene, ten years his junior, single, shapely and dressed in provocative attire that he had rarely seen worn by any other Mindanao woman—Muslim, Christian or Blaan aboriginal. George asked her out.

Marlene was still in mourning over Arcones and, according to her older sister Valmie, not attracted to George, but "she agreed to date him because out of her need at the time, Marlene at first judged him as a good prospect." That is, Marlene had her two young girls to support, George seemed to be making a good living, and he was in a position that might be of use to her, both in feeding her information about Montañer's financial shenanigans and pro-tecting her against his retaliation, since George and Montañer were friends. Unlike her passionate relationship with Arcones, Valmie told me, Marlene approached an affair with George pragmatically. After the murder of Arcones, "there was only room left for her to be realistic in matters of the heart." This, of course, was according to Marlene's interpretation of "realistic," Valmie said. "Everything in her life after Rino Arcones and her discoveries at her job became, Does this help me in my endeavor to stop this corruption? She was very much like our father in that regard."

She became pregnant, and George and Marlene's first son, Kevin Jorge, was born in 1991. George persuaded Montañer to become Kevin's godfather.

——

George may have ocassionally allowed Marlene to look at financial statements from the Cotabato office, but, nervous about
Montañer, he hesitated to interpret them for her. Marlene therefore decided to enroll in a master's degree program in public
administration at the local university to learn the skills required to
read complicated ledgers, among other things. At the beginning of
1993 she experienced an aha moment when she discovered that
although her laboratory was allotted an annual budget of 400,000
pesos, she was receiving less than half that amount.* Not wanting
to expose George by mentioning that she had discovered the
diversion of funds, she continued hounding the Department of
Agriculture for money for a new building, without luck.

The couple's second son, James Derreck, was born in 1995, and
Marlene married George, taking his name and legitimizing their
sons. George and Marlene, the two boys and Marlene's daughters
made their home in a five-room house that Marlene had purchased
with a government loan back in 1988, and which she'd been sharing
with George since Kevin was conceived. Located on a quiet, tree-
lined lane called Purok Llang-Llang Road, a few minutes from the
town square, the house was perfect for Marlene's needs. It had a main
entrance off a side porch and a driveway beside it that was protected
from the street by a high wrought-iron gate. The room that fronted
the street had been converted into a convenience store, known
in the Philippines as a "sari-sari store," which could be shuttered after
hours. The home was secure and well shaded, and the sari-sari store,
overseen by the girls, provided the family with extra income.

Marlene's mother, Pacencia, who had guaranteed Marlene's
loan for the house, now advised her daughter to keep the deed in
her own name. Pacencia did not believe Marlene's marriage to

---

*A peso was worth about four cents at the time; today it is worth about two cents.

George would last. From early on, she had noticed something about George that Marlene either had refused to acknowledge or had willfully dismissed from her mind. Pacencia didn't like the way George looked at Marlene's daughters. "Marlene was very smart, but she didn't handle her personal life well," Pacencia told me. "Not with Rino Arcones and not with George."

Marlene's daughter Rynche says that her grandmother's intuition was correct. When she and her sister, Janice, complained to their mother that George was paying them inappropriate attention, Marlene and George began to fight and, after one bad blowup, she ordered George to leave. Then, following a similar pattern that had marked her relationship with Arcones, the couple reconciled and she took him back. Thereafter, whenever Marlene thought she would be working late or had to leave town for her job, she took her daughters to stay at her mother's house.

On May 22, 1996, Marlene left Rynche and Janice with Pacencia and traveled to a National Chemistry Congress in Iloilo City. Her inquiries at the conference revealed that the Department of Agriculture had been allotting to other head offices in the country between one and two million pesos each for the construction of new laboratories, but she had not seen one peso of that amount. On her return she confronted her supervisor with the facts. Mustapha Ismael, the assistant regional director, explained that, yes, the money had been received, but it had been diverted to breeding stations because of a pressing need for better-quality livestock in central Mindanao. He brought Montañer into the discussion, and the two officials assured Marlene that in 1997 she would get the money for a new building.

In June 1997, with still no sign of construction, Marlene went to Manila and gained access to the books at the Department of Budget and Management. There she discovered the government had long ago sent her regional office eight million pesos to construct her lab. Furious, she flew back to Cotabato City, confronted Montañer and then formally filed complaints with the Legal

Division of the Department of Agriculture and its Office of the Ombudsman, a civilian body that investigated allegations to discover if they warranted criminal charges. Marlene accused Montañer of heading a Central Mindanao kickback scheme that involved the collusion of sixteen other officials and that to her mind explained why he could afford to live in a sprawling mansion and drive luxury cars.

After she filed her complaints, George approached Montañer and reminded him that they were friends and he should restrain his anger against Marlene. "I said to myself, she is on the right track and doing this for the good of the people," George told me.

In February 1998, the agriculture secretary in Manila rescinded Montañer's authority to sign checks for the regional office and began organizing a delegation of auditors to travel to Cotabato City to investigate Marlene's complaints. While awaiting the arrival of the auditors, Marlene uncovered further evidence of graft. Following the trail of various "ghost projects" for the department, Marlene determined that, in her words, "the funds for employees' social security premiums had disappeared. For a year and a half, our office was not remitting payments to the Government Service Insurance System (GSIS)." Still awaiting the arrival of the auditors from Manila, Marlene, for the first time, decided to go public, giving interviews on her findings to the local newspaper *Midland Review* and the radio station DXKR. A couple of days later, the regional office remitted the GSIS back payments to Manila. Three days after that, on May 7, the night before the arrival of the auditors, the Department of Agriculture building in Cotabato mysteriously caught fire and all the financial records went up in smoke. A security guard named Carlo Carulasan later detailed in a written affidavit for the authorities that on May 7 he was called to a meeting between Montañer and his cronies at which Carulasan was told there would be a fire and was ordered not to interfere. He also alleged in the affidavit that the fire was set by Montañer's driver, who held Carulasan at gunpoint while he turned on all the air conditioners to fan the flames. If there was any doubt that an arsonist was loose on the property, it was settled later that night when fires also consumed the offices of the cashier and the personnel division. On May 10, with the buildings still smoldering, Marlene was in the process of organizing her surviving documents for a meeting with the auditors when Carulasan, who admired Marlene's courage, warned her that he had reason to believe she might be killed before she entered the meeting. Marlene fled with her documents to Manila that afternoon and went into a witness protection program, which allotted her only one bunk in a government dorm and did not provide for the room and board of her family. She was forbidden from visiting Mindanao.

George remained behind with the boys and Marlene's sisters moved Rynche and Janice out of the house and into the home of relatives in Iloilo. A few months later Janice entered university in Davao City, a hundred-mile drive from Tacurong. Just before Janice left, she confided to Rynche that she was deeply hurt that her mother seemed to put her single-minded pursuit of her investigations ahead of them.

Montañer and his driver were eventually charged with arson by the Department of Justice, although the DOJ dropped the charges in November 1999 based on a determination that Carulasan was not a reliable witness and that investigators could find no motive for Montañer burning down his own office buildings. Meanwhile, Marlene's corruption charges against Montañer and the sixteen other officials in Cotabato went nowhere. As she later told the Center for Investigative Journalism in an interview, "An arraignment was scheduled originally in Manila. Then the respondents petitioned that it be moved to Cebu, then back again to Quezon City. After that, their lawyers filed a motion to quash. Next thing I heard, the case had been dismissed. How could that happen . . . ? I, the principal complainant and state witness, was not even told!"

Marlene had a couple of lucky breaks during her lonely two years in the witness protection program in Manila. The first was that she managed to persuade the Department of Agriculture to appoint her to the post of "action officer" within its Ombudsman Office, empowered to look into the finances of regional offices. The second was meeting Fermin Diaz, a consultant at the department with access to documents at the head office, which he agreed to monitor and hand over to her. In May 2000, despite warnings that her safety could not be guaranteed, Marlene decided to return to Mindanao, not as a chemist but as an investigator. As she told Fermin, "I am putting my life on the line for this." She said she would continue to investigate what she believed was the ongoing theft of millions from the Department of Agriculture by Montañer.

By then Marlene had not seen her family for two years. When she arrived home, Rynche moved back from Iloilo, but Janice, still deeply resentful over her mother's absence from her life and not wanting to see George, remained in Davao City. Marlene tried not to think about the difficulties her investigations were causing her family and got right to work. She went to see a veteran community lawyer named Nena Santos, who agreed to act for her if she was sued. She then began looking into the discrepancies between the books she was now officially empowered to examine in the Cotabato office and the stream of financial documents Diaz sent her from Manila. Suddenly, in early 2001, she asked George Esperat to retire from his job as regional auditor of the Cotabato office. If he didn't, she warned, she might end up including him in her complaints against the Department of Agriculture. As she later told Santos, she no longer had faith that George could resist the influence of Montañer and his "bad money."

George, at fifty-one, agreed to retire early from his job. He explained to me, however, that he'd left the Cotabato office in order to receive an early retirement bonus that Marlene wanted him to hand over to her elderly mother, Pacencia. He said Pacencia had demanded to be paid the money that Marlene now owed her for the house after defaulting on her government loan. "I was forced to retire. I had a nice job," George said. "I retired early so we could still live in the house. I was receiving a very good salary, plus travel expenses—and I gave it all up."

Pacencia, frail as her husband, Luis Garcia, and still weeping over her daughter's murder, told me she disagreed with George's recollection. "I was not demanding the mortgage," she said coldly.

Rynche indicated there was another crisis in the marriage of Marlene and George. In the midst of the turbulence surrounding George's forced retirement, the issue of his previous behavior toward her and her sister came to the fore. When Rynche told Marlene she was still uncomfortable around George, Marlene ordered him out of her house again.

"We had a minor separation, only because of Marlene and me, our relationship," George told me, adding that he had behaved as a proper stepfather to the girls at all times. "The reason we separated was because Marlene was easily irritated because of her work. I went to live for a short time with my son from my first marriage in Cotabato City."

The breakup, as George suggested, was short-lived. Vacillating in a way that had always been incomprehensible to her daughters, Marlene allowed George to move back a few weeks later. According to Marlene's sisters and Nena Santos, Marlene's justification for continually allowing George back was that she hoped his presence in the house would protect her family against renewed retaliation while she pursued her investigations of George's old friend Montañer. On the other hand, George's presence kept Janice away and still made Rynche uncomfortable. Marlene had another option, of course. If she ceased her investigations of Montañer, the danger would lessen and she could separate from George permanently. That is what her daughters wanted her to do, but it was an option Marlene refused to consider.

"Marlene believed she was working for the greater good that our father taught us," Marlene's younger sister, Lilibeth Lacorte, told me. "She was a hero, but the family suffered because her crusade always came first."

"My sister and I were hurt that she kept letting George come back," Rynche told me, adding that they both loved their mother deeply, which made Marlene's obsession with work and her marriage to George all the more painful to them. When Janice was in university, she attempted suicide. To friends and colleagues, Marlene blamed the attempt on financial problems that Janice was having. While Marlene accepted responsibility for those problems, she did so in a way that put the blame on the corrupt Department of Agriculture. Her pay at the Ombudsman Office, she said, was being processed by the very department she was investigating. "The people whom I had accused of graft and corruption were still in office and were controlling finances at the DA," she told Luz Rimban, of the Center for Investigative Journalism, a few months later. "They found a way to hit back at me. Since they filed my income-tax returns, they made it appear that I had no children and therefore was not entitled to tax exemptions. As a result, I found myself with tax liabilities of 29,000 pesos. Then I was told that my twenty-one-year-old daughter tried to commit suicide because of financial problems in school that I failed to address. I had to live with the guilt, but I believed what I was doing was for a noble cause. It helped that I was kept busy."

Marlene's sisters perceived that she was, in fact, torn by guilt, and that she suffered intensely whenever her daughters showed the effects of her neglect. But that did not stop her. According to her father, "Marlene had a fighter's will. She could not be stopped once she saw the suffering of the farmers because of evil corruption. So many of them—good people! So few evil ones—but with a power that must be smashed!"

In the midst of the disorder and torment of her personal life, Marlene decided to take a bold and dangerous step. She booked a weekly half-hour of "block time," a community slot, on Radio DXKR — her first foray into journalism. On her show she departed from the usual fare of recipes and social announcements to report on the corruption she'd uncovered in the Department's Cotabato office. As she revealed on air, she'd filed a case against Montañer and others for "the rigging of bids for postharvest facilities" — that is, warehouses and silos. A hearing on the case was set for January 24, 2001, but was postponed after police told Marlene that they had received intelligence that she was to be assassinated just before the hearing. Marlene fled to Davao. A week later, the assassins showed up in Tacurong to case her house. Before they could get down to business, however, they ran into a former *pare* who had short-changed them on a drug deal. There was a running gun battle in the public market, one of the hired murderers was himself murdered and another was arrested. When the police searched this last fellow, they found a picture of Marlene, with a shoot-here X at the bottom. The gangster confessed he'd been hired to kill Marlene although, as was typical, he wouldn't say who was footing the bill.

The fallout from this incident was threefold: the Ombudsman Office assigned her a military intelligence officer to give her round-the-clock protection; her growing public profile as an advocate on behalf of the farmers of Central Mindanao caused the district's main newspaper, the *Midland Review*, to accept her offer to write a weekly fifteen-hundred-word column, "Madam Witness," that would detail her revelations; and she decided to make the corruption story known outside of Mindanao. To accomplish this last goal, she approached the Manila-based Center for Investigative Journalism, telling her tale in a 2001 feature interview published in the PCIJ's magazine, *iReport*. In that interview, the same one in which she recounted her daughter's attempted suicide, Marlene referred to the carnage in the church when she was ten years old. Showing the mettle of her father, she threw the murders in the faces of those threatening her life.

"I am not exactly new to this," she said. *"Lumaki ako sa bala."*
I grew up on bullets.

At the beginning of 2002, Marlene ordered George out of her house
again. Rynche recollects that this time—with an armed guard protecting her—Marlene promised she would keep her resolve. Over
the next three years, she filed a flurry of graft cases—twenty-five in
all—against one official after another, including her boss Montañer;
his collaborator Estrella Sabay, the Department of Agriculture's
regional accountant for Central Mindanao; Gloria Arroyo's secretary of agriculture, Arthur Yap; Yap's undersecretaries, Jocelyn
"JocJoc" Bolante and Cesar Drilon; fourteen federal agriculture officials in Manila; a congressman; two Manila businessmen; an army
officer; a police officer; and two Tacurong politicians. All of these
cases she publicized in her weekly columns for the *Midland Review.*

Her activism led to a libel lawsuit launched by Montañer and
Sabay—a lawsuit they eventually lost—and to more attempts on
her life. In May 2002 three men tried to abduct her on the road
outside of Tacurong; the kidnapping was foiled by her bodyguard
who was following in a chase car. Ten months later, in July 2003, a
hand grenade was thrown into her house and the explosion
destroyed her living room; neither she nor her children were home.
At the beginning of 2004, with all her graft cases delayed, deflected
or dismissed, she became disgusted with risking her life trying to
change things through the corrupt judicial system and decided
to follow in her father's footsteps by entering politics. In February,
Marlene announced on radio and in her column that she was
running for Tacurong city council.

The election was scheduled for May 10, the same day as the presidential poll between incumbent Gloria Arroyo and a populist
challenger named Fernando Poe Jr. Marlene's prospects for election were promising. Her radio show and her explosive articles for
the *Midland Review* made her the best-known of the thirty-eight

council candidates; she was also the most photogenic, and drew the most media coverage and the largest crowds to her campaign rallies. Yet when the forty thousand ballots were counted, she placed last in the field, with only a thousand votes.

The tally did not surprise her, since she was certain it was fraudulent. During the campaign, documents arrived from Fermin Diaz that allowed her to trace huge amounts of funds that were deflected from their intended purpose at the Department of Agriculture and that, very likely, were used for the same kind of election fraud on a national level that had caused her loss locally. In a column called "Dare to Fail," she wrote, "It's exciting to know that my losing as a candidate was a success in proving the FRAUD of the electoral process. . . . Imagine how the administration candidates dared to use their network in cheating and vote buying. They dared to transfer all the funds from farmers."

Marlene now went to work full-time on exposing the massive diversion of agricultural funds in the lead-up to the presidential election, the biggest story in her journalism career and the one that threatened the most powerful people in the Philippines.

Ever since May 2001, when President Arroyo had beaten back the People Power III revolt launched by slum dwellers, she'd been determined to legitimize her presidency by gaining a mandate in the May 2004 election. That goal presented her with a problem. Many of the country's poor—who constituted the majority of the electorate—considered her a step down from Joseph Estrada, the grossly corrupt former movie star who had been overthrown by the Church-led and army-backed People Power II revolt that had installed her. To achieve her legitimacy, Arroyo set about laying the groundwork for victory in the 2004 election. Following the lead of presidents past, she appointed cronies to government agencies with almost unlimited funds that could be used during the campaign. They included a budget secretary named Emilia Boncodin, Secretary of Agriculture Arthur Yap and Undersecretaries of Agriculture JocJoc Bolante and Cesar Drilon. As the election approached, Arroyo's aides determined that Mindanao would be a main battleground between her and her opponent, Fernando Poe Jr., who was very popular among the poor. Three months before the election, Arroyo appointed as her national commissioner of elections a career bureaucrat named Virgilio Garcillano, the former elections commissioner of Mindanao. It would be Garcillano's job to oversee the ballot counting for the entire nation, although, with Poe favored in Mindanao, his special knowledge of the island would turn out to be an asset.

On February 3, 2004, at the start of the election campaign, Esperat learned that Arroyo's budget secretary, Boncodin, had released to the Department of Agriculture three-quarters of a billion pesos, supposedly to "cover the purchase of farm inputs"—a newly created program that was to supply fertilizer to Mindanao. Instead of the fertilizer being purchased by the department, however, Undersecretary of Agriculture Bolante secretly transferred the money to governors, congressmen and mayors via the department's regional finance officers, including Osmeña Montañer. A week later, the budget secretary released another 1.1 billion pesos, this time for a rice and corn-seed program. Five weeks after that, a half billion pesos were released to the National Irrigation Authority, the funds for this venture coming from Ferdinand Marcos's stolen wealth, which the government had recovered from his Swiss bank accounts. On April 28, yet another half billion of Marcos's recovered wealth was released for the rice program. By July 2004, Marlene had verified that in her district alone at least a quarter of a billion pesos meant for fertilizer had been used for suspicious purposes: only 28 million pesos had been requested by the officer in charge of the fertilizer program, but 248 million had been transferred to the Cotabato office. She exposed the bloated funding transfer in her column, then filed her charges against Arthur Yap and JocJoc Bolante for conspiring to defraud the government of almost all the transferred amount.

A former solicitor general named Frank Chavez filed a parallel suit of plunder against President Arroyo herself. Picking up on Marlene's research, he stated in the suit, "It appears that the modus operandi is this: there is a ranking official in the DA [Department of Agriculture] who is linked to Ms. Macapagal-Arroyo's husband, Jose Miguel Arroyo. This DA official has 'runners' who approach local government officials." Those officials, Chavez alleged, included 105 congressmen, 53 governors and 23 municipal mayors, who split much of the disbursed money with the president's husband and Department of Agriculture officials. The money was accepted as payment for help in Arroyo's campaign and (Marlene strongly suspected) for the padding and shaving of votes.

For ten months after the election, nearly every column Esperat wrote for the *Midland Review* examined the disappearance of the money that the Department of Agriculture dispensed during the campaign. Of the 432 million pesos she traced to the Cotabato office, almost none ended up purchasing fertilizer; it ended up in the pockets of the politicians and officials who could be relied on to pad and shave votes, buy votes at *barangay* festivals and funnel the money to pay off campaign expenses.

Predictably, the Arroyo government, through its spokesmen, questioned Marlene Esperat's character, replying to her charges by referring to her as "a former common-law wife," a bold pejorative in the Philippines. Marlene interpreted the insult as a sign that she was being taken seriously, and knew that when officials took journalists seriously they sometimes reacted by means other than press releases: she was fully aware that media people pursuing the darker side of the government were being murdered in record numbers. In the six months after the election, eight were assassinated. Then, on January 29, 2005, Max Quindao, the editor and publisher of the *Mindanao Truck News* in nearby Davao Province, was shot four times in the chest as he left the paper, almost certainly because of his exposure of local government corruption.

The day after Quindao's shooting, Marlene called her lawyer and asked her to bring her car over to the house. When Santos arrived, she found Marlene packing her room full of documents. She emptied all her office shelves into boxes, taped them and asked Santos to store them in a safe place. The next day, she left her children in the care of her parents and went to Davao City, where Quindao had just undergone emergency surgery. After visiting with him, she flew on to Manila to research fertilizer receipts at the Department of Agriculture.

Marlene stayed in the dorm where the Ombudsman Office had put her up during the two years she had spent under the witness protection program. In the middle of the night she awoke with a terrible stomachache and wondered if staying in the "secure" dorm had been a mistake: had she been poisoned in the cafeteria? While she moaned in her bunk, a woman from the adjoining bed approached her and asked if there was anything she could do to help. As Marlene later told her family, "I looked into her eyes and they told me the cause of the pain was not bad food or poison. She seemed to speak to me through her eyes."

The mysterious woman sat down on Marlene's bed and began massaging her stomach. A wind blew the curtains of the room inward and Marlene's research papers were lifted off the night table between the two beds and scattered onto the floor. It had been a calm night until that moment, and Marlene told the woman she was frightened. "There are bad spirits trying to harm you," the woman said. "Do not worry. I am here to help you with them. Please take a deep breath."

Marlene inhaled, felt an agonizing swelling in her abdomen, and, on the exhale, a cascade of relief as the pain disappeared. Marlene had always believed in God, but until that moment she'd had no faith in miracles or the myths of the Church. Upon the disappearance of the pain, however, she felt enveloped in an oceanic feeling of love that she was certain came from Jesus Christ. "I felt the Lord's presence in the room, filling me with light and peace," she later told her brother, Charlie Garcia. "I began to weep with such joy—I have never felt such infinite joy like that in my life. The Lord was in the room with me, telling me my soul was everlasting and with Him."

Still in a state of weeping ecstasy, Marlene embraced the woman and asked her what had happened. The woman said, "A bad spirit has left you. You are free now and one with the Lord. God Himself has determined that your work on earth must soon be concluded. You will come to Him shortly and by leaving this earthly place your work will be fulfilled, just as the work of Our Savior was fulfilled upon His leaving the place upon the Hill."

"When I picked her up at the airport in Davao, I knew I was talking to a woman reborn in our Lord," Alma Vidal, Marlene's best friend in Tacurong, related. "She said she wanted to go immediately to the Victory Church, where she told me what happened to her in the dorm. When I dropped her off at her home she said she had important work to begin."

The work she soon began was the letter to President Gloria-Macapagal Arroyo, cc'ed to her justice secretary and the Center for Investigative Journalism, and which she worked on for two weeks before sending it on February 14, 2005. Although her attention to English grammar was rather casual, her letter deserves to be quoted at length as a testament to her beliefs and investigations.

"Dear Madam President, Greetings of Peace!" it began. "First, I do not regret being a former **COMMON-LAW WIFE** of the famous Severino 'Rino' Arcones of Iloilo City, who was assassinated in broad daylight in 1989 for his pursuit of good moral ascendancy in the government"—her bold-faced, capitalized and italicized phrase a poke in the eye to Arroyo. "Being a crusader of truth in unveiling Graft and Corruption of the powers that be, his life greatly influenced me to pursue his advocacy [on] the southern island of Central Mindanao." She said the lessons Rino taught her had guided her as she filed "a series of graft cases against various presidential appointees at the Department of Agriculture, including your newly promoted Undersecretaries." Arroyo, she added, kept those officials on the payroll "notwithstanding their alleged involvement in the high profile scams within the office."

Because of her investigations, people were intent on killing her, Marlene said. She disclosed that she was aware that "lately, reports reveal that military intelligence operatives are allegedly out and tasked to liquidate the undersigned to silence her forever and [lead her to the same end] as the father of my children"—meaning Rino Arcones. She listed the people she had filed cases against, naming JocJoc Bolante first. "They were all suspects of threats to my life due to my series of exposés in my column 'Madam Witness' about their alleged involvement in hundreds of millions of anomalous government transactions." Sounding very much like her father, she said she could not be stopped: the good people of Mindanao were urging her forward. "They find me the only person who has the nerve to offer my life as a sacrificial lamb . . . by conveying to lawful authorities the acts of malfeasance and nonfeasance committed by most of the DA Presidential Appointees at the expense of the interest of farmers. . . . There is no use living in this world without [playing that] role." She admitted that she had sacrificed everything to assume that role, but "I am still here to pursue what Rino [Arcones] had started: to be the **VOICE of the MASSES**. God gave me the wisdom to comprehend and act on the people's outcry [through] writing and to have the culprits prosecuted.

"My CRUSADE," she went on, is "to PREVENT CORRUPTION." By doing so, she had "gained the ire of JocJoc Bolante" and others who were "irked [by] my crusading efforts [to] clean up the mess they have caused in the Department of Agriculture. . . . I find it imperative for me, as long as I am alive, to continue to unveil these scams for my fellow colleagues in the Press [and] the public until you LISTEN to the cries of the POOR."

She then enumerated the threats against her and the previous attempts on her life, vowing that she would continue pressing for the prosecution of Arroyo's appointees and her corrupt officials at the Department of Agriculture. "If this would mean my life, I prefer to accept the bullet than to remain silent and stare at the masses dying due to hunger. . . . I am just a small sly fry but I can make a Big Fish fall into the pit if it is **GOD'S WILL**. . . . Please spare the FOOD DEPARTMENT so it can sustain your people. I am ready to <u>**DIE for this CAUSE but you can never stop the WILL OF THE LORD**</u>."

On the day Marlene sent her letter, a terrorist bomb exploded on a bus in Manila's financial district, killing four and wounding sixty. Perhaps because of the turmoil in the capital, Marlene received no acknowledgment from the president's office. On February 28, the body of an *Asian Star Express* reporter, Arnulfo Villanueva, who had exposed the involvement of government officials in *jueteng* gambling, was found shot dead on a road south of Manila. A couple of days later Marlene met with Nena Santos in her law office and updated a point-by-point, chronological summary of a document she'd drawn up called "Department of Agriculture–National Food Authority Fertilizer Scam," then went over another summary of all her cases that were still pending with the Office of the Ombudsman. "At that point, so soon after her challenge to the president, I strongly felt she was preparing for the worst," Santos remembered. "She was brave, but she was frightened." The next time George Esperat drove down from Cotabato City to visit their sons, on March 10, Marlene invited him to move back into the house. "George was still friends with Montañer and I think she was hoping Montañer would think twice with him around the house," Santos explained. "As it was, Marlene told me Montañer conveyed a $100,000 bribe offer to her. Marlene, of course, turned it down. After that, the tension built severely. She knew what was coming."

George says he was equally worried, and remembers asking Montañer to leave Marlene alone. "We were friends," he related. "I went to him, I told him, 'Pare, do not touch Marlene. If you think she threatens you, just quarrel in the papers, do not touch.' I made him swear that he will not touch her." But after Marlene's letter, George was not convinced his lobbying could deter an attack from one quarter or another if she persisted in pursuing her cause. "I told her, 'You stop making charges in the newspapers, because, my God, they will kill you.' But she told me, 'Don't meddle with my work!'"

No one knows for certain which "reports" Marlene was referring to when she told Arroyo "military intelligence operatives" were assigned to kill her, although there was, in fact, a man of that description actively arranging her assassination when she wrote her letter. His name was Sergeant Rowie Barua, with Military Intelligence Battalion 680, a twenty-two-year veteran of the army who served as a government bodyguard for Estrella Sabay, the regional accountant working directly under Osmeña Montañer. When I interviewed Barua after Marlene's murder, he related that in January 2005 Sabay had told him that she and Montañer felt that Esperat was using the media to destroy their reputations. They therefore wanted him to hire an assassin to kill Esperat.

As he would later testify in court, Barua chose an old army buddy named Estanislao Bismanos, who, since his discharge from the military in 1983, had become a career criminal. On January 26, Barua told me, Sabay ordered Barua to ask Bismanos to come to Cotabato City. Bismanos arrived the first week in February and Barua let his boss know the killer was in the town square, awaiting instructions. Montañer then entered Sabay's office and handed her the address of Marlene Esperat, a picture of Esperat from the *Midland Review*, and a five-thousand-peso down payment for the deed. She passed all this to Barua, who went to the plaza and in turn passed it to Bismanos.

Bismanos left Cotabato for Tacurong, two hours south, and at four in the afternoon phoned Barua and said he'd taken a look at Esperat's house, and that the cost of the job and expenses would be 120,000 pesos, roughly equivalent to $2,400. Sabay agreed to the total fee, but Bismanos then got sidetracked in another criminal venture. Shortly after Marlene sent her letter to Arroyo, Sabay began pressuring Barua to execute the plan. Finally, on March 3, Bismanos hired two assistants—Gerry Cabayag as gunman and Randy Grecia as lookout—who came equipped with a motorbike they could use to surveil Esperat's house and movements.

Cabayag and Grecia motored by Marlene's house every couple of hours over a period of several days. They noted the padlocked gate at the driveway that led to the home's main entrance, and Marlene's uniformed bodyguard patrolling the premises. They also noted the convenience store that was attached to the house. On one of their surveillance passes they stopped and bought a download for Grecia's cellphone. The younger of Marlene's daughters, Rynche, who was minding the store, sold them the download. Over her shoulder they saw that the store gave access to the home's dining room. They calculated that a man could slip by Rynche into the dwelling, shoot Marlene, escape on a motorbike and make it back to the anonymity of the town plaza in five minutes. The big problem was Marlene's bodyguard—who appeared to be at her side twenty-four hours a day. The killers discussed their options. Grecia had observed that Marlene's two sons played chess on the street in front of the house every day around lunch hour and again after school. As the appointed lookout, Grecia decided to stop by occasionally, befriend the boys and pretend to watch their game as an excuse to wait for an opportunity for the guard to leave the house. If the guard questioned him, he would say he lived nearby, was doing construction work down the street and merely walked home this way.

"I remember he was a very friendly man," James, Marlene's younger boy, told me. "Some days when Kevin and I finished a game, he sat down and played chess with us."

Over the next couple of weeks, as Marlene's exposés about JocJoc Bolante and the Arroyo administration continued to appear in the *Midland Review,* Sabay and Montañer became increasingly impatient for the killers to do the job. Barua informed them that though Marlene was home much of the time, the hitmen didn't know how to get around the problem of her armed guard. A week later, Marlene solved this problem for them.

"On March 21, three days before her death, Marlene called me up and said she had a dream," her brother, Charlie Garcia, told me. "She said, 'God is trying to wake me up and He said my actions will be a catalyst because I am trying to cleanse the earth.' God Himself said that in a dream to her," explained Charlie, who is a believer in divine intercession. "She said He told her that we can't escape death, so it's a blessing that she is warned to get ready for the Holy Day when He will take her in order to expose the corruption of this land."

On Maundy Thursday, March 24—the day of the Last Supper—Marlene told her guard he could leave to spend the evening and Good Friday with his family. Sitting outside at the chess board with Marlene's sons, Randy Grecia saw the guard depart around noon, and when the minutes ticked by and he did not return, he texted Gerry Cabayag and informed him an opportunity had opened up. Cabayag arrived on his motorbike, went into the sari-sari store and asked to buy a bottle of water. Rynche placed the bottle on the counter just as a visitor arrived with her own armed guard. The visitor was Orfelina Segura, a candidate for mayor in the previous election, showing up fifteen minutes late to have lunch with Marlene and then play an afternoon game of mah-jongg. Cabayag took his water and left for a nearby bar called Strum's, leaving Grecia behind to phone him when the visitor and her guard departed.

Segura and Marlene played mah-jongg until six o'clock, when George Esperat, having a drink by himself in the kitchen, began preparing a supper of bayan fish. The couple's sons came in for dinner, Segura left and George served the meal to Marlene, Kevin and James in the dining room. Marlene tasted her fish and winced. George had made it far too salty for her taste, and she told him to go back into the kitchen to prepare her a meal of sushi.

Five minutes later, Cabayag swung off his motorbike outside the sari-sari store and asked Rynche for a pack of cigarettes. When she turned to get the pack, he slipped past her into the dining room. Cabayag's gaze met the surprised eyes of James, sitting beside Marlene, and he smiled at the nine-year-old. "Good evening, ma'am," Cabayag said, and when Marlene looked up, he shot her once in the right eye, jolting her backwards from the table and killing her instantly.

Marlene Esperat's murder, at her own Last Supper, ignited the conscience of the Philippines, just as her Christian medium had foretold. The fact that she was a mother of four shot in plain view of her young sons gave her story a heart-wrenching quality that thrust it to the front pages of the daily newspapers and tabloids, as well as to the top of the news on the major TV and radio stations. In the words of Reporters sans frontières, "The death from a bullet to the head of Marlene Esperat, nicknamed 'Erin Brockovitch' by the Philippines press, has traumatized the journalistic community, many of them women."

Six weeks after Esperat's death, on May 2, the Committee to Protect Journalists labeled the Philippines "the most murderous country" for journalists—the numbers exceeding Iraq at the time. The CPJ then joined forces with Reporters sans frontières and eight other international press organizations to send a joint letter to President Arroyo demanding that, this time, "the judicial system must not allow the instigators to go unpunished."

Arroyo at first seemed to bow to the bad press. On a hundred-degree morning two weeks later, she held a news conference in Malacañang. A frenzy of camera flashes went off as the four-foot-ten president stepped into the press hall flanked by two young boys — Kevin and James Esperat. With her hands resting maternally on the shoulders of Marlene's sons, Arroyo decried the "cold-blooded" murder of their mother and announced the creation of a $100,000 "press freedom fund" that would be used to set up a police task force to solve the unpunished killings of almost sixty journalists. "These acts of wanton violence against the men and women who form the very foundation of a free press are acts of violence against the nation itself," Arroyo told the country, the first time she'd ever acknowledged that the killings had reached a "frightening" level. "We won't rest until the perpetrators of these vicious crimes have been brought to justice and punished." Arroyo then added a sentence that would have sounded redundant to those not familiar with the Esperat case — or with the Philippines. The president declared she would "give the justice department the green light to go after the mastermind in the killing of Marlene Esperat."

Arroyo took no questions after the news conference so the journalists scrummed her secretary of justice, Raul Gonzalez. Did Arroyo's announcement mean that Gonzales would be given the "green light" to investigate the highest cabinet officials Esperat had named in her letter and exposés? "Gonzales answered with a smile," the *Philippine Daily Inquirer* reported. "'That would be a witch-hunt already.'"

While Gonzalez avoided a "witch-hunt" of high-level officials in Manila, on Mindanao the lower levels were pursued by police. Grecia, Bismanos and Barua were tracked down via the cellphone download that Grecia had stupidly purchased at the sari-sari store, and, in a sworn affidavit, Barua named Montañer and Sabay as the people who had ordered the murder. On May 20, the Tacurong City Regional Trial Court issued an arrest warrant that charged Montañer and Sabay with murder. The pair immediately filed for dismissal of the charges, and help for their cause came from none other than Justice Secretary Gonzalez, who in early June suspended the proceedings against them. To head a review of the charges, Gonzalez appointed a prosecutor who happened to be the same lawyer who'd represented Montañer and Sabay when they'd launched (and lost) the libel suit against Esperat.

Their suspicions aroused, reporters in Manila began pushing hard at three stories they sensed the government was fearful might converge: Esperat's murder on Mindanao, her allegations about the Department of Agriculture, and the 2004 national election. In the midst of their clamoring for information, one of Arroyo's own intelligence agents at Malacañang felt moved to leak tape recordings of phone conversations that Virgilio Garcillano, the president's elections commissioner, had engaged in during the 2004 ballot counting on Mindanao. The calls, which had been secretly recorded to keep track of possible election fraud by Fernando Poe Jr., revealed that Arroyo herself had phoned Garcillano fifteen times during the vote counting. On radio and television, the nation was then treated to Arroyo's deep voice orchestrating the padding and shaving of votes on Esperat's island, supplying millions of Filipinos with ringtones like "Hello, Garci, will I lead by more than a million?" and Garcillano replying, "They're doing the upward adjustment for you now."

Within hours reporters mobbed Garcillano, asking if he was concerned that Arroyo's congressional opponents would indict him or impeach his boss. "No," he blithely replied. "I helped many of them." Sheila Coronel, head of the Center for Investigative Journalism, then declared the election results in Mindanao "a symphony of fraud," and summed up the governance of the nation this way: "Since everyone is tainted with guilt . . . everyone is safe from retribution."

Outrage over the "Hello Garci" tapes, as they were dubbed in the media, now merged with the corruption cases Esperat had been pursuing at the time of her murder. To the public, everything Esperat had been alleging about the Arroyo administration suddenly made sense, and journalists across the country turned their attention to the human cost of the graft she had been laboring to expose from her home in remote Tacurong. The news became dominated by stories of the suffering of farmers caused by the rapaciousness of Department of Agriculture officials and the grotesque theft of government funds for political purposes. Marcos's stolen billions seemed to have been stolen again by a president who was more and more coming to resemble him.

Called to testify before Senate hearings into the Department of Agriculture scandal, JocJoc Bolante, the official responsible for dispensing much of the 2.4 billion pesos earmarked for Mindanao farmers, fled the country. The Senate issued an arrest warrant for him then recommended that he be charged with plunder. A Senate report on the affair concluded that the vast majority of the money under Bolante's purview had been used to bribe officials on Mindanao who had delivered the votes to elect Arroyo. "All allegations and testimony pointed to her benefiting the most in an intricate scheme of deception and fraud," the *Philippine Daily Inquirer* stated. "The fertilizer fund was misused. It was corrupted. It was intended to assure her [election] victory."

Tens of thousands of demonstrators took to the streets calling for Arroyo's impeachment, and articles of impeachment were filed by opposition members in the House of Representatives. In response, Arroyo addressed the nation on June 27. She denied that it was her voice on the tapes, while paradoxically apologizing for her "lapse in judgment" in making the calls. After the address, she issued an executive order barring officials from further testimony at congressional hearings looking into the scandals of her administration. As Garcillano had predicted, there was no reason for her to worry about impeachment. On September 6, 2005, the House voted not to pursue the impeachment hearings.

Meanwhile, down on Mindanao, the prosecutor that Justice Secretary Gonzalez had appointed to review the Esperat case recommended to the presiding judge, Francis Palmones Jr., that the murder charges against Montañer and Sabay be dismissed for lack of evidence. Palmones, who had previously approved the charges, dismissed them on August 31, just hours before the case was to have been taken out of his hands by a Supreme Court order that transferred the proceedings to a more neutral environment in Cebu, three hundred miles north.

This abrupt turnaround caused the *Manila Standard* to editorialize that "the real masterminds behind the Esperat murder" were higher up in government and that "Montañer and Sabay might have only served as conduits for the payment of the murder money."

The trial of the hired killers was set to open in Cebu on February 15, 2006. Rowie Barua was being held in Manila, and, on February 7, he agreed to meet with me in the Department of Justice Building. He was a handsome, unsmiling man of forty, wearing a white golf shirt and handcuffs. The Philippines state prosecutor in his case had assured me that Barua would be forthcoming and, indeed, he looked me straight in the eye in the interview room as he explained how he'd hired Bismanos and, from Cotabato City, had supervised the hiring of Grecia and Cabayag. But, Barua quickly added, he was not guilty "in conscience or law," because he was ordered to arrange Esperat's murder by his boss Sabay and her boss Montañer. Barua said that when his murder trial began he would testify "as to how the steps were taken, how the plan was organized, who gave the money, everything," and that his story would be backed up by the three men he had hired, all of whom had admitted their guilt and explained Esperat's killing in affidavits.

When Barua was done telling me his story, I asked something that had been on my mind for the hour I'd sat opposite him. "If you knew somebody innocent was going to get killed, why didn't you stop it?"

"Because, according to Sabay and Montañer, Marlene Esperat was doing something in the media to destroy their reputation," he said. "Since I don't know Esperat, it doesn't have any interest for me that she would be killed." Perhaps he saw by my expression that I didn't believe this absolved him of guilt. "They would kill her anyway," he added. "They already tried. There were more attempts prior to that one."

"And if he doesn't do it he might be killed himself," said Arnold Arcano, the administrative chief of the Witness Protection Group, who had led Barua into the room and was personally charged with his safety. "His family might be killed."

"That's an additional point," Barua concurred. "I did everything they instruct me because I have a wife and six children. I just did my job—if not, I would be killed and my family also would be killed."

I turned to Arcano, who was about Barua's age but with a boyishly good-natured face that I thought would be comforting to the terrified witnesses within his program. I asked him if other officials assigned to powerful people in the Philippines would act as Barua had.

Many of them would, he said. "That's the order of their boss, sir. In the case that they don't comply with the order, they and their family also will be—" He lifted his thumb and curled his trigger finger.

As the two walked out, I could only shake my head. Barua may have once been a law-abiding officer, perhaps just as law-abiding as many of his comrades, but his views and fears explained why, on the operational end, it was so easy to kill journalists in the Philippines. As for the officials who regularly gave the irrefusable orders to permanently silence reporters, Philippine history assured them they would have impunity.

The trial of the killers of Marlene Esperat opened on schedule eight days later in Cebu City. Since Bismanos, Grecia and Cabayag had admitted their guilt and Barua had turned state's witness, the initial proceedings concentrated on whether the charges against the alleged masterminds, Osmeña Montañer and Estrella Sabay, should be reinstated. They were—eventually—and then were diverted down the rabbit hole of the Philippine justice system, so easily manipulated by influences outside that system.

Over the next two years the charges were dismissed again, reinstated, raised to a higher court, reviewed by the Department of Justice and, after several repeats of this dance, returned to the Cebu court. In February 2008 an arrest warrant was reissued for Montañer and Sabay, but, as before, the warrant was never executed. On May 14, 2008, the Court of Appeals granted Montañer's and Sabay's petition for an injunction to dismiss the case. Nena Santos, acting as a private prosecutor, appealed the decision and succeeded in reinstating the charges in late October. The warrant was reissued but the pair weren't arrested. At the end of 2008 Santos told reporters that the accused were "pulling all their tricks," and that the case was running into problems that could cause it to drag on for some time.

Meanwhile, in Cotabato City, Montañer and Sabay are still officially listed as overseers of the Department of Agriculture's finances. At this writing, although charged with murder and declared "fugitives," they have good cause to be confident they will retain their posts until retirement.

In Malacañang, Arroyo too has good cause for optimism. Initially so gravely threatened, she has kept her guilt-tainted friends on side by dint of *pasalubong-pabaon*. No indictments for the crime of directing agricultural funds to her election campaign resulted from the hearings into the scandal, and on February 10, 2006, the Senate voted to end its investigation of the "Hello Garci" tapes without issuing a report. Two weeks later, on the twentieth anniversary of the overthrow of Marcos, demonstrators converged on EDSA Square, carrying signs calling for People Power IV. Arroyo reprised the tactics of Marcos by declaring a "state of emergency" — martial law. She sent her troops into the square, dispersed the crowd and tossed her "press freedom" pronouncements to the winds by ordering raids on newspapers critical of her. Today, she is working to change the constitution so she can run again in 2010.

When I'd first arrived in Manila, Marlene Esperat's colleagues told me that the death of "the Erin Brockovitch of the Philippines" had increased the chances that the people she'd exposed would pay for their malfeasance. But Marlene's killing has not been a catalyst for cleansing the Philippines. "The will of God" as she had known it was foiled. And the uproar resulting from her murder has turned out to be theater—tragic theater for Philippine journalists, eight of whom were murdered in 2008. After one of the many rulings that derailed the trial of Montañer and Sabay, I met Marlene's colleagues at a journalism conference in Toronto. This time they said that stories of Philippine malfeasance rarely had a Hollywood ending—or any ending at all.

THREE

JEWEL MOON AND THE HUMAN UNIVERSE

Manik Chandra Saha, Bangladesh

AT FIRST GLANCE THERE IS nothing particularly threatening about Khulna. Like most regional capitals in Bangladesh, it is hot and crowded, but its remote location in the waterlogged southwest has preserved its rural nature. Around Khan J. Ali traffic circle, bicycle rickshaws outnumber cars a hundred to one. Down the palm-lined lanes where a million people live, roosters crow from every backyard. And the city air, even near the jute mills and brick kilns, smells like tropical heaven.

Two unbridgeable rivers, the Ganges and Brahmaputra, are responsible for Khulna's back-country ambience. They inundate the plain to the north and east, cutting off land travel to Dhaka, and spawn a thousand other rivers that zigzag west of town, isolating it from Calcutta. All this water pools in the Bay of Bengal's tidal creeks, forming a mangrove wilderness called the Sundarbans, which walls Khulna on the south. The four-thousand-square-mile roadless jungle, a UNESCO World Heritage site, is the country's last refuge of the Bengal tiger and the sundari tree, Asia's most coveted hardwood.

There were no tourists in Khulna when I arrived after my time in the Philippines. The twenty-four-hour trip by river from Dhaka and the lawlessness of the countryside both discouraged visitors. Khulna Division, of which Khulna city is the capital, had been plagued for years by Maoist and Islamic extremists who assassinated officials, set off bombs and raped the wives of farmers who refused their extortionate demands. The fanatically motivated violence resembled the insurgencies in Colombia and the Philippines, but Khulna added its own twist to the mayhem. Here, among the shifting rivers and jigsaw islands, terrorists whose goals were radically opposed conducted joint operations, and most of their crimes were overseen by the Bengal Mafia, the real power in the division. Indeed, nowhere else in the world were alliances of murderous forces so oxymoronic. Neither theology nor ideology kept jihadists and communists from hiring themselves out to Khulna's gangsters, known in the city as "the seven godfathers."

According to local journalists, the seven godfathers wore "white clothes"—that is, they were public figures who ran Khulna's city council, chamber of commerce and mayor's office. Offered impunity in return for delivering money and votes to the government in Dhaka, the godfathers employed the extremists to illegally log the Sundarbans, steal thousands of acres a year from farmers, murder competitors and pillage Bangladesh's ocean trade at the Port of Mongla. Meanwhile, a black-uniformed unit of the federal police, the Rapid Action Battalion, maintained the appearance of law by arresting the first hapless criminal the godfathers pointed to after an assassination. "Main suspect killed in a cross fire," RAB usually stated in its press releases. Case closed.

The sanctioned gangsterism of Khulna Division was a good part of the reason Transparency International consistently rated Bangladesh at the bottom of its worldwide corruption index, and why the Committee to Protect Journalists named the country one of the five most murderous places in the world to report the news. Between 1998 and 2006, sixteen journalists were murdered in

Bangladesh, eight in Khulna Division after they'd detailed the government's alliances with "the underground groups." The most prominent on the kill list was Manik Chandra Saha, the former president of the Khulna Press Club and a winner of Transparency International's Integrity Award.

Saha was different from the slain journalists I'd encountered in Colombia and the Philippines. The division's 14 million citizens considered him a saint, and even some officials acknowledged he was Khulna's most reasoned and likable reporter. The deputy inspector general of the Khulna police wept in public when he heard Saha had been killed on January 15, 2004—the first time local journalists had ever seen him show emotion. Saha's murder precipitated a week of hysterical mourning. Nationwide *hartals,* or strikes, paralyzed the country. The prime minister's spokesman and the leader of the opposition arrived in Khulna to comfort the population. And the street where the forty-nine-year-old Saha had fallen was turned into a shrine and renamed Manik Saha Road.

For all the devotion he inspired, Saha was a rather unassuming man. He was stockily built, of middle height, with thinning hair and a voice that could barely be heard when he asked questions at press conferences. What distinguished him in a crowd of reporters were his huge brown eyes, tilted up like wingtips by high cheekbones, which gave him something of a Confucian smile, even when he was being told to shut up by one of the seven godfathers. "Manik did not know how to get angry or raise his voice," said Mainul Islam Khan, director of a Dhaka-based NGO that attempts to protect journalists. "He had no aggressive side to him, no personal agenda, no ego or inner turmoil. He was a purely innocent person. Whatever he wrote, he just laid the facts out, appealing to reason. He was motivated only by love."

That love apparently gave Saha tremendous drive. Sleeping at most four hours a night, he divided his days between exposing the region's torments and laboring to rectify them. He founded schools, libraries, cultural organizations, rural poverty councils, human rights committees, women's shelters, clinics, a theater group, a music academy, a foundation for working children and an international action forum to save the Sundarbans. Each of the underground groups had threatened to torture him to death, but he regularly traveled alone to remote villages to investigate atrocities. "If they use rape and murder as weapons," he told his worried brother Prodip, "if they steal the land and no one arrives to tell the world, then their wrongs take place in a vacuum." Trained as a lawyer, Saha exclusively represented the godfathers' penniless victims—and was penniless himself most of the time because he gave away the $250 a month he earned from his groundbreaking journalism. "There is no God to answer the prayers of the poor," he told his wife, Nanda. "It's a human universe and therefore up to humans to fulfill prayers."

Three days before his murder, Saha delivered a lecture on his brand of investigative journalism to a reporters' training session in the nearby town of Jessore. "Use the scientific method and the rules of evidence to gather facts about what is unjust and harmful," he advised. "When conveying those facts, be neither subtle nor angry. If threatened, take courage by reminding yourself that you speak for those who have no voice. Place your skills in the service of the poor and you will be happy."

Before I arrived in Bangladesh, I had searched for the motivations of journalists who had given their lives for a story and had discovered complex emotional sources for their bravery. Personal atonement, angry resistance to public enemies or compensation for infirmity had played a part with some; manly pride or religious intoxication had fueled the courage of others. But in Manik Saha I found something more difficult to explain: selflessness that seemed to come from pure goodness.

Saha was assassinated at noon, and in a way that was meant to horrify Khulna's citizens. A newspaper photo shows him lying on his stomach at the corner of Sir Iqbal and Bani Babu Roads, half a block from the Khulna Press Club. He's wearing gray slacks, freshly shined black shoes and a red sweater, but his head is missing, his bare brains spewed in a pink pool between his shoulders.

From about ten feet away someone had thrown a "cocktail" — a can, usually packed with fishing weights and gunpowder, that detonates on impact. It's a method of assassination unique to Khulna, used in dozens of hired hits because it costs less than a bullet to assemble and is all a poorly paid assassin can afford. But one look at the crime scene by journalists rushing from the Press Club convinced them that this was a specialized cocktail for a special man. Until Saha's assassination, all cocktails had been thrown at the victims' midsection from at least twenty feet away — distancing the killer from shrapnel while ensuring death to the target. Saha's assassin had aimed the can at his head, as if to send a precise message about Saha's way of thinking. "The cocktail that killed Manik was different from any before," a thirty-two-year-old colleague of Saha's named Dip Azad said. "Usually the shrapnel is everywhere and the body is riddled. But this time there was no shrapnel. The attacker was trained and outfitted with a device to target the head only. That was our first clue it wasn't a local group who masterminded the killing."

At the time of Saha's murder, seven cardboard file boxes were stacked beside his desk in the tiny apartment he shared with his wife and two daughters, four blocks from the Press Club. Each box was labeled with the name of a story he was working on: "Stealing land for shrimp farms," "Sundarbans logging," "Acid attacks on women," "Fundamentalist groups," "Anti-liberation parties," "Terrorism in the Division," and "Minorities oppression." Some of the stories were for the left-wing *Daily Sangbad*, the national newspaper for which Saha had worked since 1982; others were for the BBC's Bangla Service, to which he had been phoning in stories since 1994; and two of them, "Anti-liberation parties" and "Terrorism in the Division," were for *New Age*, a pro-government paper for which he had started writing a couple of weeks before his death.

This last turn in Saha's career had startled those at the Press Club to whom he hadn't explained the affiliation before his death. While fair-minded in its news coverage, New Age's editorials backed the ruling Bangladesh Nationalist Party, whose right-wing policies ran counter to almost everything Saha believed in. After a split election in October 2001, the BNP had formed a coalition government with an Islamic fundamentalist party called Jamaat-e-Islami, considered by Saha to be "anti-liberation" because it had sided with the Islamic military regime in Pakistan during the 1971 war that had created a secular Bangladesh out of what had previously been East Pakistan. Banned for decades, the JI had recently re-emerged as a powerful voice in Parliament, calling for an Islamic state and using the underground groups against its secular opponents. Saha had reacted to JI's rise by writing articles for Sangbad that exposed the ties between JI and Khulna's outlaw jihadist groups, detailing their bizarre cooperation with the Maoists and with the godfathers who, in turn, served the government parties in Dhaka.

Two days before his death, Saha had traveled to Dhaka to deliver a package of fact-checking material to New Age. He made the trip with a close friend, Swapan Guha, who was flying on to Bombay to attend a World Social Forum. "When we got to the capital, he asked me to drop him off at the office of New Age," Guha remembered, sitting in the Khulna office of the Working Children's Forum that he and Saha had set up in 2000. "He told me he had some important official documents to deliver for his articles." Saha then hinted that he had reasons for his latest career move. "He said that the people who wanted to kill him had no fear of prosecution but that he was now taking a step that would allow him to continue his work and change society."

After dropping off the documents, Saha visited Nayeemul Khan, the president of the Bangladesh Centre for Development, Journalism and Communication. "Manik was our representative in Khulna—he knew better than anyone the plots to kill him," Nayeemul told me. "But he would not stop writing revelations about the forces that wanted him silenced. So he had come up with this idea: It was his belief that a pro-government paper would give him protection to advance his message. It was sort of a bold strategy, but it possibly threatened the parties he criticized even more."

Not long after Saha's murder, the Rapid Action Battalion raided a camp of Janajuddha Maoists and gunned down three members "in a cross fire," claiming that they had been behind the assassination. Saha's closest colleagues in the Press Club doubted that RAB had killed the masterminds and demanded a proper investigation. Six months into its own inquiry, the Press Club's president, Humayun Kabir, was murdered in a cocktail attack, and the young journalist Dip Azad only survived another hurled cocktail because it failed to detonate against his back. By then some Press Club journalists had evidence to suggest that members of the Bangladesh Nationalist Party and Jamaat-e-Islami had used the army's intelligence service to arrange Saha's killing and that the manner of his death was indeed "symbolic."

"The government forces worked with the godfathers to hire and train Janajuddha to take off the head of our think tank," Dip Azad told me. "All these different groups come together like this," he added, holding up a tight fist. "Crime makes them brothers."

"Bangladesh is a place in which you can appreciate life's interconnectedness," Manik Saha told a Save the Sundarbans conference he'd organized three years before his murder. "That our small country with its large and poor population has tried to preserve the Sundarbans is cause for hope. That forces within our country are competing to destroy it through shrimp farming and logging is cause not for despair, but action. Ultimately, I believe, the fate of the Sundarbans will mirror the fate of our nation."

Saha was the subcontinent's leading expert on the Sundarbans. He had begun visiting this last remnant of the Bengal rainforest as a teenager, sleeping in the ruins of ancient Hindu temples overgrown by hundred-foot-tall sundari trees. He'd traveled most of its rivers and tidal creeks by the time he served as a consultant for a *National Geographic* article that was instrumental in getting the area declared a UNESCO World Heritage Site in 1999. That the Sundarbans has survived the depradations of guerrillas, godfathers and corrupt governments, with millions of people pressing on it from every side, is due in large part to Saha's activism against overwhelming odds.

Bangladesh has a population of about 150 million people in an area smaller than Florida's. Its partition from India in 1947 to form East Pakistan separated the state from its most productive rice fields in West Bengal and from its only port and industrial center, Calcutta, causing the last British governor of Bengal to predict the territory would become "the greatest rural slum in history." Today, 70 million Bangladeshis live in poverty, two-thirds are illiterate and 40 percent are unemployed. Most of the country lies at sea level, and every year cyclones move north out of the Bay of Bengal, sometimes flattening and flooding towns in fifty-mile-wide swaths. The country's politics are as disaster-prone as its terrain. Millions died in the War of Liberation that freed it from Pakistan; since then Bangladesh has seen a dozen coups, a decade and a half of martial law and hundreds of national *hartals* that have brought the country to a standstill.

Despite its political turmoil and systemic corruption, between 1971 and 2001 Bangladesh considered itself the most secular and tolerant majority Muslim nation in the world. In the last three years of Manik Saha's life, however, the alliance of the Bangladesh Nationalist Party and Jamaat-e-Islami swung the nation in the direction of politicized Islam and religiously motivated violence. Among the most sadistic of the radical Muslim groups in Khulna Division was the Jama'atul Mujahideen Bangladesh, whose leadership Saha had identified as ex-JI members. Hindus, who constituted about 12 percent of the population, suffered most at the hands of the JMB's post-2001 jihad.

Manik Chandra Saha was born a Hindu, on June 10, 1954, in the tiny village of Chalitatala, twenty miles north of Khulna. His ancestors had arrived in the thirteenth century, fleeing invading Mongols and seeking refuge in the Sundarbans. Khulna city was founded two centuries later by Sufis, a humanist and tolerant sect of Islam. The Hindus then abandoned their settlements in the marshes to form small communities in the less flood-prone north of the division. The two religions lived together peaceably until the British took control in the nineteenth century. As part of their divide-and-rule strategy, the colonizers recruited the minority Bengal Hindus as municipal officers, traders and tax collectors. The Muslims, usurped from power, refused to participate in the new order, and a social and economic fissure opened between neighbors. The division grew more volatile when Mahatma Gandhi's movement for independence from Great Britain took hold across India. Hindus were the overall majority on the subcontinent, but the western and eastern provinces of the Raj, comprising present-day Pakistan and Bangladesh, were predominantly Muslim. To Gandhi's despair, two parties emerged in the 1930s to represent different visions of an independent India. Gandhi's own Congress Party, under the leadership of Jawaharlal Nehru, voiced the Hindu desire for India to remain unified. The Muslims, under the leadership of Mohammad Ali Jinnah's Muslim League, rejected minority status in a Hindu-dominated India and called for an independent Muslim state in the west and east. Fearing civil war, in 1946 the Congress Party agreed to India's partition, which became the catalyst for some of the worst ethnic violence of the twentieth century and the greatest mass migration in history. Eighteen million Hindus and Muslims fled their homes along the border areas to cross over into India, Pakistan or East Pakistan. One million were murdered along the way.

Manik Saha's father, a member of the Hindu trading class under the British colonial system, was a prime target for ethnic violence during the days of Partition. That Krishnapada Saha survived and remained in Khulna Division to father Manik was due in large part to Gandhi—whom Krishnapada revered until his death in 2005.

On August 16, 1946, with Partition still a year away, violence broke out in Calcutta, sixty miles southwest of Krishnapada's village of Chalitatala, on the Madhumati River. Muslims and Hindus rampaged through Calcutta's slums, slaughtering six thousand people in twenty-four hours. The fraternal killing spread into the rural districts east of the city, with the Muslims pledging to drive out the minority Hindus. Horrified by the mass murder his independence movement had unleashed, Gandhi set off on a Pilgrimage of Penance through the swamps of East Bengal, preaching nonviolence to Muslims and urging Hindus to remain in their villages. Gandhi's pilgrimage succeeded in slowing and then stopping the sectarian killings, and though Krishnapada's family fled to India, Krishnapada himself heeded Gandhi's plea and stayed in Chalitatala. On Independence Day, August 14, 1947, only the crescent moon flag of Pakistan, peacefully raised in the district capital of Khulna, marked the transition to a Muslim state. "Gandhi's Satyagraha did that," Manik would later remember his father telling him, using the Sanskrit word for nonviolent political action.

After Partition, Krishnapada restarted his business, buying jute from local farmers, trading it for manufactured goods in India, and selling the goods in Khulna. Three years later, he had recovered enough of his prewar income to take a teenage bride named Chanchala, from the village of Suktagram, five miles north of his home.

Chanchala was a rarity in the district—the literate daughter of a Hindu landowner who gave her a say in choosing a husband. "My younger sisters and I were taught by our father to use our minds and be curious about everything," Manik's aunt, now one hundred and bent double from osteoporosis, told me. "When Krishnapada asked Chanchala to marry him she said yes, but only because he was a good, kind man like our father. We would not settle for less than a man like our father."

After the wedding, Krishnapada took his new bride to his home village and, two years later, their first son was born. Chanchala named him Manik Chandra—"Jewel Moon."

Saha grew up in "the real Bangladesh," as he would later refer to his home village, by which he meant that Chalitatala was a world away from the unlivable chaos of Dhaka. There may have been no electricity, phone or running water, but the town's social life and well-tended beauty were a compensation for the lack of modern conveniences. Extended families lived in communal *baris* consisting of several mud huts, a courtyard and a garden. Everyone knew everyone else's business, and life moved to a daily and seasonal rhythm that urban Bengalis still value with aching nostalgia. Every morning at Chalitatala's riverbank, young women in gold and purple saris filled spittoon-shaped *kolshis* and gracefully returned to the village balancing the jars on their heads. Out in the current, fishermen manning long-prowed boats threw gossamer nets that billowed out over the slow-moving water. Their daily catch of *hilsha* added to the two crops of rice that came from the surrounding paddies and to the harvest of vegetables; villagers had enough to eat in most years. The temperature may have topped one hundred degrees in the sun, but farmers and fishermen returned to a village sheltered by giant krishnachura trees and a market square cooled by a monumental banyan under which five hundred people could gather.

For most of the villagers, of course, life in Bangladesh had another face. Money was measured in tenths of a cent; in years of typhoon or flood there was starvation; diseases easily treated in the West went untreated. Eye infections led to blindness and appendicitis to death, parasites sapped energy, infant mortality was common, and death in childbirth was ten times higher than in Europe.

Krishnapada Saha was better off than most. His *bari* complex had tin roofs, rough wood walls and furniture. He also regularly traveled to the world beyond the village, and when Manik was six years old his father tried to give him a sense of Chalitatala's place in it. Krishnapada started by teaching Manik the concept of scale, having him draw a small picture of a tabletop with a lantern in the middle. Then he had Manik draw a picture of the house, the layout of the village and the loop of the Madhumati River. He showed him a map of East Pakistan and located Khulna on it. Finally, he took out a tiny globe of the world, put his finger on Asia and, with Manik in his arms, went outside and held the globe up to the starry sky. Before he could read, Manik understood that he lived on the twenty-second latitude of a round earth hanging in space, surrounded by other objects hanging in space.

By then Manik had a newborn brother, Prodip. Saha later recalled his mother nursing Prodip while she leaned over a newspaper that Krishnapada had brought back from Dhaka. "When I asked her what was in the paper, she read it aloud to me," he recollected to a colleague. "President Eisenhower had visited Pakistan. I had no idea who the strange bald man was, but my mother said he came from a rich country on the other side of the world." When Manik found the other side of the world on his globe, "my mother gave me a sweetmeat for being so smart. That was the first time I was rewarded for something to do with the news."

In 1963, when Manik was nine, Krishnapada took him along on a business trip down the Pusur River to the new port of Mongla, constructed at the northern end of a tidal channel as the country's proud replacement for the lost port of Calcutta. Thirty miles south of Khulna, on the east bank of the river, a road was being built through the jute and rice fields, but Manik looked west. At the river's edge was a wall of towering sundari trees, with crocodiles basking between their buttressed trunks, their tails lost in what looked like a bed of human thumbs—the trees' aerial roots. High above, macaque monkeys leapt through the branches, screaming like children. Manik's father pointed to the dorsal fin of a Gangetic dolphin creasing the water's surface as it headed up a channel.

Deep in the flooded forest, he said, the fish the dolphins hunted climbed trees—they were called mudskippers, and could breathe air. Manik's eyes, wider than usual, widened even more.

At dawn the next day in Mongla, Krishnapada took Manik across the river on a boat ride up a channel toward the Kunga River, in the heart of the Sundarbans. An hour into the journey, surrounded by the doglike barking of muntjac deer and the deafening creaking of a million species of insects, Manik saw an orange and black head in the water, twice the size of a man's. "It was a tiger, swimming between islands," he later wrote. "He emerged from the water and looked back at me with intelligent amber eyes. Our boat driver took out a rifle, but before he could shoot, the tiger delicately hopped into the jungle. I knew that tigers sometimes killed honey gatherers in the Sundarbans, but I wondered, 'Why shoot such a beautiful thing when it was about to ask me a question?'"

Saha's pleasant world of natural history lessons with his father and newspaper reading at the feet of his mother came to a sudden end in 1966, when Chanchala died in childbirth. "I was seven and very upset, but Manik was bereft," Prodip remembers. "She died an hour after having my brother Dilip. When we went to her bed to say goodbye, Manik wouldn't let go of her hand. He just wept and called her name." The household was thrown into turmoil. The baby survived, and Krishnapada, in mourning, was faced with having to take care of an infant and two young boys while earning a living at a trade that required him to travel. His family was in Calcutta, so for help he turned to Chanchala's eldest sister in nearby Suktagram.

Aunt Chapala was then sixty, childless and living alone. Her husband had succumbed to tuberculosis when she was still a teenager and her father had taken her home and made her a co-owner in his farm. A couple of years later, when her parents died, Chapala became sole owner. From that day forward Chapala oversaw the planting, harvesting and selling of rice, and all the farm's accounting. After a lifetime of managing the farm, she now agreed to become surrogate mother to her sister's three little boys.

Saha adamantly refused to leave his father's house. "My brother was a sensitive boy, but he had a will of iron," Prodip, now a high school principal in Khulna, told me. "He said the only way he'd leave Mama's house was if Auntie made him a shirt out of Caroline fabric. He thought the fabric would be too expensive for her to afford." Chapala made the shirt, and went to Chalitatala to present it to Manik. He reneged on the bargain, saying the shirt was too large, and he tearfully begged his father not to send him away. His father relented and let him stay. Left alone in the house when his father was away on business, Manik slept on his mother's side of his parents' bed, praying to God for Chanchala's magical return.

Six months after her death, Krishnapada came home from one of his trips accompanied by a new wife and her three children. He thought the surprise would comfort his lonesome son, but Manik was devastated at seeing a strange woman in his mother's place, with her own children her primary concern. She disciplined Manik for his moroseness; he drew inward, and finally went to live with his aunt and brothers in Suktagram.

The village was even poorer than Chalitatala, and Manik, without his father, was heartsick. There was no school to take his mind off his troubles, and Prodip remembers how Manik thought his life was at an end. "Then Auntie taught him something that changed him," Prodip said. "It stayed with him his whole life." Chapala suggested that Manik set up a little classroom under a banyan tree and teach the other children of the village to read. "She told him, 'Manik, do this, because the more you think about yourself, the unhappier you are.' So, even at such a young age, Manik learned to take his mind off himself by helping others. When he was unhappiest in his life, he learned to think of the poor ahead of himself. It made him happy."

The nearest secondary school was in the town of Khalia, an hour by boat on the Madhumati River, and a year later Krishnapada enrolled Manik. Because of the time the boy had missed, his father entered his birth date on school records as June 10, 1956, making him two years younger than his actual age (in news reports of his death he is reported as being younger than forty-nine). Manik spent the next four years traveling back and forth to school on the river steamer, but not without another interruption in his education. At seventeen, he took up arms during the War of Liberation.

Conflict between East and West Pakistan had been building almost since their founding as improbably linked halves of a single Muslim state on either side of Hindu India. West Pakistan was ruled by fair-skinned Punjabis who considered their culture (and race) superior to that of the darker-skinned Bengalis. Though East Pakistan was slightly more populous, West Pakistan allotted to itself the national capital, Islamabad, and the lion's share of taxes, administrative posts and development projects. Urdu, spoken in West Pakistan, was incomprehensible in Bangla-speaking East Pakistan, and both Hindu and Muslim Bengalis were outraged when shortly after independence President Jinnah read a proclamation on the grounds of Dhaka University declaring that Bangla was a "Hindu language" and that "Urdu and only Urdu" would be East Pakistan's official tongue. On February 21, 1952, a student demonstration that called for recognition of Bangla as the national language of East Pakistan erupted on the grounds of Dhaka University's Medical College. Twelve protestors were killed by Punjabi police, bloodily marking the birth of the Bangla Language Movement, which soon became equated with a struggle for independence.

The tensions between the two wings of Pakistan grew in the ensuing years. Most Bengalis wished to live in a secular state, but in 1956 Pakistan moved to make Islam the state religion, and changed the name of the country to the Islamic Republic of Pakistan. Two years later a Punjabi general named Ayub Khan seized power in Islamabad and ended freedom of speech, bottling up Bengali resentments. After ten years of army rule, leaders of East Pakistan's leftist Awami Muslim League party dropped the word *Muslim* from their name and called for a Western-style secular government, with Bangla as the official language of an autonomous Bangladesh—"the Land of Bengalis." When, in November 1970, a typhoon killed half a million people in East Pakistan but West Pakistan offered only token assistance, outrage swept the country. In the 1971 elections, the Awami League defeated the Islamist Jamaat-e-Islami party to win all but one of East Pakistan's seats in the National Assembly. Ayub Khan's successor, Yahya Khan, declared that the opening of the new National Assembly would, unfortunately, have to be postponed. Four days later Hindu and Muslim students at Dhaka University left their classes and launched a protest rally, raising the flag of a free Bangladesh beside the spot at the Medical College where the twelve students had been killed two decades earlier. The head of the Awami League, Sheikh Mujib, was arrested and a resistance force, the Mukti Bahini, was organized by a Bengali major in the Pakistan army named Zia Rahman, who captured the Chittagong radio station and declared independence. Supported by East Pakistan's Jamaat-e-Islami party, Yahya Khan reinforced his troops in Dhaka and then went on the offensive, his tanks targeting the university first, slaughtering hundreds of students. The army then turned its guns on the city, razing Hindu neighborhoods and summarily executing thousands. In the countryside, mass murder was combined with mass rape. Over the next seven months, three million civilians were killed and ten million fled to India.

In Suktagram, Manik Saha left home and met up with his Khalia schoolmates to form a local band of Mukti Bahini fighters, moving cross-country to harass the Pakistani garrison at Khulna. His young life might very well have been cut short had not India, provoked by Pakistani incursions, entered the war on the side of Bangladesh. On December 7, 1971, the Indian army entered Jessore, north of Khulna, and a week later, cut off from supplies and attacked on their flanks by freedom fighters, the Pakistanis surrendered. Within a year

a constitution was written and Bangladesh became a secular democracy with freedom of religion, speech and assembly guaranteed. A
shrine to the country's struggle for freedom was then erected on the
spot where the students had been gunned down in 1952—the only
nonreligious national symbol in the Muslim world. Called *The
Language Martyrs*, it consists of a tall stanchion arching over
smaller ones in front of the red disk of a rising sun, symbolizing a
National Mother protecting the founding children of Bangladesh.

This was an exhilarating time for Saha. He'd just graduated from
Kalia Secondary School with straight A's in math, physics and
biology and had decided to become a natural scientist. Longing to
serve his nation in some unique way, and seeing himself as a possible natural-history pioneer on behalf of Bangladesh, he set off
alone on an expedition into the Sundarbans.

Saha entered the vast swamp the way he'd motored in with his
father as a child. He carried notepads, pens and textbooks, intending to catalogue hundreds of rare species. At the place where he
had seen the tiger, he turned south into the channel of the Kunga,
its muddy banks lined with nipa palms that were stalked by herons
hunting fish—the birds, in turn, becoming meals for thrashing crocodiles. He spent his first night in a tree house erected in the sundari
forest by loggers, and the next day headed for Hiron Point on the
Bay of Bengal, camping in Hindu ruins along the way. It was
the flowering season, an intoxicating time to be in the Sundarbans,
and two days later, cleansed of the outside world, he had a transfor-
mative experience.

Saha had been attending week-long *puja* festivals with his aunt
Chapala, a devout Hindu, since he was twelve. The *pujas* were
held in honor of two goddesses: Durga, a ten-armed female warrior
who rode atop a tiger and saved supplicants by slaying devils in the
name of goodness, and Kali, a divine mother who was completely
indifferent to her children's fate and who was worshipped as the

goddess of destruction and death. To Hindus, the two goddesses were not opposed but in balance: you appealed to Durga for help when you were under duress, and to Kali for acceptance of the terrible things that made it necessary to ask for help.

Recently the *pujas* had begun to strike Saha as overwrought operas. He'd been taught the scientific method at school and had accepted it as the best way to approach questions about life. One collected data through observation and formulated and tested hypotheses through experimentation. What, he wondered, did Durga's divine goodness and Kali's divine indifference have to do with formulating and testing hypotheses about reality? And what did both of these goddesses have to do with the nonreligious National Mother?

From his sundari perches and the back of his boat, studying animals who struggled to live but always wound up dying to feed crocodiles and tigers, Saha thought about the misfortune of millions in the War of Liberation as well as the loss of his beloved mother. From the war had come the glorious birth of Bangladesh, and from his mother's death had come his realization that thinking of others ahead of himself made him happy. In Hindu terms, Durga's protective goodness had stood side by side with Kali's destructive indifference, and, overall, good had come out of the struggle.

It struck him then that Kali and Durga were intuitive attempts by people with no knowledge of the scientific method to personalize the neutral workings of matter. The National Mother of Bangladesh, on the other hand, had evolved from rational ideals that were not based on a faith in capricious grace. "If you pray to some force of good outside the natural world, like Durga, you think you can be helped," he later told his brother Prodip, "but the natural world is really completely indifferent to your fate, like Kali." Out of humanity's feelings of fear and awe, the gods were mistakenly thought to be affecting the fate of individuals from outside the tumult of matter, and independent of its laws. In fact, there was nothing outside the universe, nothing from which you were separate, and there were no external gods to intercede on your behalf. If you saw yourself as a part of the natural world—part of everything—then what you called the divine was also inside you. Why pray to gods when they were really the seamless material phenomena in front of you and inside you?

Understanding that there were no hidden gods gave Manik a sense that religion's mystification of reality actually separated people from what they thought of as divine. It was enough to know that the universe had evolved to produce man's ability to be conscious of it, that the universe derived its meaning from man's consciousness and that Bangladesh derived its ideals from man's noble mind.

For the rest of his life, Saha never deviated from his perception that what people called God was in reality the natural universe—that the natural universe was indifferent to him as an individual, but that he, Manik, was a part of the natural universe. Knowing this gave his life a meaning that others would call transcendence but that he thought of as science.

Three months after Saha returned from his adventure in the Sundarbans, he enrolled as a science major in Khulna's Salam College, proceeding with his courses in biology and physics, the latter of which introduced him to a compelling aspect of the philosophy of Bengal's Nobel Prize–winning writer, Rabindranath Tagore. In 1930, Tagore had sat down with Albert Einstein in Germany and discussed the implications of quantum physics. The conversation was recorded and published in 1961, on the hundredth anniversary of Tagore's birth, and reading it put the capstone on Manik's worldview.

Tagore began by asking Einstein about the meaning of quantum physics, which seemed to imply that the infinitesimally small packets of energy that made up the universe were governed by chance and defied the laws of causality. To Tagore, the odds that these random forces had produced the being that beheld them were too remote for a scientist to deem probable. Tagore's conclusion was that the universe should be read backwards: it existed to be beheld. "The truth of the universe is a human truth," he said. "Matter is composed of protons and electrons, with gaps between them; but matter may seem to be solid. Similarly, humanity is composed of individuals, yet they have their interconnection of human relationship, which gives living solidarity to man's world. The entire universe is linked up with us in a similar manner, it is a human universe."

Einstein accepted the premise of the universe's "organic connectivity," but he resisted Tagore's conclusion. "This is a purely human conception of the universe," he said.

Tagore replied, "There can be no other conception. This world is a human world—the scientific view of it is also that of the scientific man." He went further, arguing that organic connectivity acted like a conscious deity to produce, through evolution, a "law of goodness" that most people instinctively knew they should follow. "If in our conduct we can follow the law of goodness, we can have real liberty and self-expression. The principle of conduct is there, but the character which makes it true and individual is our own creation."

Tagore's hypothesis struck Saha as scientifically sound. If Saha can be said to have had a religion, it was his atheistic belief that organic connectivity had produced, through natural selection, a law of goodness, and that the universe that produced it was indifferent to whether or not man lived by it. Only man's consciousness made the scientific law of goodness meaningful and true. Saha interpreted the law of goodness as requiring that he put others ahead of himself, and, since living by that law promoted "real liberty and self-expression," he had a scientific code of truth he could always turn to that instructed him on the proper way to behave. Years later, when he put this code into action as a journalist and humanitarian, millions of religious Bengalis began to consider Manik Saha a saint.

Two months into Saha's first term at Salam College the indifferent universe cast Bangladesh aside, abandoning the newborn country to two decades of lonely malediction. The unrelieved misery began on October 6, 1973, when the faraway Yom Kippur War exploded among Israel, Egypt and Syria. The surrounding Arab states showed their support for their fellow Muslims by cutting oil production, quadrupling the price of crude almost overnight. Bangladesh's minuscule currency reserves disappeared in a month, an economic catastrophe that was followed by a natural one—a typhoon that caused floods throughout the south. By January 1974, the country was experiencing famine, and during the next few months over a million people starved to death.

In Khulna Division, most of the rice stored in the Mongla godowns was in the hands of three oligarchic Muslim families— Khulna's first modern godfathers. During the 1950s and 1960s the families had derived their power from collaboration with the Jamaat-e-Islami party that backed the Pakistani regime and had switched sides only when it became apparent that India would enter the War of Liberation on the side of a free Bangladesh. In the two years after liberation, the families had actually expanded their power, paying off corrupt officials in the struggling new regime of Sheikh Mujib. The head of one family had taken charge of Khulna's chamber of commerce as well as of the families' underworld operations in Mongla. He then took full advantage of Khulna's starving citizens by demanding property mortgages as collateral for food.

To the twenty-year-old Saha, the injustice was so overwhelming that he began to question whether the best way to serve his country was as a scientist. After receiving his two-year associate degree, he entered Majid Memorial College, now unsure of what he would major in. At that point Saha met a man who would have as great an effect on him as had his revelation in the Sundarbans. Ratan Sen, president of the Khulna district's Communist Party of Bangladesh (CPB), was a fifty-one-year-old lean-faced intellectual with a pencil-thin mustache and large horn-rimmed glasses. He came to Majid Memorial to deliver a speech advocating the overthrow of

Bangladesh's corrupt structure of godfather capitalism and its replacement by a planned socialist economy.

Sen was the only politician Saha had ever heard of who was brave enough to publicly attack the godfather families' hold on power. After the meeting, Saha introduced himself to the older man, who gave him back issues of the CPB weekly *Ekata* ("Unity"), every edition of which contained an exposé by Sen about the godfather clans. When Saha, mindful of Gandhi's philosophy of *Satyagraha*, expressed his fears about the human costs of a violent communist revolution, Sen explained that the CPB platform specifically rejected violence and was in favor of an alliance with the ruling Awami League government. The essence of communism, according to the party's lofty doctrine, was to educate the masses so that individuals would learn to serve others, their collective efforts coordinated by a benevolent state. Through political, humanitarian and legal action, a socialist economy that benefited the poor could be created in Bangladesh.

Saha signed up as a member that day and, under Sen's guidance, switched his major to political science and humanities. A month later he became head of the student wing of the party and wrote the text of a petition to Sheik Mujib appealing for help in the district.

Sheikh Mujib and his government were receiving desperate petitions from all over Bangladesh. Destroyed by war, typhoon and hyperinflation—with its only economy the dysfunctional black market overseen by local godfathers—Bangladesh was at a low point in its woe-plagued four-year history. In January 1975, Mujib declared a state of emergency, setting a pattern for decades to come: he appointed himself president of a one-party state that would appoint the country's six divisional governors. These governors would then follow his orders to enact wide-ranging reforms under the banner of what Mujib called "the Second Revolution."

The revolution was welcomed by most Bengalis but never carried forward. The godfathers allied themselves with the military and labeled the Second Revolution a communist coup. On August 15, 1975, the officer corps staged a countercoup, slaughtering Sheikh Mujib, his wife, their three sons and two daughters-in-law, plus seven other members of his family.

News of the coup reached Khulna just as Manik was about to take his final exams for his bachelor's degree. Sen mobilized the Communist Party's student wing, and Saha was arrested for distributing leaflets that demanded the arrest and trial of the killers of Mujib. While he sat in jail, there were two more coups, accompanied by *hartals* and violent riots. Finally, the army appointed the War of Liberation's military hero Zia Rahman as Chief Martial Law Administrator. General Zia legitimized his rule by appointing himself head of a new political party, the Bangladesh Nationalist Party, and efficiently engineered a campaign to restore order. Thousands more communists were arrested, and dozens joined Saha in the Khulna prison, including Ratan Sen. Saha not only survived the two-year ordeal but, with Sen's encouragement, studied for his missed final exams, passing them just before his release at the top of his graduating class. Sen then advised him to enter law school. "Use the law to oppose those who work outside it to oppress the weak," Saha later remembered Sen telling him. "They cannot deny the facts forever, and the law is grounded in discovering the facts."

Three years later Saha completed his law degree but was denied the bar by officials loyal to Zia. Again on Sen's advice, he returned to school to pursue a master's degree in political science. He became president of the CPB wing of the student union and, at the first rally he organized, met a Hindu woman named Nanda, who had just enrolled in a postnatal-care program. When Nanda asked him why he had named the rally "Chapala's Feast for the Poor," he said it was to honor his aunt in Suktagram.

"He told his auntie, 'I am feeding them for you so that you will know that when you die there will be many people who will pray for your soul,'" Nanda recollected, on the second floor of the mold-blackened walk-up on Ahsan Ahmed Road where Saha had lived with his family for the last four years of life. "Manik had no such belief in praying for the soul, but his auntie had no children and he meant this as a comfort to her. Manik loved his auntie as he loved his mother. He attributed to her the origins of his belief in service and kindness."

Dressed in a somber purple sari and wearing a dark mourning bindi, Nanda sat in the cramped living room that had also served as her husband's office. She had kept it exactly as he'd left it before he was killed. The desk where he once worked had a glass top under which were business cards and a 2004 *New Age* calendar with the logo promising, "News as it should be." Behind the desk were a dozen journalism awards, including a framed maroon plaque from Transparency International. "He never lived to receive the award," Nanda said, above the ringing bicycle bells on the commercial street below. "It was presented posthumously."

She took the plaque down from the wall and handed it to me. "Tragically," it read, "Mr. Saha's dedication and bravery in investigating and unmasking corruption proved fatal. With his death, Bangladesh and indeed the world has lost a committed anti-corruption fighter."

"Are you worried for your own safety?" I asked Nanda.

"What worse can happen to us?" she replied wearily. "Nothing else. The worst has already happened. His goodness was endless, in public, in private, everywhere. It can never be replaced. His heart and mind were unique in this world." She rubbed a bit of dust from the corner of the plaque. "His ideas were recognized around the world. In Khulna he used to argue in the court like a scholar, the judges thought he must have received his training in London."

Saha had started amazing judges in 1982, shortly after Zia had been assassinated in yet another coup. A liberal-minded superior court judge named Abdus Sattar had briefly replaced Zia and had loosened restrictions on banned lawyers, allowing Saha to enter the bar. Saha hadn't been practicing very long, however, when Sattar was thrust aside in still another coup, this one launched by a general named Hossain Mohammad Ershad, who now founded the Jatiya Party, which was even more right-wing than the BNP; once again martial law was declared. In the first decade of its existence, one of the Muslim world's only democracies had experienced half a dozen coups, two presidential assassinations, and martial law for the majority of the time. Ershad's military rule would last until 1990.

Saha was arrested again on March 26, 1982, two days after Sattar was overthrown, and when he got out of jail a couple of months later, the judges he'd previously impressed quietly approved his return to practicing law. "He used to go to court and argue cases for weeks and not take fees," Nanda said. "I used to ask, 'Why don't you take something?' He said, 'My clients are in jail, they have to sell their land or a cow to pay me—how can I take fees from these people?'"

Saha's reputation as a lawyer who put his clients' interests before his own sparked the admiration of Khulna's Sattar-appointed senior judge, as well as of opposition politicians, businessmen and police who managed to survive the purges and the tightening grip of Ershad. Saha was offered the potentially lucrative post of assistant Khulna magistrate, but he refused, saying he didn't want to be tainted by working for the military government. At that point, a journalist named Profulla Bhakta, the Khulna stringer for one of Bangladesh's oldest and most progressive newspapers, *Daily Sangbad*, approached him outside the courthouse. Profulla was retiring to Dhaka and told Manik he needed a progressive person to be his replacement. "Manik hadn't done any journalism before then," Saha's brother Prodip remembered. "Profulla chose him because he was liked by people in the power structure who were secretly liberal and could write well about the inside information they gave him. The fee was only one *taka* a line—maybe a dollar for a story—but my brother said yes because it was a chance to defend the poor outside the court."

The newspaper laid down a condition, however: Saha had to with-draw from politicking on behalf of the CPB. He was free to support worthwhile causes, but not in the name of the party. Saha discussed the condition with his mentor, Ratan Sen. "Sen believed in the strength of the facts as much as Manik," remembered Sharif Atiquzzaman, an old colleague of Sen's who is now a professor of English in Bagerhat. "They decided that to present evidence in an apolitical way would, at that juncture, serve the people perhaps more than to present it in a political way. So Manik made himself an inactive member of the Party. *Sangbad* hired him and he began to use his investigative skills to reveal what was going on in the city."

What was "going on in the city" involved the godfather families. Fresh faces were replacing the old guard in the three original clans, and rising in the new order established by Ershad's Jatiya Party. "The godfather structure that Khulna had when Manik was murdered first took its shape when he started at *Sangbad*," the journalist Dip Azad explained. "Most of the criminals would change parties to the one that was in power. They were in white clothes, members of parlia-ment and councilmen and the chamber of commerce, but they were all bad people from the beginning."

Many of the godfathers would figure prominently in Saha's reporting over the next twenty-two years. One official lived in a for-tified mansion that was the largest house in the division, which he somehow afforded on his $50-a-month salary. His sidekick, accord-ing to Saha's later reports, owned "a private army of hoodlums." This sidekick was now "the big brains of the criminal underworld," Azad told me. He in turn was closely allied with a city councilman during Saha's day whose specialties were guns and smuggling. Another gangster buddy was a member of parliament and a powerful busi-nessman who wielded considerable influence in the Port of Mongla. "The division's No. 1 hired killer," as Azad called him, was a politi-cian who had gotten his start in the student wing of Jamaat-e-Islami and now worked closely with a professional extortionist on good terms with the Khulna police and federal politicians. Finally, there

was a rising businessman who would go on to head the Khulna
Chamber of Commerce and become a prominent member of the
Khulna city BNP, even as he was charged with masterminding a high-
profile political murder. (He was eventually acquitted.)

Looking into the affairs of such men, Saha began his one-*taka*-
a-line journalism career. His first stories were about shrimp
farming, a business the godfathers were just then pioneering.

"Shrimp cultivation causes so many problems in Bangladesh that
it's a challenge to list them all," Saha told an international conference on human rights eight months before his murder. By then
over 370,000 acres of rice paddies had been wrested from Khulna's
farmers and flooded with salt water. Every year thousands more
acres were being stolen for the same purpose. On the books, the
land was "leased" from the farmers for five years, but the strong-
arm methods used in procuring the leases, and the fact that the
paddies became irrevocably polluted with salt, made a mockery of
the promise to return the land to rice farming after years of lucrative shrimp harvests. At the time of Saha's murder, shrimp exports
were earning the lessees roughly $300 million a year, while the
farmers who had originally owned the land were not paid even
the few dollars they had been promised when evicted. "There are
no rules or laws governing the lease of land for shrimp cultivation,"
Saha stated. "Its adverse effects on the peasants are ignored."

Saha's first sources in 1982 were a group of Hindu farmers from
Satkhira, southwest of Khulna. Several of their neighbors had been
murdered when they'd refused to sign leases, and now the salt was
leaching from the seized paddies. "Because of increased salinity,"
Saha wrote, "the cattle die, trees are destroyed, lands become
barren, drinking water becomes scarce, and local flora and fauna
become extinct." As he investigated the complaints of the farmers,
he discovered that paddies were being appropriated all over Khulna
Division, and that the police were acting like hired muscle for "the

shrimp lords." Those farmers who resisted were falsely charged with crimes, and those who complained to the Khulna authorities were beaten, forced to watch the rape of their wives and daughters, or murdered. When the shrimp lords encountered the united opposition of a village, they simply demolished dykes at the head of a tidal creek and flooded it. Hundreds of farmers, suddenly landless, were migrating to Khulna and Dhaka, where they were forced to work as van pullers or rickshaw wallahs.

"Manik carefully documented these cases," remembered Monjurul Ahsan Bulbul, one of Saha's first editors at *Sangbad*. "He was very methodical. He drew up charts with events, dates, villages and casualties, like a crime report." One of Saha's crime sheets listed seventy-seven incidents—shootings, stabbings, bombings, beatings, murders and rapes—over an eight-month period. "But he did not show personal anger at these terrible deeds against innocent people," Bulbul went on. "He was a soft-spoken man, a calm and gentle man, a man of the mind, and he stayed very reasonable in the face of the hardship he witnessed. Yet none of this was theoretical for him. He grew up in the region and he felt the fate of the farmers personally, but his reports were always factual and unbiased. His politics were clear to me, but when he put pen to paper he related only the facts."

Saha wrote an article a week for *Sangbad* and represented a score of clients in court, but his income in 1983 and 1984 was barely a dollar a day. He survived on rice and lentils that he brought back from his visits to his aunt's farm. "He could not even afford a typewriter," Nanda remembered. "He wrote his stories longhand and sent them by fax. Just before we were married I said to him, 'Manik, this will never do. Here you are a lawyer and could be a judge, you have attained your master's degree, you are a journalist, but your earnings are that of a van puller.' He said, 'We have shoes, they don't. Time will take care of us.'"

Saha married Nanda in June 1984 and divided the next few years among dangerous trips into the countryside, filing stories on what he discovered there and fighting court cases on behalf of the rural victims. The couple's one-room apartment became a counseling center and safe house for an endless string of traumatized rape victims and widows who accepted Saha's aid in launching suits. What seems to have protected him against retribution during this period was his disarmingly gentle personality, his balanced prose and his alliance with honest judges and policemen who shared his politics. "Manik was loved by a lot of people who felt great sympathy for what he was doing," remembered his longtime friend Swapan Guha. "The shrimp lords didn't like it, but they got away with their crimes because the government in Dhaka always overruled the liberal forces in Khulna."

To effect real change in Khulna, Ratan Sen urged Saha to seek political assistance from the Soviet Union. Since 1971, Moscow had been Bangladesh's largest foreign donor, part of a Cold War play for the favor of the subcontinent's three countries. Sen was Moscow's man in Khulna, and he persuaded the Soviet Ministry of Foreign Affairs to pay for a "friendship tour" for his young comrade—Saha's first trip out of Bangladesh.

Saha arrived in Moscow in the summer of 1986 and was given a supervised tour of state factories and collective farms in and around Moscow, Stalingrad and the auto-plant town of Togliatti. At each stop he guest-lectured at local universities on the problems of Bangladesh and was lectured in turn on the wonders of a centrally planned economy—even as Mikhail Gorbachev was trying to unravel that corruption-laden economy through his policy of perestroika.

If Saha had a blind spot in his worldview, it was the Soviet Union. His letters to friends during his time away describe it as a classless society. He claimed that full employment had been achieved without inflation; that the planned economy kept the country prosperous, with negligible corruption among state managers and no organized crime; and finally, that religious and ethnic hatreds had been subsumed to the higher social calling of human welfare.

Saha was promised political assistance by his handlers, given a signed copy of Maxim Gorky's early Bolshevik novel *Mother*, and returned to Khulna in 1987, driven by the idea of duplicating Soviet achievements in his homeland. Ignoring *Sangbad*'s proscription against getting involved in politics, he promptly organized a CPB protest against the dictatorship of General Ershad, was arrested and beaten, and served seven months in jail. After his release, Nanda gave birth to the couple's first daughter, whom Saha named Natasha, after a character in *Mother*.

At the end of August 1991, a few days after Boris Yeltsin declared Russia a noncommunist nation, Saha underwent a crisis of political conscience and paid a visit to Ratan Sen. Saha was deeply shaken that those who had lived under communism were now expressing their gratitude for its failure. Their recantations, including one contained in a letter from one of his Russian tour guides, made it clear to him that they had kept quiet out of fear, and that he had allowed himself to be duped.

Sen was not willing to give up his personal faith in the party. As for his acolyte's political future, he argued that the essence of their social ideology transcended the party name, and that Saha should pursue the party's ideals regardless of the banner he placed above them. Manik agreed: he would no longer act on behalf of the party but would continue to work for a just government and a socialist economy that benefited the poor. "His goals were to expose the selfish forces that were seeking to triumph over the oppressed," a colleague of Saha's named Mujibar Rahman recollected. "He continued his social activism to keep Bangladesh's upheaval that year from returning us to the past."

For by then, Bangladesh was undergoing yet another revolutionary paroxysm. An economic depression caused by years of gross corruption and the sudden removal of Soviet aid sparked a wave of national *hartals*. Millions of people took to the streets calling for an end to military rule. Khaleda Zia, the wife of the assassinated Liberation War hero General Zia, assumed leadership of the Bangladesh Nationalist Party and demanded that Ershad step down or be overthrown. She was joined by her competitor for the top prize, Sheikh Hasina, the new head of the Awami League Party and daughter of the assassinated founding father of the country. Ershad agreed to resign and was promptly jailed for corruption. A disputed 1991 election brought the conservative BNP to power under Khaleda Zia, which precipitated Awami League–led *hartals* and demonstrations that would periodically wrack the country for the next four years. As usual, the godfathers of Khulna aligned themselves with the new order, most of them switching from the Jatiya Party to the BNP.

While the country welcomed the ouster of Ershad, journalists were not sure that the 1991 constitution promulgated by Khaleda Zia marked much of a step forward. Freedom of the press was "guaranteed" but now subject to twenty-two clauses, including a proscription against publishing "official secrets" that might bring local or federal officials into disrepute. "Essentially," said Monjurul Bulbul, Saha's editor at *Sangbad*, "you could be thrown in jail without charge if the government or its appointees felt you had exposed or embarrassed them. In Dhaka, your friends could try to rally support to get you out, but in regions like Khulna, reporters were much more isolated from help. It was only a little later that I became very worried about Manik because of the assassination."

The assassination he referred to was that of Ratan Sen, on July 31, 1992. That morning, the sixty-nine-year-old Sen had held an anti-corruption rally in Shahid Hadis Park, citing Saha's reporting in a criminal complaint that he read aloud, announcing he intended to file it with the police, and marched off to the nearby police superintendent's office to deliver the complaint. As Sen approached the station, witnesses saw a man withdraw a dagger from his vest and thrust it upward into Sen, puncturing his heart.

Sen collapsed, the folder containing his undelivered criminal complaint still in his hand.

Saha's grief at the loss of his mentor reminded Prodip of the desolation he had felt after their mother's death. "We were all worried for him and what he would do." Ignoring the pleas of his family to stay away from the case, Saha began questioning witnesses and came up with a list of fifteen people implicated in the murder, including members of the Jamaat-e-Islami party and the BNP. His investigation elicited the first of many death threats he would receive before he was killed, but further detective work by the Criminal Investigation Division persuaded the authorities to lay murder charges against the fifteen, including the alleged mastermind, the head of the Chamber of Commerce, Shaharuzzaman Martuza. All of the men charged were eventually acquitted.

Saha buried his despair over the loss of Sen in a two-year blur of social activism. He formed a board of directors and fund-raising arm to establish the South Herald English School, the first in Khulna to put students on a scholarship track to attend universities in England. He drew up the curriculum and oversaw the building of a four-story facility in the center of town, the logo of which was an open book with a candle above it and the inscription, "Knowledge Is Power." While organizing the school, he became head of the Khulna branch of Udichi, a cultural organization originally founded by the Communist Party of Bangladesh that promoted Bengali traditional music. He then joined the school boards of two new kindergartens, became the founding adviser to a music academy and a theater group, and began a fund-raising drive to build what he christened the Ratan Sen Public Library.

Throughout this period of twenty-hour-a-day activity he continued his reporting on shrimp farming, discovering that the shrimp lords were appropriating hundreds of acres of supposedly protected mangroves in the Sundarbans, which even the Pakistanis had tried to preserve as a buffer against typhoons. Fertilizer and antibiotics were leaching into the soil, forming dead zones for half a mile south of the farms. In 1994 he founded a movement called Concerned Citizens for the Sundarbans and went to Dhaka to personally protest the invasion of the mangroves. After delivering a report on the illegal farms at the office of the Forestry Ministry, he stopped off at *Daily Sangbad*.

"I told him I was worried he would be the next to be murdered," Bulbul said. "He was taking on the government in an expanded way by reporting on Khulna for the BBC Bangla Service, plus engaging as an adviser for a *National Geographic* project that had to do with getting the Sundarbans set aside as a protected park. All these capacities were increasing the threats against him, so I offered him a job here in Dhaka as our senior staff reporter." Saha declined, telling Bulbul, "I am a lawyer on behalf of so many people who need help and my wife has a small job in a clinic that's a great service to many poor women. I am personally happy there in service to those who need assistance." Bulbul decided to make the offer again if Saha's situation worsened, but then he left *Sangbad* to work in television. "After that Manik opened himself to yet another set of enemies," Bulbul told me. "He began working with a very famous journalist and started his reports on the rise of the anti-liberation parties and the underground groups."

Shahriar Kabir, author of seventy books and head of the Forum for a Secular Bangladesh, initiated Saha into perhaps the most dangerous of his life's investigations and political causes. In 1996, just after the birth of Saha's second daughter, Portia (named after another character in Gorky's *Mother*), Kabir arrived in Khulna to set up an anti-fundamentalist library. "We wanted to educate young people about the War of Liberation and its ideals so they would have some knowledge to fight against Muslim militancy in the remote areas," Kabir told me in his house in Dhaka, which he said was under hostile surveillance by the army's Defense Forces Intelligence service. In recent years the fifty-five-year-old author had been jailed twice by the BNP government, was gruesomely tortured during both periods of confinement and survived a 2004 assassination attempt that took the life of his driver. "In our country Jamaat-e-Islami never gave up after their loss in the Liberation War," he went on, shifting his weight to take pressure off the six pins holding his leg bones together from the assassination attempt. "They cannot stand their own country, which has a secular soul that goes back five hundred years to the Sufis. Our tradition is tolerance. Our fifteenth-century poets proclaimed, 'Listen, O brother, Man is everything, there is no greater truth than Man!'" On the other hand, the Islamist tradition followed by the anti-liberation parties was Arab Wahabbist, famously pressed on the world by the likes of al-Qaeda. "These fanatics have seized the ideology of Islam in our country," Kabir stated. "Their goal is to grab power and impose Wahabbism."

Back in 1996, Kabir had been reading Saha's articles in *Sangbad* and thought he'd be the perfect person to head the Forum for a Secular Bangladesh in Khulna. Saha was then still living in his tiny flat, his office crammed into a nook by the door. Kabir got off the ferry packing trunks of books, brought them over to Saha's house and presented his idea. That day Saha gave up his nook and set aside the space in his apartment as a public library.

"The Jama'atul Mujahideen Bangladesh was just getting started then," remembered Dip Azad, who was first introduced to journalism at a university lecture given by Saha in 1994. "There was already another group we were dealing with, Harkat-ul-Jihad-al-Islami, which we called Huji. Both groups were lunatic jihadists." Huji's spiritual godfather was Fazlul Rahman, who would go on to sign Osama bin Laden's declaration calling for international jihad—the document that introduced al-Qaeda to the larger world. JMB and Huji then entered into a competition to be recognized as Bangladesh's "little al-Qaeda," with JMB taking the bold step of setting off a bomb during one of Saha's Udichi concerts, killing ten children and wounding fifty. "That was one level of violence,"

Azad said. "The second level was the Purbo Banglar Maoists, and they had subgroups like the Janajuddha. They had their own dogmatic ideology of violence—kill teachers, liberal politicians, journalists, anyone who wanted democracy. The third level was the godfathers, who had no ideology except 'How can I use these crazy people to do deeds I can blame on them and not me?'"

On August 30, 1998, the first of eight Khulna Division journalists was murdered by a hurled cocktail. Saiful Alam Mukul, the editor of a Jessore newspaper called the *Daily Runner*, had been aggressively exposing the gangsterism in the division and the links between the godfathers and Maoist criminals. By then the Awami League Party was in power, having ousted the BNP in yet another disputed election. Mukul argued that the names at the top had changed but the modus operandi of governance had stayed the same: the profitable links between Dhaka and the godfathers continued intact in the new supposedly "left-wing" government.

A year after Mukul's murder, Korunamoyee Sarder, one of Saha's collaborators in the fight against shrimp farming, was killed during a demonstration twenty miles southwest of Khulna city, in the village of Paikgachha. On the day Saha opened the Ratan Sen Memorial Library, he declared that November 7—the date of Sarder's murder—would henceforth be recognized as Sarder Memorial Day. He also announced that he was writing his first book, *People's Movement Against Shrimp Farming in Bangladesh,* dedicated to Sarder's memory. Then another journalist, Shamsur Rahman, was murdered in his newspaper office in Jessore. He had been working on a story about extortion and smuggling in the Port of Mongla, which was controlled by the godfathers in Khulna. The police investigation of the murder led to a number of arrests and the seizure of documents, including a hit list, with Rahman's name at the top and Saha's just below it. All those arrested were released "for lack of evidence," but Saha ignored the warnings of those on the police force with whom he was on friendly terms and went down the Pusur River to finish Rahman's story.

Mongla sits at the northern end of a narrow 60-mile channel that leads to the open waters of the Bay of Bengal. After its construction in the 1950s, it became Bangladesh's second busiest port, but by the time of Rahman's murder, about half its cargo was being routed east to Chittagong. The reason, Saha discovered, was that gangsters were waiting at the cranes to take their cut from ships. Importers and exporters had simply given up on Mongla, deciding it was worth the 150-mile detour to Chittagong. When Saha published his exposé in *Sangbad*, he received a note at his home: "Hindu dog—watch what we do to your daughter." Saha sent Natasha away to study in Calcutta's St. Thomas School and moved his family to the apartment house on Ahsan Ahmed Road, a commercial lane that was busy at all hours. The house had a gate at its entrance and was next door to a guarded bank, which he told Nanda would provide some security. "This new arrangement may protect us, but not you," Nanda told her husband. "Why can't you stop writing about these men without conscience?" Manik replied, "I cannot think about myself ahead of the people who need help. If it can be guaranteed that there will be no more pain for the people, and it will be a peaceful country, then I will stop writing."

Threats to Saha came next from an unexpected direction—the sanctum of the Khulna Press Club—an indication of how the political situation in Bangladesh deteriorated for liberals after the October 2001 elections.

The Press Club is an elite organization. To be accepted as a member a reporter must have a BA and five years' professional experience, and must be willing to pledge support for freedom of the press. The club is housed on Sir Iqbal Road in a grand old colonial building with tall stanchions at the wrought-iron front gate that opens onto a wide courtyard. Despite their pleasant headquarters, the club's ninety members are reminded each time they enter of the dangers of reporting in Khulna. The whitewashed walls at the front entrance are pockmarked with cocktail attacks, and in the main foyer, above a hardwood desk that once served as a British officer's workstation, is a wall of honor bearing four framed photos of murdered Press Club members. To the left of the wall of honor is a large room on whose walls is a magnificent stone mural that completely encircles the viewer. Carved into the pink stone is the story of Bangladesh, from Martyr's Day, 1952, to the 1971 War of Liberation, ending with the raising of the red-sun flag of the new nation. The mural was designed and commissioned by Saha, and the idea for it occurred to him right after the 2001 election.

At the time, Saha was serving as secretary of the Press Club. On the day after the BNP–JI coalition took power, a pogrom was launched against Hindus in the division. In rural areas, from Suktagram to the Sundarbans, women were raped and murdered, their husbands and fathers forced to watch then to sign over their deeds to the Jama'atul Mujahideen Bangladesh. "It was very organized—it started all at once, almost as if they were waiting to be told they could begin," Mainul Islam Khan told me as we surveyed the mural at the Press Club. When the police and local BNP leaders took no action to stop the outrages, Saha left Khulna and disappeared for a week among the division's rivers and creeks, visiting villages and documenting atrocities. He returned to file his stories with the BBC, with *Sangbad*, and with a new television station called Ekushey TV, for which he had been stringing since 2000. "I begged him not to go," Nanda told me, "but he said, 'I place my own family in their place, so I feel certain about what I need to do. If I don't write this, how will change come in the next elections? People have to see what these parties are doing.'"

This was mere weeks after al-Qaeda's attacks on the Twin Towers and the Pentagon, and Saha's stories from faraway Khulna were noticed by foreign journalists, who began citing them in the stories they were writing about Muslim terrorism. A Channel 4 TV crew was dispatched from London to Dhaka, where they filmed a

Jamaat-e-Islami demonstration, its screaming participants giving the impression that Bangladesh was a source of jihadists intent on attacking the West. The Channel 4 crew were arrested in the middle of their research and their Bangladeshi guides were thrown in jail, tortured and crippled for life. But the BNP government took note of the negative overseas publicity Saha had sparked: Khaleda Zia ordered the violence in Khulna Division stopped, then showily proclaimed the creation of an elite antiterrorism force, the Rapid Action Battalion.

"There was a lot of attention on Bangladesh because of Manik, and that's when he got his idea for the mural—to have a showpiece for journalists that demonstrated Bangladesh's fight for liberation and tolerance," said Mainul Khan, who had also served as a guide to the Channel 4 crew and had narrowly escaped arrest by fleeing his homeland. When Khan returned from his year in exile and inquired into the progress of the mural, however, he discovered there had been none. The mural had been blocked by an angry contingent of Press Club members.

"They came out of the closet and showed they were aligned with the fundamentalists and the anti-liberation parties," a Khulna editor named Gouranga Nandy told me in his *Daily Janakantha* newspaper office. "Manik decided then to run for president of the Press Club and made the mural his campaign platform."

On July 5, 2002, a Khulna journalist who had been investigating the criminal collaboration between the Purbo Banglar Maoists and jihadists was kidnapped, murdered and dumped in the river. That month, ignoring threats that he would be next, Saha published his second book, the innocuously named *Exploring Sundarbans: A Guidebook for Journalists*, which was financed by Mainul Khan's press freedom organization and George Soros's Open Society Institute. The book was a celebration of the Sundarbans, but much of it also detailed the illegal logging and shrimp farming taking place there. When Khan arrived for the book launch, Saha told him, "I am in danger. Any time I can be killed." Despite the warning signs, he put together a special for Ekushey TV based on the book. The night after it aired, August 29, the BNP government shut the station down, claiming "financial irregularities."

In late December 2002, over the objections of about a dozen journalists who were backers of Jamaat-e-Islami, Saha was elected president of the Press Club. He immediately pushed forward with his plans for the mural. At the ceremony inaugurating its commission, the Khulna City Rotarians, composed primarily of Hindus and liberal Muslims who had contributed money to the project, presented Saha with an award. "Through his fearless reporting and selfless service to our community, Manik Saha has demonstrated his complete commitment to our Four-Way Test," the head of the Khulna Rotarians told the assembly. "At every juncture he has asked the questions, Is it the truth? Is it fair to all concerned? Will it build goodwill and better friendships? Will it be beneficial to all concerned?"

The mural was finished by November 2003, but the reporters opposed to it began lobbying for its dismantling, signing a petition that declared, "This project has prejudiced the reputation of an esteemed organization that has made unbiased reporting its ideal." The petition was personally presented to Saha by a delegation of the pro–Jamaat-e-Islami reporters. That afternoon, in his Press Club mailbox, Saha found an anonymous note: "You have made enemies of your friends and worse enemies of your enemies."

On January 1, 2004, the last day of his term as Press Club president, Saha was scheduled to be the keynote speaker at an antiterrorism conference he'd organized at the Hotel Royal International. Nanda asked him not to make himself a public target by offending the officials in attendance, and he pondered putting his speech aside and simply moderating an opening panel discussion. Then he returned to his original plan. "If I give in to my fears," he said, "I will be unhappy knowing I did not convey the ways our population are suffering by the inaction or collusion of the government."

"They will kill you," his wife told him.

"If I die, it will be for my country. If I am a threat to this government, it is because they hate the reason we are a nation. They can never kill that reason."

The Hotel Royal stands at one end of the Khan J. Ali traffic circle, with two statues of crouching Bengal tigers decorating its courtyard. About twenty Rapid Action Battalion officers were arrayed at the entrance when Saha arrived, unguarded and on a bicycle rickshaw. Abdul Khan, the deputy inspector general of the Khulna police, greeted him in the lobby and accompanied him to the upstairs dining room, where the police, journalists and politicians were assembled. Syed Habib, a former treasurer of the Press Club who had known Saha for twenty-four years, remembers that Saha's talk "did not back away from what was wrong in the division." Saha began with the emergence of the Maoist and jihadist groups in the 1990s, their unfettered progression from political and religious violence to profit-oriented criminality, and completed his introduction by describing the explosion of terrorism after the 2001 elections. He then catalogued two and a half years of acid attacks, rapes, murders and bombings committed against the Hindu minority. After each described incident, Saha named a suspect then said, "case unsolved" or "mastermind still at large." The police began to shift uncomfortably in their seats. "Manik made it obvious how terrible their investigations were. How could he know all this and not them? Either they are not intelligent or they are corrupt." Saha ended with a mission statement for the police: "Arrest the terrorists and criminals and protect the innocent."

Inspector General Khan, whom Saha considered his most trustworthy ally on the force, approached him after his speech. "He told him, 'We are friends for so many years—be especially careful,'" Prodip Saha remembers his brother relating. "He said, 'I know so many forces in our district are offended by your work, and they are more powerful than the law.'"

Saha went home and discussed with Nanda how to protect

himself. The Maoists, the jihadists, the godfathers, the government parties, the police protecting the illegal shrimp farming and logging—even the JI reporters in the Press Club—all wanted him silenced. He pondered leaving the city, but then said, "I cannot stop my work here. I know there are more people trying to do good than there are doing bad. I must think of a way to continue."

A few days later, Saha came up with the idea to publish his exposés in *New Age*. The paper was relatively new, but its conservative editorials supporting BNP economic policies, combined with its news articles that highlighted the ruinous effects of the Awami League's *hartals*, had opened doors to interviews with the BNP leadership that were closed to other papers. Khaleda Zia now cited *New Age* in her speeches as an objective voice on her successes, whereas she considered Saha's paper, *Sangbad*, an enemy and the BBC Bangla Service little better than a foreign-owned subversive organization. If Saha could get himself installed on the staff of *New Age*, he reasoned, perhaps those who wanted to kill him would conclude that he was connected to powerful people who valued his voice and were capable of retribution.

He phoned *New Age* in Dhaka and asked if they needed a stringer in Khulna, saying he had numerous breaking stories about underground groups. "They said that because of his reputation they would be willing to take him on as their Khulna senior correspondent," Nanda told me. "He was delighted. He thought this was a new beginning for him, that once he began publishing he would be okay." The one wrinkle was that *New Age* accepted stories only by e-mail, in order to facilitate editing. Saha was still writing his stories longhand and sending them to *Sangbad* by fax, so he went to the South Herald English School and spent three days in a classroom teaching himself word processing and how to use an e-mail account. His first stories published in *New Age* were straightforward pieces about Awami League versus BNP wrangling over the allocation of development funding. On January 10 he sent in two linked stories: one detailed an illegal logging operation taking place in the

Sundarbans, and the other the logging operation's connection to "the anti-liberation parties' underground political activities." Normally these kinds of stories from the veteran Saha were accepted by *Sangbad* without fact-checking, but, as he was a rookie writer for *New Age*, the paper wrote back asking that he back his facts with documentary evidence. Saha was hesitant to courier the material, which included signed reports from his government sources. He thought about going to Dhaka and back by ferry, but there was an Awami League public meeting scheduled for the morning of January 15 and making the three-day round trip would cause him to miss it. Then he remembered that his friend Swapan Guha was driving to Dhaka to catch a flight to Bombay. And so, on January 13, the pair set out at dawn, on the labyrinthine road that took them eighty miles north, then east, then south, crossing rivers on two hour-long ferries and arriving in Dhaka by nightfall. Guha dropped Saha off at *New Age*'s headquarters in the upscale Tejgaon neighborhood near the National Assembly Building. Saha left his package at the editorial office desk, then took a bicycle rickshaw to his final meeting with Nayeemul Khan, president of the journalists' NGO for which Saha was the representative in Khulna.

"He was quite frank with me because we go back many years," Khan told me. "He said he was terribly afraid for his life but at the same time he would remain in Khulna and continue his work. I said that if it was me, I would be more subtle in my reporting. You know, Manik was substantive in all he wrote, but he was definitely not subtle with the evidence he presented. And being a Hindu made him doubly vulnerable. I certainly didn't think being affiliated with *New Age* would give him any protection at all in Khulna—the physical and psychological geography of that place makes life very cheap. Anyway, I did not have a good feeling when we said goodbye."

Saha caught the 3 a.m. Rocket ferry in Old Dhaka and arrived in Khulna twenty-four hours later, Thursday, January 15. He went home and slept his usual four hours and awoke around seven and had a meal with Nanda, Portia and Natasha, who was home from Calcutta on a midterm break. Then he went to his desk to prepare for the public meeting of the Awami League in Hadis Park, about six blocks north of his house.

At 10:45 that morning he received a call on his desk phone. Standing just a few feet away, Nanda gathered that Manik did not know the caller. She heard him ask the man to meet him at Hadis Park. "The man refused," Nanda said, "but told him he will see him at the Press Club at 11:45." The Press Club was just a couple of blocks from Hadis Park, so Manik agreed to the man's request. "He is the mystery man whose identity no one has been able to discover," Nanda told me. "All we know is that he was unknown in the city, or he would have been recognized when they later met at the Press Club. Before Manik left the house I reminded him that right after his meeting we had a luncheon put on by Shikhya Niketan School. Manik was the ex-president of the school and would give a speech. He said not to worry, the meeting at the Press Club would be short. I said goodbye to Manik for the last time at eleven that morning."

Saha walked into the street and held his hand up for a bicycle rickshaw. On Ahsan Ahmed Road there were always at least fifty of them within hailing distance, their chinging bells perhaps the world's most musically pleasant alternative to car horns. He climbed into one heading toward the park.

At one end of the park's parade ground, under an awning beneath palms, the city executive of the opposition Awami League party was announcing candidates for a blue-ribbon committee that would draw up fresh ideas for tackling the corruption of the city. By 11:40 the voting was over and Saha turned to leave for his meeting at the Press Club. Just before he walked away, he seems to have changed his mind about going alone and asked Dip Azad to go with him. "I answered yes, but then another journalist said to wait and we will go together. Manik couldn't wait and so he went alone. I will regret forever that I did not accompany him. We learned from our investigation there was an undercover group of four Janajuddha at the rally and they were in communication by cellphone with two other groups. One group had waited outside Manik's house when he left, but the street was too crowded for them to take action. This other group was at the park but, again, they could not get close enough. The third group was near the Press Club."

A number of journalists were just leaving the Press Club when Saha got out of his rickshaw and entered the courtyard. The unknown man was waiting for him in the lobby. Some said they thought he could be local, others that he was in city attire, which indicated to them he might be from Dhaka. "People come and go all the time in the Press Club, there are so many interviews a day there," Habib said. "This man was hiding in plain sight."

The meeting Saha had with the mystery man lasted no more than ten minutes. At five minutes to noon, Nanda called Saha on his cellphone to remind him of the luncheon engagement. He left the Press Club, hailed a rickshaw going south on Sir Iqbal Road to pick up his family, and had gone half a block when, at the corner of Bani Babu Road, someone from behind him called, "Manik!" Saha stopped the rickshaw and got out. The man walked to within three steps of him and then hurled the cocktail at his face, exploding his head and sending bits of his bloody skull and scalp spraying into the open storefronts.

Dip Azad received a call on his cellphone from his *Daily Jugantor* newspaper office saying there had been an explosion down the block. He ran to the scene, joining the crowd of journalists who were just arriving from the Press Club. There is a newspaper photo of Azad and several of his colleagues, taken a few moments later. Azad's hands are extended and his face is contorted in horror as he turns toward two journalists, one of whom has his fingers interlocked over his heart and the other of whom is holding his head and crying out at the sight in front of them.

Twenty weeping men wrapped Saha's decapitated body in a sheet and carried their crimson-soaked burden to the Khulna Medical College Hospital. As the news spread, the city of a million reacted as one. Shops were shuttered and thousands of rickshaws converged on Iqbal Road, until the mass of tightly packed people stretched for a mile in every direction. All day people thronged the streets, the men wailing and beating their chests, while several hundred Hindu women whom Saha had helped in his career gathered at the hospital, their keening drowning out a spontaneous rally held there by Communist Party members. By radio, cellphone and ferry, the news swept the countryside, the inhabitants of each tiny village from the Ganges River to the Sundarbans assembling under their central banyan, Muslim women smashing their household trinkets in a ritual of grief while Hindu priests led their flocks in mourning prayers.

Saha's murder headlined the nation's TV stations that night and statements of condolence were offered by BNP prime minister Khaleda Zia and her AL opponent, Sheikh Hasina. "Nab the killers and give exemplary punishment to them," Zia ordered her police in Khulna. Hasina, on the other hand, blamed "the coalition government for this bomb attack—not an isolated incident but part of a systematic campaign of repression against journalists."

The next day at dawn, Saha's body was released to his family and colleagues. Dignitaries arrived from Dhaka by military helicopter and accompanied the coffin as it was carried in an open van to lie in repose at a dozen city landmarks, including the Press Club and the Ratan Sen Public Library. At Communist Party headquarters, the general secretary of the Khulna branch read a eulogy over his fallen comrade: "A man of pure humanity devotes his life to others, expecting no reward on earth, no reward in the hereafter—that is the definition of a saintly hero. Manik Saha, who gave his life willingly for us, now assures mankind of the power of goodness in the face of a preponderance of evil."

At 4 p.m. the funeral van, followed by 100,000 people, rolled through the city streets toward the ferry port, where it turned south down a narrow lane. A few steps before the Rupsha Crematorium the van paused in front of a temple to the goddess Kali—the divine mother whose indifference to the fate of her children helps them to accept the trials of mortal life. A Hindu priest blessed Saha's body and soul and committed it to its journey onward: "Lead me from the Unreal to the Real," he chanted, "from Darkness to Light, from Death to Immortality." As the van left the temple, members of the Communist Party of Bangladesh, offended by the religious service they knew their comrade did not believe in, ran up to Saha's coffin and draped it with a hammer and sickle flag, startling those at the head of the procession. With the flag covering the coffin now, Saha's body was rolled across the dirt street toward a fire pit filled with sandalwood logs. Dip Azad and several other journalists lifted the plank bearing their colleague's body and laid it upon stanchions over the pit, positioning Saha's shoulders toward his home villages of Chalitatala and Suktagram. They poured canisters of ghee mixed with camphor on the pyre and then set it ablaze.

Twelve days later, Saha's ashes were taken by his family to the edge of the Sundarbans and spilled into the Kunga River. They merged with the water and drifted slowly south, through the sundari forest, past the basking crocodiles and the questioning eyes of Bengal tigers to the sea.

Under the moonlight, the mile-wide Madhumati River seemed still as a lake. A galaxy of fireflies winked on and off between the ferry and the shore and it took some time before I could discern that several hundred of the pinpoints belonged to kerosene lanterns. Prodip Saha had phoned ahead to his brother Dilip to tell him we were coming to meet Aunt Chapala. On the shore, under the silhouetted krishnachura trees, the entire village had turned out to greet the ferry. "No foreigner has ever visited Suktagram," Prodip told me, putting a hand on my shoulder. "Everyone wants to see you."

The diesel ferry pulled to the dock and its loud engines were suddenly replaced by a vast stillness. An old man in loose pajama pants and cotton kameez stepped onto the dock, pronamed to Prodip and embraced him. Prodip introduced me to the elderly mayor, who led us up the incline to where the village residents were gathered on the dirt street. As we approached, they silently parted then closed in behind, giving us an advancing pool of space within which we moved through the village.

A hundred steps on we passed under the town's enormous banyan then followed a path through a mango orchard until we arrived at a corrugated iron hut. On the porch of the hut, in a plastic chair, sat a tiny, nearly bald woman in a white cotton gown. The villagers crowded onto the porch, keeping a respectful distance from the century-old person in the chair. She held a hand up and stroked my face, my shoulders and then my chest, holding her open palm there a moment as if feeling my heart beat. "God bless you," she said, rubbing my shirt. "You have come for my Manik. How can I serve you?"

"Auntie," Prodip said, kneeling beside her. "He would like to talk to you about Manik as a child."

"Manik was my power and strength," she said in a high voice. "How could it happen that Manik left me behind? He was my strength."

"Aunt Chapala," I said, "he told everyone he received his goodness from you."

"What I could do, I did," she replied. "I gave him whatever was inside me. My sister died and I brought her sons to me. What is done is done by God, the Creator. And everything now is in God's hands. I have no understanding."

"Manik's goodness made him a saint," I said.

She nodded, pulling a shawl over her head. "In this world there is so much that is terrible. I have lived a hundred years and should be in despair. But I remember my Manik as a little boy, he walked in the street, and if he saw anybody walking without shoes, he used to ask, 'Don't you have any shoes?' and if he heard they didn't, then he gave his own shoes to them and he went barefoot. That is why he was my strength. As he gave his shoes, so he gave his life."

Prodip looked at me then back at Chapala. "Auntie, he wants to know where you received the goodness that you taught to Manik."

She smiled and looked toward the land she had inherited. "Myself, I got my goodness from my father. My father was a famous person for his goodness. His kindness and his good behavior were known in all the district."

"And where did his goodness come from?" Prodip asked.

"From his father," she replied.

"And his?" I asked.

Finally she understood. She turned to me, laughed and stroked my cheek, then held her hands up to the stars. "It comes down and is in all equally," she said, her voice rising so high it sounded as if she were singing. "In many people, goodness is hidden because they do not give it. But in my Manik goodness was not hidden, because he gave it. So young a child! And yet he understood that giving made him happy. Giving goodness and feeling good are the same. And so my Manik was happy."

On the return trip to Khulna, Prodip and I stood on the stern of the ferry, watching the lanterns of the town grow dimmer and merge with the fireflies. Suddenly he began to weep. "How could this have happened to such a good man? How?"

FOUR

ANNA HAD NO ROOF

Anna Politkovskaya, Russia

IN THE FALL OF 1995 I WAS
writing an article about Russian
gangsters in Vancouver when I
heard about the murder of a journalist in a faraway city on the
Volga River. Because of its huge
car plant, Togliatti was considered the Motor City of Russia. It
was also considered the gangster capital of the country, which, as
Russian crime experts quipped, meant that it was probably the
gangster capital of the globe. A Vancouver intelligence officer told
me that targeted murders in Togliatti were practically a daily occur-
rence, although there were almost never any arrests. "The killers all
have serious *krysha*," he said, using the Russian word for "roof," the
nation's metaphor for protection, influence and impunity.

By early October 2006, when I set out for Russia, five more journalists had been murdered in Togliatti, another twenty had been
murdered in other parts of the country, and in each case the masterminds had gone unpunished. At the time I boarded my flight, the
youngest and most lionized journalists on the casualty list were
Valery Ivanov and Alexei Sidorov, two strikingly handsome editors
of the newspaper *Togliatti Observer*. Press freedom organizations I'd

phoned in Moscow told me the duo had pioneered crime reporting in Russia after the fall of the Soviet Union.

Ivanov was only thirty-two when he was shot in the head outside
his Togliatti apartment building on April 29, 2002. Taking up his
best friend's mantle as editor-in-chief, the thirty-one-year-old
Sidorov was stabbed eleven times a year and a half later, also
outside his apartment building. Throngs of loyal readers had
attended both editors' funerals, some carrying banners bearing the
newspaper's motto: "We Print the News Others Are Afraid Of." In
a city where bus drivers went unpaid while low-ranking officials
built million-dollar dachas, there was a lot of news to be afraid of.

As was the case with all the other murdered journalists, the
Russian government seemed to have a reason for protecting
the killers of Ivanov and Sidorov. That reason was almost certainly
krysha, a word Ivanov himself had used to explain why murderers
in his hometown so often went unprosecuted. Krysha had popped
up in almost every one of his many discussions of Russian organized crime, politics and corruption. "Krysha is at the core of our
corrupt civil structure," he'd declared. "It has replaced the constitution as our law and replaced the ruble as our currency."

Krysha had entered the Russian lexicon in the late 1980s, when
Ivanov and Sidorov were still in their teens. The Soviet economy
was collapsing and budding entrepreneurs, sensing the winds of perestroika under the administration of Mikhail Gorbachev, found they
could go into private business—*if* they bought a roof from either
party bosses or the local *banditsky.* After the Soviet Union itself collapsed in 1991, and President Boris Yeltsin launched his program of
economic "shock therapy," privatizing state-owned industries all at
once, a roof became the route to riches. Factories like Togliatti's
car plant were acquired from the state at bargain-basement prices
by men with serious krysha—usually Yeltsin-backers, former party
bosses, rising oligarchs and gangsters, some of whom fell into all
four categories. "That is exactly how, during the Yeltsin years,
organized crime syndicates were born and grew to maturity in

Russia," the journalist Anna Politkovskaya wrote in her 2004 book *Putin's Russia*, a polemic against the reign of Yeltsin's chosen successor, the former KGB colonel Vladimir Putin, whom Yeltsin had appointed president on December 31, 1999. "Now, under Putin, they determine what happens in the state."

In Putin's regime, no less kleptocratic than Yeltsin's but more abundant in appointed officials who used force to stifle the media, krysha was king. Safety inspectors sold krysha to airline companies, old age homes and nightclubs, giving Russia the worst accidental death rate in the world. Police chiefs sold krysha to murderous multimillionaires, who promised to limit their criminality to the boardroom and to maintain the appearance of order. "Legitimate" businessmen bought krysha from government ministers, who licensed the transfer of their untaxed riches to Swiss banks. And from his Kremlin seat atop his mountain of krysha, President Putin awarded chunks of the commodity to Chechen warlords, regional governors and gangs of patriotic bullies who intimidated his critics. All of Russia revolved around the need for krysha, the purchase of krysha, the maintenance of krysha. With madhouse logic, the withdrawal of krysha meant being jailed for having purchased krysha, a system of control that ensured that anyone of accomplishment was guilty of a crime from the first rung of his career onward. Krysha was why Russia was one of the most dangerous places in the world to work as a journalist. All reporters understood that anyone who exposed the excesses of krysha could be murdered with impunity by those who possessed that krysha.

I'd left home hoping that Anna Politkovskaya, the most vehement living critic of Russia's criminal modus operandi, could explain what it took for men like Ivanov and Sidorov to stay on a story after being warned their deaths were imminent. Following up on an e-mail from her was on my mind when I'd landed at Moscow's Sheremetyevo Airport on the evening of Saturday, October 7, 2006. "You will please confirm in Moscow if I am available for Tuesday. Have a safe trip. A."

The press freedom organizations that had recommended
Politkovskaya to me were amazed she was still alive. In the previous
six years her books and articles had insulted and enraged Putin and
his *siloviki*—the political class of ex-KGB cronies he surrounded
himself with—and the senior ranks of the army, the mafia and the
gangs of crazy fascists who'd posted a wanted poster of her on
the Internet. A lean, handsome woman of forty-eight, financially
comfortable and with two grown children—one of whom was
expecting a child—Politkovskaya risked everything to pursue the
story that made her famous in the West. Since 1999, she'd made forty-
eight dangerous trips to Chechnya, many of them illegal, exposing
the atrocities committed in the rebellious southern republic by the
Russian army and the sociopathic warlords Putin had placed in
power there. On several occasions, Politkovskaya had narrowly
escaped the fate of the twelve journalists murdered contract-style
since Putin had become president. But, as she'd recently written in
an essay for English PEN, "the poisoning, the arrests, the threats in
letters and over the Internet, the telephoned death threats, the weekly
summons to the prosecutor general's office" would not stop her.

On the new superhighway into town, passing big-box superstores,
luxury car dealerships and a forest of construction cranes, I could see
why Politkovskaya was having so much difficulty convincing her
countrymen "that Putin's vertical system of authority, founded on
fear and total subservience to one individual, himself, was not
working." On the contrary, the polls showed that over 70 percent of
Russians were fans of Putin's rule. With oil prices coincidentally
soaring from $10 a barrel to $60-plus during his six years in power,
revenue from Russia's vast reserves had allowed Putin to restore economic order after the chaotic Yeltsin years of national default, currency devaluation and runaway inflation. He'd also restored Russia's
pride in itself by reviving the country's influence in the world, as
well as its anti-Western posturing. It didn't seem to matter to most
Russians that Putin used his prosecutors to charge political opponents with crimes, jailed them or drove them into exile, since he'd

used those same prosecutors to crack down on the ubiquitous extortion of small-businessmen by street criminals. If many human rights groups had had their licenses revoked, if the independent media had mostly either been shut down or placed under state control, and if Russia was slowly returning to the monocratic state it had been during Soviet times, at least the country now had a leader who was strong, sober and paid government pensions. Oil and gas money had trickled down into the pockets of city dwellers, and the loss of the drunken Yeltsin's democratic reforms seemed like no loss at all.

To Politkovskaya, however, it seemed a catastrophic loss. She was working on yet another exposé of army-sponsored torture in Chechnya, and had appeared two days earlier on Radio Liberty to promote the article's upcoming publication in her Moscow-based newspaper, *Novaya Gazeta*. In that interview, she'd denounced and insulted Ramzan Kadyrov, the Putin-appointed prime minister of Chechnya, whose government she'd previously claimed had threatened her with death. Her interview with Radio Liberty had taken place on Kadyrov's thirtieth birthday, a milestone that made him eligible to be appointed president of Chechnya, a position his father had held until his assassination in May 2004. "I am conducting an investigation about torture today in Kadyrov's prisons," she'd told her countrymen, in the quiet, patient voice that often infuriated her macho targets. "I plan to say that these people were abducted . . . and were then killed. . . . Kadyrov is a puppet . . . he's a coward. . . . I only have one dream for Kadyrov's birthday: I dream of him someday sitting in the dock, in a trial that meets the strictest legal standards, with all of his crimes listed and investigated."

The hotel I checked into in southeast Moscow was a decrepit Brezhnev-era tower near the last stop of the No. 7 subway line. At $150 a night, the Moskvich was the cheapest available in the world's most expensive city. I got what I paid for, both in Soviet-era facilities and Soviet-era treatment of guests. The porter did not rise from his couch to help me as I struggled with my suitcase around a mop leaning from a slop bucket in front of the entrance. His eyes above his dangling cigarette were glued to the TV, which was blasting a manic variety show. The logo at the bottom of the screen said NTV, one of the country's most popular channels. Before Putin's ascension to power, NTV had been an independent station that had produced the best investigative news shows in Russia, exposing government corruption and bringing the Chechen war into the homes of Russians. In April 2001, Putin, unhappy with NTV's coverage of himself and the war, had its studios raided by a SWAT team, pulled it off the air, engineered its acquisition by the government's energy corporation, Gazprom, and driven its owner, Vladimir Gusinsky, into exile. Variety shows and positive-spin news were now NTV's usual fare, even in times of national crisis, such as the takeover of an elementary school in Beslan by Chechen terrorists in 2004—an event Politkovskaya had been flying from Moscow to cover when she'd been poisoned on the flight. Russia's other privately owned stations had suffered the same fate as NTV. In her English PEN article, Politkovskaya had written that "what is shown on television and written about in the overwhelming majority of newspapers is emasculated and doused with ideology." Politkovskaya—Russia's most famous journalist *outside* Russia— was banned from television, and most Russians, 80 percent of whom got their news from state-controlled television, had never heard of her.

The hotelier within her fortress check-in island declared *"Nyet!"* when I asked if she spoke English. When I pointed to a bilingual line in the Moskvich's brochure that said "Our customers are welcome to services of our professional interpreters," she brushed it aside with the back of her hand, as if to say, Don't bother me with what's promised on paper. She disappeared into a back room with my passport to photocopy it, dropping my tissue-thin Ministry of the Interior registration slip, which had to be stamped by every hotel I stayed in. Keeping track of foreigners was still a preoccupation of the

Ministry of the Interior, and being stopped by a cop without that slip in my passport meant a $500 curbside krysha payment.

The desk lady reappeared yawning, noticed my registration slip on the floor, retrieved it, stamped it and then threw me a key for a "tourist room." I took the screeching elevator to the eleventh floor and approached a plywood door whose splintered jamb made it appear as if the room had been broken into a dozen times. Braided wiring hung in loops from a water-stained ceiling that met smoke-cured, bubbled wallpaper. In the middle of a scratchy velour sofa was a towel the size of a dishrag and a used bar of soap. A hundred and fifty dollars didn't even get me a phone that worked. When I finally got somebody from downstairs to replace the phone, I called the local researcher for the Committee to Protect Journalists to let her know I'd arrived, only to learn that Anna Politkovskaya had been shot dead in her apartment building while I had been in the airplane on the way to Moscow. I quickly turned on the television. The story dominated the hourly cycle on the BBC World Service. The Russian stations gave it a minute.

"Today is the day of versions," the Glasnost Defense Foundation's chairman, Alexei Simonov, told me on Monday at his headquarters in the Russian Union of Journalists building, about a mile southwest of the Kremlin. "October 7 was Putin's birthday. Was this his present?" he asked rhetorically, referring to Politkovskaya's murder. "Just previously it was Kadyrov's birthday. Was it *his* present? Or it might have been done by somebody from the other side, who just did it because everybody would think—"

He broke off to light a cigarette, shaking his head as he exhaled. He had a terrible cold and two tears rolled down his cheeks, but I didn't think they were from his illness. "Anyway, it was absolutely professionally done. There were four very controlled shots, contract-style. And now she is gone."

A reliable version of the facts was now being put together by Politkovskaya's colleagues at *Novaya Gazeta*, Simonov said. Early Saturday afternoon she left her apartment house and drove six miles south on an errand for her pregnant daughter, Vera, and her mother, Raisa, who was in a hospital near the banks of the Moscow River. About 2:20 p.m. she stopped off at a supermarket called Ramstore. A frame from the store's surveillance camera showed her wearing a long black coat and black slacks and carrying a large black purse. The camera also picked up a man and a woman following her. She purchased five bags of merchandise and then drove north, parking her car near the front of her apartment house. At 4:01 p.m., carrying two heavy shopping bags, she edged through the slatted wooden door of her building and rode the elevator up to her apartment, then came down for the other bags. A man with a baseball cap pulled low over his eyes, also captured on a surveillance camera, stood at the entrance to the elevator as she emerged. He raised a semiautomatic Makarov pistol with a silencer and shot her in the heart, lungs, shoulder and, as she lay on the floor, the head. Her purse was not stolen and the killer left his weapon at her feet—trademarks of a contract hit.

Simonov's phone rang for the twentieth time that morning, since he was the man to call when a journalist was murdered in Russia. "Fifteen years of this idiotic life protecting the lives of journalists—you become known. *Da!*" he shouted into the receiver. It was the *Los Angeles Times*. "Today is the day of versions," he said into the phone, wiping his cheeks.

I took his picture, then stood up and took pictures of his display cases, crowded floor to ceiling with turtle dolls and sculptures— wooden turtles, glass turtles, rubber, brass and plastic turtles. Simonov had chosen the symbol when he'd founded the organization in 1991. "Glasnost is a turtle crawling toward free speech," he'd told me.

He was the spitting image of Ezra Pound, sans the poet's anti-Semitism, since Simonov was Jewish. When he'd told me his heritage I'd said that if Jews were allowed to consider themselves Russian, then I was Russian too. My grandmother had dreamed in Russian until she died at 101, eight decades after leaving for America. "Yes, yes, you are permitted to be a Jew and Russian," he'd said, "but you are totally illiterate—deaf and dumb besides. You shouldn't come to a country where you are illiterate on what is written! How can you get from place to place? You will get into trouble and then I will have to spend time on you."

He got off the phone now and lit another cigarette from the tip of the one he was smoking. "The funeral and burial for Anya will be held tomorrow, at two o'clock, at Troekurovskoye Cemetery. You should go to it before leaving for Togliatti. Her father was buried there just two weeks ago. Her mother is very ill from cancer, and Anya was visiting her in the hospital in the weeks before she was killed. Things were not happy for her at the end."

"Did you know her personally?"

"Yes, yes, I knew her, for many years. I wouldn't mind calling her a friend, but I think she had a lot of colleagues and very few friends. I wasn't one of her friends. She was a member of our jury that hands out the Sakharov Prize for Journalism as a Deed. She was not an easy person with which to debate the merits of an issue. To be honest, she assailed her best allies in print for meeting with the president in a human rights forum, including me. She was totally uncompromising."

"I suppose she had to be in Putin's Russia."

"Well, that is an issue I fought with her about. If you don't talk with someone, how will he know your point of view?"

His phone rang again, this time from Togliatti. Today was the third anniversary of Alexei Sidorov's death, and that morning the staff of the *Observer* had held a ceremony at the Aisle of Heroes in Banekenskogo Cemetery, where Ivanov and Sidorov were buried side by side. The deputy editor wanted to include Simonov's views on Politkovskaya's murder in her coverage of the Sidorov memorial. When Simonov hung up he lit another cigarette off the one he was smoking. "At the rate we are going," he said, "every day will be a remembrance day for the murder of one journalist or another." He blew his nose, then stared into the cement courtyard, silent for the first time in our hour and a half together.

By the time she was murdered, Anna Politkovskaya had been writing about the Chechen war for seven years, and Ramzan Kadyrov, the Putin-approved prime minister of Chechnya, was only one of her many targets. She'd exposed hundreds of cases of torture, kidnapping for ransom, pillage, rape and murder, naming the Russian officers responsible even as she continued to send dispatches from the districts the officers controlled. In retaliation, she'd been arrested, beaten, and had suffered a mock execution in a concentration camp. After surviving her poisoning in 2004, she published an article called "Poisoned by Putin," causing her friends to suggest it was time for her to stop commuting to the lawless Caucasus. At the very least, her colleagues urged, she should soften the language she used to expose the crimes and insult the honor of the most dangerous men in Russia. She ignored their advice, continued her acid reporting from the rubble of Chechnya, until, with death threats coming at her from every quarter, the contract killer finally caught up with her in her Moscow apartment house.

Politkovskaya was still being mourned when I visited the murder scene a couple of weeks later. The front of her building in northern Moscow was banked with dozens of bouquets of fresh flowers, its wall papered with memorial editions of *Novaya Gazeta* published after her funeral. One of the editions showed a full-page photo of Muscovites standing twenty deep around her open coffin—the third funeral for a murdered *Novaya* journalist since 2000. At the second funeral, in 2003, she'd told the reporter who shared her office, "I will be next."

And yet Politkovskaya had had a lot to live for. Born into an elite

Soviet family, she'd had a genteel childhood, had become a journalist at twenty-two and, since 2001, had won a string of international
awards. She had two handsome and successful children and was
thrilled about the prospect of becoming a grandmother. In addition,
with three books published in the West and a fourth being translated, she had an income that was well above that of most Russian
journalists. She knew how to spend her money, too: her apartment
at 8 Lesnaya Street was on the top floor of a sandstone building
near Tverskaya Ulitsa — Moscow's Fifth Avenue, just a forty-
minute stroll from the Kremlin. It rose above elegant shops and
overlooked a cathedral's gold onion dome that made even a
cloudy day seem sunny.

I looked away from that dome and placed a bouquet against her
wall, wondering exactly why she had pursued the Chechen story in
ways she knew would inevitably fulfill her own prediction.

To find an answer I walked east on Lesnaya, then turned south.
Eight blocks from Politkovskaya's home I entered a narrow alley
that the FSB (the successor to the KGB) had kept under surveillance
since September 1999 — the start of the Second Chechen War. At
the end of the alley was the ground-floor headquarters of a refugee
center named Civil Assistance. I had an appointment to interview
the center's sixty-four-year-old director, Svetlana Gannushkina,
who had been close to Politkovskaya and knew how she'd first
found her calling as a defender of Chechens, which had turned
into a passion to expose Russian atrocities to her own country and
the world.

The reception area of Civil Assistance was crowded with dark-
skinned people from the North Caucasus, most of whom took one
look at me and held their children close. A caseworker told me that
FSB agents had raided the place in the night and hauled out a political refugee named Rustam Muminov. "They're scared because
they think you're from the government," she said, pointing to my
briefcase. "Everyone is now feeling a little panicky." She led me
into a tiny kitchen, the only quiet spot for an interview.

Soon Gannushkina, a no-nonsense matron with boy-cut hair, pushed through the door, shouting into her cellphone, apparently at an FSB officer: "Don't you know that Muminov faces torture and execution? Don't you know that the European Court has ruled that Muminov should stay in Moscow?" She listened to the reply, then snapped her phone shut. "He says the matter's 'concluded,'" she told a couple of caseworkers trailing her. "Muminov is on a jet flying home."

She shook my hand firmly and pulled back a chair. "You know what my first thought is?" she asked me. "It's that I have to pass this story to Politkovskaya, she will follow it to save his life. But now there is no Politkovskaya to pass it to."

Politkovskaya's murder was being uniformly described in the West as an example of everything that was going wrong in Putin's Russian, one more example of the country's "criminality, corruption and culture of impunity," in the words of the *New York Times*. And yet, perhaps out of discretion, something not publicized in the West was her combative relationships with the people who were her natural allies, who she was in the habit of attacking almost as vehemently as she attacked her enemies. She never cultivated her own krysha—people who could offer an investigative journalist such as her protection. Whenever Politkovskaya established a relationship with someone who could provide her with a roof, she discovered an excuse to put a hole through it.

Vyacheslav Izmailov, the military affairs correspondent for *Novaya Gazeta* and a former army major who had the power to pull strings to save Politkovskaya's life, recounted the painful moment when "she called me a coward to my face," and then gave him the silent treatment for a year.

Oleg Panfilov, the head of the Center for Journalism in Extreme Situations, who spent most of his time helping journalists like Politkovskaya, told me, "She didn't appreciate when other people had their own opinions about Chechnya. She always thought that only she knew what was happening there. We quarreled publicly several times."

Her deputy editor, Vitaly Yaroshevsky, said, "She could turn into your enemy in a second."

Any attempt by her colleagues to give nuance to the causes of the Second Chechen War, to add complexity to the reign of Vladimir Putin or to attempt to modify the president's authoritarian policies by engaging in dialogue with him was met by a stinging attack. She had accused many of her liberal allies of being "sweetened up" by the Kremlin, "tuck[ing] their tails between their legs," "playing games," making "sordid compromises" and "never straying beyond the bounds of what was permissible." Galina Mursalieva, the woman who shared her office at the paper for seven years, summed up Politkovskaya's relationships with most anti-Putin politicians, journalists and human rights workers: "She had numerous and endless conflicts with many people. When it came to sharing an office, it was only me who was willing; not many people could take her kind of personality."

Not surprisingly, Politkovskaya's coverage of the Chechen conflict and her constant fighting with colleagues wore her to a frazzle. "I saw her crying a million times," Mursalieva told me. "She would always weep openly, she was a very emotional person." In her last published photo, taken just before her death, the one-time svelte and photogenic journalist appeared gray and haggard.

"My memories of when I first saw her and when I last saw her are of two physically different people," Svetlana Gannushkina told me in the kitchen of Civil Assistance. "She lived through so much. She didn't eat properly, she hardly slept, but she always said her goal in Chechnya was more important than she was. All she wanted was to tell what was happening to the civilians."

On the wall behind Gannushkina were children's drawings of sunflowers, each of the petals inscribed with a thank-you note from a Chechen child. Gannushkina followed my gaze to the drawings. "If not for Anya, no one would have known what Russia's conduct of the war was doing to the children. Sometimes she snuck into Chechnya by hiding in the trunks of cars, sometimes she disguised herself as a peasant woman. She went where no one else would go."

"Did she ever turn on you?"

"Yes, of course, there were many black cats that ran between us," she replied, glancing at the floor as if those cats were running through the room even now. "She attacked me on several occasions, wrote me angry letters saying she was embarrassed by my behavior, that I didn't meet her standards because I met with the president. But I viewed it like this: she was a young woman who was risking her life. I tried not to take it personally."

She gazed for a moment at the tea and plate of cookies in the middle of the table, then looked up at me through her big glasses. "I must tell you, our relationship was one of cooperation rather than friendship," she admitted. "We liked each other and felt great sympathy for one another's views, but Anya was not an easy person to get along with. I don't know anybody who had a loving friendship with her. Many colleagues admired her, but they couldn't give her warmth and love. Not Anya—that sharp, abrupt person! And yet, you know, towards needful people, she was never impatient, never critical, and always loving."

She indicated the needful people in the reception area. A lot of them were Chechens, seeking help at the center because they'd had a run-in with the Moscow police, who routinely harassed anyone with the dark complexion typical of the North Caucasus. Chechnya was a part of Russia, and Chechens were Russian citizens who had fled their homes because they'd been bombed to rubble, but they were treated as if they were all plotting terror, often arbitrarily jailed or "deported" from Moscow. In *Putin's Russia*, Politkovskaya called this policy "the machinery of racially based state retribution"—that is, payback for a hostage-taking at a Moscow theater in 2002, among other things. "Racial attacks and purges supervised by the police have become commonplace," she wrote. "In a single moment people's lives are ruined, they lose their home, their jobs, any sort of social support, and for just one reason: they are Chechens. Their lives in Moscow and many other cities are intolerable: drugs are slipped into their pockets, cartridges are pressed into their hands, and they are promptly sentenced to several years in prison. They have been quite openly made into pariahs and find themselves at a dead end, with no chance of escape. It is a way of life that leaves nobody unscathed, regardless of age."

Politkovskaya seemed profoundly ashamed of her country—its leadership, its society and even the people who believed they were fighting to change both. "This whole system of thieving judges, rigged elections, presidents who have only contempt for the needs of their people can operate only if nobody protests," she'd written in 2004. "We have emerged from socialism as a thoroughly self-centered people."

I wondered whether her use of the plural "we" was a journalistic device, or if she was ashamed of herself, too. "Alexei Simonov said you might know of a catalyst that launched her career as a human rights champion," I said to Gannushkina. "He said you were there at the beginning."

"I can tell you to the day," Gannushkina replied. "It was on August 27, 1996."

She clasped her hands on the table and leaned forward without saying anything for a moment, as if ordering events in her mind. "I first met Anya in late 1995," she said finally. "She was the same difficult personality, but not the same journalist. Back then Anya had the ambitions of a paparazzo. She was after hot hooks, hot items, characters who would give her a popular people-scoop. She carried her taste for prosperity and high urban fashion to all her interviews, even with me."

Politkovskaya was then thirty-seven, a reporter with the liberal newspaper *Obshchaya Gazeta*, known for its aggressive exposés of Boris Yeltsin's corrupt privatization program and of the disastrous First Chechen War, which had been raging for a year. While her own reporting occasionally explored the themes of privatization, she rarely if ever mentioned Chechnya. Indeed, she most often profiled the foibles and fancies of the cosmopolitan intelligentsia with whom she rubbed shoulders. As the daughter of Soviet-era United Nations diplomats, then as the wife of Russia's most famous TV journalist, for most of her life Politkovskaya had enjoyed similar social privileges. In the midst of the post-Soviet depression, while millions of Russians were reduced to selling trinkets in kiosks, Politkovskaya had been able to send her teenage son to England's Taunton boarding school and swathe her angular figure in Europe's best fashions.

"As a reporter back then, Anna was looking for personality conflicts," Gannushkina explained. "That included conflicts within our own struggling organization. In one of our interviews she actually fished for conflicts among the staff at Civil Assistance. I told her, 'But I want to defend the people who need us—office politics are not important.' She told me that readers first needed to be interested in our relationships; she needed some personal conflict in order to write a story about us. I told her, 'Journalists should not violate our Hippocratic standard: First do no harm!' When I refused to give her any hook, she got angry."   •

It was Gannushkina's first encounter with Politkovskaya's temper. Most of the people I'd spoken to attributed her prickly character to her western Ukrainian forbears—legendary in Russia for their supposed hotheadedness—although things also had not been going well for Politkovskaya at the time, making her fuse even shorter than usual. Her famous husband of seventeen years, Alexander "Sasha" Politkovsky, had been drinking heavily for months, ever since the director of his public television station, an old friend, had been assassinated.

Gannushkina guesses that personal turmoil may have made Politkovskaya susceptible to a change in focus, from "looking for a successful scoop to looking to the needs of others." On August 26, 1996, with school starting in a week, Politkovskaya called

Gannushkina proposing a human-interest cover story about big-eyed Chechen children entering a Moscow elementary school for the first time.

"I said I had to disappoint her because, first of all, Chechen children were not going to Moscow schools," Gannushkina told me, imitating the patient tone she'd used to explain the situation to the touchy Anna. "The mayor had ordered that children whose parents were not registered in Moscow could not go to the city's schools." However, because the Russian government was in the midst of pressuring the Chechen president to sign a truce to end the First Chechen War, and Grozny had been shelled recently, "I told her we would soon have many refugees from Chechnya who were in an absolutely terrible situation. I said she could come down and meet Chechen children if she wanted to."

And so Anna swooshed in wearing her high-society clothes, only to be brought up short by the sight of a hundred people sitting shoulder to shoulder in the hallways. Here were mothers who had just lost children, husbands who had just lost wives, children who had just lost both parents, all of whom had traveled for days without a shower or proper food. The staff was taking down the details of each person, moving from the merely wretched to the catatonic, from bloodily bandaged adolescents cradling baby siblings to old people begging for medical attention.

"Anna at once understood that all of this was inflicted by our Russian army as a negotiating tactic," Gannushkina told me. "She was a beautiful and fashionable woman, good looks and good clothes were very important to her, and she brought those priorities through the door." But Gannushkina could almost see her looking inward as she posed two radical questions to herself: Who am I? What am I good for? And then she changed.

"One of our employees was interviewing people to make a list of dead relatives, but there were so many who needed immediate help that she had to stop making the list. Anya put her story idea aside and took over. She said she would compile the list for us and she would publish it, with some words about each of the dead. That was her first act as a human rights–oriented journalist."

"She went from being a feature columnist to a human rights activist right then?" I asked.

"That very day she started a fund-raising campaign for the people in our center," Gannushkina declared. "She raised $500 by the end of the day. Then she started working on new stories, telling their tales. She became very involved in their individual fates, she started doing the same work as I did, acting as an advocate for them, but through her paper."

Scoops went out the window and the Hippocratic ethic became Politkovskaya's journalistic code, Gannushkina said. "If she got the news that someone needed to escape Russia, she phoned me first. We would help him escape, and only after the person was safe would she write it up, even when she knew someone else would write about it first.

"You could see her physically change, too," Gannushkina added, "like a dancer modifying her movements to a new repertoire, taking her quick, sharp aggressive attitude and redirecting it to a cause. That was the beginning of her relationship to Chechnya. She tried to protect and defend these people until her last day."

The sight of atrocities inflicted in the name of one's country could turn any journalist into a human rights advocate, but Politkovskaya went a lot further than most. In the ensuing years she literally broadcast the fact that she was willing to die—not just *risk* death—to get the Chechen story out. "I think the Second Chechen War is such a cruel and unjust war, that in reporting this war you have no right to think of yourself," she told PBS television a couple of years before her murder. "You just don't have this right! If you are the transmitter of this truth, and I think of myself as simply a transmitter, that is worth a life."

As I left Civil Assistance I reflected on what the Moscow

researcher for the Committee to Protect Journalists had told me after we'd attended Politkovskaya's funeral. One by one, Anna's colleagues had eulogized her beside her open coffin, where she lay on a bed of white silk, her lower torso covered in roses, a white band across her forehead concealing the bullet wound. "They said she knew she would be murdered," Masha Yulikova said.

Yulikova and I were standing at the back entrance of Troekurovskoye funeral hall, a mold-stained Soviet monolith rising four stories high on a hill that overlooked power plants and the outermost ring of highways that belted the city. Low clouds and rain did nothing to cheer the scene. The mourners standing under their carapace of black umbrellas were mostly middle-aged or older, many of their heads as white as that of the journalist they'd just honored. There were almost no young people, and not one face from the North Caucasus. The Chechens had a reason for not being here, Yulikova told me: they were too frightened of the Russian authorities to show up at the funeral of the woman who had lived and died for them. Young Russians had another reason: they simply had never heard of Politkovskaya, since she'd been banned from Russian TV and very few if any of them read *Novaya Gazeta*. Perhaps a couple of thousand people had traveled to the western suburbs to pay their respects, along with a hundred members of the international press, who had followed them into the huge hall and filmed them from an upstairs gallery. Putin spoke the truth that day when he told a news conference of foreign journalists in Dresden, where he had once worked as a KGB agent, "She was well known in journalistic circles, in human rights circles and in the West, but her influence over political life in Russia was very minimal."

As we made our way back to town, I shared with Yulikova some of the cases I'd covered. "Like Anna, they all knew it was very likely they would be murdered but they kept at it, so I'm trying to find out—"

"What was their motivation," she finished my sentence.

"Exactly. Not who killed them, but why they pursued a story to the death. How far back do I have to look for that motivation is always the question."

"I suspect not so far," Yulikova said, as we descended into the Kuntsevskaya subway station. She gave the matter a moment's thought, then, speaking for herself and not the CPJ, suggested a personal explanation. "I think these people could be very unhappy in their private life. So unhappy that they don't care if they get killed. Maybe they don't have enough faith?" She waved back toward the funeral hall, which was as bare of religious icons as the subway station.

"I know she was raised an atheist," I said, "so she probably wasn't thinking about serving God."

"I feel about her that she couldn't find anything else to do besides defending people," Yulikova said above the roar of the incoming train. "This is why one person at the funeral said she defended those who couldn't find anyone else to help them. I think this was very much the reason she risked her life."

"What would you do if somebody said they'd kill you if you kept at your work?" I asked, because her work wasn't exactly risk-free in Putin's Russia.

"I would stop doing it," she declared, without hesitation. "The difference between someone like me and Anna is that the CPJ can find anther person who can replace me—nobody's life depends on me alone. But with Anna, she knew there were no other people who would do her work, that everyone was too scared or just not interested in going to Chechnya to tell what is going on."

Unfortunately, most Russians did not *want* to hear what was going on. That reality had struck Politkovskaya as among the most shameful aspects of her country, the reason so many atrocities could take place in the first place. Even many of the most liberal people in Russia—the 150,000 who read *Novaya Gazeta*, for instance—wanted to look the other way.

"People call the newspaper and send letters with one and the same question," she wrote in A *Small Corner of Hell: Dispatches from Chechnya.* "'Why are you writing about this? Why are you scaring us? Why do we need to know this. . . ?' For one simple reason," she answered. "As contemporaries of this war, we will be held responsible for it. The classic Soviet excuse of not being there and not taking part in anything personally won't work. So I want you to know the truth. Then you'll be free of cynicism."

Russian cynicism—the product of a thousand years of authoritarian rule—tormented her. That "Putin's war" was supported by most Russians and passively accepted even by those who questioned it proved to her that "our society is sick. Most people are suffering from the disease of paternalism, which is why Putin gets away with everything, why he is possible in Russia." She knew her bitterness toward Putin's regime was rare in the nation. Indeed, in all respects, from her outraged writing to her risk taking, Politkovskaya was a rare Russian. Looking into the deep structure of her life, I began to wonder if her exceptionality might have been due to the fact that she was not really Russian.

Anna Stepanova Mazepa was born in New York City, on August 30, 1958, to Ukrainian parents who had been victims of Stalin's USSR. In the 1930s, Stalin's forced collectivization of Ukrainian farms had caused millions to die of starvation in an engineered famine that was meant to destroy the Ukraine as a political force within the Soviet Union. But after Stalin's death, Nikita Khrushchev came to power. Khrushchev had been raised in the Ukraine, proudly attended public events in Ukrainian peasant dress and, in a speech to the 20th Party Congress eighteen months before Anna's birth, exposed the criminal nature of Stalin's regime.

Khrushchev's affinity for the Ukraine benefited Anna's father, Stepan Mazepa, a foreign-policy analyst from Chernigov who was soon appointed to serve with the Ukrainian delegation to the United Nations. Anna's mother, Raisa, an academic from Kerch, at the eastern tip of the Crimean Peninsula, received a co-appointment and gladly accompanied Stepan to New York. What they had seen in their Ukrainian youth melded with what they experienced in New York and turned them into a liberal-minded, westward-looking couple who believed in the UN's Declaration on Human Rights and European-style social democracy. Their Manhattan household was filled with banned books, their minds filled with banned attitudes about freedom of speech and thought. All of this would be Anna's intellectual foundation, but what her colleagues say Stepan Mazepa also gave his daughter was a fighting name. "When Russians heard Anna was a Mazepa," Oleg Panfilov told me, "they stepped back." To a Russian it was as if Anna's maiden name was Attila.

Three hundred years ago Ivan Stepanovych Mazepa was the *hetman* (ruler) of the Cossacks and today is considered the super-hero of Ukrainian history, his name associated with do-or-die battle, romantic patriotism and the hearty culture of the wild steppes. Say "Mazepa" to a Russian and he pictures a band of hard-riding war-riors charging down on a Muscovite outpost, taking no prisoners and torching everything in their path. Mazepa fought Peter the Great for independence until his forces were overwhelmed by a Muscovite army in the Battle of Poltava in 1709, which ended in the massacre of thousands of his followers, his death in exile and the subjugation of his country by Moscow for the next three centuries. But Mazepa's spirit was never extinguished, and Russians tended to think that Politkovskaya wrote with a *bulava*—Mazepa's battle mace.

Anna's warrior lineage notwithstanding, the Mazepa ferocity was not evident in her father. "My grandfather was a kind and gentle person," Anna's son, Ilya, told me shortly after his mother's murder. "My grandmother is equally of that nature. From them my mother learned how to respond to people's troubles. The reason they were so sympathetic to others' troubles was that they were originally very plain people from western Ukraine and grew up among so much trouble. They studied and one day managed to become accomplished, but they never forgot the suffering they had seen, or the causes."

Unlike many Soviet diplomats with one eye on their careers and the other on the KGB, at the height of the Cold War, Anna's parents made sure their daughter was registered as a native-born American citizen, which entitled her to a U.S. passport for life and, once she reached her majority, to vote in American federal elections. This act of foresight may have contributed to Stepan's recall to the Soviet Union as Khrushchev's fall from power approached in 1964. In Moscow, speaking English and Russian, Anna entered a grade school reserved for party bureaucrats and embarked on an education in Russian literature. A prodigy, by eleven she was reading a book a day off her father's shelves, from Chekhov to Dostoyevsky to Tolstoy. Then, as a teenager, she discovered a forbidden female poet who would have an impact on her sensibility for the rest of her life.

Marina Ivanova Tsvetaeva, little known in the West, was regarded by the Soviets as an iconoclast and by Russians generally as one of the most psychologically complex and morally ambiguous figures in their literary heritage. The fact that Anna took this fiercely anti-Soviet, emotionally volatile, sexually omnivorous and ultimately tragic woman to heart was an early sign that she was to be her own person.

Tsvetaeva, like Politkovskaya, was born to the metropolitan elite, in 1892. Immediately after her marriage at twenty to a czarist military officer, she embarked on a series of passionate love affairs with both men and women, all the while proclaiming her marital devotion. In Moscow she witnessed and opposed the Communist Revolution, while her husband, Sergei Efron, joined the Whites in the ensuing civil war. Alone in Moscow with her children and suspected by the Reds, Tsvetaeva had no way to support herself and her youngest child died of starvation. She consoled herself by carrying on a love affair with a female actress, later writing a book of poetry about the adventure, called *The Mistake*. By the time she fled Lenin's Russia in 1922, she had written several books of poetry in autobiographical, diary format, including *Swan's Camp*, an allegory of the White Army's struggles. She reunited with Efron in Berlin, and they spent most of the next two decades living among Russian émigrés in various capitals, where her books of diary-form poems were largely ignored by her fellow expatriates.

In the late 1930s, Efron turned on his anticommunist comrades, became an agent for the Soviet secret police and took part in the assassination of a Soviet defector. Charged with murder by French authorities, he fled to the Soviet Union. Tsvetaeva was questioned about her husband by the French police, who judged her insane. Ostracized by the Russian émigré community because of her husband's betrayal, Tsvetaeva followed him to Russia in 1939. After the German invasion in 1941, Efron was executed as a potential counterintelligence agent and Tsvetaeva, at forty-nine, almost certainly suffered the same fate, although the Soviets listed suicide as her cause of death.

Politkovskaya's early admiration of Tsvetaeva's radical independence and her immersion in the passionate woman's erratic career—Tsvetaeva was the subject of her university thesis—gives some clue to what was to come in her own life. Both were from the same social class and married risk-taking men at twenty; in their handsome youth and careworn last years, they bore a strong physical resemblance; both opposed a murderous Russian regime, and both of their lives ended violently, at about the same age. In all four of her books and many of her articles, Politkovskaya emulated Tsvetaeva's staccato diary style, and the poet's tumultuous mix of fatalism, idealism and outrage are evident in much of Politkovskaya's writing.

"In life, you strive to get from the superficial to the real," Politkovskaya wrote in A Small Corner of Hell. "There it is, you think, right around the corner. Oh no, again you're out of luck, it's just a mirage. And you think that if you dig deeper into yourself, you'll find it. But vanity is vanity, and you're right back, running in circles after new, more vivid sensations and impressions, only to face defeat again. Here, in the smoldering ruins of Grozny, there's nothing to see except suffering, your own and others. Yet it is precisely here that life is the most real. . . ."

Anna did not have many friends in high school, and those she did have thought she would never get married: no man, they said, would ever put up with "a devil in a skirt." Not surprisingly, the contrarian Anna defied all their predictions by becoming the first among them to lose her virginity and the first to get married.

In 1975, when she was a seventeen-year-old high school senior raptly reading Marina Tsvetaeva, the tall, ruggedly handsome Alexander Politkovsky and some companions walked into the family's apartment with Anna's older sister, Elena, a university classmate of Alexander's. Anna's parents were away in New York, and though Anna was five years Sasha's junior, the two had what Sasha called "an encounter" that rapidly evolved into a love affair. Because of the age difference, Anna's classmates began referring to Sasha as "the old man," which Anna interpreted as flattering to her taste in men.

Anna entered the University of Moscow's journalism program in 1976, and two years later married Sasha, who had graduated from the same program and was then embarking on a journalism career. The wedding was held in his two-hundred-square-foot apartment, which somehow accommodated what Sasha described as "an insane number" of their bohemian colleagues. Anna's parents were not impressed by her new husband's poverty, nor amused by his antics. Instead of formal dress, he showed up for his wedding wearing a worker's cap with a flower stuck in it, and carrying a backpack containing a bottle of vodka and a loaf of black bread—his wedding presents for Anna. "I meant it as a joke, but they didn't recognize it as such," he told a Moscow newspaper.

Anna had never cooked a meal in her privileged life and, after Ilya was born, spent hours on the phone with her mother jotting down recipes for breakfasts as simple as oatmeal, gradually working her way up to eggplant and tomato dinners. "She became an excellent housewife and mistress of the house before my very eyes," Sasha reflected. Their second child, Vera, was born in 1980, and, despite being a full-time mother, Anna graduated on time, writing her thesis on Tsvetaeva while juggling diapers and baby bottles.

Sasha remembered that Anna didn't take kindly to the fact that he was often away from home, pursuing his journalism. "I was, after all, working, and she was left to tend the children. Basically, the entire household hung on her." And she was envious of his career, which led to screaming matches in their cramped apartment. "After yet another colossal argument," Sasha said, "I would go into the kitchen and write. And later still, when we made peace, we laughed that the text was unusually good. Life is a strangely striped creature — and ours was unusually so."

Anna got her first job, a part-time position in the letters-to-the-editor department of *Izvestia*, when Vera was still an infant. It was "a Soviet shit house," Sasha said, a rat's nest of backbiting and innuendo, filled with informants, conspiracies and counterconspiracies. Two years later, Anna moved to Aeroflot's in-house magazine, *Air Transport*, primarily because of its perks. "Every journalist got free tickets all year round," she told the *Guardian* years later. "You could go on any plane and fly wherever you wanted. Thanks to this I saw the whole of our huge country. I was a girl from a diplomatic family, a reader, a bit of a swot; I didn't know life at all."

Then, in 1986, Gorbachev declared his policy of glasnost, and Anna moved to a new people-oriented tabloid called *Megapolis-Express*. At the same time, Sasha's career took off toward what he called "the height of my glory," co-hosting a show called *Vzglyad* (*The View*), which eventually made him the Dan Rather of Russian TV news. When Boris Yeltsin took his heroic stand atop a tank in August 1991 — foiling a communist attempt to topple Gorbachev — communist rule and the Soviet Union collapsed, putting Yeltsin, as president of Russia, in charge of a new nation with new rules — liberal democratic ones. Journalists like Anna and Sasha felt euphoric over the disintegration of the old regime; it meant they had a limitless future. Still, their relationship remained stormy, and that, combined with their absorption in their careers, had an effect on their children, especially their teenage son, Ilya. "My behavior was not very good," Ilya told me. "They sent me away to Taunton boarding school in 1992, when I was fourteen. . . . They thought it would help me be less wild." (He said he remained wild through his teens, though he eventually graduated from the University of East London, with a major in business economics, and procured a job with a prominent public relations company.)

In 1994, Anna got her first big break when she was hired by *Obshchaya Gazeta*, which had got its start in 1991 during the coup and since then had made a name for itself as a critic of Yeltsin's administration. Its sixty-four-year-old editor, Yegor Yakovlev, was a tempestuous figure who had begun his journalism career during Soviet times and believed the purpose of a newspaper was to help people think "correctly," which in his view meant giving favorable coverage to the liberal politicians he supported and unfavorable coverage to the politicians (liberal and otherwise) he didn't. Anna was hired to work in *Obshchaya*'s cultural affairs department doing interviews and profiles.

Helped by Sasha's ready access to Moscow's liberal elite, she did well, her portraits of the conflict-ridden lives of Moscow's intelligentsia and artists garnering the paper a readership beyond liberal circles. As usual, though, Anna ran into people problems. "Her professional life was difficult," Sasha remembered. "She had big problems—there were lots of complications and lots of drama everywhere."

A year into her tenure, on March 1, 1995, Sasha's best friend at Russian Public Television, Vladislav Listyev, was shot dead as he entered his apartment block in Moscow. Listyev, the director of the station, had taken the controversial step of banning private advertising on the channel, thus torpedoing the lucrative contracts of a number of advertising agencies owned by Russia's corrupt business elite. Paul Klebnikov, a *Forbes* journalist who himself would be murdered in Moscow nine years later, alleged that an oligarch infuriated by the cutoff in advertising was behind the killing.

Sasha was devastated by the murder, his grief made worse by the fact that those at the station who had supported private advertising gained the upper hand. "My bastard colleagues did all they could to make work impossible for me after the murder of Vlad Listyev," he later reflected in a newspaper interview. "That was definitely the reason I started drinking. After Vlad's murder, I had to drink myself to sleep."

Sasha's collapse into alcoholism ruined him as a husband and father. By the summer of 1996 he was staggering home with strange bar buddies, singing and arguing with them in the living room until the wee hours.

At the end of August, with her son, Ilya, about to enter another year at boarding school in England, Anna made her call to Svetlana Gannushkina and proposed her story about Chechen schoolchildren. The next day she had her epiphany at Civil Assistance.

Politkovskaya used the skills she had learned profiling Moscow's chic to depict the lives of the poor, giving a human face to suffering. Chechens were not her only subjects. Ethnic Tatars, Tajiks, Georgians, Azeris and Armenians all wound up at the doorstep of Civil Assistance, where she was soon working as a volunteer. Politkovskaya went beyond telling the stories of the bigotry and hardship they faced in Moscow. She tried to find them apartments and schooling for their children, fighting an official city policy that said "nonresidents" weren't entitled to either.

In the midst of one of her battles, she sought the help of Major Vyacheslav Izmailov, a bald, barrel-chested man with a quiet voice and a thoughtful, very unmilitary mien. She first met him at the May 9, 1998 Victory Day parade in Red Square, where she was manning the *Obshchaya Gazeta* publicity booth. She handed him a cup of coffee and learned that in his twenty-seven years of service, Izmailov had fought in Afghanistan for two years and in Chechnya until the troops left in late 1996. He was not only a Jew who had risen fairly high in an organization with ingrained currents of anti-Semitism, but he had done something unheard of for a Russian officer. In June 1996, trying to arrange a prisoner exchange, he had discovered that the Chechens he thought he could barter for Russians had all been shot on the orders of a general named Vladimir Shamanov. When I interviewed Izmailov in the cafeteria of *Novaya Gazeta*, he explained what happened next. "In order to get our soldiers back, I had to reveal to the Chechens we had no prisoners to exchange because we had killed them," he told me. "The Chechens proposed a deal. If I announced on Radio Liberty that we had executed our Chechen prisoners, they would return our soldiers. I agreed. But I was so outraged that we had killed our prisoners that I also wrote an article for a magazine in which I named Shamanov as one of the perpetrators."

"You were in a war zone, Shamanov was your commander and you exposed him for murdering prisoners?" I asked.

"That's correct. Right after that I learned Shamanov ordered me shot, but he couldn't find any soldiers to carry out the order. Instead, they came to me and told me that I should go into hiding. I refused to run, my own soldiers protected me, and then the war ended and we withdrew from Chechnya." Admired by liberals in Yeltsin's administration who were critical of the Chechen War, in Moscow Izmailov found a roof that protected him and allowed him to speak out. "At the time I met Anna," he said, "I was contributing articles to *Novaya Gazeta*, so she knew she could trust me."

About two weeks after their first meeting, Anna showed up at Izmailov's army office, saying she needed government housing for a group of Armenians who'd been evicted from a Moscow hotel because they had no residency permits. She'd tried to help them by writing advocacy articles in *Obshchaya*, and, when that didn't work, she'd filed suit on their behalf and accompanied them to court.

"Typical for Anna, when the judge decided in favor of the City of Moscow, she started to berate him, and he threw her out of the court, threatening to arrest her if she came back. She took the Armenians to her office and they were living there. So I found some empty barracks and that was the start of our cooperation. Then I retired from the army and went to work for *Novaya Gazeta*. I arrived at a very interesting time for journalists, for all Russia, because that was when Putin began his rise."

In July 1998, Yeltsin, with his sobriety and his country in a tailspin, appointed the forty-five-year-old Vladimir Vladimirovich Putin as head of the FSB. Putin believed in order, loyalty and patriotism — which Yeltsin concluded made him a good choice for top cop in a nation that was falling apart. Nine years earlier, Putin had endured the greatest shock of his life when crowds of East Germans stormed his KGB office in Berlin as the Wall came down. He drew a pistol and tried to obtain instructions from Moscow on how to handle the situation, only to learn there were no instructions. Putin was witness to the end of the Soviet Union's extraterritorial empire, and he never forgot it — and never accepted it.

Two years later, he was back in his hometown of Saint Petersburg when twelve of Russia's historical republics declared independence and the Soviet Union ceased to be. He judged the event "the greatest geopolitical catastrophe" of the twentieth century. One of those republics, on the north side of the Caucasus mountains, was Chechnya. It was the only one of the self-proclaimed independent states that Yeltsin refused to let go.

Russia had ruled Chechnya since 1859, when Czar Alexander I won a war of conquest against Islamic clans that for centuries had run their own affairs in the mountains. It hadn't been an easy campaign; it took the Russians forty years to subdue thousands of guerrilla fighters expert in raiding for spoils and kidnapping for ransom. Russian generals gave the republic's capital a name that matched their treatment of resistors. In Russian, Grozny means "Terrible."

The clans signed a peace treaty but never truly accepted defeat. They became part of a nationalist movement whose Islamic adherents believed they would eventually overthrow the Christian invaders. Over the years these rebellious clans evolved into mafia-style criminal syndicates that turned Chechnya into the Sicily of Russia, giving Russians the impression that all Chechens were innately criminal, and that those who had moved to Russia were branch managers of a Chechen underworld empire.

In 1919, Lenin promised the Chechens land and liberation in return for their help in winning the struggle against the reactionary Whites in the civil war. They agreed to help, and Lenin lived up to his promise, at least insofar as Chechens were rewarded with an autonomous republic within the USSR. When Stalin consolidated his power in 1928, he reversed the policy, collectivizing the land and brutally suppressing Chechen national aspirations. In 1942, as Hitler's divisions struck south from Rostov toward Grozny, some Chechen clans sided with the Germans and attacked the Red Army's lines of supply from the rear. Eighteen months later, when the Germans had been thrown back across the Dnieper, Stalin took revenge. He loaded every man, woman and child in Chechnya into boxcars and, in the middle of winter, transported them to Kazakhstan. Of the half-million people who made the trip in February 1944, an estimated 150,000 died. Thirteen years later, as part of his de-Stalinization plan, Nikita Khrushchev allowed the Chechens to return to their homeland, but by the time of the collapse of the Soviet Union, Chechnya was anxious to throw off the yolk of a nation that had conquered, ruled, expelled and almost exterminated its citizens.

The man who declared Chechen independence in October 1991 was General Dzhokhar Dudayev, who until March of that year had commanded the USSR's nuclear bomber fleet in the Baltic. Yeltsin believed that Chechen secession would start a chain reaction among all ethnic provinces still within the Russian Federation, causing the collapse of Russia itself. But instead of attacking Chechnya, as war hawks within his cabinet urged him to do, Yeltsin imposed a trade blockade on the breakaway republic and urged the international community not to recognize it. For the next two years Chechnya held an uncertain status, considering itself independent while Russia regarded it as still part of the Federation.

Some accommodation might have been arrived at through negotiation had not Dudayev, seeking to prop up his shaky regime, disbanded Parliament, declared himself dictator and put his nation on a war footing with Russia. Thousands of ethnic Russians fled the province. Such a challenge could not go unanswered, and in December 1994, Yeltsin ordered his forces to invade, thinking he was in for a short campaign.

To the surprise of the world and the horror of Russia, Chechnya turned into another Afghanistan for Russian forces. Yeltsin had grossly underestimated both the deterioration of his own conscript army since the collapse of the Soviet Union and the strength and determination of Chechen forces led by two fiercely capable resistance fighters: a ruthless guerrilla commander named Shamil Basayev and an ex–Red Army colonel named Aslan Maskhadov. Their fighters were all volunteers, imbued with the memory of Stalin's genocide and supplied with Russian equipment bought openly in Grozny's markets.

To his credit, Yeltsin allowed journalists full access to the war zone, sticking to his credo that a free press was necessary for Russia's transformation into a liberal society. As a result, Russians were exposed nightly to the horrors of the street fighting in Grozny as well as to a deluge of editorials appealing to Yeltsin to end the war. In June 1995, Basayev took the fight to Russia itself, invading a hospital in Budyonnovsk, seizing a thousand hostages and killing 150 doctors, nurses and patients before Yeltsin's prime minister negotiated the release of the survivors and allowed Basayev and his men safe passage to Chechnya. When rebel forces drove the Russians out of Grozny in August 1996, Yeltsin fired the hawks who had urged him to go to war and opened negotiations with the new Chechen leader, Maskhadov, who had replaced Dudayev after he was killed during a Russian attack.

During those negotiations, Yeltsin bombed Grozny one last time, causing the exodus of Chechen refugees that Politkovskaya encountered at the Civil Assistance refugee center. In the final truce, Yeltsin agreed to lift the blockade, withdraw all Russian troops and allow the country to be run by Maskhadov as a de facto independent state until 2001, when a final round of negotiations was scheduled to determine the republic's status.

In the three years between her first story about Chechen refugees and her first trip to their country, Politkovskaya's personal life continued to darken. Sasha lost his job at Russian Public Television and completely abandoned himself to the bottle. "She once had a nervous breakdown," Sasha told a newspaper, in response to a question about how Anna had handled his drinking, although he added that most of the time she stood up to him like "an iron lady." In the late spring of 1999, after a number of household fights, he broke the news that he wanted out of the marriage.

Politkovskaya's emotionally raw state at the end of her marriage pushed her over the edge at work, leading to a final blowup with her editor at *Obshchaya Gazeta*, who for some time had been ordering her to revise her material and change the focus of her reporting. Without taking any time off, in June 1999 she went to work for *Novaya Gazeta*. A twice-weekly tabloid, the paper had been founded in 1993 by a journalist named Dmitry Muratov, helped by a financial donation from Mikhail Gorbachev. *Novaya* considered itself the leading liberal democratic newspaper in Russia, valuing honesty and independence above all. When Anna arrived it had a circulation of about 100,000 and was unique among

Russia's papers in that its shares were 100 percent owned by the seventy or so journalists who worked there. (The paper is now 51 percent owned by its journalists, the rest of its shares split between Gorbachev, who owns 10 percent, and billionaire banker Aleksandr Lebedev, who owns the remaining 39 percent.)

Anna's first day of work coincided with that of Galina Mursalieva—the woman who would go on to become her office mate. Muratov assigned his new hires to cover Moscow's culture scene, and they sat beside each other in the newsroom. "I know that Anna was really suffering greatly from the end of her marriage," Mursalieva told me. "At the beginning we had some small quarrels, some misunderstandings, but I really liked her drive and didn't fight with her like others did. Our relationship was probably helped because I stayed covering social and cultural affairs but she immediately moved to human rights. She threw herself totally into her work. She produced three articles for every issue."

Politkovskaya's articles in June and July that year were a series about the sadistic hazing and murder of conscript soldiers by their drunken officers, a subject she would return to repeatedly in her career, relying for her sources on a group called the Committee of Soldiers' Mothers and on Vyacheslav Izmailov. While writing these exposés, she began lobbying the editor Muratov to send her to the Caucasus, a prospect that terrified her parents and children. "She told me they couldn't understand why she wanted to go to such a place," Izmailov said. "They were absolutely opposed to it and condemned her for thinking about it. Perhaps they worried she was only reacting to her domestic grief. I didn't know about her private life, but I did know Chechnya was not a place children would want to see their mother go."

For by then all the hopes that had been born in Russia's military withdrawal had vanished and Chechnya had turned into one of the most dangerous stories in the world to cover. Shamil Basayev, funded in part by Osama bin Laden, had declared a jihad against both Maskhadov and Russia, and the republic had plunged into criminal chaos, with Basayev's forces (sometimes more interested in profit than in jihad) extorting money from the few businesses still running. Meanwhile, the mountain clans and the Chechen mafia—it was often hard to tell them apart—had taken full advantage of the state of anarchy to expand their drug, weapon and kidnapping-for-ransom trades. Warlords ruled the republic outside the capital. To bolster his appeal to the Islamic faithful, Maskhadov declared he would rule the country under sharia law, then sent troops still loyal to him into the field to restore order. By the time Politkovskaya asked to be sent to the Caucasus, Chechnya was enduring a multi-sided civil war, with clans fighting one another as well as Maskhadov's forces.

On August 7, 1999, Basayev tried to precipitate an Islamic union in the Caucasus by leading his renegade force in an invasion of the Russian republic of Dagestan, to the east. The same day, Yeltsin promoted Putin from FSB chief to prime minister. Putin immediately ordered the Dagestani militia and the Russian troops in the area to drive the rebels back. Thousands of Chechens and Dagestanis fled the fighting in the border area. As the refugee crisis developed, Muratov agreed to send Politkovskaya to Dagestan.

She flew to the capital, Makhachkala, then moved overland to a Dagestani border hotel called the Pearl. Her first dispatches were all on the same theme: a condemnatory account of the Russian government's indifference to the refugees living in camps around the hotel grounds, who were surviving thanks to the charity of the Pearl's owner and Dagestani businesses. "The present catastrophe in Dagestan has once again shown that ordinary people are a hundred times better and purer than our authorities," she wrote. "At best our clumsy and unresponsive regime thinks only of itself and does nothing." She then turned her critical gaze on Russia's human rights organizations, including, by implication, Civil Assistance. "One other sad observation," she wrote. "Unlike the Chechen war in 1994–6, not a single Moscow human rights organization has done anything to aid these hapless people—and yet several of these organizations are specifically for refugees and not lacking in resources. Only the Dagestanis today are helping the people of their republic and this does not bode well. Moscow is thereby sowing the seeds of separatism. When they take root and begin to grow, the federal authorities will complain that you can do nothing with these people."

Putin knew what to do with "these people." In his view, Yeltsin had humiliated Russia by negotiating with Basayev during the hostage-taking in 1995, and overall had been too lax in pursuit of victory in the First Chechen War. Putin asked Yeltsin for permission to send the Russian army in force to retake Chechnya, predicting that the conflict would be "resolved within a week and a half or two." Yeltsin agreed.

By the end of August, Basayev's forces had been driven out of Dagestan by local forces and, from what the public could tell, the fighting appeared to be over. Then, between September 8 and 16, as the Russian army was massing in the Caucasus, bombs brought down a number of apartment houses in the cities of Moscow, Volgodonsk and Buinaksk. More than three hundred people were killed, and Russia was thrown into a state of shock and ethnic hatred. Fifteen thousand Chechens were deported en masse from Moscow, and another 62,000 were made to register as "foreigners."

No Chechens took responsibility for the three attacks, however, which was unusual for the rebels. Then, on September 22, a week after the last bombing, witnesses in the town of Ryazan called the police when they saw three strangers carrying large sacks into their apartment-house basement. The police discovered the sacks contained hexogen, the explosive used in the other bombings. A day later, two of the culprits were identified and arrested. To the shock of the police, the two men produced FSB identification. When the police called Moscow, the FSB ordered their men released, sent their agents to Ryazan to seize and destroy the powder, and, as the incident began to be talked about in the town, publicly announced that the sacks had contained sugar and that the arrested agents had been conducting "a training exercise."

An investigation by journalist Pavel Voloshin led him to allege in *Novaya Gazeta* that the evidence strongly suggested that the FSB had been behind planting the explosives in Ryazan, a suggestion Politkovskaya endorsed, further alleging that the agents had been attempting to provide a pretext for Putin to invade Chechnya. But the Russian people took scant notice. Putin had proclaimed on television that Chechens were behind the slaughter, promising to "corner the bandits in the shithouse and wipe them out." With the overwhelming support of the Russian people, he launched an aerial assault on Grozny. On October 1, 1999, the Russian army crossed the border and the Second Chechen War began.

Politkovskaya's family begged her to cover the invasion from Dagestan, but she was too filled with outrage at the sight of wounded teenagers returning from the front to listen. "Where are the human rights activists?" she wrote. "The intelligentsia, the conscience of the nation? Where has all that army of socially active people gone. . . . ? The minds of the majority are becoming rapidly and totally militarized: they talk of 'wiping out,' 'crushing,' and 'smashing' the enemy, while the minority, faced by this rising tide of military euphoria, lapse into a state of apathy."

She arrived in Grozny as artillery shells and aerial bombs were leveling it, block by block. She sheltered in basements with civilians, then joined a column of refugees in the flight west to Ingushetia. "We are the people caught in the bombing," she wrote in her first wartime dispatch. "Grozny is behind us. We run as a herd from the war and its battles. When the time comes, and you have hit the ground face down, assuming a fetal position, trying to hide your head, your knees, and even elbows under your body— then a kind of false, sticky loneliness sneaks up on you, and you start to think, 'Why are you crouching? What are you trying to save? This life of yours that no one cares about?'

"Why is it false?" she asked herself. "Because you know perfectly well that this isn't really true: you have a family, and they are waiting and praying for you. And it's sticky because of the sweat. When you're clinging to life, you pray a lot. . . .

"Still, there is loneliness. Death is the one situation where you can never find companionship. When the diving helicopters hover over your bent back, the ground starts to resemble a deathbed."

While on the trek west, Politkovskaya heard about a hundred or so ethnic Russians left behind in Grozny, trapped in an old-age home; thirty of them were bedridden, and most of the others were suffering from dementia. "What can you Russians do right, if you can't even save your own old people from being bombed?" the Chechen refugees asked her. In Ingushetia, she began investigating the story and discovered that the home's staff had abandoned their charges without water or heat, and that those who could walk were venturing out amidst the shelling in search of food. When she got back to Moscow a few days later, she began lobbying *Novaya Gazeta* to take up their cause.

For help she turned to Izmailov, now her paper's military affairs correspondent. Politkovskaya laid out her plan: Izmailov would urge his contacts in the military to coordinate the rescue operation while Politkovskaya coordinated transport and housing. But neither civilian officials in Moscow nor the military were the least bit interested in helping. Politkovskaya refused to accept that nothing could be done. She went door to door until she had shouted down, arm-twisted and embarrassed the Ministry of Labor into at least finding homes for the old people outside the war zone.

She burst into Izmailov's office with the good news. "Let's go, it's all arranged!" Izmailov remembered her urging. "But I knew it wasn't arranged," he said to me. "I was very doubtful of the logistics of the operation because there were none. Anna had negotiated for a place where the old people would go, but I had to find a way to get them out of the home and bring them through the lines to a place where the Russian federal troops were. 'Don't worry, you'll do it!' she told me, but she didn't know the kind of people I would have to deal with on the Russian side."

Izmailov and Politkovskaya flew down to Ingushetia and made their way east through the columns of refugees to Grozny, where they discovered street-to-street fighting taking place within blocks of the old-age home. It fell to Izmailov to arrange a cease-fire. Risking his life, Izmailov left the Russian lines on their first night in Grozny and made his way to the Chechen side, where he met with fighters in a bombed-out building near the home and somehow persuaded them to cease firing long enough for the old people to be led or carried out of the war zone. There was a problem, however: the Chechens insisted on doing the leading and carrying, since they didn't trust the Russians to come behind their lines and then leave. Izmailov returned to the Russian side and reported the bad news to Politkovskaya, who failed to see that trying to persuade the Russians to hold their fire while the Chechens came out with the old people was even more dangerous for him than running back and forth between the lines. "Go, go go! Get started!" she told him.

The general in charge of the Russian attempt to take Grozny was Vladimir Shamanov, the same man who had ordered Izmailov shot three years earlier for exposing the murder of the Chechen prisoners. "Now, in the midst of combat, Anna was telling me to go to General Shamanov's headquarters and arrange the cease-fire from the Russian side."

"Did you do it?"

"I did. He refused to call a cease-fire and told me he'd have me shot for asking. I told Anna, 'We can't trust Shamanov not to shoot at the Chechens. We have to get an order from Moscow.' Anna and I had a big argument then because she said she was sure that Russian troops wouldn't shoot at these old and mentally deficient people. But I said she didn't know Russian soldiers, that they would shoot—I knew them, and I knew Shamanov."

The argument escalated to a larger issue. "What we were doing was extremely dangerous," he said. "And our agreement was that she would do it my way. But now Anna said there was no time to do it my way. I understood her concerns because those old people could die, but I said it was impossible to move them right away. She wanted me to go back to Shamanov, and when I said it wouldn't do any good, she shouted at me, 'You're a coward, do you hear those words? You are a coward!'"

"I wasn't polite to her," Izmailov remembered. "I was quite harsh because she called me a coward to my face. Suddenly she burst into tears, she said that she had a family, a son and daughter, and her relatives condemned her and said it wasn't her job to save old people here and she had to live for her family. But while crying, she insisted that she'd come to Grozny and risked her life and I didn't understand what she wanted to do, what she *had* to do, and she *would* do it, with me or without me."

In the end, she did do it—without Izmailov's or Shamanov's help. Using the same tactics of persuasion she'd employed with Russian officials in Moscow, she enlisted a platoon of soldiers in the area from the Ingushetian Republic, who were fighting on the Russian side against the rebels. Then, via radio, she persuaded the Chechens to allow their fellow Muslims into their perimeter to lead the old people across the lines. Standing with Russian soldiers at the front line, she watched as the Ingushetian soldiers brought the old people through the battle zone.

"All 103 people escaped alive!" Izmailov told me, his expression still reflecting his amazement at the feat. "The majority of them are still alive. Anna's energy and will saved these people. It was she and she alone who accomplished it.

"The only casualty was our relationship," he added, sighing in recollection. "Whenever I spoke to her after that, she always turned it into a fight. I would return the argument and then she refused to speak to me for a year. When you disagreed with Anna, she could get you back."

———

After her rift with Izmailov—the one man at the newspaper who had the pull to rescue her if she were taken prisoner by Chechen or Russian forces in the battle zone—colleagues began to question her judgment as well as her self-control. She won the Russian Union of Journalists' Golden Pen Award for her coverage of Chechnya, but when congratulations came her way, she complained that her editors were cutting the heart out of her stories. She embarrassed her employer by going public with her beefs in a column, which was reprinted two years later in A Small Corner of Hell: "Not even my newspaper, which opposes the current party line, is eager to print my reports from Chechnya. And if they do, they sometimes cut out the toughest parts, not wanting to shock the public. There are fierce arguments within the editorial staff over this issue, and it is more difficult than ever for me to publish the whole truth."

Anna became sullen and uncommunicative, giving other colleagues the kind of silent treatment she was giving Izmailov. "Even close friends don't believe my stories after my trips to Chechnya, and I have stopped explaining anything, and just sit silently when I'm invited anywhere," she wrote.

There is every possibility that Politkovskaya's reporting had traumatized her. Her marital collapse may have exacerbated the trauma, for she seemed always between tears and anger when back in Moscow. Her columns during this period paint a picture of her wandering alone through a war zone, observing things no one wanted to know and no journalist wanted to cover.

"Only the very strong in body and mind can endure Grozny today," she wrote from that city. "Everywhere there are ruins, filth, hunger and hordes of thin, homeless dogs." The horrors of the war caused her to feel profound shame not only for her country, its people and its leaders but also for her own profession. "No journalists come here," she wrote bitterly when she got to a destroyed town called Shali, its streets filled with "tubercular" people "out of their minds with hunger." She was too ashamed to reveal to them that their graphic stories of hardship would probably be edited from her columns. "I am silent about this, simply because for the people around me, who have suffered so much, I am the first civilian from *there*, from the other, non-war world. . . . There's no one else they can tell what's going on." They begged her to call Moscow's attention to the fact that the government handouts were not enough to live on. "Of course, I promise to tell them this," she wrote. "But I promise very quietly. I don't even actually promise, but just nod and whisper something. And I don't explain either. It's hard to tell the condemned that, first, the Kremlin doesn't give a damn about my report and, second, the situation in Moscow regarding the war in the Caucasus is very complicated, and no one knows anything about it, because they don't want to." Russia's leaders, journalists and citizens showed only a "bacchanalia of indifference" toward the most terrible crimes committed in their name.

One of those crimes struck very close to home. On July 16, 2000, Igor Dominkov, her newspaper's special projects editor, was attacked by five men at the entryway to his apartment building and died after spending two months in a coma. *Novaya Gazeta*'s journalists suspected the mastermind was a former regional vice governor whose wayward economic policies Dominkov had investigated. Though the attack shocked her as much as the rest of the staff, Politkovskaya left on schedule for another trip to Chechnya, and on July 24, she conducted a confrontational interview with Ramzan Kadyrov's father, Ahmad, a former rebel who'd once declared that, to win independence, "every Chechen would have to kill 150 Russians." He'd switched sides, however, and Putin had just appointed him president of Chechnya, replacing Aslan Maskhadov's insurgent regime with one now agreeable to remaining within Russia. Politkovskaya published the verbatim transcript of her interview with Ahmad, appending a postscript he was not happy to read, accusing him of paying only lip service to truth and the interests of ordinary people.

By then Russia's heavy losses to rebels who were indistinguishable from civilians had turned the conflict into "a dirty war," which became the title of Politkovskaya's first book. Chechens who were not allied with Kadyrov's clan were treated as enemy sympathizers until proven otherwise. After the new regime took power, Russian soldiers and Kadyrov's militia men entered villages they had just shelled and conducted *zachistkis*, or mop-up operations. Suspicious males were sent to "filtration centers," where rebels were to be separated from non-rebels. This required interrogation, which was facilitated by means of "the pit" — a six-foot-deep hole in the ground with slats over the top that left it open to the elements. Every so often the prisoner would be taken out and beaten, given electric shocks, sometimes raped and sometimes murdered. Many units went beyond even the questionable protocol of the *zachistki*, indulging in sprees of pillaging, random rape, and kidnapping for ransom.

Much of Politkovskaya's lonely journalism from 2000 onward centered on exposing the Russian army's criminal conduct of the war and its atrocities against civilians. In her dispatches, she named the officers responsible and also launched a one-woman campaign to help villagers whose homes had been destroyed, who were starving and freezing, and whose men had been taken prisoner. She filed these stories while moving among the troops responsible for the atrocities. That is why severe alarm bells were set off when *Novaya Gazeta* received word, on February 21, 2001, that Politkovskaya was missing.

"Anna was last heard from when she was in a village named Khatuni," Izmailov told me, referring to a town twenty-five miles south of Grozny, in the Caucasus Mountains. "I immediately knew how serious the situation was. Khatuni was the headquarters of the 45th Regiment, attached to the Chief Prosecutor's Department here in Moscow and responsible for holding rebels seized during the mop-up operations. Everyone was afraid to go there, even the prosecutors. They knew if they witnessed the atrocities, they themselves could be shot, and no soldier would testify it was murder. When I was serving in the First Chechen War, the 45th ordered the murder of a journalist for exposing what they were doing."

Politkovskaya had entered this most dangerous of areas because she had received a petition for help from ninety families living around Khatuni. Their relatives were being tortured within the compound of the 45th Regiment, and they themselves were starving, freezing and sick. "Anna was their last resort," Izmailov said. "She was fully aware what she was walking into, she was terrified, but she went."

She arrived in the area on February 18, in the company of a female Chechen human rights worker named Zainap Gashayeva. Together the women began documenting the cases of the civilians. Then, on February 20, Anna and Gashayeva went to the 45th Regiment compound in Khatuni. They wanted to find out what was happening to the sons and husbands being held by the Russians.

"At the time, Anna was still not speaking to me except to say something angry," Izmailov recounted. "She got her press pass for Chechnya from a government official, a friend of mine. When I asked him how she was doing, he said the officials and the military couldn't stand having her around. Instead of conducting interviews like a journalist, where you listen and take notes, she would launch into an attack. Or else she demanded they do something not in their power. Some respected her courage, but in Khatuni she had no allies, only enemies."

Gashayeva remained outside the compound as a lifeline while Politkovskaya went in to speak with the commanding officer. Hours passed and, as it began to get dark, Gashayeva became worried. There were no phones in Khatuni or the nearby villages, so when Politkovskaya had still not emerged by the next morning, Gashayeva traveled fifty miles to Ingushetia and called a human rights group, who passed on the news to Izmailov, who phoned his army contacts, who told him Anna was being held prisoner. "I immediately knew if we didn't rescue her that day, she would be dead."

Anna must have known that walking into the compound meant being tortured, murdered or both. She had reported on, and was in the process of investigating, numerous acts of torture and murder committed by Russian federal forces or officers from a special operations unit, the OMON, a militia brought in from other parts of Russia for "antiterrorism" duty in Chechnya. One month earlier, an OMON captain named Sergei Lapin had led an operation that Anna was convinced had ended in the torture and murder of twelve Chechen civilians. And yet she entered the very compound where many of the atrocities were taking place.

"Did she really think they'd let her out alive?" I asked Izmailov.

"I honestly don't know. She was just so ashamed of what Russia was sponsoring she probably couldn't help herself." Then Izmailov smiled. "But first she was given a tour of the compound by the commander," he said. "She was a very good journalist when she wanted the facts."

The commander was Colonel Aleksei Romanov. In that instant assessment of needs that both great journalists and grifters are expert at, Politkovskaya saw that more than anything else Romanov wanted to go home. She therefore got him talking about his kids, the pain of their growing up without him, and the lousy war. Then, knowing soldiers think as much about food as they do about family, she asked for a tour of the mess hall, which he explained was so well stocked that his men didn't have to raid neighboring farms for cattle. At that point, she enquired innocently about the pits, and he showed her those too, explaining that they had originally been dug for garbage but that his commanding general had flown in and decided they could be used to hold Chechens.

"We only put militants in there," he told her.

"Then why do you let them out later, if they're militants?" she asked, hinting that most who'd been tortured in the pits were innocent.

"You know very well," he replied, and walked away. Two minutes later, she was put under arrest. Her guards ordered her to remain motionless in the freezing cold while they appraised her with smirks. After an hour, an armored vehicle pulled up and the soldiers used their rifle butts to push her inside, where they accused her of being an ally of the terrorist Shamil Basayev. They drove her across the base and dragged her into an interrogation center, where a number of officers took turns grilling her, each one reminding her that they could behave as they wished since "they work for the FSB and answer only to Putin." They went through the contents of her purse, and graphic insults to her womanhood were followed by sexual propositions. Then they began to beat her in the ways in which torturers are trained—inflicting bone bruises that cause hematomas to rise, which are then targeted so that the victim comes to dread a particular kind of agony in a particular place. While the expert beating was taking place, other officers concentrated on breaking her down psychologically, leering at pictures of her son and daughter from her purse and explaining how her children could be tortured and abused.

After three hours of this, a fat colonel with bulging eyes entered the room and ordered Politkovskaya to stand up—he was going to take her outside and shoot her. She limped ahead of him through the cold and darkness, expecting each step would be her last. He announced, "Ready or not!" at which point Politkovskaya heard a "burst with pulsating fire all around me, screeching, roaring, and growling." It was not a bullet to the brain, she realized, because she could hear the colonel cackling as she lay crouching on the ground in terror. He had led her directly under the muzzles of a multisequence rocket launcher and had fired off a salvo. "Get up, bitch," he commanded, then pushed her into a bathroom and ordered her to strip. When she refused, he told a drunken FSB agent to take her out into the dark, where she again expected to be shot. After walking her in circles the agent threw her into a cell, where she began vomiting violently and begged to use a bathroom. "The bathroom? All right, but with an escort," he said. "We have to make sure you don't get rid of your bugging devices."

Izmailov knew he only had hours to save her, if she hadn't already been killed. He called a friend who phoned the chief of the investigative department of the army, who phoned a general in Chechnya, who placed a call to the 45th Regiment, which claimed that Politkovskaya was not in Khatuni, and had never been there. "That was the most dangerous message I could have received," Izmailov said. He called every one of his other government contacts, trying to reach as close to Putin as he could; when nothing seemed to be working, he went on Radio Liberty, Echo Moscow and other radio stations with the news that Anna Politkovskaya was missing in the vicinity of Khatuni. He did not receive confirmation that she was still alive until February 22.

"Everybody here was relieved," he told me, "but I could just picture her insulting her captors and one of them losing control and shooting her. The next day was the anniversary of Stalin's Day of Deportation, and they could always say they'd been attacked by the militants and Anna had been killed by enemy fire."

Izmailov's publicity campaign and phone calls saved Anna's life. He finally reached a minister of the Chechen government who, worried about an international backlash, ordered a helicopter to take Politkovskaya out of Khatuni. She arrived back in Moscow on February 23, but Izmailov was not there to greet her. "I didn't want to go to the airport because I was sure she would pick a fight with me over something," he told me. "Instead, our editor Muratov met her. The first thing he said was, 'Anna, you have to thank Izmailov for your rescue—he saved your life—if not for him, you would be dead.'" Muratov drove her directly from the airport to the Echo Moscow radio station to do an interview. He then called Izmailov and told him to come to the station. "I was still hesitant, but I went.

When she saw me, she gave me a big hug and kissed me. She said, 'We shouldn't quarrel anymore, okay?'"

"Was that your last quarrel, then?" I asked.

He chuckled, ran a hand over his scalp and said, "With Anna?" He took a deep breath, filling his barrel chest, then sighed. "I can say she never called me a coward again."

Galina Mursalieva placed her palms a few feet apart, showing me the distance she'd sat from Anna for seven years. She was Anna's age, with raven hair, huge dark eyes and a warm, patient manner. We were sitting in the Pyramid Café, in central Moscow, not far from the offices of *Novaya Gazeta*. "I knew she wasn't the kind of person who could come back from Khatuni untouched," Mursalieva said. "Chechnya had a psychological impact on her, and it just built up every trip. Everyone is saying she was a brave soldier, she was not afraid of anything. But she was actually terrified. We were not as close as sisters, but we had a fellowship, and she showed me signs no one else saw."

I asked her what signs she had seen.

"After she wrote an article about what went on in Khatuni, she received hate mail from so-called patriots. Her hands started to shake and she would cry hysterically and just keep saying, 'How can they say these things? How can they think these things?' Because the things they wrote were shameful and sadistic. They said, 'You're an enemy of the Russian people, and it won't be good enough to kill you.'"

The official reaction to Anna's article on what she'd endured was just as unsympathetic. The United Group of Forces in Chechnya, which included Ahmad and Ramzan Kadyrov's militia, issued a terse press release calling her allegations "a lie and a provocation"—implying that if she returned to Chechnya she might be treated worse.

And yet within weeks she began planning her next trip, all the while writing articles that used her ordeal as an example of the even more egregious abuses thousands of Chechens had experienced. She included in her catalogue of victims six young men who were hauled out of their pits in Khatuni, informed "they had nice asses" and then raped by Russian soldiers.

"How did she get the courage to overcome her fear and continue on the same path?" I asked.

"Anna never became a grown-up," Mursalieva explained. "She could giggle a lot like a little kid, get angry a lot like a kid—her first reaction always dominated her, whether it was laughing or crying, just like a kid. So she took all these children's habits into her adult life and she stayed a child, so much so that it hurt. And like a little child that doesn't learn to be realistic about the dangers of doing something, she would go back to do the thing that terrified her."

I asked if Anna received satisfaction from the love and gratitude of Chechens, quoting a passage she had written in *A Small Corner of Hell*: "When these people find out you're a journalist they cling to your clothing, hands and feet, as if you're a magician, as if something essential depended on you."

"No, she was not motivated for herself," Mursalieva commented. "She only mentioned that it was pitiful to see people so needy. My feeling is that Anna couldn't stand to see suffering, suffering upset her very much, and so she always tried to stop it. Even with animals. For instance, almost every day someone would bring some stray cat or dog or a sick bird to the office and Anna would always take them home. She always had two cats, two dogs and several birds in her apartment. When she got back from Khatuni, there was a mangy dog in the office. She said to me, 'My kids are going to have a fit if I bring another one home!' She was laughing and crying at the same time."

That compassionate side, so sensitive to the suffering of the helpless, contrasted, however, with the way I'd heard she could turn on friends. And when Anna turned on friends, I said, she wrote and said things that hurt them.

Mursalieva defended her colleague by insisting that Anna's temper was only aroused on points of principle, which usually had to do with a wrong imposed by Russia's powerful, and not sufficiently opposed by its intelligentsia. "She was so ashamed that we as a nation could cause such suffering that whenever she saw it, she wanted to stop the suffering," she said. "She believed she was the last hope of people from all over Russia. They wrote her letters and spent their last pennies on tickets to come to Moscow to seek her help, and she *always* helped them. I don't know any other journalist who did that. Even if she was on a deadline, she would meet for hours with very old people who came to the office. She would listen to them and then go to their villages trying to help them. She never gave up. Most people, they see a wall, they understand you can't break through. And you start thinking, 'Why do I need to break my forehead?' But Anna never saw it like this. She always thought that she had to break through the wall."

"Even if it meant breaking her own head," I said.

"I would say to her, 'You have to switch away from this subject because this is so dark and you can do nothing to lighten it,' but Anna could never close her eyes. She always saw through the eyes of the people who needed her to defend them. She always had the eyes of others in her mind. Most of us live according to the Russian saying: A bad peace is better than a good war. But Anna always thought, 'If it's a war, it's a war, so I will fight them.'"

She fought them by returning to Chechnya, and in September 2001 she produced an exposé that would reverberate for years. "Disappearing People" was based on her confirmation of the accounts she'd heard in Khatuni about the militia OMON's kidnapping and killing of civilians. She named the lead perpetrator, Captain Sergei Lapin, and his accomplices. When she returned to Moscow, her newspaper received an e-mail from someone using the name "Cadet"—Lapin's nickname—warning that the sender had "trained as a sniper and intend[s] to visit Moscow."

To the surprise of her friends in the liberal journalism community, after the e-mail Anna moved to Vienna. Most thought she had sensibly chosen to flee, when in fact she had been awarded a fellowship to work on the book that became A Small Corner of Hell. Her colleagues wrote and urged her to stay in Austria, but when Anna learned that a rumor was spreading she had run away from "Cadet" Lapin, she immediately returned to Moscow. She claimed that after only two months in quiet Vienna she'd become bored and wanted to get back to covering news.

Big news awaited her. Putin had handed control of the Chechen war to the FSB, and the press passes she had been able to finagle from Izmailov's contacts were discontinued. Anna decided to break through this wall to her reporting. She began sneaking across the Ingush border into Chechnya, sometimes in the trunks of cars, other times disguised as a peasant — all this with a death threat from Sergei "Cadet" Lapin still hanging over her head.

On February 9, 2002, alarm bells again went off in her newspaper offices when Politkovskaya was out of touch for three days. This time she was on the run from the FSB, which had gotten wind she was in the country without a press pass. Villagers in the Khatuni area tipped her off she was being hunted, and she crossed west over the mountains on foot. "I wanted to stay alive!" she told the Guardian afterwards, implying the FSB might have killed her. "It was terrifying. I reached the village of Stary Atagi at dawn. I stayed there for a day and a night, keeping my head down." On the third day, she made it across the border to Ingushetia, reporting in Novaya Gazeta that she had been "hiding from the FSB, which wanted to intervene in our investigation of the killing of civilians."

Politkovskaya's heroics had first begun to receive the attention of the foreign media after her Novaya Gazeta articles on Chechnya were translated into English and published in A Dirty War in 2001. Awards committees noticed her too. She won the Amnesty

International Global Award for Human Rights Journalism, the PEN American Center Freedom to Write Award and the Courage in Journalism Award sponsored by the International Women's Media Foundation. "Getting the awards did not make her happy," Galina Mursalieva told me. "Because whenever she took an award, she tried to make her points about Chechnya at the microphone. But the custom was you were only allowed to say a few words. She said, 'They won't let me speak!' She became very frustrated with her Western audiences."

She also had little use for bleeding-heart audiences when they did let her speak. "This spring I have been in Amsterdam, Paris, Geneva, Manila, Bonn, [and] Hamburg," she wrote in May 2002, at the end of a campaign for support against Russia's conduct of the war. "Everywhere they invite me to make a speech about 'the situation in Chechnya,' but there are zero results. Only polite Western applause in response to my words: 'Remember, people are continuing to die in Chechnya *every day*. Including today.' It's a clear, obvious, unbelievable worldwide betrayal of humanitarian values."

Five months later she was on another speaking tour when a terrorist attack organized by Shamil Basayev rocked Moscow. On October 23, 2002, during the second act of a play called *Nord-Ost*, dozens of heavily armed Chechens burst into a theater on Dubrovka Street, sealed the entrances, and threatened to blow up everyone inside unless Russian troops were withdrawn from Chechnya. Politkovskaya, lecturing in Santa Monica, California, received a call from her paper telling her the hostage-takers wanted to talk to her in person. The next call came from her twenty-four-year-old son, begging her not to fly home to Moscow. "Please don't do this!" Ilya told her. "We can't take it anymore! You don't know what's going on here!"

"It's a difficult conversation," Politkovskaya recounted later, writing in the present tense she often used in her columns. "My son feels desperate; he is very upset. He's tired of worrying about me. He can't even express in words how tired everyone around me has gotten from these experiences that take up their whole lives as I cover this infernal, endless Second Chechen War. My son gets furious when he doesn't get a definite promise I won't come."

She took the next plane to Moscow and, on October 25, went straight from the airport to the theater, where an FSB agent pointed a finger at her and warned her not to contribute to Chechen propaganda. Carrying boxes of juice and sandwiches for the hostages, Politkovskaya brushed by the agent and entered the theater. Beyond the lobby more than nine hundred people were cowering in their seats, satchels of explosives hanging over their heads, guarded by black-clad men and women wearing suicide belts and holding Kalashnikovs and hand grenades. She set to negotiating with one of the terrorist leaders, Abu Bakr, who refused her entreaty to free the children in the theater, saying that when Russian soldiers conducted their village mop-up operations, they did not spare children. ("To be quite frank," she told journalists later, "I didn't know what to say. I knew he was quite right.") After relating more tales of oppression to justify their act, the fanatics allowed Politkovskaya to leave to tell their story. The next day, fifty-seven hours into the siege, Russian Special Forces pumped sleeping gas into the theater's ventilation system and stormed in. The gas killed 129 of the hostages. None of the hostage-takers survived the assault.

Politkovskaya excoriated Putin for launching a "murderous" rescue operation. "The secret military gas was chosen by the president personally," she wrote. "Many people died [because] the identity of the gas was not even revealed to the doctors charged with saving lives." Equally shameful to her was that the vast majority of Russians accepted Putin's argument that the atrocities his forces committed daily in Chechnya had nothing to do with the motives of the hostage-takers. Rather, Politkovskaya wrote, Russians considered the president's rescue as "a triumph for Russia over 'the forces of international terror. . . .' It was a shame about the people who died, of course, but the interests of society must come first."

In the wake of the hostage-taking, an "antiterrorist" pogrom was launched against Muslims across Russia, dubbed Operation Whirlwind. "Let us look at the ethnic purging that followed that act of terrorism," she wrote, "and at the new state ideology Putin has enunciated: 'We shall not count the cost. Let nobody doubt that. Even if the cost is very high.'"

From the Urals to the Baltic, thousands of bearded men were rounded up by OMON militia, thrown into jail, interrogated, beaten and told they would have to go back to where they came from. Skinheads rampaged through Muslim markets while the police stood by. Mosques were desecrated and copies of the Koran seized as "evidence." Bad as this was, in Chechnya the Russian army's retribution was slaughterous, with troops fanning out across the republic, reducing homes to rubble, arresting the young men and hauling them off to the filtration camps, where they were thrown into the pits. "What sort of a nation are we, the Russian people?" Politkovskaya asked. "A depraved society wants comfort and peace and quiet, and doesn't mind if the cost is other people's lives."

She was again barraged with "patriot" hate mail, and her articles were returned and defaced with the words "Stick it up your ass" and "Your dollars come from the CIA."

Politkovskaya returned to Grozny in February 2003, this time to offer testimony to a prosecutor who was weighing evidence against Captain Sergei Lapin, recently arrested because of her campaign to seek justice for his victims. Her visit was officially approved by Russia's Office of the Prosecutor, but, in lawless Chechnya, guns and wrath counted more than stamped documents.

The prosecutor of the case treated her like a criminal: she was interrogated through the night, not allowed to call her newspaper and not allowed to use the toilet. Then, in the early hours, she was ordered to leave and had to make her own way to the bombed-out home of a friend, who expressed amazement that she had not been kidnapped or shot. When she returned to Moscow she discovered that Lapin had been released on his own recognizance and that thirty of the documents relating to his case had disappeared. She promptly went to press with an article that announced she still had copies of those documents and that Lapin should be brought to trial.

In July 2003, another journalist at *Novaya Gazeta* was killed, this time the deputy editor of the paper, Yuri Shchekochikhin, who was poisoned while covering a scheme of money laundering, weapons trafficking and illegal oil smuggling, allegedly engineered by the FSB and the Prosecutor General's office. The authorities attributed the death to "a rare allergy" and, citing the issue of "medical privacy," sealed the coroner's report and wouldn't allow the dead man's own family to see it. At the funeral, Politkovskaya told Galina Mursalieva, "I will be the next."

Six months later, Simonov, Gannushkina and other leading lights of the human rights movement met with Putin at his first Presidential Human Rights Forum. In critical articles and in the diary she was intending to publish, Politkovskaya charged that the activists had played right into Putin's agenda, giving his autocracy credibility by attending the forum. They were "brought in closer to the Kremlin and sweetened up," she wrote. "It is a recurrent Russian problem: proximity to the Kremlin makes people slow to say no, and altogether less discriminating. . . . In Russia, the best way to subjugate even the most recalcitrant is not money, but bringing us in from the cold, at arm's length at first. The rebellious soon begin to subside. . . . Now even the admirers of Andrei Sakharov and Yelena Bonner are beginning to talk about Putin's charisma, saying he gives them grounds for hope."

The Glasnost Defense Foundation's Alexei Simonov recalled the shock he and his colleagues felt when they read Anna's columns and received her letters after the event. "She was always convinced she was 100 percent right," he told me. "Maybe she was accurate on her eyewitness reporting, but in this case she never phoned us to get the facts about what we were trying to accomplish. We were not cozying up to the Kremlin. It was a very hurtful thing to say to many brave and well-meaning people who were trying to have an effect on the president."

"Did you tell her that?" I asked.

"Of course I told her, but with Anna it made no difference."

She never apologized and her relationships with her allies were never truly patched up. As they often did, however, the liberals who were hurt by Politkovskaya swallowed their feelings. They were fully aware of the risks she was taking to tell the story of Chechnya.

Eight months after the forum, in late August 2004, Politkovskaya traveled to Chechnya to interview the man she described in her published diaries as "the deranged Ramzan Kadyrov" in his fortified home in Tsentoroy. Ramzan had taken over from his recently assassinated father, and in three months had earned a reputation for being the most ruthless political leader in the North Caucasus. Politkovskaya wrote in her diary that she was not confident she would get out of the twenty-seven-year-old prime minister's fortress alive. "They hold people prisoner in their cellars in Tsentoroy, and torture them like gangsters. No prosecutor challenges any of this. It is all hushed up. They know better than to poke their noses in. Tsentoroy is above the law, by Putin's will. The rules that apply to other people do not apply to Ramzan. He can do as he pleases because he is said to be fighting terrorists using his own methods. In fact, he's fighting nobody. He is in the business of robbery and extortion, disguised as 'the fight against terrorism.'"

She was kept waiting for seven hours before Kadryov appeared, surrounded by armed men. He sat down and put his leg up, "his foot, in a sock, almost level with my face." During the interview, Kadryov said to her, "You personally are the enemy. You are worse than Basayev"—a reference to the Chechen jihadist who had orchestrated the worst acts of terror against civilians. The comparison encouraged one of his aides to say, "You are an enemy of the Chechen people. . . . You should have to answer for this."

After the hour-long interview she was put into a car with three fighters, ostensibly to be taken back to Grozny. "I get into the vehicle and think that somewhere along the route, in the dark, with checkpoints everywhere, I am obviously going to be killed." But the driver she believed would be her assassin spent the ninety-minute drive to Grozny telling her about his career as a fighter and why he had joined Kadryov. "I know he is not going to kill me," she wrote, describing the end of another round of reporting in Chechnya.

Two days later, on the morning of September 1, the first day of school, another terrorist disaster struck Russia. In the town of Beslan, North Ossetia, bordering Chechnya, over two dozen militants, guns blazing, seized the elementary school and herded 1,200 children, parents and teachers into the gymnasium. They dragged one of several men they'd just murdered into the center of the gym as an example to the rest. "We've taken you hostage, and our demand is that Putin withdraw the troops from Chechnya," a gunman declared.

When Politkovskaya heard the news in Moscow, she rushed to the airport with one thought in mind: "Look for the Chechen separatist leader, Aslan Maskhadov, let him come out of hiding, let him go to the hostage-takers, and then ask them to free the children."

The airport was crowded with Russian and foreign journalists trying to get to Beslan. All flights to the Caucasus were postponed by the authorities, however, and she was told her prospects of getting on a plane to another southern destination were slim. While waiting, Politkovskaya used her cellphone to try to locate Maskhadov, something she knew was risky since her line was probably tapped and communicating with Chechen fighters was against the law. Suddenly a man approached her and introduced himself as an airport executive. "I'll put you on a flight to Rostov," he told her, referring to a city about three hundred miles from Beslan. In the minibus to the plane, he shared some information with her: the

FSB had instructed him to put her on the flight. "As I board," she later recounted, "my eyes meet those of three passengers sitting in a group: malicious eyes, looking at an enemy. But I don't pay attention. This is the way most FSB people look at me."

She refused the in-flight meal, but at 9:50 p.m., close to Rostov, finally accepted a glass of tea. Ten minutes later she felt an agony of stomach pain and realized she was about to pass out. She called out to the stewardess for help and heard her shout, "We're landing, hold on!" That was the last thing she remembered.

"Welcome back," said a nurse bending over her in hospital, half a day later. The nurse informed her that she had been close to dead when she was brought in. Then she whispered, "My dear, they tried to poison you," adding that all the tests done on her blood had been destroyed "on orders from on high."

Weak and very ill, Politkovskaya watched events in Beslan from the hospital, aching for the families and the children. The authorities and state television were claiming that only 354 people were being held hostage, but Beslan residents were holding up signs behind the backs of compliant reporters saying there were far more in the gym. "By September 3, the families of hostages are in a total news blackout," Politkovskaya wrote. "They are desperate; they all remember the experience of the Dubrovka theatre siege. . . . They remember how the government lied."

The lead actors were the same in this siege. The Chechen terrorists claimed allegiance to Shamil Basayev; and Putin, on state television, was promising that "our principal task in the current situation is to save the lives and health of the hostages." But the relatives of the hostages were less passive this time. "The school is surrounded by people with hunting rifles. They are ordinary people, the fathers and brothers of the hostages who have despaired of getting help from the state; they have decided to rescue their relatives themselves. . . . After the theatre siege in 2002, the hostages made this harrowing discovery: save yourself, because the state can only help to destroy you. And it's the same in Beslan now. Official lies continue. The media promote official views. They call it 'taking a state-friendly position,' meaning a position of approval of Vladimir Putin's actions. The media don't have a critical word to say about him."

Just after 1 p.m., September 3, an explosion went off within the gymnasium; apparently one of the terrorists, accidentally or purposely, set it off. This caused the fathers and brothers of those surrounding the school to open fire. The terrorists, thinking a rescue operation had been launched, returned fire. At that point, Russian Alpha commandos blew a hole in the gym wall to allow the hostages to escape, then launched an attack. But the attack was not coordinated: various sectors of the police and military and the civilians surrounding the school all joined the fray, and the firing was chaotic. The building caught fire. By the end of the battle, 396 hostages had been killed—42 more than the total number of people the government had claimed had been taken hostage—and over 700 were wounded.

In her coverage of the event, "Poisoned by Putin," Politkovskaya turned her wrath on her colleagues in the media. The oligarch owner of *Izvestia*, Vladimir Potanin, had fired his editor-in-chief, Raf Shakirov, for "deviating ever so slightly from the official line" in his reporting on Putin's handling of the affair. "You might think," she wrote, "that journalists staged an action of protest in support of Shakirov. Of course not. The Russian Union of Journalists and the Media Union kept mum. Only a journalist who is loyal to the establishment is treated as 'one of us. . . .' Putin declared that the Beslan tragedy had nothing to do with the Chechen crisis, so the media stopped covering the topic. . . . We are hurtling back into a Soviet abyss, into an information vacuum that spells death from our own ignorance. . . . If you want to go on working as a journalist, it's total servility to Putin. Otherwise, it can be death, the bullet, poison or trial—whatever our special services, Putin's guard dogs, see fit."

———

After her poisoning, Politkovskaya began to speak openly about her possible assassination to colleagues, the media, and to audiences who attended her overseas speaking engagements. Izmailov remembers that a few days after she moved into her flat on Lesnaya Street, she told him her building was being watched. He took it as a bad sign. "*Novaya Gazeta* had a stringer in Chechnya who wrote under the pen name Mainat Abdulaeva," Izmailov told me. "In autumn 2004, Mainat was visited by Chechens in uniform—they were followers of Kadyrov—and they said, 'If we don't find and kill Politkovskaya, we'll kill you.' I went to Chechnya and took Mainat to Moscow and, with the help of Simonov and the GDF, sent her abroad. But Anna refused to leave Russia. Each time she came back from a lecture tour, she found a lot of people who needed her help. From 2004 on, we knew her murder could happen at any minute."

That fall she brought a human arm back with her from Chechnya so that grieving parents could determine if it belonged to their dismembered son. She stored it in her freezer while she phoned around for a lab willing to test its DNA. With the arm still in her freezer, she set to finishing work on the galleys for her latest book, *Putin's Russia*. "Putin has, by chance, gotten hold of enormous power and has used it to catastrophic effect," she wrote in the closing chapter. "I dislike him because he does not like people. He despises us. He sees us as a means to his ends, a means for the achievement and retention of personal power, no more than that. Accordingly he believes he can do anything he likes with us, play with us as he sees fit, destroy us if he wishes. . . . I dislike this typical Soviet Checkist as he struts down the red carpet in the Kremlin on his way to the throne of Russia."

Ignoring the advice of all around her to tone it down, she continued to hammer at the FSB. "To this day," she told the *Guardian* on her book tour in London, "there's torture in any FSB branch in Chechnya. . . . Some have been tortured in such an intricate way that it's hard for me to believe that it was done by people who went to the same sort of schools that I did, who read the same textbooks."

To the Moscow newspaper *Kommersant,* she stated, "I was poisoned by FSB agents, and the KGB's Thirteenth Laboratory, which makes the poisons, is operating again."

At the same time, her periodic blowups with her colleagues at *Novaya Gazeta* continued. In July 2005 she wrote a polemical piece about the kidnapping and murder of a young Chechen allegedly by "Kadryov's troops." When the piece was spiked, she wrote in her diary, "*Novaya Gazeta* wants to stay out of trouble, so it is best not to give Ramzan Kadyrov too much grief, since he is in favor with the president."

"In her articles she very often used cynicism and sarcasm to express her points," *Novaya's* deputy editor, Vitaly Yaroshevsky, told me. "It was my opinion she was too cynical, too sarcastic. She certainly didn't like it when somebody interfered with her articles. She could turn into your enemy in a second. She quarreled even with the editor-in-chief when he tried to edit her material on sound journalistic principles. None of which is to say she was not extraordinarily brave and had our respect. One of her articles led to a conviction of the officer she reported on."

That officer was Sergei Lapin, sentenced in 2005 to eleven years in jail for torture. There was another row in the office when Muratov refused to allow Politkovskaya to go to Grozny to attend the sentencing. "There was a bitter exchange between them," a human rights activist named Natalya Estemirova commented. "She had worked so hard on this case; she had found the only lawyer in Moscow who would agree to go to Grozny; she had persuaded Amnesty International to pay his fees, and she had even gotten Russian TV channels to broadcast the trial." Nevertheless, Lapin's bosses were still at large, and there was no guarantee that Lapin himself would be immediately led away in chains. As it turned out, the Supreme Court overturned his conviction, and Lapin did only eleven months.*

---

*A year after Politkovskaya's death, Lapin was retried and convicted on the torture charges and sentenced to ten and a half years in jail.

———

Politkovskaya made her last trip to Chechnya in August 2006, two months before her murder. In her essay for English PEN, she admitted that she was tempting fate by showing up the same day one of her exposés of the Kadyrov regime was published. "A few days ago, on August 5, I was standing in a crowd of women in the central square of Kurchaloi, a dusty village in Chechnya," she wrote. "I was wearing a headscarf folded and tied in the manner favoured by many women my age in Chechnya. . . . This was essential if I was not to be identified, in which case nobody could say what might happen."

The *Novaya Gazeta* article on the stands that day featured her article describing a beheading she'd alleged was sponsored by Kadyrov's vice premier, with the headless body left in the street as a lesson to all who might defy young Ramzan. "I reached Chechnya at exactly the same time as the issue of our newspaper with the article," she wrote. "The women in the crowd tried to conceal me because they were sure the Kadyrov people would shoot me on the spot if they knew I was there. They reminded me that Kadyrov's government has publicly vowed to murder me. It was actually said at a meeting that his government had had enough, and that I was a condemned woman." And yet here she was in the belly of the beast, protected only by the sisterhood of headscarved women around her. The "people in Chechnya are afraid for me, and I find that very touching. They fear for me more than I fear for myself, and that is how I survive."

In the end, she said, her enemies may have made her into a "pariah," but she would not yield an inch—except to admit that she was hurting. "Of course I don't like the constant derisive articles about me that appear in other newspapers and on Internet sites presenting me as the madwoman of Moscow. I find it disgusting to live this way. I would like a bit more understanding.

"The main thing, however, is to get on with my job, to describe the life I see, to receive visitors every day in our editorial office who have nowhere else to bring their troubles."

A month later, Politkovskaya's mother Raisa was diagnosed with terminal cancer, and on September 22, her father died of a heart attack while on his way to see her.

Politkovskaya's last two weeks of life were split between taking care of her father's burial arrangements, visiting her mother, giving denunciatory interviews, and writing articles about Kadyrov and Putin with titles such as "Vindictive Collusion." She hoped to finish her last article, "We Declare You a Terrorist," on Sunday, October 8.

Izmailov last saw Politkovskaya on October 5, the day she gave a Radio Liberty interview in which she told Russians that Kadyrov was "a coward" and that she had exposed "one criminal case about the abduction of two people carried out with the participation of Ramzan A. Kadryov."

"She looked very tired," Izmailov told me. "It seemed to me that she had become very much older. She admitted it was very difficult for her to work in Chechnya, and that many people didn't understand why she was so dedicated, why she kept going there, but she said that if not for her, none of the tragedies she wrote about would be known. People had had enough of Chechnya and she was very, very ashamed of that. Her two kids loved her and visited her, but they didn't understand her devotion to her subject. Her husband had left her so many years ago. It's very difficult to live such a life. She was feeling very alone at the end."

Anna's office-mate Galina Mursalieva was at home on the afternoon of October 7. "I got a call from the editor," she told me. "He didn't explain anything, just said drop everything and come to the office immediately. I called a colleague and he told me Anna had been killed. I forgot everything, my driver's license, my cellphone, and just got in my car and drove to the office. Up to the minute I got there, I didn't believe it was true. I just didn't believe that nothing could be done to save her. I knew they had shot her but I wanted to believe that *something* could be done, perhaps a blood transfusion—that she could be saved. When I reached the office, there were quite a lot of cameras there, and then I knew. Everyone took pictures of Anna's table, and I just sat at my desk, looking at her chair."

At 8 p.m. three detectives entered her office. They stayed until the early morning, cataloguing and boxing Politkovskaya's files. "It was the most devastating thing in my life to see all her papers and private things taken out of her drawer," Mursalieva said. "The detectives were just shocked by the quantity of letters. One of them told me, 'We go to such cases very often, but I've never seen so many letters.' I told them, 'They're from people all over Russia who need her help.' Then I helped them sort through quite a lot of criminal cases that Anna was investigating. They thought they might give some clues to the identity of who killed her."

A year later, eleven men were arrested in connection with the murder of Anna Politkovskaya. They included Russian Interior Ministry officials, a police officer, several Chechen criminals, a Chechen politician and an ex-FSB major named Pavel Ryaguzov, who was accused of supplying Anna's address to the killers. Neither the shooter nor the mastermind were among those arrested, and Yuri Chaika, Russia's prosecutor general, declared that Politkovskaya's murder had been ordered from abroad with the aim of destabilizing Russia. Ramzan Kadyrov, now president of Chechnya, hailed the arrests. "Only if those responsible are punished will attempts to murder journalists, businessmen and politicians cease," he said. One by one, however, seven of the men arrested were released from jail. "Some of the detainees have been released, it's true," President Putin told a news conference in Germany on October 15, 2007. "It speaks to the quality of the investigative work. In general they are on the right track." By the second anniversary of Politkovskaya's death an ethnic Chechen, Rustam Makhmudov, had been named as the shooter, although he remained at large. On October 15, 2008, two of Makhmudov's relatives and a Moscow police officer went to trial on charges of being accessories to the murder. The mastermind, according to the authorities, remained unknown, although one of Anna's deputy editors testified that he believed the killers were working on behalf of the FSB, whose agents, he said, had been tailing her before she was killed.

On January 19, 2009, press freedom advocates awaiting a verdict in the murder trial learned that yet another *Novaya Gazeta* journalist had been killed—the fourth since 2000. Anastasia Baburova, just twenty-five years old, was in the midst of investigating ultra-nationalist groups in Russia when she and a human rights lawyer who had once represented Politkovskaya were gunned down in Moscow. The journalist and the lawyer, Stanislav Markelov, had just left a press conference where Markelov had protested the early release of a former army colonel who'd been imprisoned in 2003 for raping and murdering a young Chechen girl.

A month later, on February 19, the three men accused as accessories in the murder of Politkovskaya were acquitted, even as journalists at *Novaya Gazeta* declared that the prosecution's case had been inept and that it was the mastermind who should have been on trial. At this writing, it is more likely that *Novaya Gazeta* journalists who protest impunity will themselves face prosecution. New legislation is now being backed by Vladimir Putin that will allow the Russian authorities to charge any government critic with treason, a crime punishable by twenty years in prison.

Three weeks after Politkovskaya's murder, I took the subway from *Novaya Gazeta* back to the Moskvich Hotel. I was still, as Simonov called me, "totally illiterate," and "deaf and dumb besides," but I'd become acutely aware of something that needed no translation, something that was universal to our species and that, I felt, had driven Anna Politkovskaya. Yes, she was filled with selfless outrage at the atrocities she'd seen, and wanted to help the victims. Yes, she'd endured a breakdown and trauma that probably inclined her to take chances that invited her fate. But shame, I believe, was what drove her. Shame for the period during which she hadn't reported the First Chechen War and its atrocities. Shame that twenty-first-century Russians could continue to perpetrate such atrocities; that ordinary Russians could support them; that fellow *liberal* Russians wanted to look the other way; and, finally, that Russians had embraced a KGB colonel who was the unconcerned author of those atrocities, one who was herding them gleefully back to the authoritarian state from which they'd emerged.

Mercifully, there was a woman at the front desk of the Moskvich who spoke a few words of English. Over a blasting game show on the TV, she helped me book a cab to the airport, then handed me the bill and asked, "You enjoy vacation?"

I told her I wasn't on vacation. "I'm writing about Anna Politkovskaya."

She inclined her head with a pleasant expression.

"Who?"

FIVE

THE BOYS FROM CAR CITY

Valery Ivanov and Alexei Sidorov, Russia

TOGLIATTI SPRAWLS FIVE HUNDRED miles southeast of Moscow, just above a massive hydroelectric dam that strangles the Volga River. Endless blocks of dilapidated housing projects are ringed by fuming chemical plants, cement factories and—the jewel in the industrial crown—the 1,500-acre car plant known as Avtovaz. The plant was the brainstorm of the founder of the Italian communist party, Palmiro Togliatti, who, in the 1950s, persuaded Fiat to partner with the Soviet Union to build Socialism's Detroit. The dam was constructed, the eighteenth-century town of Stavropol was flooded, and a hundred square miles of birch forest made way for a dynamic new city. In 1966, the first boxy Lada rolled out of Avtovaz, and by the time the Soviet Union collapsed twenty-five years later, the plant was producing a million cars a year.

Then came Avtovaz's abrupt privatization: the company's government directors cornered the shares and Togliatti's criminals cornered the directors. By 2004, Avtovaz was losing $30 million annually to mobsters, four gang wars for control of its production had left five hundred dead, the city's treasury had been heisted by corrupt officials, and six journalists who'd covered the mayhem had been murdered with impunity. Togliatti's 750,000 residents were so used to hearing about bodies floating in the Volga that when they saw a headline like "Another Record Day!" they instantly assumed it referred to rubouts.

Most of the inside information we know about the villainous world of Togliatti during that bloody decade comes from the journalism of the city's most honored and beloved newspaper editors, Valery Ivanov and Alexei Sidorov. Best friends since college, they had begun their groundbreaking reporting just after Avtovaz's privatization in early 1993, when Ivanov was only twenty-three and Sidorov twenty-one. Three years later, Ivanov founded the *Togliatti Observer*, hired Sidorov as his deputy editor, and together they began writing daily exposés about the evolving but always corrupt relationship between the city's politicians, the mafia, the police, and the directors of Avtovaz. Nothing was too risky for their tabloid paper. When gangsters threatened to hang them from their heels or offered them bribes, they put it on the front page, just under their cheeky motto, "We Print the News Others Are Afraid Of." When they were served libel notices by the mayor or city prosecutor, they published the legal correspondence. And when the FSB promised them years of imprisonment for revealing state secrets, Ivanov told the officers, "The file we have on you is thicker than the file you have on us." In 2000, Ivanov won a seat on city council, where for two years he both investigated corruption as a committee chair and exposed it in his paper as a journalist. Many of Togliatti's citizens hoped he would become their next mayor. Perhaps too many.

After Ivanov was murdered contract-style in front of his apartment house in April 2002, Sidorov at first refused to take over his position, fearing he was next. Then, a few weeks later, he made the decision to throw himself into the line of fire. He not only became editor but launched two overlapping investigations that he predicted would rock Togliatti's power structure. One was an inquiry into the murder of Ivanov. The other was the completion of the last story Ivanov had been working on—a task Sidorov accomplished on October 9, 2003, the night he left the newspaper office for the last time. The documents he was carrying, which proved the story, were not among the possessions police said they found on his body after he was stabbed to death near his front door.

I was met at the Samara airport, forty miles south of Togliatti, by Alexei Mironov, who had started working at the *Observer* shortly before Ivanov was murdered and had recently succeeded the editor who had replaced Sidorov. The interim editor had tried to lighten the focus of the paper with good-news coverage and celebrities, causing its readership to plunge. "The investors like young editors," Mironov, who was thirty-one, told me. He wore dark-tinted glasses and, though reserved and somewhat bookish, seemed alert to everything going on around us, darting glances over my shoulder and around the arrivals lounge. On the drive to Togliatti we discussed the murder of Politkovskaya, then I asked if he was under threat, too.

"They would not be so stupid to kill a third editor here," he replied. "Still, we have to be cautious." He said that local authorities throughout Russia had interpreted Putin's swat-team takeover of NTV as giving them a green light to use force against independent newspapers like his own. And that included murderous force against editors, journalists and financial backers. After Sidorov's murder, in fact, the *Observer*'s investors had bailed out. The new ones kept their identities secret.

Mironov told me that the paper had thoroughly investigated the motives for the editors' killings and had come up with a card deck of suspects but no incriminating evidence. "Don't expect any murder-solving breakthroughs on your visit," he advised. I told him I hadn't come to Togliatti to investigate the murderers, but the victims. From Colombia to Russia, outraged politicians, cops and gangsters killed journalists for pretty much the same reason, but each journalist risked being murdered according to his or her own compelling logic. I said I was seeking answers to three questions. Why, in a town where journalists were being murdered one after another, had Ivanov and Sidorov defied the threats from all directions? Why, when they'd barely earned enough to live on, had they said no to fat envelopes pushed their way? And why had the frightened Sidorov stayed on a story that had possibly gotten Ivanov murdered and that Sidorov could reasonably expect might get him murdered, too?

Mironov looked at the flat road ahead for a pensive moment. "Yes, each had his personal reasons," he remarked, "but for both of them, this was their home." He fell quiet for another moment, then added, "If you are a journalist and you are too fearful to expose the men who are stealing your city, then you can feel you are betraying your home. And if you stay a journalist, you can feel you are being humiliated each day."

The *Observer* occupied the first floor of an office building on Lenina Street, in the Central District, a few blocks north of the mayor's office and the city council building. Unlike the headquarters of most city papers, no logo faced the street. Instead, a small faded sign was screwed into the redbrick wall beside what looked like a service entrance at the back of the building. The first thing you saw on entering through the heavy steel door were photos of Ivanov and Sidorov on the corridor wall, with a couple of the frames wreathed in black crepe. They were both dark-haired, acutely intelligent-looking men who bore a close enough resemblance to each other that they could have been handsome brothers. In one photo, Ivanov, wearing a jacket and tie, looked directly at the camera, a smile crinkling his eyes, while the younger, frailer Sidorov, in a sweater, leaned his head on Ivanov's shoulder, his arm around his neck. Sidorov looked boyish and vulnerable, almost as if he were clinging to his friend and editor.

"You can see, they were different personalities," Mironov said, while I photographed them. He led me down the narrow corridor, off which were a couple of offices with about a dozen reporters working at computers. He took a seat behind his desk in the editor's office, the walls lined with awards the newspaper had won over the years. "Ivanov was an optimist and an idealist, very forceful in his manner, a fluent public speaker," he said, glancing through his messages. "He was threatened many times but it was not in his nature to show fear. He would joke about the threats."

And Sidorov?

"Sidorov was much gentler and more sensitive than Ivanov. He was very frightened, and he spoke of it." The two journalists had met at a school newspaper in college, after which Sidorov had stood in his older friend's shadow, following his lead and seeking his approval. "After Ivanov was shot, Sidorov told us he didn't have Ivanov's abilities as a businessman. Naturally, he was worried he would be killed, too. But he was loyal to the memory of Ivanov, and I think that made him take the job and drove him forward, despite the threats against him."

We ran down the list of people I wanted to interview, each of whom had threatened Ivanov and Sidorov, and Mironov scratched off a gangster named Igor Filipov—"murdered"—and another named Igor Sirotenko—"too dangerous. Anyway, I don't know where he is now."

While Mironov called the people on my list, the Observer's lead crime reporter, Oleg Novikov, came in. A baby-faced man with the build of a wrestler, he was dressed all in black, Russian gangster–style. He'd got his start in journalism in his native city of Samara and, because of his ability to get along with volatile sources, Ivanov had hired him in 1999, then put him in charge of the investigative unit that specialized in the town's narcotics scene. He seemed like he could handle himself in a street fight with the Chechen drug dealers he still wrote about. He had been working with Sidorov on Ivanov's last story, attempting to trace the millions of dollars that had gone missing after a powerful gangster named Dmitri Ruzlyaev was murdered. After Sidorov was killed too, Novikov had sworn in an affidavit that "it's probable the reason for Alexei's murder was his intention to publish the article and name all the names of the people who received a percentage of Ruzlyaev's money." He'd added, however, that "Sidorov did not tell me these names."

"Ivanov was killed for many reasons," Novikov said now. "Primarily for his investigations but also because he would have been the next mayor. It's one of the most powerful positions in Russia, just behind the mayor of Moscow. They had to stop him."

"Who's 'they'?" I asked. "The politicians? The gangsters?"

"Same thing," Mironov chimed in, between calls.

"So who killed Sidorov, then? The same people?"

Novikov raised his huge hands, palms up. "The documents he was carrying went missing, but these things come down through several layers. To get rid of somebody it's nothing to give the criminals the nod from above. Somebody just says, 'I don't like him.' His assistant hears, the assistant says the same thing to his assistant. Finally, a criminal hears and there is a murder."

"Did they mention any specific threats on their last days?"

"They were too busy with the articles that caused the threats," Novikov replied. "They were actually both in good moods on their last day. If you go through our back issues, you'll see how many people they pissed off and for how many years."

"We'll be here all day if we list them," Mironov cracked, as he left the office to arrange an interview for me with the deputy editor, Rimma Mikhareva.

On his thick fingers Novikov enumerated three of those who were particularly offended by Ivanov and Sidorov. "One thing I can tell you: neither the killers nor the ones who ordered the killings have to worry."

Mironov came back in the office. "Rimma Mikhareva says she has time to talk now."

And so, through the eyes of others and the murdered editors' own journalism, I began to get to know Ivanov and Sidorov. I addressed a thousand questions to their friends and enemies, the reporters in the newsroom, the parents of Sidorov, the wife and sister of Ivanov, the city councilmen with whom Ivanov had worked, and the police chief who had first investigated Sidorov's still-unsolved murder.

Valery Ivanov's writing career was signposted by three very different works. In 1978, when he was nine years old, he wrote a novella called *Hero of Dugon*, about alien cannibals who invade a peaceful planet. For help, the citizens turn to a once-disparaged wise man who forgives their insults and uses telepathic powers to persuade the cannibals to eat one another.

Twenty-two years later, as part of his campaign for a seat on city council, Ivanov published a six-page memoir in his newspaper. "The greatest reward of my early career was the interest and appreciation of the people," he wrote, recalling his first year as a journalist, when he'd used the pen name Hamlet. "Hamlet became the people's hero who uncovered the mafia."

Then, in 2002, on the day before his murder, Ivanov composed a poem that is today inscribed on the polished face of his black marble gravestone.

In this chaotic world
Pulling us to the darkness
Oh, my Lord, give me strength
To keep Thy kindness.

In this world without ethics
Where everyone is alone
Oh, my Lord, can't You see
How much we need kindness?

Ivanov's first written work, his older sister told me, was influenced by his mother; his last by his father. His career was the embodiment of the two. "He was an ethical idealist," Stella Ivanova explained. "He was ambitious, he sought glory, but not power for its own sake. He wanted the power to change things for the good and be recognized for doing that."

"As a hero?" I asked.

"A hero of the helpless."

Valery Ivanov was born on November 5, 1969, in Abkhazia, then an autonomous republic within Soviet Georgia. He was plagued by colds and allergies, as well as by the bullying of Abkhazian classmates who had been taught by their parents to hate Russians as occupiers. He didn't play sports, went straight home after school and had few friends. Stella, an auburned-haired computer programmer in Samara, said her mother read children's books to Valery after school, reassuring him that his strength of mind would compensate for his frail body.

"My mother was descended from Turks and she had an iron will," Stella told me in Togliatti's Sicilian Pizzeria, near where Valery had lived. "She read him stories about real children with real problems and told him, 'Knowledge will give you understanding, and understanding will give you confidence. Because when you understand the wrong behavior of others, you will have the power to protect the people they harm.' I remember that all her children's stories had this moral for us: 'Understand what is wrong and use your mental strength to change it.'"

Valery's father, Yvgeny, a music teacher, offered another perspective on dealing with bad people. He was a much gentler sort than his wife, and read fairy tales to Valery, after which the two would compose their own tales, again with a predominant moral — that kindness is more powerful than cruelty. "My father truly believed that if you have kindness you need nothing else," Stella said. "He told us that you can yell at a music student, you can hit him, and he will play, but not so well or originally as if you are kind to him. He will do more if he loves his teacher than if he fears him."

When Valery entered the second grade, the verbal bullying of his classmates became physical, and the family decided to move a thousand miles north, to the new city of Togliatti, where housing—always scarce in the Soviet Union—was relatively easy to obtain. They took up residence in the Avtozavodsky business district, whose amenities drew professionals and party bureaucrats. To the east was the working class Central District, home to baroque government buildings that had been relocated from Stavropol before the old city had been flooded. Farther east was the river port district of Komsomolski, where Valery's future partner, Alexei Sidorov, lived.

The move to Togliatti did not improve Valery Ivanov's social life much. Even in the authoritarian Soviet Union, the young city had a subculture of ethnic gangs, chiefly Chechens, Tatars and Georgians who ran prostitution and gambling rackets and were not averse to random acts of hooliganism in all three districts. Valery came straight home from school every day and for entertainment read voraciously, dreaming of joining the circus or the air force, or traveling to outer space on a Soyuz rocket. His favorite author was Jules Verne, and after writing his space fantasy, he made a career choice. "Right after I stopped dreaming of becoming a famous clown, cosmonaut or fighter pilot," he wrote in his newspaper memoir, "I decided to become a writer, or at least a journalist. I made the decision at nine years old, after I finished *The Mysterious Island*. Captain Nemo had a friend who was a reporter. I liked this reporter more than the greedy captain."

Ivanov began his career by composing humorous news articles about his school, an activity his teachers believed detracted from class decorum. By the time he was in secondary school, he was known as the class troublemaker. His parents were frequently called in to be lectured by the headmaster, who said Ivanov's essays on Russian history drew antisocial conclusions regarding the loyalty of the southern republics—an insight based on firsthand experience but assessed as dangerously precocious for a Soviet-schooled fifteen-year-old. Ivanov's grades were never more than 3 out of a possible 5, and because of his conflicts with party-minded teachers, he eventually lost interest in school.

As he emerged from puberty, his allergies diminished and he became physically tougher, socially extroverted and openly sarcastic in his retorts to his teachers' criticism. Girls were paying him attention now and one invited him to enroll in her folk-dance class, where he became adept at leaping about with sword and tambourine in the Cossack and Hopak Ukrainian traditions. Folk dancing did not help his grades, though, and he failed his first entrance examination for the teaching college in Samara, the region's capital, where many students with no interest in engineering wound up. He took a year off and went to work in a steel shop attached to Avtovaz, keeping a diary of the daily concerns of his co-workers and writing poems about them, each one titled with a worker's name.

At eighteen, he took the teaching college entrance exam again and passed. A year later, he met two people at the college to whom he would remain devoted for the remainder of his short life: his future wife, Elena, and his future partner in investigative journalism, Alexei Sidorov.

Sidorov was a native Tolyatin, as the locals call themselves. His father, Vladimir, of Jewish heritage, was originally from Penza, about two hundred miles west of Togliatti, and had moved to the new city when the plant opened in 1966, eventually becoming an engineering professor at Togliatti's Polytechnic University. Tatanya, Alexei's mother, was from Chilyabinsk, a top-secret military town in the Urals, and was the daughter of a colonel in the Red Army. Alexei, born on his parents' first wedding anniversary, December 29, 1971, was an only child.

He was a hypersensitive boy, with few friends and no interest in sports. His parents remember him sitting in front of the television set at five years old, tears pouring down his cheeks, inconsolable because a cartoon rabbit had been caught by foxes. He showed an early love of nature and was close to his maternal grandfather, Colonel Pavel Yanko, who would take him on walks in the Zhiguli Hills above the Volga. Under the birch trees overlooking the river, Alexei would sit enthralled as his grandfather related his dangerous adventures during the Second World War.

In grade school, Alexei began reading a book a day, concentrating—partly because of his grandfather—on Russian military exploits. Still shy, polite and soft-spoken, his grades in academic subjects were always a perfect 5. Then, as he entered his teens, he went through a personality change, and his reading at the time contributed to it. "He was such a sweet boy, but on the inside he yearned to be tougher," Vladimir Sidorov told me in his apartment in the Komsomolski district, not far from where his son was murdered. "He wanted to be different from what he was, more like his grandfather, and he discovered a literary model."

Alexei became enamored with a rebellious figure in Soviet literature, Mikhail Saltykov-Shchedrin, a nineteenth-century satirical journalist and novelist who, in *The Story of One Town*, bravely mocked the czar's bureaucracy that lorded over the fictional town Glupov, or Sillytown—based in part on Vladimir Sidorov's hometown of Penza. The Jonathan Swift of Russian literature, Saltykov-Shchedrin lampooned the greed of the urban autocracy in contrast to the dire poverty in the provinces. Banished from Saint Petersburg to Penza for good, he wrote the novel *The House of Greed* (Alexei Sidorov's favorite), then turned to fables that eighty years later would influence George Orwell's writing of *Animal Farm*.

"My son developed a vicarious mental relationship with Saltykov-Shchedrin," Vladimir Sidorov told me. "Alexei was not a rebel in personality, but that was the kind of personality he was drawn to. He wanted to model himself on someone with the qualities he didn't naturally have."

At the end of his life, Saltykov-Shchedrin summed up his mission as a writer in words that Sidorov later taped to his bedroom wall: "The sole object of my literary work was to unfailingly protest against the greed, hypocrisy, falsehood, theft, treachery, and stupidity of modern Russians."

In the midst of this intellectual awakening, Sidorov began to write socially conscious stories in Saltykov-Shchedrin's style— highly literate fables about herd animals and their cruel overseers, which he said were inspired by observing the long lines of tired Avtovaz workers queued up to take the bus to work in the morning. In the fall of 1989, at seventeen, Sidorov entered the Samara teachers college, telling his parents he intended to become, not a teacher, but a writer. Two weeks into his first semester, he showed up at the school newspaper, where he introduced himself to a star student reporter named Valery Ivanov.

Ivanov was now so confident about his abilities that some at the school newspaper considered him rude and aggressive. He preferred to think of himself, in his sister's words, as "honest and audacious."

This was a time of great promise in Russia. Gorbachev's policy of glasnost made it permissible for journalists to criticize the state and its officials, at least in theory, and Ivanov took full advantage of the new freedoms by making excursions into the countryside and interviewing farmers about the bribes they were forced to pay state truckers to transport their privately grown vegetables to market. His low grades, however, coupled with his critical articles about the university administration, caused him to be expelled at the beginning of the next term. One month after Sidorov met him, Ivanov took a job as a private tutor in the countryside, a stretch he later referred to as his "year of exile."

By then Ivanov had become romantically involved with Elena, an attractive accounting major one year his senior. "He was a rebel who went his own way in everything, and the funniest boy I'd ever met," Elena told me, sitting beside her sister-in-law in the Sicilian Pizzeria. "Before he got thrown out of school, we lived in the same co-ed dorm. I first met him when he came to our room with some other boys to help us hang shower curtains." For Elena's amusement, the theatrical Valery turned the curtains into a sari, a sail and then a parachute. They kissed for the first time a couple of months later at a school New Year's party, and after Ivanov was expelled, he walked twenty miles each way to visit her on Saturday nights. When he was accepted back into school a year later, he proposed, and they were married in November.

Friends who saw Ivanov and Sidorov at work on the school paper during that 1990–91 school year remarked that the quiet, painfully shy Sidorov always had his eyes on the older Ivanov, as if studying him for cues on how to behave. Voluble, sociable and a natural director of the events around him, Ivanov accepted this hero worship as his due but never took advantage of it, respectfully asking Sidorov's advice on grammar and complimenting him effusively on his writing. When Ivanov briefly wore a bohemian beard, Sidorov grew one; after Ivanov married Elena, Sidorov married a stunning student he'd met at the college, named Olga. Like Ivanov, Sidorov began writing articles about social conditions in the Samara countryside. Finally, even though Sidorov's grades were exemplary and he could have attained any academic goal he wanted, when Ivanov quit school for good in June 1991 and got a laborer's job, Sidorov dropped out too, and took a job in a Samara machine shop.

"From the very beginning, my son recognized that Ivanov was going places," Vladimir Sidorov said. "Alexei lived within his mind, like an artist, but Ivanov was a leader. I think that when Alexei looked at Valery he saw a self-made man—the forceful businessman, the wheeler-dealer, the politician. My son was none of those things and never would be any of those things. He just had faith that Ivanov would lead the way and provide him with opportunity. Later on, he was willing to do everything he could to help make Ivanov successful so he could thrive under his wing."

Ivanov now had a daughter to support, however, and for a while article-writing took a back seat in his life, as it did in Sidorov's. Then, in late 1992, an opportunity presented itself to Ivanov that would set him, and his loyal friend, on a path that, a decade later, would end in their murders.

While Ivanov and Sidorov had been away in Samara, the lid had come off the old regime in Togliatti, creating a lawless atmosphere in an already volatile town that produced 2 percent of Russia's gross national income and employed 110,000 assembly-line workers. In the face of Boris Yeltsin's plans to privatize Avtovaz, the city's criminal groups began scrambling for position. Two Slavic gangsters in their late twenties emerged to dominate the city's multiethnic gang scene. Vladimir "Mate" Vdovin, a martial arts master who ran a car-parts theft ring out of Avtovaz, formed a pact with the Tatar gangs. Dmitri "Big Dima" Ruzlyaev, Vdovin's former best friend and bodyguard, allied himself with the Chechens. As shares of Avtovaz were acquired by the company's onetime government directors through a series of backroom deals and phony front companies—indeed, as *all* business in the bustling town was corruptly privatized—the gangsters saw no reason why they shouldn't get in on the heist. That set the stage for a war to see which gang would control Togliatti's legitimate and illegitimate enterprises.

The first major gang violence in post-Soviet Russia (later called the First Gang War) erupted in the fall of 1992 over control of three criminal rackets: *adgrus*—a protection fee that "ensured" Ladas were delivered to dealers from Avtovaz; *obshchak*—an underground bank set up by the gangs to buy krysha from the authorities; and *naperstok*—a gambling shell game popular along the Volga. After street battles that involved as many as a hundred gunmen and a dozen tit-for-tat murders, the First Gang War

ended in a truce, with Vdovin taking nominal control of the
obshak bank, and with the *adgrus* protection fee and the *naperstok*
gambling racket split between Vdovin and Ruzlyaev. With hundreds of millions of dollars to be gained from the infiltration of
Avtovaz, no one expected the truce to last.

Curiously, to readers of Togliatti's newspapers, all this violence
had occurred with no names attached. Typically a public shoot-
out would take place, two or three bodies would be picked up,
rumors and gossip would sweep the city, but, aside from the bare
details of the event appearing on the back pages—usually in the
context of a reassuring quote from a policeman claiming an isolated crime had been "solved"—the First Gang War had gone
almost unreported. This self-censorship, the order of the day in
Soviet times, arose partly out of terror of the gangsters and partly
out of an age-old Russian penchant to accept things as they are,
borne of a knowledge that nothing will really change and that only
trouble will come down on the bearers of bad news.

Observing this willful silence, a short, crew-cut literature professor at the Samara teachers college, Alexander Kynazev, perceived
a great opportunity. He called the school's former newspaper star,
Valery Ivanov, and told him he was thinking of launching a publication. Ivanov phoned Sidorov and brought him along to a job
interview with Kynazev. After explaining that their inexperience
was an asset in the new Russia, Kynazev hired them. He decided to
name his newspaper *Vse i Vsya*—"Everything and Everybody." He
said he would launch it in the spring of 1993.

"Not the least of Kynazev's great strengths was his complete freedom
from ideological dogma," Ivanov wrote in his memoir seven years
later. "There were no taboo topics. Kynazev told his young journalists, 'You have to write about everything, no matter what the
circumstances. People have the right to know what happens around
them.' In short, we had full freedom, and we used it."

To a twenty-three-year-old freshman journalist sent out to find news, Togliatti was a candy store, and Ivanov felt like the only kid among the shelves. "Our colleagues from other newspapers," he later remembered, "thought that the main goal of journalism was to publish government reports." The more timid Sidorov, however, told Kynazev he was a little fearful of plunging into articles about gang warfare, and, at his boss's direction, began his professional career by reporting on the scandalous liaisons between monks and prostitutes. Ivanov jumped right into an article about the gangs.

"The most difficult part was to begin," he wrote. "I knew there were killings, but I didn't know who was doing the killing or who was being killed. There were no facts and no reasons supplied by the police. They hid all useful information and gave me no clue about what was really going on." Some Togliatti police officers told him there was no organized crime in the city because there had been none in the Soviet era. ("If we don't have organized crime, why should we fight it?" they said.) Other officers warned that none of what was taking place was his business and that if he pursued the subject he would cause himself trouble. Ivanov ignored the veiled threat and continued to troll the city for a police source who would be sympathetic to his ends. He wound up in a late-night meeting with an investigator who instructed him to enter the station disguised as a criminal informant. After keeping Ivanov cooling his heels in the booking room for hours, the officer finally called him in and secretly gave him a fifteen-minute rundown on the main gangland players.

Ivanov was thrilled by the cloak-and-dagger episode, and over the next two weeks he staked out various locations where he had been told he could see for himself what was going on. Indeed, once he knew what to look for, all he had to do was stand at the back gate of Avtovaz to witness gangsters buttonholing car dealers to collect *adgrus*. Dealers who refused to pay were invited into a Mercedes and taken for a ride into the Zhiguli Hills. If they still refused, a dead dog was thrown on their lawn or their children were approached. It was useless to report the threats to the police because the police provided the gangsters with krysha. Ivanov titled his article "The Blood-Colored Car," and also named Vladimir Vdovin and Dmitri Ruzlyaev as chieftains of the city's two most powerful crime groups.

"The Blood-Colored Car" was among the first articles published on organized crime in Russia, and the first in the state of Samara. "We felt ourselves pioneers who discovered secrets for our readers that, before our exposés, were carefully hidden aspects of life in Samara state," Ivanov later remembered. "We didn't get a lot of money, but money wasn't important to us at all. My biggest reward for this accomplishment was the interest and appreciation of the people. . . . For the first time, my readers started to talk openly about organized crime." In large part because of this article, President Yeltsin established what would later become known as the Central Agency for Combating Organized Crime, with a counterpart in the Samara region. Ivanov was suddenly famous, or at least his pen name was. For safety's sake, he had published the article under the byline Hamlet. In his memoir, he expressed his joy at attaining what he had been after since he was nine years old. "Hamlet," Ivanov wrote, "became the people's hero who had uncovered the mafia."

The police didn't see it that way; they invested their energies in denying the story, announcing that Hamlet was probably guilty of criminal mischief for unnecessarily alarming the public. When this tactic proved counterproductive—sales of the magazine actually increased—they called him in for interrogation. They threatened him with prosecution for revealing classified police information and pressured him to reveal the name of his cop source. Ivanov countered by citing Boris Yeltsin's constitutional guarantees of freedom of the press, hinting that he could make a call and tap a Kremlin friend with krysha. The police let him go without gaining any information, and Ivanov returned to the magazine in triumph.

His exhilaration about writing for *Everything and Everybody* was short-lived. When Kynazev attempted to edit his next article, the headstrong journalist was furious, complaining that he "literally felt raped." Kynazev, the literature professor, replied coolly that he knew what good writing was and published the article with his stylistic changes. At the beginning of 1994, after barely eight months at the magazine, Ivanov quit in a huff and moved with Elena and their three-year-old daughter, Maria, to Togliatti. He left a publication that, largely because of his spectacular reporting, now had a circulation of 120,000, the highest in Samara state. He walked into the offices of a Togliatti business magazine called *Million* and was hired the same day.

Despite its name, *Million* did not have the budget to hire Sidorov and, left behind in Samara, the younger journalist's life and career began going in the opposite direction of Ivanov's. His short marriage to Olga was falling apart and he was miserable working under Kynazev, who now seemed interested in covering "everything" only so long as it increased readership. After Ivanov quit, Kynazev became most interested in "everybody"—scandal.

Years later, Vladimir Voronov, the editor of a competing publication, *Samarska Weekly*, called Kynazev "the most scandalous editor in Samara . . . the father of yellow journalism. . . . The main criteria of *Everything and Everybody* was a complete absence of journalistic standards. . . . They talked about who drinks with whom, who sleeps with whom . . . their low information arising from even lower sources."

Monks sleeping with prostitutes was not what Sidorov was interested in writing about anymore. When he offered to cover business, as Ivanov was doing, Kynazev said no, and assigned him to a series of stories about the sex lives of local celebrities. Sidorov hung on at the magazine for a few more months, but when he and Olga divorced in 1994, he quit and went back to work at his old job in the Samara machine shop.

After a time, he retreated to Togliatti, taking up residence in a small apartment his parents rented for him, where he spent his days staring at the walls and chain smoking. Realizing his twenty-two-year-old son was obsessing about his failures, Vladimir Sidorov took him down to the Polytechnic University and got him a job finding part-time work for students at the school's employment agency. Alexei hated it. By the end of 1994, he seemed more and more depressed and directionless, perhaps all the more so because Ivanov was excelling at *Million*. Ivanov was now the head of *Million*'s one-man organized crime department, but, to Sidorov's despair, the magazine still had no budget to hire him.

By then Togliatti's Second Gang War was in full swing, this time over control of the cars coming off the day and night shifts at Avtovaz. Dmitri Ruzlyaev's coalition of gangs went to war with Vladimir Vdovin's bunch, shooting up the streets, killing sixty-six people in less than a year and earning Togliatti an international reputation for being the most violent and gang-ridden city in Russia. Because the killers Ivanov covered appeared in court and then were set free, he took the corrupt behavior of the court system personally: "I felt insulted by this [lack of] reaction to my articles, and decided to make the authorities act." He began tracking all arrests of gang members and following their trials, reporting on the often-faulty memories of officers on the stand. As his chronicle of illogical acquittals length-ened, Ivanov incurred the unified wrath of the arresting officers, the judges and the criminals. *Million* received gangster death threats, and then a prosecutor and judge who were trying a shooting case he was reporting showed up at the *Million* office to tell Ivanov they knew where he lived. He carried on covering the trial to its end, after which the prosecutor and judge launched a libel suit, not basing their suit on a defamatory remark by Ivanov but on the way he contrasted the facts of the case with the suspended sentence of the accused. *Million* refused to print a retraction, and as the regional newspapers began to give coverage to the filings in the suit that Ivanov sent reporters, the judge and prosecutor realized they were doing themselves more harm than good and dropped their case.

With that victory under his belt, Ivanov began planning a series of articles about the direct connections among the courts, the police and the gangs run by Vdovin, Ruzlyaev and another up and coming gangster named Igor "Sirota" Sirotenko. But the editor of *Million* was growing tired of dealing with death threats and lawsuits. In addition, the directors of Avtovaz, the main advertiser in the city, had just informed the editor that they were unhappy with the bad press Ivanov was bringing down on their heads. The editor told Ivanov he didn't need the headaches he was causing, Ivanov said he wasn't willing to write about anything else, and, for the second time in a row, he quit.

By then the lonely Sidorov had invited his ex-wife Olga back into his life—such as it was. She took up residence in the tiny apartment his parents were still paying for but, unemployed and with no prospects, he was in despair at the thought she would have to support him. Then, on a cold day in February 1995, getting on the bus to visit his parents, Sidorov heard a familiar voice call his name. His heart leapt. It was Ivanov.

After updating each other on their stalled careers, Ivanov suggested to Sidorov that maybe they should team up and start their own paper. "My son came to our apartment and told us the news right away," Vladimir Sidorov remembers. "I don't think I'd ever seen him happier or more excited. 'Where will you get the money?' I asked him. 'Valery will do it,' he said."

Between them the young duo had only $100 in savings but, using his contacts from *Million*, Ivanov was able to call on dozens of potential investors, every one of whom asked for editorial control of the newspaper. He later admitted that what he was really looking for was a selfless arts patron, a mythical Russian figure known as a

"Savva Morozov." In fact, most people with money in Togliatti were tied in with one racket or another, and no one was interested in having a newspaper they owned investigating their allies in politics, business and possibly organized crime. In addition, some potential investors suggested to Ivanov that they wanted to use the paper to investigate their competitors while leaving their own questionable activities unexamined.

Any doubt that media investors saw themselves as the opposite of a Savva Morozov was eliminated on October 15, 1995, when Andrei Ulanov, editor of a people-oriented weekly called *Togliatti Today*, was gunned down in front of his apartment building—the first murder of a journalist in the city. Though the murderer was never found, most local journalists concluded that Ulanov was killed for one of two reasons: either he had threatened to expose the criminal activities of his investors when they demanded payment of a debt, or a powerful investor had demanded that Ulanov write a glowing profile of him in the face of the figure's well-known nefarious activities.

Ivanov spent another couple of months in a fruitless search for a white-knight investor until, at the beginning of 1996, he had a brainstorm: "We could earn the necessary funds ourselves . . . ! If the businessmen we talked to could do it, we could, too." In any other nation besides topsy-turvy Russia, what he did next would have been considered ethically borderline. Ivanov started a company called Togliatti Cars and used it to purchase from the gang-infiltrated Avtovaz the rights to buy 150 Ladas a year for private sale. This meant that he had to negotiate with the company's gang-affiliated "brokers," who charged *adgrus* premiums to insure on-time delivery to car dealers like himself. He also started a travel business, Ooo Sun! Agency, booking vacations to the Black Sea beaches of Sochi. At the time, like the car business, the Russian travel business was notorious for being riddled with organized crime fixers, since getting to the front of the line on Aeroflot's perpetually overbooked flights was almost always arranged by bribing shady middlemen.

Vladimir Voronov, the editor of the competing publication *Samarska Weekly*, was highly critical of Ivanov's business ventures in a piece he wrote about Ivanov and Sidorov years later. "What is this: journalist-dealers?" he rhetorically asked. "Yes . . . ! They were dealers and only part-time editors." Alexei Mironov, however, insisted to me that Ivanov had made no compromising business arrangements with criminals. "If he had been interested in getting wealthy in Togliatti," he said, "he wouldn't have used the paper to attack its power structure but to serve the power structure's interests." The Glasnost Defense Foundation's lawyer, Karen Nersisyan, after years of studying Ivanov's business relationships as part of his investigation into the two editors' murders, also saw no problem with what Ivanov had done to get the paper going—and then to keep it going until, close to his death, he found idealistic investors. "Look, this is Russia," he laughed, as if that explained everything. "In Russia, it's almost impossible to form a business without encountering criminals, since most businessmen *are* criminals. My findings are that Ivanov was an honest man. He formed his business so his paper could be *independent* of criminal investors and advertisers. But, listen, not to say he wasn't still Ivanov the go-getter. I do think he had a double motive for entering the car business, but it wasn't to reap profits from criminals. It was to gain sources in Avtovaz who *knew* about the criminals."

That is exactly what he gained. Ivanov quickly made contact with aggrieved Avtovaz investors, security guards and auditors, who, for the rest of his life, fed him tips and documents on gangster infiltration of the company and on the collusion of company directors in their thievery.

At the same time as he founded these business ventures, he set up a nonprofit center for investigative journalism, called the Bureau of Investigations and Analysis. The BIA was headquartered, courtesy of Sidorov's father, in a tiny office in the Polytechnic University, with a single desk and computer. The municipal elections of September 1996 were approaching and Ivanov and Sidorov began research on four questions, the answers to which they intended to publish in their first issue of the *Observer*: Who really ran the city? How was the city's budget spent (or stolen)? What was the relationship among the city government, the police and the organized crime elements in Avtovaz? And how much was the city losing from this relationship?

It wasn't too long before they made a remarkable discovery of corruption, even for Russia.

"There was a coup in the city and nobody had found out about it!" Ivanov related in his newspaper memoir.

Just after a city council election in the spring of 1994, a cabal of Togliatti's bureaucrats had secretly rewritten sections of the municipal constitution to render the newly elected council and mayor technically ineligible to hold office. All the old councilors and the vice mayor were reinstalled for another term while the status of the new slate was supposedly straightened out. To reinforce the constitutional coup, gangsters threatened the ousted candidates, but since Togliatti's newspapers were in the habit of only printing government news releases, the whole affair sounded to the public like one more confused incident in the transition from rule-by-appointment to democracy. Not to Ivanov, who was tipped off to the details of what had gone on during his investigation of the city's finances. "The right of the people to decide who was going to govern the city was stolen," he wrote. "As a result, for two and a half years . . . the city was run by the bureaucratic apparatus and the commercial organizations allied with it."

Ivanov and Sidorov began preparing a pre-election exposé, along with profiles of each incumbent candidate that told a story diametrically opposed to their official biographies. By August 15, 1996, all the articles were on the computer and slated to be put on disk and shipped to the printer for the first edition of the *Observer*. That night, the BIA/*Observer* office was broken into and the computer and all the documentary evidence were stolen. Before leaving the premises, the thieves sledge-hammered the office's fax machine, printer, telephones and shelves. In addition, Ivanov's spiral notebooks, containing all the poems he had written since he was nine years old, were nowhere to be found when he rummaged through the catastrophe in the morning.

Ivanov repressed his personal anguish at the sight, quoting Pushkin to Sidorov: "Our heavy fetters will fall, jails will open, and freedom will greet us joyously at the door!" Working from memory, he said, they would rewrite the entire issue in just two weeks. As they feverishly typed, they received word that they would be attacked again. "I visited them, to see if they were okay," Vladimir Sidorov told me. "Valery was all over the little office, a whirlwind. My son was working quietly. When Valery went out, I said, 'Are you all right, Alexei?' He said, 'Yes, of course, we have no time, we have to work.' I said, 'But are you safe?' Because a journalist had been murdered in the city the year before and I was worried. He didn't answer me, but he looked at me from the corner of his eye. So I hugged him before Valery came back. 'Remember who you're up against, please,' I said."

"To secure the paper and put the enemy off the scent, we changed the time and place where the paper was to be printed three times," Ivanov later wrote. He also hired three guards with automatic weapons and bulletproof vests to protect the newspaper's delivery to the printer. As a final flourish, like Luther nailing his challenge to the wall, Ivanov stopped the presses to insert his new motto on a banner at the top of page one: "We Print the News Others Are Afraid Of."

"Our edition went off like a bomb in the city," Ivanov wrote. "For the first time ordinary citizens were shown the real picture of the people who ruled our city, and how the rights of voters were violated. It's fashionable to say that Russian people don't care about politics and have a profound lack of interest in who rules them. The first issue of the *Togliatti Observer* proved this viewpoint completely wrong. Our office phone rang nonstop for three weeks. People called to thank us for not being afraid to write about the inner workings of the local government. . . . They offered to help with money out of their pensions when they learned that we had been robbed. Others called just to talk with the 'brave' journalists. In short, we could see with our own eyes that the city needed our paper."

In the aftermath, a progressive mayor was elected: Sergei Zhilkin, who promised to reform the secrecy and corruption of city council. At the beginning of 1997, just after the murder of a Togliatti reporter working on a story of personal scandal for *Everything and Everybody*, the *Observer* won a municipal journalism prize for coverage of the election. As part of the award, the city council granted the paper a three-room office in the Central District. Ivanov, listed on the *Observer's* new business cards as publisher and editor-in-chief, and Sidorov, as deputy editor, purchased new equipment and hired two part-time reporters to put their second edition out. This one chronicled the racketeer wars that had been taking place in the city over the last half decade, offering detailed portraits of all the mob bosses and their seamless links to Avtovaz and beyond. "We connected the criminal underworld to the city police, the federal authorities and the business world," Ivanov wrote in proud glee. "We offended everybody with influence. The gangsters threatened us, law enforcement agencies said what we published was all lies and those in city authorities we exposed condemned us."

One Chechen mob leader showed up in person at the *Observer* and threatened to put holes in the editors' heads. That night, Sidorov conceded to his father that he was terrified. "I said to him, 'Why state their names to enrage them then?' My son said if it was up to him he'd be more indirect in the writing, but Ivanov wanted to go straight at them. Then he got angry with himself for confiding his fears. He said, 'No, we're doing the right thing, we're saving the town. Ivanov knows what he's doing and he'll pull it off.'"

"You see, my son had such faith in Valery," Alexei's mother, Tatanya, recollected as she sat with her husband at their dining-room table. In front of them were the family scrapbooks, chronologically arranged from the time when Alexei had wept at the sight of the cartoon rabbit caught by foxes. Tatanya looked over her clasped hands at the photo of her boy with his head on Ivanov's shoulder. "He always felt that Valery was shrewd enough to get them through everything. He trusted that Valery knew what he was doing."

In fact, what saved the young journalists during this dangerous period was a blossoming of the seeds that Ivanov had astutely sown in the minds of the police back in 1993. "Nobody believed the paper was independent!" he later wrote. "Everyone thought some huge power was giving us a roof. The gangsters thought the police supported us. The police thought we were supported by the FSB in Moscow. The FSB thought we were supported by the oligarchs and politicians. No one thought we were just a couple of journalists who got together and started a newspaper."

As their readership climbed, they began putting out a weekly, then a daily, and moved into a modern brick office building on the city's main drag, Lenina Street, within walking distance of city council and the mayor's office. Thanks to Ivanov's sources within the dealership department of Avtovaz, in mid-1997 the *Observer* broke the news that there were now well over two hundred gangsters working inside the plant, with full access to the company computers. Through threats, payoffs and manipulation of the books, the mobsters were stealing cars and spare parts worth millions of dollars, driving Avtovaz, which produced 75 percent of Russia's vehicles and should have been profitable, into the red. The company owed hundreds of millions of dollars in unpaid taxes, and things were only getting worse. Ivanov, having now accrued a bank of underworld sources who saw it as in their interest to inform on their enemies, revealed that Dmitri Ruzlyaev, in partnership with former policemen working for a security firm called Forpost, was in control of half the plant's production lines. Ruzlyaev and his allies were channeling their profits into a private fund called Kontinental, also run by former police officers, who'd supposedly established the fund to aid law enforcement. The stakes for control of the plant were immense, and a third gang war for control of Avtovaz broke out. In the fall of 1997, Ivanov and Sidorov reported that two hundred people had been murdered in the last twelve months.

Largely because of the publicity generated by the *Observer*, President Yeltsin's Minister of Internal Affairs in Moscow ordered the Samara authorities to launch a crackdown on Avtovaz, called Operation Cyclone. On October 1, 1997, three thousand regional and federal officers invaded the factory, seizing computers and discovering five hundred cars ready to be driven off the premises with no documentation. In the new year, a hundred plant employees, officials and gangsters were charged, including Dmitri Ruzlyaev, whom the authorities declared the criminal kingpin of Avtovaz. Two months later, Ruzlyaev was released on bail and rumors were rife in the underworld that he hadn't just bought his way out but had cut a deal in exchange for information about a group called the Shekinsky gang. The thirty-five-year-old Ruzlyaev attributed the rumors to efforts by the police to undermine him, but the rival gang apparently believed the cops. On April 24, 1998, Shekinsky hitmen shot Ruzlyaev dead outside his mansion. In the fall, Ruzlyaev's vast fortune was seized by the police as proceeds of crime. Six months later, in April 1999, while Ivanov was making his first inquiries into Ruzlyaev's business holdings, the FSB, under the control of Vladimir Putin, launched a criminal case against the *Togliatti Observer* for publishing state secrets.

The official reason for the investigation was absurd, according to Ivanov. The state secrets that Ivanov and Sidorov had revealed in their newspaper concerned a scandal that was directly related to the Avtovaz raid and was on everyone's lips.

Most of the records connected to the hundred cases now before the courts were stored in the regional police headquarters in Samara. On February 10, 1999, as the employees in the building were getting ready to leave work for the day, a fire broke out on the third floor. The blaze blocked the only escape route down the main stairway, and by the time the fire trucks arrived, a dozen people had jumped to their deaths. The rest of the employees, crowded at the fourth-floor windows, begged for help from the firemen, whose ladders reached only up to the third floor. Ammunition exploded behind them and the building collapsed. In all, seventy-seven people died in the blaze, which coincidentally consumed the records of the hundred Avtovaz cases. The next day, the Togliatti police station also burned down, taking all copies of the documents with it.

In their coverage of the fires, Ivanov and Sidorov compared the results of their own investigation with the explanations offered by the police and the Ministry of Internal Affairs. According to the authorities, the Samara fire was a tragic accident, the result of a lit cigarette tossed into a wastepaper basket, and the Togliatti fire was another accident. The *Observer*, however, reported that the Samara fire had broken out in three separate places at the same time, and that an earlier fire in the same building had been contained and extinguished. It seemed clear to Ivanov and Sidorov that some person or persons was allowed access to the buildings—the two most secure facilities in the region—in order "to burn the documents and destroy the evidence in the corruption cases."

"The Minister of Internal Affairs was furious," Ivanov later wrote. "He came to Togliatti and shouted, 'I want this paper closed down!'" Shortly after that visit, the FSB launched its criminal proceedings against them.

One by one, the paper's twenty or so staff were ordered to the offices of the FSB for interrogation, where they were told that unless they revealed their sources, they were going to jail. "We learned that they had every employee of the newspaper under twenty-four-hour surveillance" and, by their questioning, they "let us know they knew every detail of our family history back to 1917." The KGB may have changed its name to the FSB, Ivanov wrote, but "they still knew how to do their old jobs."

None of the *Observer's* employees broke under the FSB questioning, and Ivanov went on the offensive. "We ran a counter-investigation against some FSB agents that could have resulted in a *huge* scandal for them. . . . As a result," he noted dryly, "the regional prosecutor's office recognized we had committed no criminal offense and their case against us was dropped."

In the wake of the FSB investigation, Ivanov's cop contacts dried up and he found it impossible to procure documents that listed Ruzlyaev's seized assets, which Ivanov estimated as high as $30 million and which should have gone into the city treasury. What agency of the city police was holding these assets? Was the cash protected against theft? Was the property secure from being transferred into the portfolios of corrupt officials? He received answers to none of these questions.

Ivanov added this story to a lengthening list of reasons why the authorities were so anxious to shut down his paper. Perhaps the most anxious of the politicians was the very mayor whom Ivanov had helped get elected, Sergei Zhilkin, whose financial dealings with a company called Ada Trade House the *Observer* had begun to expose in 1998. Through leaked documents, Ivanov had discovered that a financial backer of Zhilkin's 1996 campaign had been using Ada Trade House to siphon off millions of dollars in taxes due to the city. With the disappearance of Ruzlyaev's wealth, the fires of 1999 and the city "turning into a feeding ground for the authorities," Ivanov came to the conclusion that gangsters were just "a small part of the criminal pie." The major crimes were being committed by officials. "Billions of rubles were being stolen by these bastards." Petty officials "drove expensive cars and were buying $200,000 boats while at the same time old people were going hungry on their tiny pensions. . . . Soon we stopped being satisfied with only publishing exposés. We got tired of barking at a caravan that kept going. This was our entry into politics."

Ivanov founded a political movement and, in 2000, announced he was running for city council in the fall elections. On the front page of the edition that contained his memoir, the *Togliatti Observer* published a political cartoon of Ivanov on horseback, slaying a dragon with a quill pen.

During the campaign, Sidorov took over editing the paper, assigning stories with an unabashedly pro-Ivanov bias. As in any political campaign, there were charges to counter. One was that Ivanov had become too close to his gangster sources; another was that he was in the habit of fattening his wallet by blackmailing his journalistic targets. Among Ivanov's critics were the head of the Togliatti Chamber of Commerce and Vladimir Voronov, the editor of *Samarska Weekly*. Voronov later claimed in an article in the *Weekly* that he'd "received a letter on *Observer* letterhead, signed by Sidorov, filled with insults and threats—a virtual invitation to a shoot-out. The important part of this letter was, 'We at the *Observer* are tough, so you'd better watch yourself. Don't get involved because you don't have any business looking at our dirty linen.'"

"It was totally out of character for Sidorov," Ruslan Gorevoy, former information officer of the Glasnost Defense Foundation, told me. "Sidorov was gentle, whereas Ivanov was what we call a *krutiye parni*, a tough guy. Yet that letter was real, I saw it, and Sidorov had written it. Sidorov was such a close friend to Ivanov, I think he just adopted his style in defense of his friend."

"You mean it was Ivanov's style to write that kind of a letter?" I asked.

"It was. I think that Ivanov was a bad guy, but Sidorov wasn't. Ivanov and I once clashed over an article I wrote about his business tactics. Ivanov told me everything I'd written was lies. I told him to sue me. Then he asked me how much I earned, and that he would offer me more."

A year before I talked with him, Gorevoy had written a book for the GDF, *Murders of Journalists in Togliatti*, which detailed the cases of each of the six journalists killed in the violent car town. The section on Ivanov was not kind, often making him seem as unprincipled as the people he exposed. Gorevoy quoted allegations from Voronov stating that Ivanov "was always proposing deals. He said, 'If you pay, I won't publish.' These were not just mere threats, they were followed by actions. Businesses in the city and officials at Avtovaz paid him money for not publishing articles that contained information that was compromising to their companies."

Following publication of the book, the GDF's chairman, Alexei Simonov, distanced himself from Gorevoy's findings, advising journalists who wanted to know more about such allegations to speak to Gorevoy—who quit the GDF during the controversy. Two hundred members of the Samara Union of Journalists signed a petition denouncing the book and demanding the GDF retract Gorevoy's charges. "They wanted to lynch me," Gorevoy said. "When I said, 'Let's go to the courts and let justice reign—if I lose I will pay you the award,' they said, 'No, it's not a valid reason for a lawsuit.' They couldn't specifically address the reason that I was wrong, and I stand by my report that Ivanov had another side to him. The journalists of the Samara region were just blind to it."

Oleg Panfilov, director of the Moscow-based Center for Journalism in Extreme Situations, told me he had looked into the matter and Sidorov's letter to Voronov was authentic. It had been written in response to Voronov's first claims that Ivanov's business ventures were corrupt. Although Panfilov didn't put much stock in Gorevoy's sources, some Samara regional journalists he'd spoken to thought Ivanov had been unethically capitalizing on Togliatti's gang wars. "There was an article in *Izvestia* by Igor Korolkov, a respected journalist," Panfilov told me. "It alleged that Ivanov gave different coverage to gang members in return for information, playing one side against the other. . . . Otherwise, I have no information on whether he took any money from anyone, but I can tell you that 80 percent of Russian journalists would not refuse being bought or extracting bribes. If I were you, I would just deal with the matter by saying we have a very irresponsible press in Russia. Freedom of speech is so new to us. That makes for a very fertile climate for irresponsible behavior and irresponsible allegations."

Still, the overwhelming number of sources I spoke with in Samara categorically refuted the charges. "Ivanov was in politics," the GDF's lawyer Nersisyan told me. "People take sides, they make charges. Ivanov fought for what he believed in. He had a temper— he made plenty of people angry. Gorevoy created a huge controversy by quoting the charges of the people who were angry with Ivanov, for one reason or another. This is Russia. Either they kill you or kill your reputation, sometimes both."

Ivanov was elected as part of a slate called the December Party, named after an 1825 revolution that had ended with most rebel leaders shot. His new party managed to elect only four members out of seventeen on council, but Ivanov found himself in a powerful position that made up for his minority voice.

Two of his elected colleagues, Borislav Greenblat and Sergei Andreev, remember the heady day when Ivanov strode through the portal of the sandstone building off Central Square, saluted the bronze bust of Vasily Tatischev, founder of Stavropol, and entered the wood-paneled council chamber. "He finally had access to all government documents related to the city's finances," Greenblat told me, sitting in Andreev's office beneath a photo of Mikhail Khodorkovsky, the oil oligarch and government critic whom Putin had jailed in 2003 on charges of tax evasion.

Also elected was a new mayor, Nikolai Utkin, a prominent city businessman who, according to Greenblat and Andreev, correctly assessed Ivanov as a threat to the established order of Togliatti. "The entire structure of Togliatti is based upon corruption," Greenblat said. "At the head of this system is the mayor. You can guess how he felt about Ivanov."

"I know the exact name of Ivanov's killer," Andreev added. "Corruption—the entire system. Valery did the bravest thing possible. He came in these chambers with a torch to light the darkness. They couldn't let him live."

When Ivanov opened up the finances of the city, he found a tangled web of contracts for city services entered into with front companies. One of the most convoluted of these contracts was for the purchase of gasoline to run the city's fleet of buses. Ivanov discovered that contracts had been awarded to men with criminal backgrounds who were connected to senior-level bureaucrats, some of whom were in the prosecutor's office, supposedly guarding against corruption and cronyism. Ivanov inquired at the gasoline head office and determined that the city was paying far too much for the fuel delivered. In council, he demanded that the gasoline contracts be opened for competition, a move opposed by Mayor Utkin's majority United Russia Party—Vladimir Putin's chief political organ.

Losing in council, Ivanov decided to attack from another direction: he set to work researching an article exposing the non-competitive contracts, assigning the writing to Sidorov. Ivanov interviewed bus drivers and discovered that their salaries were months in arrears. The explanation they'd been given by the city was that their paychecks had been spent on gasoline to run the buses. "In other words," Councilman Andreev told me, "the gasoline brokers and the officials were getting filthy rich and the bus drivers weren't even getting their usual kopeks."

The *Observer* published its exposé on the contracts in December 2001, under the headline "Black Gold." With the facts laid bare, the bus drivers went on strike and Avtovaz's workers could not get to the plant. The strike lasted until well into January 2002, when Mayor Utkin agreed to form a committee that would review the gasoline contracts. "No one on council wanted to head the committee because they were afraid they would be murdered," Andreev remembers. "Valery took the post, canceled the contracts and opened them up for bidding. By awarding them to the lowest bidders, he saved the city well over a million dollars that year. Just by cleaning up that *one* aspect of the city administration."

In the midst of the gasoline scandal, the Fourth Gang War exploded in Togliatti and a Moscow-based TV documentary crew showed up in town and asked Ivanov and Sidorov to go on camera and profile the situation in Avtovaz. The pair agreed, and laid bare what they knew about the rise and fall of Dmitri Ruzlyaev, his competitors and successors, their incomes and their ties to the region's power structure. Referring to law enforcement as "the wardens of order," Ivanov stated that some of these wardens "fight the bandits, but many secretly partner with them . . . and some use them for profit in ways that combine fighting and partnering."

The series was shown across the country as *Criminal Russia*, and, coupled with "Black Gold," lined up just about every powerful force in the Samara region against the *Observer* editors. Not stopping there, Ivanov assigned Sidorov an article called "Cold War," a 6,500-word cover story about the decade-long rivalry behind the two biggest gangs in the city and the covert police plots to set them at each other. This was partly done, Sidorov wrote, in order to seize "their commercial organizations" and "improve the well-being of law-enforcement agencies." The article was published on March 1, 2002, with no byline, although the writing had Sidorov's satirical touch: "Sirotenko's men demanded money, threatening that unless the payment was made, the director's head would be used as a watermelon, given that it was also round and could be sliced." The gangsters in the article were not sensitive enough to distinguish between literary styles at the *Observer*, and all the resulting death threats came Ivanov's way.

———

In the newsroom, concern for Ivanov's safety grew. In the past sixteen months, two more journalists had been murdered in the city. One of them owned Lada TV, Togliatti's only television station, which had been reporting on local politicians when the owner was shot to death; the other victim was the senior editor of Lada, who was run down by a car in his driveway a month later. Rimma Mikareva, who would become the deputy editor of the *Observer* after Sidorov's assassination, said a colleague offered Ivanov a gun, which he refused, saying, "I'm not even sure which hole the bullet comes out of." Another colleague said he would hire Ivanov a bodyguard, which Ivanov also declined, saying he preferred to go to the bathroom alone. "He had lots of warnings, he knew he might be murdered, but he didn't take it seriously," Mikareva told me. "His attitude was, Have they murdered me yet? No. So, they won't murder me now."

Then a call came into the paper from one of the subjects of "Cold War" — Igor "Sirota" Sirotenko, a bull-necked, flat-nosed mobster with an old wound over his left eye that kept it permanently half-closed. Sirotenko asked Ivanov to meet him for supper at the Zhiguli Restaurant. He said the meeting was not for him but because his Chechen ally, Suleiman "Bibi" Akhmadov, had asked him to convey a message. Ivanov had once interviewed Bibi, and the *Observer* had published a mug shot of the Chechen sociopath, who was so bushy-browed his eyes were perpetually in shadow. "These two were the worst in the region," the *Observer's* crime reporter, Oleg Novikov, told me. "The most killings, the least human, the best connected. No one would have thought anything if Ivanov had said no, but he agreed to go. He thought it would be a good interview."

When Ivanov arrived at the restaurant, Sirotenko hugged him like an old friend, whispering into his ear, "Shall I kill you now or later?" Ivanov replied, "Later sounds better to me." They then sat down to a meal of borscht, whitefish and black bread. Ivanov told his colleagues that during the meal Sirotenko explained that he was a man of peace. Hadn't he made peace with his old enemy Suleiman, the Chechen madman nobody could reason with? As a sign of that peace, he was here on Suleiman's behalf. Sirotenko took out a fat manila envelope and put it on the table in front of Ivanov, saying, "Suleiman doesn't like the way you wrote about him. Take the money and stop writing about him. Then there will be no trouble." Ivanov refused the money but promised he would listen to Suleiman's side and present it in an article. Sirotenko responded, "My friend, if you don't take this money, somebody else will. And they are going to kill you because this will be their payment."

"Valery didn't take the threat seriously," Councilman Greenblat told me. "He felt it was too odd a way to threaten somebody. Why didn't Suleiman threaten Ivanov himself? His belief was that the gangsters liked the attention he gave them in the *Observer*. They were uneducated thugs, and he made them feel like big, famous men. Maybe Suleiman was threatening Valery through Sirotenko, not because Suleiman really wanted to kill Valery but to impress Sirotenko. On the other hand, maybe Sirotenko just wanted to see his name in print again."

At the time, the consensus of Ivanov's friends and colleagues was that Ivanov was more inconvenient to the government and the authorities than he was to the gangsters. His enemies in the mayor's office, the business elite and the police were feeling increasingly uncomfortable about the possibility that he might be elected mayor in 2004. In addition, they perceived a more immediate threat. "Many people suspected he was working on an article that would cover the entire situation of Togliatti," the lawyer Karen Nersisyan told me. "As it turns out, that was the article Sidorov would later try to finish for his friend."

In March and April 2002, in conjunction with Oleg Novikov and Sidorov, Ivanov analyzed the events that had precipitated the city's four main gang wars. At least two of them, the 1998 and 2000 wars, seemed to have been caused by agents provocateurs working for the police within the gangs. The goal of the police was twofold: to instigate the gangsters to weaken and kill one another (good from a law enforcement perspective), then to move in, seize the dead criminals' wealth and redistribute it among the members of the regional power structure. In effect, the region's officials were richly profiting from a murderous criminal enterprise.

"Not just Togliatti, *all* of Russia is a criminal enterprise," Nersisyan explained. "All such organizations as the city police, prosecutors and federal forces give krysha to top businessmen. In return, they always get a certain percentage of the businessman's profits, from 10 to 30. But in Togliatti, the businesses are so rich and the amount of money so huge that the authorities decided, Why should we give krysha and take only 10 or 30 percent? We want everything! And so, behind the scenes, these forces decided to become owners of the businesses — not just of Avtovaz, but the oil, gas, car parts and cement companies. They did it so well it was like a how-to manual on the procedure for the rest of the country."

"Who runs the city, then, the gangs or the government?" I asked.

"Neither. The businessmen run the city, and the officials and police are part of the business structure. Whether they own the business secretly or publicly, they are behind everything and, in one form or another, work with very violent criminal organizations. The authorities had the ties within the bandit organizations to spark the wars. These organizations were very wealthy, and when one lost, the authorities could seize the wealth. The most famous of these cases was Dmitri Ruzlyaev's. Thanks to the work of the authorities, Ruzlyaev was eliminated by the Shekinsky gang, and his wealth was seized by the authorities."

It was this complexly braided relationship that Ivanov was seeking to expose at the end of his life — in one sweeping article that would name all the individuals in the "organs of the state" and among the "wardens of order" who had profited from the murder of Ruzlyaev. The story would ruin the *Observer* if Ivanov got it wrong, and proof would have to come from documents that showed where Ruzlyaev's millions had ended up. But Ivanov admitted to Novikov and Sidorov that he could not find *any* documentation of Ruzlyaev's wealth, never mind whose portfolios it was now fattening. Yet *some*body had to have it because, he said, he had inside information that Ruzlyaev's gang was demanding its return.

At 6 p.m. on Sunday, April 29, 2002, Ivanov attended a meeting in the city council building with Borislav Greenblat. "I was the last councilman to see Ivanov alive," Greenblat told me. "We discussed the behind-the-scenes deals going on with the privatization of state buildings in the Avtozavodsky District. Valery said it was nearly criminal to award the best property in the city to friends of the administration. He wanted to make the transactions public."

Ivanov left city hall for home at 8 p.m., driving his Niva hatchback west through the green space that separated the Central District from where he lived in Avtozavodsky. Monday night was shopping night for the Ivanov family, and he picked up his wife, Elena, at his apartment house, 21 Gaya Street, a gray six-story building across the street from a small park. They drove to the neighborhood supermarket and filled the car with a week's groceries. At around 10:40 they left the supermarket, arriving home ten minutes later. Ivanov turned the wheel of his car and rode up onto the curb, the car now tilted away from the house. He got the groceries out of the back seat and approached the building's black metal doors with Elena. On the right was a brightly painted, red and green bench. It was an unusually warm night for April and some of the building's old women were seated under birch trees, just budding out in the late Russian spring. A group of neighborhood teens were across the street in the park, listening to a boom box playing a song from the Russian girl group, Tatu. Ivanov and Elena passed the old ladies and went upstairs with the groceries. A few minutes later, Ivanov came back to park the car. He had opened the car door and had one foot on the floorboard when the teens in the park saw a slim man about twenty-five to thirty years old come up behind him, pull a Makarov pistol from his dark jacket and put it against the back of Ivanov's head. The man fired once. Ivanov lurched forward, rebounded off the car and fell onto his back. The assassin put the gun above his heart and fired again, then dropped the gun and walked quickly away.

Ten miles east, in his apartment in the Komsomolski District, Alexei Sidorov received a call from an *Observer* photographer who said Ivanov was reported shot. When he arrived at the scene, Sidorov saw his friend lying in the road beside his car with his arms, as he put it later, "in a crucifixion pose." Ivanov's sports jacket was open and medics were still working on him, but there was no hope. A few minutes later a white sheet was draped over Ivanov's body.

"He phoned to tell us it was Valery and not him," his mother remembered. "He was using his professional voice—things were going on all around him—so I said, 'Are you safe?' He said, 'It's terrible, Momma, terrible. I'm very scared.'" Sidorov started to weep over the phone, then pulled himself together and said he would call back in the morning. "I told him, 'Leave! Leave there! Leave the city!' But he said he was going to the newspaper."

Sidorov next phoned a liberal investor in the newspaper, Gennady Shakarov, and showed up at work with two of Shakarov's bodyguards. "He was distraught," Novikov told me. "There was no color in his face. His hands were—" He held out quivering palms. "But he wanted to help us prepare the news stories about the murder of his best friend."

"We all looked to him as the new editor," Rimma Mikareva says. "He told us, no, he didn't want to be the editor, he didn't know how to manage the paper. He said he would work as just a journalist and we would find a new editor later."

Later that day, a personal note of condolence arrived at the paper from the Samara governor, and the vice mayor offered a $200,000 reward for any information about the murder. An hour later a spokesman for Avtovaz promised another $100,000. In the afternoon, the city council passed a unanimous motion requesting that the prosecutor general solve the crime as quickly as possible.

"Ivanov's killing made a huge impression in Washington, New York, London and Paris," Nersisyan recalled. "Such a reaction was not what the masterminds expected. Many people who'd had conflicts with Ivanov tried to deflect attention from themselves by offering support."

One official who could not bring himself to participate in the outpouring of sympathy was the mayor of Togliatti. Nikolai Utkin did not interrupt his vacation abroad and did not send a letter of condolence.

On May 2, a funeral attended by hundreds of loyal readers was held in the city center. The cortege wound through the streets to Banekenskogo Cemetery, at whose entrance stood the marble grave of the gangster Dmitri Ruzlyaev. Ivanov was laid to rest in the Aisle of Heroes, the same row in which local soldiers who had died in the Chechen and Afghan wars were buried. A black marble gravestone was raised a few weeks later, with a photo of Ivanov, his cheek resting on his fist, embedded in the stone. On the opposite side, engraved on the wings of a soaring pen, was the poem he had written in his notebook the day before he was killed.

Over the next several weeks, Russia's deputy prosecutor general, Vladimir Kolesnikov, issued bulletins stating that the city police had the case well in hand: they had a composite sketch of the gunman from the witnesses, and they were using their full resources to locate him. But the police refused to make this composite sketch public or share it with Sidorov, explaining that the killers and the people who ordered the killing were known and would be named shortly. A couple of days later this statement was retracted by the chief prosecutor, Yvgeny Novozhilov.

During this period, Sidorov continued to refuse the editor's job. He told Marakeva and Novikov that he did not have the business sense to be an editor-in-chief, and that he was worried he would be killed if he accepted. He chain smoked, drank endless cups of coffee and functioned on almost no sleep. "He was bereft and very, very frightened," his father said. "And yet everybody at that paper was looking to him for guidance. Would the paper continue? Which direction should it go? Should it keep investigating that whole corrupt society of Togliatti, or turn into something else?"

"Sidorov had been psychologically dependent on Ivanov for his strength and courage," Nersisyan told me. "Everything he'd done since college had been with him and for him. And now Ivanov had been murdered, he didn't know what to do. He could take over and risk being murdered, or he could not take over and maybe see Ivanov's work disappear. He was out from Ivanov's wing, but could he fly by himself? He didn't know."

In the midst of Sidorov's anxiety and grief, Councilman Greenblat, who had assumed control of the gasoline committee after Ivanov's murder, informed Sidorov that something unsettling was happening with the gasoline contracts. The companies that had bid against each other after Ivanov had opened up the contracts appeared to be coming under the sway of the front companies that had held the contracts before Ivanov's election. "They were quietly forming a monopoly so that they would all present the same high bid when the contract was negotiated again," Greenblat told me. "At the head of that monopoly were the same old figures. The same people who held the gasoline contract before Ivanov's murder got it again after his murder."

On one of his sleepless nights, Alexei Sidorov slipped the Mel Gibson movie *The Patriot* into his video player. "It was his favorite movie," his father told me. "He'd seen it ten times." It is the story of a farmer, Benjamin Martin, who refuses to fight in the American Revolution because of the horrors he's seen in the French and Indian War. Martin's son is killed in front of him by the British, and, seeking justice, he forms a ragtag militia and launches a guerrilla war. He loses his other son in battle and his farm is burned, but he plays a pivotal role in winning independence for the Colonies.

The next morning, Sidorov phoned Gennady Shakarov and said he would take the post as editor. When his appointment was made public, the *New York Times* phoned to ask the new editor about the threats to his life. Sidorov told the *Times*, "They can't kill us all."

Sidorov may not have been a businessman, but he now had to become one in a hurry. Without Ivanov's direction, and with his own journalism on the back burner, the *Observer's* readership steadily declined over the summer of 2002. In September, the paper became the object of a hostile takeover bid, which in Togliatti is often literally hostile. A conglomerate called Media-Samara, owned by a local magnate named Vladimir Avetisjan, informed Sidorov that if he refused to yield control of the newspaper, Avetisjan would simply drive the *Observer* out of business. On September 10, Sidorov received an unsigned letter that said, "Just to remind you, 134 days have passed since Valery Ivanov's murder."

At his parents' urging, Sidorov did something his best friend had never done: he fled town, booking himself on an Ooo Sun! flight to Sochi. When he returned in October, the pressure continued. A blogger with a regionally popular Internet magazine phoned him up for an interview that he said he would post online verbatim. The blogger started out matter-of-factly, asking Sidorov about the paper's circulation, then put Sidorov on the defensive by claiming the number was inflated to conceal the *Observer's* decline. The blogger then moved on to questions about the paper's findings regarding the murder of Ivanov, to which Sidorov responded, "The police investigation will have to answer who killed Valery. Why he was killed is another matter. He was killed because of what he wrote and his political activities."

"On what grounds does the *Observer* base such an assessment?" the blogger asked.

As Sidorov explained the quality of the staff and its fact-checking process, the interview took an openly antagonistic turn. "Was Valery Ivanov an honest and law-abiding person?" the blogger asked. And then, "Does the paper garner a share of its income from blackmailing its interview subjects? Could this be the reason for Ivanov's end?"

Suspecting Avetisjan was behind the interview, Sidorov phoned the media magnate and came away from the conversation visibly shaken. He called a staff meeting and announced, "We have to be ready for anything. The paper could be under serious threat of some violence." After the meeting, Sidorov lost his courage and left town yet again—this time for two months. While he was gone, Avetisjan hired away two of his best crime reporters. When he returned, his accountants informed him the circulation of the *Observer* and its advertising revenue were approaching such low figures that the paper could go under.

Sidorov faced a crisis decision. Media-Samara was breathing down his neck, yet if he unleashed himself and his staff, once again breaking the kind of stories that had made his paper both famous and well read, he risked kicking over the nest of hornets that had swarmed Ivanov.

In the spring of 2003, Sidorov met with his liberal-minded investors, got an infusion of cash to bridge him through the summer, then called another staff meeting. "He said he was going to concentrate on a return to our strong suit with a number of explosive stories," Novikov said, adding that he felt confident his new boss was finally rising to the challenge, "just like Ivanov."

One of Igor Sirotenko's gangster allies was a manic forty-four-year-old named Igor Filipov, previously convicted of rape, murder and banditry. That he was still on the street, the head of his own gang as well as the main enforcer for Sirotenko, said a lot about Togliatti's bribe-receptive judiciary. Sidorov said he was going to target Filipov in an article whose hook would be the death threats he'd learned the gangster had made against a businessman named Vladimir Zaharchenko. The police had refused to act on the threats and Sidorov told the businessman to phone him the next time Filipov put the squeeze on him to sign over his company, Spetsroi Machines. While Sidorov was researching Filipov's background, the Spetsroi office was sprayed with gunfire and Zaharchenko was left for dead. He survived, Sidorov went with the full story, and the police had no option but to arrest Filipov and investigate his businesses up and down the Volga. With Filipov in custody, the gangster's enemies moved to take over some of his turf. By the time he was released with no charges, he was a markedly poorer man.

The police warned Sidorov that Filipov was in an unpredictable state. Sidorov replied that Filipov was a lackey of Sirotenko and would not murder a journalist except on his boss's orders. At that moment, in fact, Sidorov was preparing another bombshell story— this one about Sirotenko himself. Through murder and intimidation, the gangster had secretly seized control of Togliatti's largest construction enterprise, the Zhiguli Quarry, from which almost all gravel for the city's concrete was dug. The quarry was Sirotenko's richest money-making enterprise but, until Sidorov published his exposé in June 2003, nobody knew that Sirotenko was "King of the Mountain." The directors of the Zhiguli Quarry Corporation demanded a retraction. Sidorov refused. They threatened a libel suit that would drive the paper into bankruptcy. Sidorov sent them the documents he had unearthed that backed up the article. Fat envelopes were offered. Sidorov was unyielding. "Our public buildings are being built with blood," Borislav Greenblat announced at a city council meeting, demanding a police investigation. None was launched.

Death threats arrived at the newspaper, but Sidorov ignored them, even though Sirotenko, the presumed author of the threats, had even more impunity than Filipov. The *Observer's* backers were happy: subscription rates had increased, along with ad rates, and the threats of a takeover from Avetisjan had receded. Gone was the frightened expression Sidorov had worn for months after Ivanov's murder. "He was achieving a sense of himself as cleaning up the city," Nersisyan said. "His main goal now became to find out who killed Ivanov and why. The secondary goal was to continue the journalistic investigations that he had started together with Ivanov. The biggest and most far-reaching of these stories was finding out what happened to Ruzlyaev's wealth."

"We worked on the Ruzlyaev story very quietly," Novikov told me. "There were too many members of the power structure involved to let it leak. Alexei wouldn't even tell me the names he suspected were involved."

"Because of the danger?" I asked.

"He wasn't thinking that way anymore. He wanted to finish Valery's work and didn't want anything to interfere. He was only waiting for a break."

The break came in late August 2003, thanks to a bit of luck and Sidorov's own artful manipulations.

Earlier that spring, after years of fruitless negotiation with the authorities for the return of their murdered boss's wealth, Dmitri Ruzlyaev's gangland comrades had instructed a lawyer named Fedulov to inform the police that unless their dead leader's spoils were equitably divided, they would publicize the fact that his millions were making their way into the pockets of senor policemen, prosecutors and politicians. Shortly after Fedulov had conveyed this information, the police charged him with tax evasion.

The tax-evasion case proceeded in typical Togliatti fashion. By the summer, Sidorov learned from his sources that Fedulov was getting close to a deal with the authorities: in return for the gang's silence, he would be found not guilty, and some of the wealth would be returned to his clients. Unfortunately, the Shekinsky gang were not happy when they heard of this deal. The rules that governed the Togliatti underworld and its liaisons with the police dictated that Ruzlyaev's spoils should be shared with them, and they were now getting tired of waiting for their payoff after all the good they had done for law enforcement by getting rid of Ruzlyaev. They ordered their own lawyer, a man named Kazeev, to intercede in the negotiations and cut a side deal that would give them their due. To get standing in the bargaining (so to speak), they "persuaded" Fedulov to accept Kazeev as his defense lawyer. Suddenly, the lawyer for the gang that had murdered Ruzlyaev was defending the lawyer for Ruzlyaev's gang, with Kazeev implying that unless Fedulov was found not guilty, all the officials who could now afford mansions and yachts on Zhigulevsky Lake would be exposed.

Novikov suspects that Sidorov was talking to one or both lawyers, because the editor knew exactly what methods of persuasion the Shekinsky gang had used to get Fedulov to agree to have Kazeev defend him. Sidorov also knew that if Kazeev lost the case, the Shekinsky gang and Ruzlyaev's gang would probably kill both the lawyers. "In the last months, four lawyers had been murdered in Samara," Novikov told me. "Fedulov and Kazeev could be five and six."

At the beginning of September, Sidorov became suddenly confident he could procure the documentary evidence that would name the officials who had pocketed Ruzlyaev's money. With that end in mind, he gave two assignments to Novikov: the first was to pull together all their research on Ruzlyaev's wealth into a preliminary draft; the second was to research and write another article, entitled "Why Lawyers Are Killed."

The lawyer article was published at the end of September, and it gave a sympathetic portrait of the plight of Russian lawyers who represented mobsters. Both Fedulov and Kazeev were comforted by the article, particularly because, Novikov would later swear in an affidavit, the same week the article came out, "the case against Fedulov took a dangerous turn and it looked like Fedulov was going to be found guilty." The authorities had apparently had their fill of both gangs. Fedulov, even if he escaped assassination, was looking at ten years in Siberia; Kazeev would be lucky if the Shekinsky gang let him move there.

Sidorov now reviewed Novikov's draft of the Ruzlyaev exposé, and told him to be prepared to insert the names. A week later, early on the morning of Thursday, October 9, Sidorov called Novikov into his office and excitedly told him he had been shown the Ruzlyaev documents, he knew the names of the police officers who were getting the money and he was about to be handed the documents that would enable him to follow the money into all the other officials' pockets. "This evening I'll have the documents and we'll begin our work after that," Sidorov said. He told Novikov that he had a meeting at 8 p.m. with the person who would hand the documents over, and that they should be prepared to publish the article Wednesday, October 15, the day after the Fedulov verdict. Sidorov then called a staff meeting, at which his reporters noticed he was unusually energized, although he said nothing about the upcoming Ruzlyaev bombshell.

Some time before eight, Sidorov left the office for his meeting. He returned half an hour later carrying a folder.

"He was beholding the fulfillment of Ivanov's life's work," Nersisyan told me. "That was Sidorov's goal in life at this point. This article he was so excited about would encapsulate the entire situation in Togliatti, and in Russia, since Togliatti was so emblematic of the nation."

About 9 p.m., Sidorov received a call from his wife, Olga, reminding him that there were friends at the apartment visiting them. Sidorov, who had been planning on working through the night, apologized and told Olga he would leave the office immediately.

He gathered up his folders and CDs, told the security guard he would finish his work at home and began the drive east to the Komsomolski District. He had progressed less than a mile from the office when the security guard at the paper phoned him on his cell-phone to tell him he had forgotten what looked like important financial documents on his desk. Sidorov returned to the office to retrieve the documents then headed home again. Along the way he stopped at a corner store and bought several bags of groceries for the gathering. About a block west of his apartment house, he turned into a commercial parking lot that faced a four-lane boulevard called Kommunisticheskaya Street. The attendant saw him leave the lot carrying the plastic shopping bags. Sidorov crossed the street and walked east a block, then turned into a grassy quadrangle, bordered on the north by a patch of forest and on the south by his nine-story apartment house.

Except for a weak light thrown by a bulb above the front door, the quadrangle was dark. Just then a young couple came out of the steel door of the building. As they rounded the corner of the build-ing, they saw two men approaching them in the dark, followed by Sidorov, who was being followed in turn by a third man. Sidorov turned the corner and a woman crossing the quadrangle and another woman looking out her first-floor window saw the man fol-lowing Sidorov speed up and come abreast of him about ten steps from the entrance to the apartment house. In an attack that lasted no longer than a few seconds, the man stabbed Sidorov eleven times with what police later determined to be a *zatochka*, or shiv, a homemade pick used in prisons. Three of the blows were deadly: two to Sidorov's heart and one to his pancreas. The coroner later determined that the fatal blows were the first to be delivered, and the rest were wounds to Sidorov's arms as he tried to defend himself.

Sidorov was still standing after the attack. The witness in the quadrangle and the woman at her window, unaware Sidorov had been stabbed, saw the man go through his pockets and shopping bags and then take off across the park toward the trees. Sidorov staggered forward to his entrance and pressed the button to his apartment on the eighth floor. When Olga answered he said, "Help," and then collapsed. She raced downstairs and found him slumped below the buzzer, his shirt soaked in blood. The police arrived twenty minutes later, but by then he had bled to death in Olga's arms. The documents and CDs the *Observer's* security guard had seen him leave the office with were not found at the scene.

For the second time in eighteen months, a funeral was held for a *Togliatti Observer* editor. The column of grieving readers and staff again made its way through town to the Aisle of Heroes, where Sidorov was laid to rest beside the man he had followed loyally for a decade and a half and for whose memory and ideals he had given his life.

The day after Sidorov's murder, the police arrested a twenty-nine-year-old welder named Yvgeny Maininger, who lived in an apartment house on the west side of the quadrangle and whom the police had long considered of interest to them. A young woman identified Maininger as being at the scene of the crime just before the police arrived, but Maininger explained that he had been returning home from a nearby café and had only witnessed the aftermath of the murder, then had gone to his apartment. Maininger's father accompanied his son to the police station and, after a few hours, was informed that during questioning Maininger had assaulted police officers and would be held in custody.

On Maininger's third day in jail he confessed to the murder, saying he had asked Sidorov for some money for vodka, that Sidorov had refused and insulted him, and that a vicious fight had broken out, during which Maininger had pulled his homemade *zatochka* and repeatedly stabbed the journalist.

To anyone who knew the gentle Sidorov, the story of him insulting the workman then engaging in a street brawl was ludicrous, but the police ended their investigation and charged Maininger with murder. On October 21, the deputy attorney general, Vladimir Kolesnikov, formally announced, "The investigation has determined that the murder of Alexei Sidorov was perpetrated solely for hooligan reasons. The murderer has been caught. The speculation alleging that the killing was done because of Sidorov's professional activities is untrue."

The Glasnost Defense Foundation, suspecting a cover-up, sent an investigative team to Togliatti. Karen Nersisyan, after talking to Maininger and questioning the witnesses whose story contradicted the police version, agreed to act as Maininger's lawyer. On November 3, 2003, Maininger withdrew his confession. "The police worked him over for three days," Nersisyan told the *Togliatti Observer*. "After what he went through, a person would confess to anything."

Some months later, a BBC crew showed up in Togliatti with Nersisyan and went to the nearby café where Maininger claimed he'd been dining at the time of the murder. Two witnesses stated on camera that Maininger had been in the café at the exact time of the killing. The BBC then brought the witnesses to the Justice Building and, through a closed door, tape-recorded a meeting between Nersisyan and the city prosecutor. The prosecutor told Nersisyan he had no interest in interviewing the witnesses outside his door or taking their statements.

In June 2004, after the BBC broadcast its revelations about the incurious attitude of the prosecutor, Paul Klebnikov, the American editor of *Forbes Russia*, phoned Nersisyan in Togliatti. Klebnikov told Nersisyan he was working on a book about murdered Russian journalists, and wanted to research the cases of Ivanov and Sidorov. At the beginning of July, Klebnikov flew down to view testimony at the trial of Maininger. "He told me Togliatti was the most visible example of what was happening to the editors of independent publications who were writing about the links between gangsters, corrupt officials and high ranking police," Nersisyan later told the *Observer*. "He collected material in Togliatti and Samara about gross corruption in the economic spheres. I told Klebnikov that immediately after the court proceedings I would get in touch with him in Moscow."

On July 9, a few days after returning from Togliatti, Klebnikov was leaving his Moscow office at 10 p.m. when a car pulled up beside him and one of the passengers shot him nine times. The Russian authorities attributed the murder to Klebnikov's writing on Chechnya and charged two ethnic Chechens, who were eventually acquitted in a trial that was closed to the public and the media. "Many people knew about Klebnikov's investigations of the murders of Togliatti's editors," Nersisyan told the *Observer*. "Maybe the bad guys did not want a journalist with lots of influence and connections to stick his nose in this business and they decided to get rid of him."

Finding Maininger guilty after the BBC broadcast would have been too great an embarrassment, even for Russia. On October 11, 2004, the welder was acquitted.

A few days later a woman named Svetlana Okruzhko phoned the *Observer* claiming to have "important information," then asked for a meeting with Nersisyan and Vladimir Sidorov. "She told us she was the common-law wife of the driver of the getaway car used by the killers of my son," Vladimir Sidorov told me. "She said her common-law husband was in hiding in another city and had the CDs and documents that were taken from Alexei the night he was murdered." Okruzhko explained that she and her husband, Yvgeny Marzinkevitch, needed help. They were being hunted and wanted to use the documents as bargaining chips with Russia's prosecutor general to enter a federal witness protection program.

The woman swore out an affidavit addressed to the prosecutor general stating that two hired killers had been led to Sidorov by a lookout, and that the killers had no idea their target was a famous journalist. When they heard on the getaway car's radio that the police were setting up roadblocks, they panicked, fled the car and left the CDs and documents behind with Marzinkevitch. "These documents," Svetlana Okruzhko wrote, "contain serious facts about corruption and dishonesty among police officers in Togliatti, in the Internal Investigation Branch, on the city level and on the regional level. At the Samara regional level, the prosecutors who were investigating organized crime groups are accused of corruption."

Nersisyan took Okruzhko's affidavit to Moscow and gave it to the GDF's Alexei Simonov, who wrote a cover letter to the prosecutor general and asked him to investigate Okruzhko's claims personally. He specified that the investigation should be done without the participation of the Togliatti authorities. Nersisyan then contacted Okruzhko and arranged for her to come to Moscow with the CDs and documents to hand over to the prosecutor general. By then, however, the prosecutor general had acted on the affidavit, sending it to the Togliatti authorities. The woman never showed up in Moscow, and when Nersisyan tried to reach her, he discovered that her phone was dead and the couple had disappeared from their flat. "I have no information on whether she's still alive," Nersisyan told me. "Our prosecutor general has washed his hands of her affidavit and her fate."

Two days before I left Togliatti, Vladimir Sidorov accompanied me to the Aisle of Heroes in Banekenskogo Cemetery. The mown lawn around the grave sites of Alexei Sidorov and Valery Ivanov was dappled with golden birch leaves, looking exactly, Vladimir said, as it had on the day Alexei was buried there three years before. He placed a bouquet of carnations in an urn on the ledge of Alexei's headstone, then turned and pointed to Valery's poem. "'Oh, my Lord,'" he read aloud in Russian, "'can't You see how much we need kindness?'"

The next day I went to the *Observer's* offices for a scheduled meeting with Colonel Sergei Korpilov, the police chief of the

Komsomolski District where Sidorov was murdered. Korpilov insisted that he and his officers had taken the crime investigation seriously, and that they'd arrested the right man: Maininger had murdered Sidorov because the editor had refused to give the welder spare change for vodka.

"It's very sad to lose a child—the father's emotions overwhelm his reason," Korpilov explained, referring to Vladimir Sidorov's pleas that the real killer be found. "It keeps him from seeing that Maininger is guilty. I understand his emotions as a father. He doesn't want to accept that his son died by a simple act of hooliganism, a casual act. Of course, there is a lot of talk that he died because of his activities here. But we have facts that he was killed by casual incident."

We were sitting two steps from Ivanov's and Sidorov's desk, now manned by their young successor, Alexei Mironov. Even here, and with a photographer circling him, Korpilov seemed completely at ease, almost avuncular in his knit sweater. At the start of the interview he'd told me he was one month from retirement and was thinking about settling in Florida.

"Everyone I talked to told me the people who ordered Sidorov murdered had krysha," I said. "Sidorov was on an article about high-level corruption when he was killed."

Korpilov lifted his arms and shrugged. "One of the theories was that Alexei Sidorov received some information and was about to publish it here, but there are no documents to prove it, just words, just rumors. In Russia—" He paused to smile at an attractive female reporter named Marina Novikova, who had persuaded him to talk with me. "Here it's cheaper to kill someone than to discuss a problem." He turned a friendly gaze back on me. "Because in Russia, there is no man, there is no problem. But in Alexei Sidorov's case, I can tell you, there is no evidence to support such a conjecture."

Suddenly there was a lot of activity in the corridor. Radios crackled. Male voices outside the door shouted to others in the parking lot. Then the door to the editor's office was thrown open by a fellow in a trench coat who came forward and whispered something into Korpilov's ear. Korpilov pushed his chair back. The interview was over.

Novikova stayed behind as Mironov escorted Korpilov out of the building. A year after Sidorov's murder, Novikova had left the *Observer* to have a child. She now worked as a reporter at a less dangerous newspaper, *The Square of Freedom.*

"What do you think of what Korpilov was telling me?" I asked.

"If he wanted to find the real killers, he could," she replied, rolling her neck in circles to release the tension. "He himself says he hasn't encountered a murder where he can't find the killer."

"Did somebody stop the investigation from above?"

"Of course. When a murder of a journalist happens here, immediately a special message is sent to Moscow—every time. Kolesnikov stopped the investigation," she added, referring to Russia's deputy prosecutor general. "Kolesnikov right away announced, 'Sidorov's murder is an act of hooliganism.' If he said so, who will contradict him? The same thing happened with Valery Ivanov's murder. Alexei Sidorov was continuing the work that Valery started. Everything is connected."

"This gangster Dmitri Ruzlyaev was murdered in 1998," I said. "That's a long time to stay on one story about police corruption."

"Not just police corruption," she reminded me. "The prosecutors and politicians also took Ruzlyaev's wealth. It took years to get the documents to prove it."

"But the documents are gone now."

"No, somebody has them. Those documents are real." She stood up and rolled her neck again. "It's too dangerous for me to say more." She extended her hand and shook mine with a tight grip. "You're leaving the city, but I have to remain here. These people all have plenty of krysha."

—

Before I left the city, Alexei Mironov and I attended a rally for Anna Politkovskaya in Central Square, arranged by an organization called Open Alternatives. It was raining and there were only about fifty people gathered in front of the stage. Circling the spectators were half as many uniformed policemen, most in camouflage uniforms and visored helmets.

Mironov explained my book project to the woman in charge of the demonstration and she invited me out of the rain and into her car, where she said, "Things are more difficult now for us than you can imagine. Can you say a few words of encouragement from the stage? Just so they know the international press is watching."

"I don't know any Russian."

"I will translate," she offered.

A representative of Open Alternatives was now standing silently on stage, cupping a candle. Beside her a colleague held a framed picture of Politkovskaya out to the audience. Leaning against the back of the stage were framed photos of Ivanov and Sidorov. I looked at the line of riot police. Beyond them were two men in trench coats, uniformed cops holding umbrellas over their heads. A third man in a trench coat was crouched behind a tripod, his head close to a video camera that was aimed at the stage.

I agreed to say a few words, but as we approached the stage I realized that if I brought attention to myself here, the police might seize my research and harrass my sources. "I can't let them see me advocating anything," I said.

She looked from the stage to the police. "Of course, I understand."

We walked back toward Mironov, who was now in the crosshairs of the camera. "Can I ask you a favor, please?" she said.

"Of course."

"When you get home, please explain why you couldn't speak."

SIX

SOLID KHALID

Khalid W. Hassan, Iraq

 FOUR YEARS INTO THE SLAUGHTEROUS Iran-Iraq War, the wife of a Baghdad car mechanic named her firstborn child Khalid, which means "He will live forever." Twenty-three years later, on July 13, 2007, at the height of the Sunni-Shiite violence that had emerged out of the American invasion of Iraq, Khalid W. Hassan was on his way to work at the *New York Times* Baghdad bureau when a group of men caught up with his car and shot him dead. That night, his mother laid his body to rest in a cemetery that had recently been opened to accommodate the thousands of victims from both sides of the civil war. Samira Hassan chose for her son's gravestone a Koranic verse that reflected the hopeful yet fatalistic name she had given her boy at birth: "Do not think that people who are killed in a holy cause die; they are still alive with God."

At the time of his murder, Khalid Hassan's name was attached to some of the most dangerous stories ever covered by a journalist in Iraq. He'd barely survived several of these stories, and one—after he'd been kidnapped by insurgents—had earned him a *Times* bravery award. From the beginning of November 2003, when the

Times had hired him at the age of nineteen, until his death four years later, Hassan had filed his reports in the paper's walled compound, just across the Tigris River from the Green Zone. He'd known that as an employee of Americans he faced being murdered every time he made the forty-five-minute commute from his apartment in Saydia, Baghdad's most violent neighborhood; and yet, after that perilous journey, he often left the relative safety of the compound to interview witnesses at car bombings. He weighed three hundred pounds and was easily recognizable to insurgents, but, lumbering amidst the flames and the body parts, he'd somehow managed to survive long enough to report eighty stories with headlines like "At Least 130 Die as Blast Levels Baghdad Market."

Over one hundred journalists were killed in Iraq during Hassan's tenure at the *Times*, most of them Iraqis. One of the victims, Fakher Haider, a *Times* stringer in the southern city of Basra, had said goodbye to Hassan in Baghdad just before driving off to his fate. "God willing, we'll see each other soon," Haider had told the young reporter. "Either here," Hassan had replied, indicating the newsroom, "or there"—pointing to the sky.

There was a tremendous outpouring of emotion at the *Times* bureau after Hassan's murder. The bureau chief, John Burns, wrote the news story, and eight of Hassan's Western colleagues posted online reminiscences. These leading lights of American war reporting painted a portrait of an easygoing young man who had made fun of his size and his passion for Western pop culture by nicknaming himself "Solid Khalid," as if he were one of the big-boy rappers he habitually watched on MTV. Solid Khalid was a goateed computer whiz who'd never finished high school, who'd been supporting his mother and four sisters since his parents had split up when he was a young teenager and who'd learned to speak an unaccented and slang-filled English from TV and movies.

I was instantly drawn to Solid Khalid's street smarts and moxie. He'd endured wars, dictatorship, poverty and family hardship to flower into a self-taught reporter who presented himself to the world as something of a dandy no matter his size. "In a city of bombs and rags, Khalid always dressed as if he had a dinner date," wrote *Times* correspondent Paul von Zielbauer. "Like men everywhere, he had the winsome quality of a young buck that wanted people to know he had his life in order: the latest cell phone on his hip, the funkiest websites on his computer, the most colorful Turkish-made golf shirts tucked into his expansive waistline." Dexter Filkins, the *Times'* premier war correspondent, recollected that Hassan "had taken to America and its gadgets and its liberties like no other son of the Muslim world I had ever met." Anecdotes abounded about how Solid Khalid would return to the bureau after risking his life for a story, switch the TV sets from Al Arabiya and Al Jazeera to The Movie Channel and MTV, then settle back with a big bowl of buttered popcorn and divide his time between social networking websites, text messaging and gabbing on his cellphone. "I would wander into the newsroom at one or two in the morning and I'd find him sitting there, looking like an American teenager lost in his own world," Filkins wrote.

Shortly before his murder, Hassan had summarized for reporter Damien Cave what he and his fellow Iraqis wanted out of life: "We just want the same things everyone wants. We just want to live our lives."

A little over a year after Hassan's death, when a decrease in the number of car bombs made a research trip to Baghdad feasible for me, I began placing calls to the Iraqi *Times* reporters who'd known Solid Khalid in his own language. Some had moved to the U.S. or Canada; others were still living in Baghdad but worked for other news organizations. Like Hassan prior to his murder, their names were obscure to most readers of the *Times*, since they'd rarely received the lead byline for the stories they'd covered. As a few of them explained to me, they were all fluent speakers of English but less fluent in writing it, and their eyewitness accounts and interviews had most often been credited in a line at the bottom of articles, as in "Khalid W. Hassan contributed reporting for this article." In truth, they'd been the Tenzing Norgays to the bureau's Edmund Hillarys—their guides, interpreters and protectors, and their eyes and ears at mass casualty events that were sometimes too dangerous for American journalists to attend.

Although they'd all risked their lives by working for the *Times*, they told me that Solid Khalid had differed from them in one important way: he had openly tried to live the life of a cosmopolitan Westerner in a Muslim society that had gone mad. In almost every aspect of his life, Hassan had thumbed his nose at caution and convention. In his last months he had become engaged to a divorcée who was twice his age—older than his mother—which was unheard of in a conservative society like Iraq. He'd also taken terrible chances in his violent neighborhood. "His area was filled with very radical insurgents like al-Qaeda and the Shia militias," a reporter named Abdul Razzaq al-Saiedi told me, adding that Solid Khalid had walked the streets of Saydia dressed and accessorized like a Manhattanite. "And that could mean only one thing to the insurgents: he worked for the Americans," Razzaq said. "Where else did he get his money? They once came to his door and warned his mother that he should quit [the *Times*]. But he wouldn't change his habits or move from Saydia." Solid Khalid, he said, had been handed one of the most dangerous jobs in the world when he was still just a teenager, and from that moment until his death he'd refused to bow to the terror.

"Khalid will be a different case for you because he was so young," Ali Adeeb, the bureau's former manager of the Iraqi staff, told me. "But I don't think he would look strange in your book. He would just be his own person, murdered very early in his career. Good luck on your research. It won't be easy."

I landed at Baghdad International Airport in October 2008 and was immediately deported—a not unusual experience for an author arriving with a visa and a letter but no important-looking ID from a major news organization. With the help of the Iraqi consul in Amman, I tried again two days later and got in. After a ride in an armor-plated sedan that skirted Hassan's neighborhood, I moved into the Hamra Hotel, a concrete tower ringed by blast walls and defended by twenty armed guards. The Hamra was in Karada, the "best" neighborhood in Baghdad outside the Green Zone. Hassan had lived in the worst. In his last two weeks he'd driven to work in a rattletrap Kia. I, on the other hand, would be touring his city in a two-ton Beemer protected by flak-jacketed Iraqis sporting Kalashnikovs with the safeties switched off.

The next day, I set about trying to figure out what had made Solid Khalid tick. Where, I wondered, had his raw talent come from? What had driven him to lead such a stubbornly provocative life in a country overrun with insurgents and fundamentalist fanatics?

The Martyrs' Cemetery where Khalid Hassan is buried stands beside the Bridge of the Imams in the Adhamiya District in northern Baghdad, on the east bank of the Tigris River. The city may be thirteen hundred years old — the storied setting to A Thousand and One Nights — but there are no old gravestones in the cemetery's rows. All the dead are new, the ground is raw sand and the view of the Tigris is blocked by freshly erected blast walls.

Until a couple of years after the American invasion, this riverside patch was a soccer field. Then, on August 31, 2005, thousands of Shia pilgrims walking across the bridge panicked when a rumor swept the crowd that a suicide bomber was about to blow himself up. The pilgrims' fear was well founded. The bridge linked the predominantly Sunni neighborhood of Adhamiya, infiltrated by al-Qaeda-in-Iraq, with the predominantly Shia neighborhood of Kadhimiya, ruled by Shia militias, and bombs targeting crowds were frequent in the district. A thousand people died in the ensuing stampede, and the soccer field below the bridge was bulldozed and turned into an emergency graveyard. Hundreds more bodies were added over the following two years, many headless, some with holes drilled into them by power tools, the surrounding skin burned black with acid. A few bodies had been found with their heads jammed into their slit stomachs.

Two former colleagues of Khalid Hassan explained this gruesome history to me in my hotel room, four miles down the Tigris from the Martyrs' Cemetery. They were describing the ritual washing and burial of Hassan at the cemetery, which had taken place just eight hours after he'd been murdered on the other side of the river from my hotel.

"The Imams' Bridge was named to be the symbol of a peaceful link between the Sunni and Shia," Wisam Habeeb, a fifty-two-year-old freelancer who used to work for the *Times*, told me. "The Sunni imam was named Al Adam, from which you get 'Adhamiya.' The Shia imam was named Al Kadhim, from which you get 'Kadhimiya.' So they named the bridge in 1957 to link the two sects that held their different views of Islam."

"Obviously, nobody pays attention to links now," said Khalid al-Ansary, a thirty-two-year-old Reuters journalist who left the *Times* not long after Hassan's murder. "For thirteen hundred years they have been fighting each other over their differences."

Staring at a photo of Hassan's gravestone on my computer, al-Ansary thought of something to lighten the moment. Because there had been two journalists named Khalid in the bureau, the Iraqi staff had called al-Ansary "Slim Khalid" (Khalid Dhaeef), and Hassan "Fat Khalid" (Khalid Al Simeen). "That was the reason Fat Khalid changed his name to 'Solid Khalid,'" he explained. "Whenever someone would call him 'Fat Khalid,' he would make a pose and say, 'I am *Solid* Khalid—call me by a name that accurately describes me.'"

"Was Solid Khalid killed by Sunni extremists or Shia militia?" I asked. I mentioned that Abdul Razzaq had told me he was reasonably certain the assassins were al-Qaeda—Sunnis—based on a Koranic passage that was texted to the Hassan family after the assassination. John Burns, on the other hand, in his news article about the murder, had mentioned the possibility that Hassan had avoided a Shia-controlled roadblock near his home, and that it could have been Shia gunmen who had followed him.

The two reporters discussed the matter in Arabic then informed me that it was impossible to know which faction had finally caught up with Hassan. "There is an Iraqi saying," al-Ansary said, above a deafening convoy of Chinook helicopters passing close over the Hamra's roof. "'Everyone is on the death queue.' Danger finds all Iraqis, from which direction, orchestrated by whom, you can rarely tell for sure."

"I happened to flee Saydia when al-Qaeda moved in," Habeeb pointed out. "Our names were on their death list—they knew we worked for the *Times*. I begged him to get out of our neighborhood, but he wouldn't move. He told me he just laughed at the young men who'd joined al-Qaeda in the neighborhood—he wouldn't let them drive him out. But if you speak to his fiancée, she will tell you that he knew what awaited him. On his last night he said to her, 'This is the last time you might see me.'"

Khalid Waleed Hassan al-Nabhani was born in Baghdad on January 12, 1984, a descendant of the ancient Sunni Arab tribe of Bani Nabhan, from northern Palestine. His mother, Samira Ahmed, and his father, Waleed Hassan, were cousins from a large extended family that had fled Palestine in 1948, during Israel's War of Independence, an event known by Palestinians as "the Catastrophe." Khalid's paternal great-grandfather had led the clan into exile, first to Jordan and then, a few months later, to Iraq. When this patriarch died, Khalid's grandfather, Hassan Mousa al-Nabhani, became head of the clan. According to what Khalid later told his Iraqi colleagues, it was Mousa, not Waleed, who most influenced the path Khalid would take in life.

Hassan Mousa had lived long enough in the green Galilee to make returning to his homeland from desolate Iraq a lifelong dream, although Iraq was inhospitable in more ways than just its

aridity: the country was riven by coups and countercoups, the plot-
ters always calling for a return to the country's glory days while
generally delivering political and economic chaos.

At school, every Iraqi child is taught about these ancient glory
days, the nation's lifeline to self-respect amidst so much tragedy.
Civilization was born five thousand years ago in the fertile lands
between the Tigris and Euphrates rivers. The origins of writing,
mathematics, epic literature, astronomy, the calendar, universities
and the codification of law can all be traced to Mesopotamia, "the
land between the rivers." Conquered by the Persians in the sixth
century BC, Mesopotamia was retaken by Arab disciples of the
Prophet Muhammad eleven hundred years later in the Battle of
Qadisiyah. A dispute over the succession line of the Prophet then
resulted in another battle near the Iraqi city of Karbala, giving birth
to the Sunni-Shia split in Islam, whose main fault line has run
through the center of Iraq ever since.

In AD 762, Iraq's capital, Baghdad, was founded, and went on to
become the intellectual hub of the Islamic world. For five hundred
years it was the most prosperous and beautiful city on the planet,
with universities, gardens and palaces lining the banks of the wide
Tigris, which irrigated the surrounding fields. This storied era
came to a violent end when Mongol invaders sacked Baghdad in
1258, destroying its waterworks and burning its palaces. In 1534
the Ottoman Turks seized the millennia-old land, and remained
in control until ousted by the British at the end of World War I.
Following their usual divide-and-rule strategy, the British drew
Iraq's modern borders to encompass three competing peoples: the
Sunni Kurds, who formed the majority in the mountainous north;
the Sunni Arabs, who were in the majority north and west of
Baghdad; and the Shiite Arabs, who were in the vast majority in
the south and who constituted about 60 percent of the total population. To keep the Shiites from uniting around a national ruler,
the British installed as king a Sunni, who favored his fellow Sunnis
in many government appointments.

In 1932, the year after Mousa Hassan was born, the British nomi-
nally granted Iraq independence, but the discovery of vast reserves of
oil meant London would not stop meddling in Iraq's internal affairs
for decades. Violent revolts occurred regularly, until in 1958 a leftist
military coup finally overthrew the British-favored monarch and
reversed his pro-Western policies, nationalizing the country's oil
and industry while once again disrupting its shaky economy.

Mousa tried to live his life apart from all this turmoil. When he
was in his twenties he began buying and selling grain on the
Baghdad market, but business was not where his heart lay. In 1964,
a year after the Arab Socialist Ba'ath Party seized power in yet
another coup, he entered Baghdad University's College of Arts,
graduating with a major in English literature in 1968, the year a
rising Sunni figure in the dictatorial Ba'ath Party, Saddam Hussein,
was appointed vice president.

Mousa hoped to make his way as an English teacher and poet,
but as his family grew larger, he looked around for better-paying
opportunities. His English skills and grain-trading experience
earned him a post as a representative of Iraq's state-owned grain
company, and throughout the 1970s he made frequent trips to the
United States and Canada, negotiating import deals for wheat.
These trips cemented his liberal democratic leanings: he became
one of the few Iraqi Palestinians who supported Egyptian president
Anwar Sadat's peace settlement with Israel in 1979, and a few
months later, when Saddam Hussein muscled his way to the presidency, he attended secret meetings of an organization opposed to
the Ba'ath Party. Saddam's mass executions of his political rivals
and his tightening grip over every aspect of life, however, persuaded
Mousa that he should stop attending the meetings. Until some
unforeseen miracle occurred, he would have to find his joys in his
private life.

From his travels he had accumulated a private library of hundreds of volumes of American and British literature, as well as the
complete works of the modern Syrian poet Nizar Tawfiq Qabbani,

who was a rarity in the modern Arab world for his bold verses about sex and the empowerment of women. "Love in the Arab world is like a prisoner" was how Qabbani summed up his attitude toward the strictures on women in his culture. "I want to set love free. I want to free the Arab soul—its sensuality and body—with my poetry." It was an ethic that Mousa would one day preach to his grandson Khalid, although Mousa's own son, Waleed, was always deaf to such pronouncements.

Waleed Hassan was born in 1960, and as a teenager was more inclined to tinker with big American cars than to read books and listen to sermons about the benefits of women's liberation. He quit high school at sixteen, took a vocational training course, then worked at industrial jobs until, on January 5, 1980, he married his cousin Samira, a heavy-set woman of limited education who'd been raised to be a mother and housewife. With a loan from his father, Waleed opened an American-brand "car-fitter" shop in Adhamiya, not far from the Bridge of the Imams. According to Khalid's mother, now living in exile in Larnaca, Cyprus, "Waleed was making a good living and at first we were happy.... [Waleed's] skills were much in demand." His car shop, however, was filled with fewer of the Malibus and Caprices he loved, than with military vehicles that had been disabled in a war raging to the east.

That war had been launched by Saddam in September 1980, ostensibly because Iran's new revolutionary Shia leaders were attempting to overthrow his Sunni-dominated government and replace it with traitorous Iraqi Shias. Saddam invoked the memory of the Battle of Qadisiyah in his "defensive" crusade, while the Iranians named their military operations after the city of Karbala, where seventy-two Shiites had been massacred by Sunnis in AD 680. Mousa believed Saddam's war had two goals that had nothing to do with the protection of the country: the conquest of large swaths of Iranian territory and the uniting of Iraqi Arabs—Sunni and Shiite— behind his fascist dictatorship. The result was that huge numbers of soldiers from both sects and nationalities became cannon fodder in a stalemated struggle. A month after Khalid Hassan's birth, the war escalated, with a major Iranian assault. In two days, 25,000 soldiers died, including those whose burns proved to UN observers that, to repel the attack, Saddam had used mustard gas. In one of the final battles of the war, in March 1988, Saddam launched an offensive in the northern border region, gassing Kurdish Iraqis whom he suspected of trying to gain their independence by siding with Iran, killing five thousand people in the town of Halabja. By the time little Khalid had reached his fifth birthday and the war had finally ended in a UN-brokered cease-fire, the total casualties for both sides stood at one and a half million. Not an inch of ground had been gained by Iraq; the war proved only that Saddam would go to any length to enhance his absolute hold on power in Iraq—and expand it to other realms if he got the chance.

As a Palestinian, Khalid Hassan would never have full Iraqi citizenship, the result of a decision by the Arab League that was meant to guarantee "the right of return" to the heirs of refugees from Israel's War of Independence. This hazy national status set little Khalid apart from his Iraqi schoolmates at Al Ahrar Primary School in Adhamiya, although there is little doubt that he didn't fit in for other reasons. From glimpses he gave of these early years to colleagues, it appears his size made him the brunt of jokes, and that he had avoided social contact during recess. Even among fellow Palestinians he had no friends, and his mother, Samira, recalls that "during recess he would go to the library in the school and read a book, not like his classmates, who preferred to play naughty games in the yard."

His one friend was his grandfather. Mousa, disappointed in the blue-collar Waleed, treated little Khalid like his own son, and many of the books Khalid read during primary school were in English, a language Mousa had begun teaching Khalid when he was six, expanding the curriculum to encompass world history and literature. "Khalid told me that from elementary school forward, Mousa insisted that he read all the English books in his home library, hundreds of books," Wisam Habeeb told me. "In addition to that, he made Khalid avail himself of the public library to read poetry, plays and history—especially history. Because Iraqis live in their history."

Mousa had a lot of time to spend with his grandson. When Khalid was six and a half, Saddam, undaunted by eight years of fruitless war with Iran, had invaded Kuwait, and four days later a near-total financial and trade embargo had been imposed on Iraq by the UN. The stringent UN sanctions were kept in place after Saddam was driven from Kuwait, aimed either at getting him to disarm or at sparking a coup that would oust him from power. While the sanctions drove the economy into a catastrophic depression, ending Mousa's career as a government grain trader and forcing him into retirement, they had no effect on Saddam. By dint of his mafia-like Sunni tribal alliances and mass-murdering ways, Saddam continued to rule the country from the luxury of his many palaces, winning a 1995 referendum on his presidency with 99.96 percent of the vote. A joke among Western journalists in Baghdad at the time was that there were 40 million Iraqis: 20 million people and 20 million billboards of Saddam.

During the postwar period, Waleed and Samira had four daughters, the last of whom was born in 1997. Pictures taken of Khalid with each of his successive sisters during these years show him getting steadily chubbier. He later told his closest colleagues that his parents' marriage began to fall apart as one daughter followed another and his father increasingly indulged a penchant for going to nightclubs and spending the family income on his own pleasures. Today, Waleed attributes his failed marriage to Samira's inability to ration the family's diminished resources during the sanctions, but it was a view Khalid didn't share. "Khalid told me he disliked his father," a *Times* computer technician and driver named Ehab Ahmed said to me. "He loved his mother, his sisters and his grandfather deeply, but he had no kind words for his father. His father was the only person I ever heard Khalid say he disliked."

After the birth of Khalid's youngest sister, Waleed lost his garage business and the family was evicted from their apartment. Grandpa Mousa, who had just been diagnosed with terminal cancer and was living on his retirement checks, was unable to provide financial assistance. Waleed procured a job across town as a night watchman at Thiqar Primary School for Boys, which allotted him a small room for his wife and five children. According to what Khalid confided to his colleagues, Waleed continued his bad habits, until in November 1997, when Khalid was thirteen, Samira gathered her children and left him.

She moved three miles south of the school to a tiny apartment in the residential district of Saydia. To support her family, Samira left home each morning at dawn to clean the houses of wealthy Ba'ath Party members who lived in neighborhoods surrounding what is now the Green Zone, not returning until late in the evening. Agonized by his mother's toil and pain, Khalid told Samira, "I, your son, will be your husband." To his sisters he said, "I, your brother, will be your father." He walked five miles across Baghdad to the Market District and bought a bagful of combs and hairbrushes for a dollar, then walked back toward Saydia, selling his wares from the curb and door to door. Not yet fourteen, he began cultivating a talent for salesmanship that he polished over the next three years until he became a master at striking up instant intimacies with complete strangers—an ability that would be a valuable asset for a journalist. "I showed them I cared about their problems," he later told his fiancée, Nidaa Al Salmani. "They told me of their hardships and then they bought my combs."

In time, he also gained another important skill. On his daily trips to the Market District he passed through a bazaar known locally as Technology Street, which was filled with video arcades that adjoined the camera shops in Al Tahrir Square. Since Khalid gave his mother all the money he earned and could not afford to play the video games, he got another job washing cars at Saydia's Al Rahman Parking, and with the extra cash he began spending his weekends and evenings (and quite a few school days) in the arcades. He soon discovered that some of the arcade stores held caches of smuggled computers and pirated videos of popular American films and TV episodes. He struck a deal with a couple of shop owners who allowed him to use their products in return for quietly hawking videos in the market. When he wasn't playing video games, he taught himself computer programming and watched films like *Pulp Fiction* and the first episodes of *Sex and the City*. He'd heard about the wondrous wealth of America from his grandfather but hadn't realized that the U.S. was a nation where no one had anything to do with their families and everyone had sex at the drop of a hat.

Khalid took to the world of electronics as naturally as he had to salesmanship. By the time he turned seventeen, in 2001, he was an expert in computers. He was also (thanks to his grandfather) probably the best-educated student at Waheid Hazair Preparatory School for Boys, but his confidence as a salesman, computer wizard and family breadwinner caused him to look beyond school for a future. He never prepared for tests, and, noticing his failing grades, his mother asked him, "Dear son, don't you want to use your intelligence to become an engineer?" Khalid replied that Iraq was filled with unemployed engineers, some of whom washed cars beside him in Al Rahman Parking. He was considering quitting high school and going into some kind of computer-related business when, during the first week of classes of his senior year, on September 11, al-Qaeda's hijacked planes struck the Twin Towers.

East of the famous copper statue of Saddam in Central Baghdad's Firdos Square, the dictator's deranged son Uday ran an organization called the Iraqi Olympic Committee. On the ground floor, Uday kept racehorses in stables that adjoined rooms where he held women he'd kidnapped and used as sex slaves. A few floors above these chambers, he published a thin newspaper, *Babil*, which he'd founded after Iraq's loss in the first Gulf War. Uday's stated goal for *Babil* was to demonstrate to Iraqis that the regime was still open to the world, despite the stranglehold of UN sanctions. Toward that end he had hired several government-approved journalists to search through foreign newspapers for articles to translate and republish, often with a lot of rewriting by censors. After the September 11 attacks, Uday decided to publish an expanded edition of *Babil*. As soon as Khalid heard Uday was hiring, he went down to the Iraqi Olympic Committee and offered his expertise in computer graphics and English. That was the last time Khalid ever saw the inside of a school.

He was put on the night shift, at first assigned to laying out each day's edition and then, after January 2003, to searching the Web for articles that Uday thought showed the opposition of foreign leaders to President George W. Bush's increasingly bellicose pronouncements about Iraq. The reporters at their computers were supposed to scan the world's news reports through Uday's eyes, remaining unaffected by exposés of Saddam's quarter-century reign of terror that had seen as many as 200,000 Iraqis executed and countless others tortured in prisons. To ensure that the minds of his employees were not being stained, Uday would drop in unannounced in the middle of the night and grill the reporters on their attitudes toward what they were reading. Khalid later described to one of his colleagues, Zaineb Obeid, the fear he would endure during these visits: "Zaineb, you should have seen us when he walked in and just stood there behind our backs! We'd keep working and then he'd say, 'Stand up. What is your name? Where are you from? What do you think of this article?' No matter what we said, he would just stare with his examining eyes, looking into our brains with threatening judgment. Oh my God, it was like we were awaiting execution! I couldn't even breathe! And I thought, 'This is the society we live in, under this crazy person?'"

Three months later, on March 19, 2003, Baghdad was rocked by the tremendous explosions of U.S. cruise missiles—Bush's "shock and awe" tactic aimed at destroying Saddam's command centers and palaces. Suspecting that Uday's *Babil* would be a target, Khalid did not go into work, instead watching the bombardment with his mother and sisters from his Saydia apartment window. Internet connections for *Babil* were wiped out that night, but the BBC Arabic Service remained on the air, and Khalid and his colleagues were aware of the rapid progress made by American troops moving up from Basra. Two and a half weeks later, tanks from the U.S. Army's Third Division entered the western outskirts of Baghdad then moved in columns up Airport Road, which ran along the northern border of Saydia. Three days later, in front of a small gathering of about 150 apparently celebrating people, the U.S. Marines pulled down the statue of Saddam in Firdos Square. Five days after that, on April 14, amidst the unrestrained looting that had broken out in the city, the international media staged a job fair at the Palestine and Sheraton hotels just off the square. Dozens of newspapers and television stations suddenly needed translators and fixers, and hundreds of Iraqis who spoke English showed up to apply. Khalid Hassan was one them.

"We were all really happy when the statue came down, but none of us could believe Saddam was really gone," Hassan's future colleague Khalid al-Ansary told me. "We were also not happy another country had invaded us to overthrow Saddam. The city was lawless with all the looting and burning, but the Americans were protecting the Oil Ministry. Our feelings were very mixed."

Al-Ansary, who had a degree in English literature, met Hassan for the first time at a tent the BBC had set up on the roof of the Palestine. "Khalid was ahead of me in line," al-Ansary remembered. "He started to talk to the BBC recruiter and I was astonished by his American accent. I asked how he learned to talk like that, and he told me from his grandfather and American movies. He was so full of enthusiasm and easy in his manner that even the BBC interviewer at first thought he was raised in America. I got the job at the BBC, but perhaps because he was only nineteen and without a high school diploma, Khalid did not. Instead, he moved to another recruiting center and CBS TV hired him."

It was at CBS that Hassan first began to refer to himself as a journalist. "He discovered himself there," I was told by Zaineb Obeid, who had been hired by the *New York Times* during the job fair. "He was so proud to be working for this American news station with so many attractive people. Whenever he would later tell me about CBS, he would always say, 'I entered another world from the one I had known and this is the world I want to stay in. I love Americans. They talk only about the present and the future, not the past. They are free of the past.'"

Khalid at first did well at CBS. He worked long hours scouring the city for stories he could hand to reporters, using his ability as a salesman to lay the groundwork for interviews with people who would talk about relatives they had lost to Saddam, about the invasion and about the looting. When he was assigned a computer, he began searching the Internet for Jihadi websites, translating the threatening videos and giving his work to reporters as news stories. The CBS staff felt they had a gold mine in Khalid, and he felt he had a gold mine in them: his first paycheck was more than he had ever made in a year. He took a personal e-mail address, khalidcbs@yahoo.com, which he kept to the end of his life.

It wasn't too long into his tenure, however, that Khalid began using his computer for purposes other than work—as any nineteen-year-old would, given what was suddenly available to him over the unmonitored Internet. He started with dating and swinger websites and progressed to carrying on torrid electronic affairs with middle-aged American women, who seemed to have no reservations about sending him provocative pictures of themselves. He interspersed his virtual dating life with frequent visits to porn sites that again featured mostly middle-aged women, a fascination almost everyone I spoke to described as his bent. It was only a matter of time before two things happened: the CBS mainframe began to get infected with viruses from the porn sites, and complaints were made to the bureau chief by Iraqi employees who were deeply offended by what he was looking at on his screen.

Khalid was warned that such activities were forbidden in the newsroom and told that if he wanted to carry on affairs or look at dirty pictures, he should do so privately at one of the Internet cafés that were sprouting up all over Baghdad. Khalid promised he would behave and then used his expertise to disinfect the mainframe. But, working on the night shift, he returned to perusing the "mature women" websites again and again. Finally, in late October, he was fired for inappropriate use of the computer.

In any other place beside Baghdad in 2003, being fired from one news organization would close doors to others. But for Khalid, with his MTV accent, computer skills and recommendations from CBS reporters who loved his work, it was a seller's market. He walked into the *New York Times* bureau, in a cheery, ocher-walled private house beside the Sheraton Hotel, and was hired by the bureau chief, Susan Sachs.

By this time the American occupation of Iraq had begun to deteriorate. The weapons of mass destruction that had been used as a justification for the invasion had not been found, the Jordanian embassy and the United Nations headquarters in Baghdad had been destroyed by massive car bombs, and because the Americans had not developed plans for reconstructing the country's infrastructure after the invasion, there were only six hours of electricity a day.

Amid the increasing restiveness on Baghdad's streets, Khalid took public transportation to work, riding in a crowded minibus. The route took him east from Saydia, across the Jadriya Bridge over the Tigris, through the declining neighborhood of Karada and along the riverside Abu Nawas Boulevard opposite the Green Zone. He was as proud of his affiliation with the *Times* as he'd been of working for CBS. According to Abdul Razzaq, who joined the *Times* at the same time as Khalid, the rising tide of Iraqi resentment at

the occupation had not discouraged Khalid from acting dangerously brash in public. "We usually hid our press credentials unless
we needed to show them," Razzaq told me. "Khalid wore his badge
on his chest in the minibus, as if he were telling everyone, 'Hey, I
work for the New York Times.' He was very full of himself; he
wanted everyone from Saydia to Karada to know who he worked
for, but it was very stupid behavior. I told him that, and he said, 'Ah,
no problem—come on, it's a new country.'"

Every Iraqi I spoke to who worked with Hassan at that time recalls
that he acted as if Iraq truly were a new country. He hadn't yet
turned twenty, was fifteen years younger than anyone else in the
bureau, and here he was in the most important newspaper in
the world with world-famous reporters like Jeffrey Gettleman
dependent on his smarts. "I'll never forget the day Khalid and I went
to a hospital to cover my first suicide bombing," Gettleman recollected years later. "This was January 2004, and Khalid waltzed into
the emergency room wearing his floor-length black leather trench
coat—think Keanu Reeves in The Matrix, Iraqi-style—and strutted
straight into the trauma ward. He gave off such a self-confident,
authoritative air (he was all of nineteen, too) that victims and their
family members mistook him for a doctor.

"While we were interviewing a man taped up in bed, some poor
guy crept up to Khalid with an X-ray of a relative and asked him
to take a look. Without missing a beat—or blowing his cover—
Khalid, who watched way too many American TV shows, apparently including ER, grabbed the X-ray from the guy's hands, gave
it a very professional snap and held it up to the light. He closed
one eye, scanned the black and white bones for the perfect amount
of time—not too long, not too short—and rendered a verdict.

"'She'll be fine,' he said."

For his current roles as translator, fixer and researcher, Hassan
was paid fifteen hundred dollars a month, and although it was just
a small fraction of what the Westerners earned, it was an enormous
amount for a young man in an Iraqi city with a million unemployed.

He moved his family into a larger Saydia apartment that provided him and his mother with their own rooms and his four sisters with two rooms. He appointed his eldest sister to be his bookkeeper and secretary and set off on a shopping spree, buying a generator, cologne, clothes, a $400 Sony Ericsson cellphone, the complete works of D.H. Lawrence, a DVD player and CDs of every group on the charts in the United States. "He was enthralled with the financial and political freedom and being in the middle of it all," remembers Zaineb Obeid. "Just overjoyed, and so proud of himself. He had a U.S. military pass and could travel anywhere. He attended conferences in the Green Zone, he arranged interviews for the foreign reporters with high-ranking officials and he came up with story ideas at meetings. Everybody respected him. He was just in heaven."

Then something happened to Hassan that caused him to begin hiding his press credentials on the minibus. On March 31, 2004, insurgents in Fallujah, a Sunni town thirty miles west of Baghdad, ambushed four private military contactors working for Blackwater USA. The contractors were killed and dragged out of their vehicle by a mob who set their bodies ablaze and hung their corpses from a bridge that crossed the Euphrates. Footage of the event appeared on television stations around the world, and the U.S. military committed itself to "pacifying" the city. On April 4, two thousand troops surrounded Fallujah and called in air strikes, triggering a rebellion throughout central Iraq by Sunni forces.

Into this war zone three *Times* employees, their driver and, in a chase car, several guards plunged to cover the story: Jeffrey Gettleman was the reporter; a woman named Lynsey Addario was the photographer; and Khalid Hassan was the translator and fixer. The main road to Fallujah was blocked by the U.S. military, so Gettleman and Addario decided to skirt the town by the back roads and cover the situation in Ramadi, ten miles up the Euphrates River from Fallujah. In a village along these rural roads, a minivan cut them off and dozens of masked men brandishing Kalashnikovs and rocket-propelled grenades surrounded their vehicle, firing their guns triumphantly into the air. The chase car made a U-turn and headed back to Baghdad. Addario later remembered turning to Gettleman and saying, "We are going to die now."

Khalid got out of the car to negotiate. He was immediately surrounded by enraged gunmen who shouted questions at him all at once, leading him to believe that they weren't interested in answers and that at any moment he would be murdered. "I was thinking not that they would kill me but *how* they would kill me," he later told Ehab Ahmed, referring to his dread at having his throat slit. "Then I thought of my mother and sisters and how they would get along without me. I tried to think of something to say that would get us out of this, but no one was listening to me."

He was shoved in the minivan along with Gettleman and Addario and driven to the militia compound, where they were hauled before the insurgent commander. Guns were pointed at them and Khalid surmised that a life-or-death decision was about to be made. "I calmed myself by pretending I was selling the commander something," Khalid later told Ahmed, recollecting the tone he'd used. "He had a need, his problems, and we wanted to help."

Gettleman had the same idea, and Khalid translated what the journalist said, using his salesman voice: they were in the area to cover the Iraqi side of the conflict, particularly the violence being visited on ordinary citizens by Americans.

The commander demanded to see Addario's photographs, and she showed him pictures she had taken that morning of the Mahdi Army, the militia of a rising Shiite cleric named Moqtada Al Sadr. Had the journalists' kidnapping occurred a year later, these photos might have infuriated the commander, but the Sunni-Shia civil war had not yet broken out, and both sects had a common enemy. "He scrolled through scenes of heavily-armed men trolling the streets of Sadr city, manning funeral processions of civilians allegedly killed by the Americans, and seemed satisfied," Addario wrote.

More grilling followed, but the commander's mood had softened toward his prisoners. He ordered that they be taken to a house, where they were instructed in the rationale behind the insurgency and in the civilized nature of their captors. A few hours later, to their astonishment and infinite relief, they were released.

When Ehab Ahmed greeted Khalid at the *Times* compound that evening, Khalid said, "We came pretty close, we lost all hope. But you know, that's my job, and I'm glad I was able to perform it well. I feel good that I didn't lose my cool. Maybe I was able to help get us out of there."

A celebration was held on the roof of the bureau, where Khalid learned that the new bureau chief, John Burns, had also been kidnapped and released, in Najaf, sixty miles south of Fallujah. Khalid was later presented with a *Times* certificate of bravery, which he proudly hung on his wall at home.

The shared danger cemented Khalid's position as Gettlemen's translator, and, in Burns's view, also cemented Khalid's standing as an employee of the *New York Times*.

Despite his near-death experience, Khalid returned to Fallujah by himself just two months later, after an air strike killed seventeen Iraqis in a poor neighborhood. The citizens were enraged by the attack, and Khalid, in his new role as contributing reporter, offered his eyewitness account, stating that he saw "gunmen with straps of bullets crisscrossing their chests at checkpoints," and quoting a resident who vowed to fight the Americans: "It's not only Fallujah people who will stand up to them, it's all of Iraq."

Hassan conducted his interviews even though many in the town would have considered him one of "them" and though some of the bandoliered gunmen might very well have been from the same group that had kidnapped him in April. "I will go wherever it takes me and do whatever I am asked," he told Ahmed. "Perhaps by shedding light on these situations, the authorities in Washington will realize there is a grave situation developing that must be addressed in a better manner. That is why we are journalists."

Hassan's night shifts, which he pulled every couple of weeks, were safer than his day shifts, but Ahmed remembers that they brought Khalid problems from a direction that had nothing to do with the insurgency. As was his habit, Hassan took advantage of the quiet and privacy by switching the TV channel from Al Jazeera to MTV. While listening to the music, he dated American women over the Internet and skimmed through his favorite porn sites; and, as at CBS, the sites infected the office computers with viruses. It didn't take long before the ten Iraqi staff figured out who was responsible.

By the summer of 2004, partly because of his nighttime pursuits, Hassan began to have trouble with some of his colleagues. Newsrooms throughout the world are known for being competitive environments, with more than their share of unresolved resentments, but many of the Iraqi staff I spoke to reflected that there was an added layer of tension at the *Times*' Baghdad bureau. There were two distinct groups of reporters at the paper: the Western staff, who were on permanent contract and whom the Iraqis called "the foreigners"; and the locals, who had no contracts and who could be fired at any time. "You can notice it from the first day, from the very day that you came to the newsroom, you would notice the [Iraqis] are competing with each other for the attention of the foreign reporters," one Iraqi journalist no longer with the *Times* told me. "But Khalid didn't care to participate in such competition. He never told rumors about people to the foreigners. He was confident, he was clever, he delivered good stories, and whenever he was outside the *Times* compound in the dangerous world with a foreign journalist, he was really brave."

While Khalid was a favorite of the most daredevil reporters at the *Times*, his youthful flaws made him an easy target for those who could not accept that this kid who spent his time infecting their computers with porn viruses had achieved such esteem. And while he could use his salesman skills to talk himself out of a dangerous situation on the street, he was helpless at maneuvering in a complex office environment where his habits made him vulnerable to jealous colleagues who could inform on him. "Khalid had a big body, but he was a boy, a totally innocent boy," Ehab Ahmed told me. "I tried to offer him advice when he got into trouble with his colleagues, but the problem was he didn't know how to deal with people maturely—he had no social skills." It seemed to Ahmed that Khalid's total range of social contacts was limited to people he'd met online and communicated with electronically or by long-distance phone calls. "He had no personal friends," Ahmed said. "Only his mobile phone, his computer, his DVD player, his books— those were his friends. So nobody taught him, 'Khalid, this is how you are supposed to behave when people are feeling jealous of you. If they are angry about something you have done, they will use it against you, they will bully and mock you and make trouble.' But because he never had a social life as a boy, he never learned to be a social person."

"How did he react when someone mocked him?" I asked.

"He would cry. Sometimes when we were alone together, he would tell me what they were saying about him to the foreigners and he would cry. The tears would come down his face like a little boy. It was very sad. They always made fun of him. The foreign staff would never make fun of him, but the Iraqi staff were unkind to him."

Khalid himself would sometimes prompt this ridicule by dint of his ingenuousness. On January 12, 2005, he showed up for work carrying a big cake in a box. He wanted to throw himself a twenty-first birthday party, but when the Iraqi security staff saw him opening the box, they laughed in his face. "It's unusual in Iraq for an adult to make a birthday party," Ahmed said. "Some of the staff made fun of his intention, and when he brought the cake out of the box, he was so nervous he dropped it upside down to the ground. Everyone laughed at him, so he got very mad and cried in front of everyone. That made them laugh even more."

Zaineb Obeid, who worked with Khalid for two years before transferring to Knight Ridder, remembers that while Khalid was extremely sensitive, he also had a capacity for swallowing his feelings after a crying jag and then moving on as if nothing had happened. When she tried to offer him sympathy, "he told me not to say anything more because that would make the problem bigger—'I don't know what's wrong with those people, but let's forget about it.'" He had learned to endure taunts as the fat kid in the schoolyard, and he could push them from his mind and press on. "The foreigners respected his talents and abilities, and he based his confidence on that," Obeid recalled. "Everybody wanted to work with him, and they told him his work was exceptional. That was all he cared about—'I'm a journalist who reports a war in my country, not an office person. So let them say what they want.'"

"You should see my room," Solid Khalid announced to Zaineb after the birthday-cake incident. "It's a whole different world: I have my DVD player, all my books, my TV, video, Internet, a satellite connection—I have everything in my room I need. I don't leave it—I just ask my sisters and mom for lunch and dinner because when I'm off work, I don't want to leave that heaven."

This "heaven" contrasted with the hell Khalid was covering as a journalist. Car bombings were becoming a daily event, sometimes with scores of casualties. Garbage workers were being murdered by insurgents aiming to turn the population against the occupation, and the entire city began to smell like a dump. Power stations were being sabotaged as fast as they could be repaired, leaving most of Baghdad without air-conditioning as the June temperature climbed into the hundreds.

There was trouble in the south of the country, too. On August 2, 2005, an American freelance reporter named Steven Vincent was murdered in Basra. Vincent had just written an opinion column in the *Times* revealing that the police in Basra were taking their orders from Shiite religious groups and that these groups were using the police as violent enforcers of their political and economic power. Corruption and extrajudicial killings now reigned in Basra,

Vincent had reported. Secular women in the local university were being forced to adhere to Islamic codes of dress, and a "death car" drove around town carrying thugs from assignment to assignment. Hundreds were being murdered every month. "The entire [police] force should be dissolved and replaced," he quoted one human rights advocate as saying. Not surprisingly, the powers that ruled Basra had no use for reporters like Vincent nosing around their criminal business.

Ehab Ahmed, Khalid Hassan and a number of other *Times* staff bravely drove down to Basra to investigate the complex story that Vincent had unearthed. They were met by a local *Times* reporter, Fakher Haider, who had covered the murder of Vincent for the paper. Haider was a lean thirty-eight-year-old whom the *Times* journalist James Glanz would later write "exemplified what an Iraqi stringer must be." Haider knew the streets and the numerous Shiite factions who ruled them. He could get by the checkpoints and talk his way out of almost anything. "Khalid really liked Fakher from previous visits to Basra," Ahmed remembered. "Fakher treated him with respect and Khalid tried to learn from him. It was very dangerous for Khalid [as a Sunni] in that Shiite area, and he listened when Fakher spoke and watched him to see how he behaved. Like all of us, Khalid thought of Fakher as someone to look up to."

In September, Haider arrived in Baghdad to collect his paycheck. He stayed for two days, rooming in the area of the *Times* compound where the Western reporters lived. On his second day he went to Saydia to get some car parts at a shop Khalid had recommended. As Fakher was coming out of the shop, a car bomb exploded, one of the some twenty detonating daily in the country. He was not wounded, but Khalid al-Ansary remembers him returning to the compound "shaken and pale from what he had seen, and this man had seen a lot."

Haider said goodbye to al-Ansary, then discussed with Ahmed and Hassan their plans for an upcoming visit to Basra. "We'll see each other soon, *inshala*," he said to Khalid on his way out.

"*Inshala,* either here or there," Khalid replied, meaning Baghdad or Basra. "Or there," he added, meaning heaven.

A week later Haider sent in a story about clashes between British soldiers and the corrupt Shiite militia. Shortly afterwards, on the night of September 18, a police car pulled up in front of his house and Haider was taken in for questioning. Early the next morning he was found dead on the outskirts of Basra with a bullet in his head.

The *Times* staff had barely absorbed the shock of Haider's murder when an attack was launched against the Palestine and Sheraton hotels, which were protected by the same concrete blast wall that ran along the front of the bureau half a block away. On October 23, a car bomb blasted a hole in the wall in front of the hotels and a cement truck that was following behind got partway through then detonated. The deafening explosion sent up a two-hundred-foot mushroom cloud; glass shattered throughout the hotels and every window in the *Times* building blew out. A couple of seconds later the truck's radiator landed in the bureau's back-yard. Twenty people were killed on the street. The reporters in the compound—which also contained the offices of the Associated Press, Reuters and the BBC—felt as if they were under siege.

It was during this period that Hassan received his first targeted threat. He was at work when Sunni insurgents showed up at his apartment and told Samira that they wanted to speak to her son. When she said he wasn't home, one of them said, "Tell Khalid Hassan to quit his job"—indicating to her they knew exactly where he worked. Samira told her son that she wanted to move, and he reluctantly agreed, transferring his "heaven" into an apartment complex just a few blocks away. When Samira said the location still left them vulnerable, he explained to her that the insurgents in Saydia were like street gangs: they controlled neighborhoods, and the move would take them out of this gang's orbit. There may have been some limited truth to that, yet Khalid made no attempt in his new neighborhood to hide his expensive accessories, which was evidence to everyone on his block that he worked for Westerners.

He walked around with a Bluetooth in his ear and dressed like he was on his way to an L.A. nightclub. Khalid al-Ansary, who had started at the bureau in 2004, viewed Hassan's attire as a dangerous but sincere political statement, observing that when colleagues told Hassan he was asking for trouble, he always replied, "The insurgents don't tell Solid Khalid how to dress." Those who had little patience for Hassan thought his behavior part and parcel of the immaturity that was causing him other problems in the bureau.

In November 2005, a forty-one-year-old woman named Yusra al-Hakeem joined the paper. A former engineer with a son Khalid's age, she was startled when the twenty-one-year-old journalist wasted no time in making advances. "When I first went there he was trying to be close to me," she told me. "I was shocked. I kept saying, 'I'm your mom's age! Watch your words! Watch your behavior! Behave, boy!' He was like a big baby who didn't know how to behave."

"I don't know how to define the word *mature*," Ali Adeeb, the newsroom's manager of the Iraqi staff, told me, "but if you want to say maturity means that you are consistent in your behavior, he wasn't consistent. He had different sides to his personality. For someone his age, for sure he was a smart guy, and when it came to the Internet, computers, software, mobile phones—he was really into this stuff and he understood everything. The other side was his childishness. He would make up excuses for being late, then come to me and say, 'I want to leave early.' And this would happen very often, just like a kid in school with poor attendance habits. Sometimes he would give translation work to others that I asked him to do because he was just not in the mood to do it."

Adeeb had been hired as manager of the Iraqi staff in part because of his natural ability to defuse confrontations and get warring parties to all face in the same direction. He had tried to calm the roiled waters around Khalid by explaining to people offended by him that, because of his physical size, it was easy to forget how young he was. But even the mild-mannered Adeeb had enough when he sent a Christmas e-card to the Western office manager, Jane Scott Long, and out leapt a sex site. "I said to her, 'Oh my God, I sent it from a normal greeting site!' So she replied, 'I know it's not you, but we have a virus and I know it's because of Khalid.' He was always Suspect Number One. All the time, whenever we had a porn virus, we would think, 'Khalid!' Finally I gave him a last warning: 'Listen, you cannot do this in the newsroom!'"

That stopped the viruses for a bit, partly because Khalid appointed himself as the office cop, scanning the system at frequent intervals and reporting to Adeeb everything he discovered. "See, here is a virus and it wasn't me."

His immaturity notwithstanding, the articles Khalid filed during this period read like a catalogue of the hellish events engulfing Iraq's civilians: "3 Truck Bombs Kill at Least 62 in Iraqi Town"; "24 hurt as Bombs Shatter New Year's Calm in Baghdad and Kirkuk"; "4 Schoolchildren Are Killed as Baghdad Violence Surges."

A week after this last article, on February 22, 2006, a terrorist attack occurred that precipitated all-out civil war between Sunnis and Shiites. In the city of Samarra, about forty miles north of Baghdad, the Al-Askari Mosque, one of the most holy sites for Shiites, was destroyed by powerful bombs. During the next two weeks, the morgues of Baghdad filled with 1,300 bodies, each atrocity committed by one side leading to an atrocity by the other.

Four months after the mosque bombing, Hassan began the closest relationship of his life with a person outside his family — a father figure who lived near his apartment in Saydia and who drove him to and from work each day for most of his last year. Wisam Habeeb was a Muslim East Indian of Kashmiri descent whose family had moved to Iraq from Lebanon in the 1940s and who bore such a close resemblance in looks and temperament to Mahatma Gandhi that his friends had nicknamed him after the man of peace.

Habeeb was born in Baghdad in 1956, and, as a sensitive teenager, he'd had ambitions to be an artist. Economic reality persuaded him to enter Baghdad's High School of Commerce, and through the 1980s and '90s he worked for various European companies as a translator. Like many English-speaking Iraqis, after Saddam's statue came down he got a job with the foreign media, first with the BBC and then with the *Guardian*. In August 2004, he was threatened with beheading for working with the occupiers and switched to Japan's NTV. His reporting on the insurgency and Iraq's complex political parties was exceptional, and a couple of years later he decided to accept an offer from the *New York Times*. He started at the bureau on June 16, 2006, and when Hassan learned they lived just a few blocks apart, he asked for a lift.

On weekdays, the four-mile ride from the housing blocks of Saydia to the *Times'* upscale neighborhood in the Abu Nawas district took forty-five minutes—twice as long if there were roadblocks. "I spent more time alone with Khalid, going and coming, than anybody else except his family," Habeeb said. He was curious about this twenty-two-year-old who could go from a serious man who risked his life for his work to a silly kid who found humor in pornographic e-mail and sometimes seemed interested in gadgets more for their novelty than for the journalistic service they performed. From these sessions in the car, Habeeb learned details of Hassan's early upbringing and what was on his mind as events unfolded over the following year. I sat with Wisam for hours as he recollected those commutes: "He was obviously secular, but he was also Palestinian, and I wondered about his politics. I discovered he had serious views which were well thought out." Unlike almost every other Palestinian Iraqi, Khalid had never liked Yasser Arafat and had strongly disapproved of his tactics during the Intifada, which included sending out young people as suicide bombers. "Khalid accepted that the Jewish state was here to stay," Habeeb recollected. "Peace would come only when Palestinians learned to look forward and not backward. His model in the Arab world was Sheikh Zayed

Al Nahyan"—the late president of the United Arab Emirates. "He appreciated that he'd preached and practiced tolerance, and that he was the only Arab leader who thought about the future more than the past. He knew the man's whole biography: he said he had never fought a war with his neighbors, whereas here in Iraq Saddam never stopped fighting them. And what did it give us? Thousands upon thousands of fatherless children who'd grown up in poverty and were now insurgents. These were very perceptive insights."

"The more we talked," Habeeb went on, "the more I was startled by his range of knowledge. He received a lot of wisdom from his grandfather, and he had read all the great American authors, plus Shakespeare's plays, all the poems of Nizar Qabbani, many works of Middle Eastern and European history. Despite our age differences I could have serious discussions with him. On the other hand—"

He paused, laughed out loud and then recalled a cartoon Khalid had e-mailed to him, which Habeeb later forwarded to me. A horrified cat is looking up the backside of a woman bending over a food bowl—a not so subtle swipe at an office overseer who loved cats, and one that could have got him fired.

Wisam said that to understand why Khalid so frequently combined the silly with the high-minded, the responsible with the reckless, you had to consider where he'd come from and what he'd lived through as a boy. His job at the *Times* gave him the opportunity to some day achieve what Habeeb thought was his potential to be a truly great journalist, but it also gave him the opportunity to indulge his hunger for what he'd been deprived of as a child. "He never got to play."

"All of that silly side I attributed to his age," Habeeb added. "But you know, the essence of youth is that they do things older people wouldn't do—and that includes the very bold and brave things that push the human race forward. The silly things they grow out of. But sometimes their brave and bold deeds don't allow them to grow out of their youth. It gets them killed."

—

On January 10, 2007, George Bush announced what would become known as "the surge," but the effects of thirty thousand additional U.S. troops, a new commander and a new counterterrorism strategy would not be felt in the seven months that remained of Khalid Hassan's life. The civil war became instead more violent and bloodier, with one of the single worst mass casualty events of the war occurring just three weeks after Bush's announcement.

On February 3, a truck containing over two thousand pounds of explosive detonated in the middle of the Sadriya Market in Central Baghdad at the height of the Saturday-afternoon shopping hour. The explosion in the mostly Shia neighborhood killed almost everyone in the surrounding crowd and collapsed the apartment houses overlooking the market, turning the streets into what one witness called "a swimming pool of blood." The detonation could be heard throughout the city and the rising black smoke was visible for fifty miles. Eight journalists at the *Times* went to work on the story, including Khalid Hassan. He traveled to the market and found a scene of unimaginable carnage. For blocks around the central crater, red firehoses snaked over blasted bodies half buried in bricks, blackened cars lay on their sides and the helicopters roaring back and forth over the streets barely drowned out the high-pitched screams of the wounded and the mourning. "The Americans are the sons of dogs because they do nothing to protect us," the *Times* reported one elderly man bellowing. The death toll from this single event was over 130, with at least 300 wounded, bringing the total number of dead from half a dozen bomb attacks in just three weeks to 400, and the civilian death toll from the last 33 days to almost 2,500, a figure that included the score of bodies found every morning on the streets of Baghdad, murdered in the night and dumped like carrion.

Driving home from work with Habeeb, Hassan said that the people who did such things could not be permitted to win in Iraq or they would take over the whole world. Then, to distract himself from what he had seen, he slipped an Elton John CD into Habeeb's car stereo and sang along with "Rocket Man." He went home to his room and watched several episodes of *Desperate Housewives* until he fell asleep. A few days later, when he sold his DVD player to Zaineb in order to trade up to a better one, he declared, "The things I watch on DVD are not valued by very educated people. But they are very important to the world because they are about love. They are opposite to what is going on in our country."

Twelve days after the bombing—"the day after St. Valentine's Day," as Hassan would always tell the story—he visited a company called Atheer Telecommunications, where three of his uncles worked. He showed up as a reporter researching a feature on how businesses were coping during the ever-increasing violence.

In the back of the office sat a relatively new sales manager, with jet black hair falling to her shoulders and a blouse that was open at the neck. She had the complexion of a Caucasian, her full lips adorned with pink glossy lipstick and her almond eyes accentuated by dark mascara. Nidaa Al Salmani was twenty years older than Khalid, but one look at the slim woman as she stood up in high heels and reached over her desk for some papers convinced Khalid that he would marry her.

The social norms at Al Atheer were different from those at the relaxed *Times* bureau. Hassan couldn't just express a romantic interest in Nidaa the way he had with Yusra al-Hakeem, since Iraqi standards of decorum forbade self-introductions. Instead he approached his uncles about the woman and discovered she was a divorced college graduate, with no children, living alone with her widowed mother. His uncle Adil deduced that Khalid was not thinking about his news story anymore and led him over for an introduction. "The first time I saw him, I had no romantic feelings," Nidaa told me in Baghdad. "He was a boy and I didn't trust him—maybe he was bad or insincere. The thought didn't come into my mind to be attracted to him."

When Khalid got back to the *Times* compound, he phoned Nidaa and told her how impressed he was by her. The next day he found an excuse to visit Atheer, and the next. On his rides to and from work, all he could talk about with Wisam was Nidaa.

Iraqi courtship follows formal rules, which Khalid now had to abide by. No private meetings are permitted. At some point, when the woman believes the suitor is appropriate for marriage, she allows the conversation to enter what's called a "prenuptial period." If during this period she comes to believe the suitor is serious, she brings in her male relatives, who interview the prospective groom. Nidaa was still some way from taking that step.

"At the beginning of his calling upon me, I was afraid," she remembered. "How could I go down to his age, or he climb to mine? But after two weeks, after he came to find me so many times at Atheer, I began to know him. He was so sensitive, with a huge heart and so many intelligent opinions and fresh ways of thinking. Always he joked, he made me laugh. He talked about his work, what he did at the *Times*, the serious business, but also the funny things at the office. His mind was much older than his age. His heart was so big and he cared so much for his responsibilities in life and work. You know, I lost my father so long ago and I didn't have any brothers or sons, so he became for me like my brother, like my son. He was like a baby for me, like a baby bear."

"You mean a teddy bear?" I asked.

"I mean he was comforting to me. Day by day our relationship developed, and I discovered he's really a man. When he wants something, no one can stop him from getting it. He thinks in this way: 'If I want it, I *must* get it.' So when he fell in love with me, he insisted on getting me."

On March 8, three weeks after they had first met, Nidaa agreed to allow Khalid to begin his prenuptial courtship of her. Two days later he set off on a dangerous mission to cover a Shiite religious festival.

———

By name, Khalid Waleed Hassan was identifiable as a Sunni, and Shiites across Iraq were roiling with hatred at Sunnis for the market bombings and other mass casualty events recently committed against them. The weekend of March 10, millions of Shiites were congregating in Karbala for a passionate religious occasion known as Arabeen. The annual pilgrimage to the city fifty miles southwest of Baghdad commemorates the fortieth day of mourning following the slaying by Sunnis of the Prophet's grandson, Imam Hussein, in AD 680. That event defines the great schism between Shiites, who believe a member of the Prophet's family should have inherited his mantle, and Sunnis, who believe his successors were rightly chosen by the community of Muslims. The commemoration often involves bloody self-flagellation by mourners expressing their grief for the death of Hussein, as well as expressions of rage at Sunnis for the ancient injustice and all the trials they've endured since. Saddam had banned the pilgrimage for twenty-five years and the Shiites now had a lot of pent-up emotion to express.

To cover the event and produce an online video report, two *Times* reporters, Edward Wong and Diana Oliva Cave, caught a ride on a military helicopter with the Iraqi vice president, but there was no room in the aircraft for their interpreter, Khalid, who drove down. It was a journey that, as Cave stated in her memorial to Khalid, "was quite dangerous."

The Westerners and Khalid met up in the town of Hilla, across the Euphrates from Karbala. "He was beaming as usual—and probably on his cellphone. He was always on his cellphone," Cave recollected.

At that moment Khalid was almost certainly on the phone with Nidaa, for he had spent the entire car ride to Hilla talking to her. "I told him, 'Why do you go to such a dangerous assignment? You are like a man going to his death,'" Nidaa recollected. "He said, 'God is the only one who knows when I am going to die. Meanwhile, neither you nor I know anything about my fate. Let me go to Karbala and see the event there—at least I can try to understand it and convey to the world what's happening in the city. This is the job for which I am paid, this is my country and this is my life.'"

"Our drive from Hilla to Karbala was unbelievable," Cave wrote. "As we approached, we saw people everywhere, some of whom had been walking for 10 days to get there. The vice president told us that there were about 7 million pilgrims this year, the most ever. Khalid was Sunni, so this was particularly overwhelming. Nonetheless, his curiosity was immense and infectious."

Khalid "charmed the vice president silly over dinner, I think they even offered him a job," she wrote. When it came time to go to the mosque, however, the vice president decided it was too dangerous for the journalists to accompany him, especially with a video camera, and had them escorted to an SUV, where they were told to stay locked inside and wait for him. "Khalid was not satisfied," Cave recalled. "He really wanted to help me get the footage I needed. Feeling he'd be safer because he was an Iraqi, he hurriedly asked me for my camera and darted out of the vehicle, trying to keep up with the vice president." After he had disappeared into the crowd, the driver put the car in gear and pulled out of the parking spot. Neither Cave nor Wong spoke Arabic and couldn't explain the grave danger Khalid would be in if he returned to this spot and couldn't find them.

"Eventually the car pulled over at a hotel on the far side of town, where we were told we would have to wait for the vice-presidential entourage to return," she wrote. When the vice president did appear, Khalid was not with him, and their concern for their fellow reporter rose by the minute. "Then, all of a sudden the door of our vehicle swung open, and a sweaty, breathless Khalid fell in. He was practically crying with relief. But before we could even ask him a question, he extended his arm and in his hand was my camera. He handed it to me and said, 'I think I got it.'

"If you watch the Arabeen video report, some of the most important shots—the ones among the chanting Shiites in front of Imam Hussein Mosque—were filmed by Khalid. He had tried to follow the vice president, but was quickly swept into the raucous crowd and could not keep up. But despite being lost, fearful, and a Sunni in a crowd of hard-core Shiites, he had held up the camera, and gotten the shots we needed."

Not long after Khalid returned from Karbala, a truck bomb set by Sunni extremists went off on his block in the middle of his workday, killing about forty people on the street and blowing out half the foundation to his apartment house. His sisters were at school and, miraculously, his mother, who was in the apartment, was uninjured. She ran out of the building before it caved in, destroying most of the family's possessions. "Only life is important," he told his mother and sisters in the hotel room he rented that night. "Inanimate objects mean nothing," he added, dismissing the loss of his gadget-filled "heaven." To his colleagues at the *Times* he sloughed off the catastrophe as just another average day in Baghdad.

"Even in the face of tragedy that most people back here in the States could not comprehend, he managed not to lose his sense of humor," *Times* reporter Marc Santora later wrote. "I remember looking at the pictures [of the building] he had snapped on his cellphone camera, and his ability to still crack wise about the incident struck me."

Khalid moved the family half a mile south to a rental complex called Shoqaq Al Saydia. He took a three-bedroom flat on the ground floor of a concrete building with a scooped archway that gave the place an Arabian flair, then phoned Nidaa's male cousin, Osama, and asked to visit his beloved's home in Mansour, north of Saydia, to request her hand. Several of Nidaa's male cousins held a meeting and the prenuptial interview with Khalid was arranged for the evening of April 4. Khalid showed up in a suit and tie and was interviewed by the group while Nidaa and her mother sat in another room. Finally, Osama went into Nidaa's room. "He's a good man, he loves you, he has a good future because he has a job with the *New York Times*," Nidaa remembers Osama saying. "Never mind his age, he's exceptionally clever. I'm satisfied this will be a good marriage for you." Nidaa went to Khalid and told him she agreed to his proposal. He began to weep. "My dear Nidaa," he said, "I promise to give you a good life, a happy life."

Two days later the couple held an engagement party with both sides of the family, during which the ebullient Khalid reconciled with his father. On Monday morning he showed up for work in a state that approached ecstasy, totally oblivious to the raised eyebrows in the office when he passed Nidaa's picture around. "She's an *old* woman!" Abdul Razzaq, then thirty-seven, remembers thinking. "A single old woman, and this young man is crazy in love with her! Of course she's not going to say no—you take what you can get! He was showing all of us her picture, saying, 'What do you think, what do you think?' So I told him, 'Khalid, you're still young, why are you involved in this very complicated relationship? Here you are in Iraq, for goodness' sake! People will never accept such a match as normal.'"

Wisam Habeeb suspected that Khalid's fetish for older women, combined with his poor self-esteem because of his weight, might be causing him to make a mistake. When he pulled into the driveway of the Shoqaq complex that evening with Khalid, he decided to follow his colleague inside. "I spoke to his mother and asked frankly, 'Why does your son like this older woman? Did you not have a close relationship with him to cause him to dream about women his mother's age? Was he deprived of your love?' And I discovered then that she was very upset about the relationship, she said that she blamed herself because when Khalid was young she was busy with his four sisters and working as a cleaning woman. She said that she wanted the relationship to end."

Samira set about trying to torpedo the engagement, and by June she had nearly succeeded. According to what Khalid told both Nidaa and Wisam, his mother gave him an ultimatum: "If you marry her, don't ever bring her to the house. If you want to visit me, come alone. And if you don't want to visit me, I will consider you dead."

Khalid wavered. "My mother disagrees with this," he told Nidaa. "She refuses to go along with our relationship. I don't know what to do." Nidaa was furious. She told Khalid maybe it was time they parted ways for a while. Khalid replied, "Okay, you have your own life, I have mine." On June 13, Nidaa, wondering what she was doing with this childish boy, left for a two-week vacation in Lebanon and Jordan.

As soon as she was gone, Khalid realized what he had just done. He went to Yusra al-Hakeem in tears. "He told me, 'Yusra, I can't get over this, I need to talk to you! I need advice! My fiancée has left me and I don't know what to do!' I felt so bad for him," she explained to me, "but I was leaving for Jordan and the United States the next day and I had no time to discuss the matter with him. I still feel bad, because that was the last time I saw Khalid."

That night, Khalid phoned Nidaa in Beirut, and then continued phoning her, half a dozen times a day, throughout her vacation, until, just before she returned at the end of June, she accepted his apology. The couple got re-engaged, setting the marriage date for September 15. To help celebrate, Khalid's father used his contacts in the car business to get his son a deal on an old Kia. Khalid then told Wisam he would be driving himself to work from now on.

On June 28, Khalid contributed his penultimate story to the *Times*, with the headline "Sectarian Attacks Kill Dozens in Baghdad." It was an example of the open warfare wracking his own mixed Sunni-Shiite neighborhood. Just across the district line from Saydia, in Baya, "a rush-hour bombing killed twenty-five people," he reported. Another article in the *Times* around that period declared, "By general consent, Saydia is one of the worst areas of Baghdad, if not the worst." Sunni insurgents, driven from their strongholds in other parts of the city, were flooding in, assassinating local Shiites, who turned to the extremist Mahdi Army for protection. Death squads hunted each other in the streets, set off car bombs and took potshots at residents from rooftops. Thousands were fleeing the district.

Khaldoon Khalid, one of the bodyguards who accompanied me around Baghdad, and who had lived not far from Hassan in Saydia, recollected the horror taking place in the streets during Hassan's last two weeks. "Every day, every hour, the Mahdi Army and Sunni extremists bombed, mortared, shot and tortured," he told me in our armored car as we sat at a roadblock not far from Khalid's house. "They burned apartment houses. One house near us" — he flicked his thumb against his forefinger, as if striking a match — "thirty-six people dead."

On July 7, Wisam Habeeb was throwing some bags of garbage into an alley being used as a local dump when a teenaged boy came up behind him and shouted, "Do not throw your garbage there!"

There had been no garbage pickup in Saydia for months, since the insurgents had killed the garbage men to make life unendurable in the neighborhood. Habeeb looked across the street to another alley, also filled with garbage. He figured the boy lived above this alley and had had enough of the sulfurous stench. "Should I throw it over there?" he said.

"Nowhere!" the boy said. "Your garbage has beer bottles, whiskey bottles. This makes them outraged."

"Who is 'them'?" Wisam asked.

"Al-Qaeda. They have moved into our neighborhood and are making threats against everyone."

Wisam ran upstairs and told his wife, Sundus, "Pack immediately, we are moving." He burned all the stories he had been working on for the *Times* and moved across town to the Babylon Hotel in Karada, about a mile south of the *Times* and opposite the new American embassy being constructed within the Green Zone. The area was heavily patrolled by American forces, and while Wisam couldn't afford to stay in the Babylon for more than a week, he thought that would be enough time to look for an apartment in an area that was marginally safer than Saydia—or at least one where he would not be actively hunted by a local branch of al-Qaeda. "It was a question of percentages," he told me. "Nowhere was safe, but Saydia was now a hundred percent unsafe for a journalist to live. The jihadis had informants who wrote down license plates—they knew everything and made up assassination lists. So when I went to the *Times* that day I told Khalid, 'You must get out now. Al-Qaeda is in our neighborhood.' He said he knew all about it and it didn't bother him. 'These mujahideen are just kids,' he said. 'Some of them used to be students with me. I saw them on their bicycles carrying their Kalashnikovs. I just laughed at their silliness.' I said to him, 'Khalid, if you say you laughed at them, it's even worse. They are crazy people. Even if you are not afraid of them, there are mortars coming in every day from Baya.' All he said was, 'There is no place to move. One place is the same as another. That is my home and I will not leave it because of them.'"

"It was a strange reaction," Wisam added. "His mother was telling him, 'Khalid, please, we must leave Saydia,' and he cared very much for her safety. Also, he was moving away in September after his wedding, so why not move now? Instead, he made jokes about getting good interviews. He was very young and very stubborn and he would not be driven out."

Khalid's last story for the *Times* was about an al-Qaeda member who'd just been hanged by the government for a bomb attack at a Shiite mosque that had killed a prominent Shiite cleric as well as eighty-four other people. A couple of days later, on July 10, he visited Nidaa at her Atheer Telcom office and asked her to come with him to look at some furniture he was thinking of buying for their apartment. When she said she couldn't leave work just then, he seemed crestfallen. "He looked very tired, very sad, so I asked him, 'What is the matter?' He said, 'Maybe it's near the end for me.' I said, 'What are you talking about?' He said, 'Maybe I will never see you again because I will not change for these people.' Then he kissed me and went to work."

The next day, a colleague of Khalid al-Ansary's who worked for Reuters was murdered east of Karada. "He was my second colleague to be killed, after Fakher Haider," al-Ansary told me. "We were very close. He had two kids. I was very upset. I took my family and we went to Syria the next day, to get away, to forget. That's where I was during the next few days."

On his way home from work on Thursday, July 12, the last evening of his life, Khalid Hassan stopped off at Nidaa's house in Mansour. "We discussed the wedding and the furniture for the apartment," she remembered. "Then I had to make supper for my mother, so Khalid got up to leave. I saw him through the window, he put the key in the car door, but then he returned. He came in and said, 'Nidaa, I feel like I am never going to see you again.' I said, 'Khalid, shhh! You must stop talking that way! *Ithkur Allah rooh!*" Trust in God and return home safely.

The following day, Friday—the Muslim day of prayer— happened to be Khalid's day off. It would have been a good time for him to stay at home: The threat of car bombs around mosques was so extreme on Fridays that the government had declared that all cars should be off the streets between 11 a.m. and 3 p.m. Nevertheless, late Thursday night he called Nidaa and told her he'd informed the bureau he would be going into work. "He wanted to report on the very dangerous situation near the mosques," she told me. "He was so brave, he would not think of the danger to himself."

In the morning, as soon as he awoke at 7:30, Khalid phoned Nidaa and spoke to her for an hour on his Bluetooth while he washed and shaved and dressed. Some time after 8:30, he pulled his rusted Kia out of the Shoqaq compound and headed east toward Saydia Road, the main thoroughfare that led to the Jadriya Bridge across the Tigris. There was only one direct route to Saydia Road, Industry Street, and somewhere along it he ran into trouble. At 8:45

he sent a text message to his boss, Ali Adeeb: "Hi Ali, My area is blocked. I'm trying to find a way out."

"He sent the sentence in English and Arabic," Adeeb told me. "He wanted to make clear I understood he wasn't just making his usual excuse for being late, so in the second sentence he used an Arabic idiom, *'zaghoor atlaa min enda.'*" The idiom implied he was in a tight spot that he needed to get out of—possibly a roadblock, which in that disputed region of east Saydia could have been set up by Shiite militia or Sunni extremists. Either one would have been bad news for Khalid.

He got through or around whatever was blocking Industry Street and found his way to Saydia Road. Four lanes wide, Saydia Road runs north and south; today the road has a concrete median that prevents U-turns, but when Khalid turned onto it and headed north to the bridge, it was undivided.

A mile from where he entered the thoroughfare, on the left side, is Baya Benzene, the main filling station for the region. South of the station Hassan hit traffic that was backed up in both directions with cars waiting to fill up. My security guard, Khaldoon Khalid, was a witness to what happened next. He was perhaps a dozen cars behind Hassan, headed to the Hamra Hotel compound, where he worked for the security company that defends the facility. Not until the incident made the news did he learn who was in the car ahead of him.

"Traffic was stopped," Khaldoon told me, where we had pulled to the side of the road opposite Baya Benzene. "Then I saw two men go out from a Mercedes a few cars behind Hassan. They went up with rifles and—bang! bang! bang! Then they walked back to their car."

Hassan was wounded in the torso, but, amazingly, he'd been hit only once. He turned the wheel of his car sharply, honked his horn, and the startled drivers waiting to fill up on his left allowed him to make a U-turn. Khaldoon saw Hassan talking on his cellphone as he crossed the center line. In two brief calls he told his mother, then his father, that he'd been shot but was okay.

As Hassan completed the U-turn, an Opel behind the Mercedes made a U-turn and cut him off. Two gunmen got out and sprayed Hassan's Kia with bullets, hitting him in the head and neck. They reached in through the window, took his Sony Ericsson phone from the car seat, then went through his pockets and left the scene with his wallet and *New York Times* press credentials.

Wisam Habeeb was in the Babylon Hotel when he got a call from Khalid's weeping mother, who told him her son had just been murdered. Wisam drove immediately to the *Times* bureau, where he phoned Khalid's father, reaching him at Baghdad's police headquarters. He learned the boy's body had been thrown in the back of a truck alongside other unidentified murder victims picked up that day in Saydia and driven to the station. Kahlid's father and uncles had identified the body where it lay in the truck. The police then put Khalid in a body bag for them, and they brought it to the morgue in Yarmouk Hospital. From there Khalid's body was transported by the municipal authorities to the Abu Hanifa Mosque, which adjoins the Martyrs' Cemetery in Adhamiya.

That afternoon the family held a small funeral service for Khalid in his apartment, then drove to the mosque, where Wisam and Ali Adeeb were waiting for them. "We went inside to where the imam washes the body," Wisam recalled. "It was in a special room built of marble. Khalid was on a stone tablet. We prayed to his body and then the imam rubbed him with white linen and put perfume on him—it made him smell of roses. I thought, 'Well, Khalid, here you were a boy who had not hurt anybody and had tried to do good for your family, your country and the world. You were too brave.'

"In the cemetery, I told the grave keeper to please put Khalid gently in the ground. And then he was gone."

All that day the Westerners at the bureau reflected on Khalid's life as a journalist. "Among colleagues who reminisced about him on Friday," John Burns wrote in his article about the murder,

"Mr. Hassan was remembered for a willingness to venture into some of Iraq's riskiest war zones, his occasionally imprudent enthusiasm, and a quirky humor."

Ehab Ahmed was in Damascus when he heard about Khalid's death, having just fled there after being threatened with beheading. "I cried for him," he told me, from where he now lives in Vancouver, in safety. "I cried because he was just a boy and he stood up to the people destroying our country. He had a terrible life. He was such a good guy, all he wanted was a normal life. But he would not flee Saydia to get it."

Shortly after the murder, Wisam and his wife fled to Damascus. When Samira relocated to the city with her daughters at the end of the summer, she asked the couple to move into her apartment. "She wanted to be close to someone who had been close to her son," he said. "Before I returned to Baghdad to continue my work, I reminded her of his gravestone and said that his reporting still lived. I told her that all the murdered journalists, they still live."

JOURNALISM AS AN ACT OF COURAGE

BEFORE HE WAS MURDERED, Manik Saha enjoyed taking time from his reporting to read *Aesop's Fables* to children at the school he'd founded in Bangladesh. I often picture him reading "The Wolf and the Kid."

A kid goat stands atop a roof. When he notices a wolf passing through town, he cries out, "Murderer and thief! What are you doing here near honest folks' houses? How dare you make an appearance where your vile deeds are known?" The wolf looks up and replies with the moral of the fable: "Curse away, my young friend, for it is easy to be brave from a safe distance."

None of the journalists in this book kept a safe distance from the wolf in their towns. Like Manik Saha, they all leapt to do battle with the jaws of death. I have spent the last several years trying to understand why they did that.

By visiting their homes and asking questions about their murders, I was given a glimpse of the mortal threats they each had faced. But only a glimpse, for I was always doubly protected. I stood atop the safe roof of my foreign citizenship, and I had another roof on top of that one—allies who guided me through my research. By contrast, the murdered journalists had all stood alone and unprotected, neither on a roof nor under one. They had committed themselves to a life-and-death struggle whose outcome they had predicted.

I think the best way to understand their motives is by recogniz-
ing the extent of the corruption and violence in their homelands.
As journalists under threat, they had three options: they could flee;
they could agree to stay silent; or they could continue to expose the
murderers and thieves who dominated their countries. Making
that decision took time. The consequences were weighed. They
struggled with themselves and finally pushed their fears aside. I
think anyone can identify with the dangerous decision these men
and women made *if* one remembers that they were standing up
for their homes. They did not arrive from somewhere else to seek
adventure in exotic Neiva, Tacurong, Khulna, Moscow, Togliatti
or Baghdad. They lived where they died, and they tried to defend
the towns where they lived.

In the chapter about Anna Politkovskaya, I noted that there is a
prize in Russia awarded annually for "Journalism as a Deed." The
phrase sounds vague in English, but in Russia, where deeds have
always involved a degree of peril, its meaning is clear. Journalism
as a deed is an act of courage. In Russia it is understood that the
consequence for exposing a powerful figure is sometimes death.
When journalists make the decision to carry on in the face of
threats, they cease being mere messengers and become unarmed
combatants. They enter the public arena to battle an opponent who
stands at the head of an army.

Local journalists in lawless countries are aware they will probably
lose that battle. At the same time, they generally believe that something good will arise from news of their loss. And therein lies the key
to understanding the hearts of the journalists I have written about. I
am now convinced that, whatever their individual psychologies, they
saw themselves as acting for the sake of the many victims in their
tormented communities. In the West, stable governments and
honest police officers help raise journalists above the deadly jeop-
ardy they may face because of their reporting. But in towns where the
government and police are in league with killers and bandits, there
is no safe vantage point, and risky deeds are required. By leading the

charge against corrupt forces, journalists set an example for others to follow. They know from the outset that they might be the first to fall, but they charge onward, believing that, months or years in the future, their fellow citizens will find their courage and join their struggle.

The journalists in this book lived and died for that higher purpose—the source of their own courage. Convinced that the outcome of events could be affected by their reporting, they were unstoppable except by murder. There is little doubt that many of them wanted to be recognized for their heroic journalism, but that is something different from merely wanting attention. Did they care about impressing the opposite sex? Some did. Did they have hopes for personal advancement? In a minor way, yes, but not if it meant sacrificing their ultimate goal: advancing the cause for which they were willing to give up all personal advancement.

Hundreds of journalists have given their lives to right wrongs and to hold the powerful accountable. Not all journalists who have been murdered were so high-minded, of course, but if you read the brief biographies of victims on the website of the Committee to Protect Journalists, you will notice a pattern. The vast majority used their reporting to expose and confront the malevolent powers that plagued their homelands. They defied impunity, and they paid the price.

In the last decade, two journalists in the relative safe zones of the United States and Canada have paid that price. Their murders, while rare, stand as a warning. In my hometown of Vancouver, a newspaper publisher named Tara Singh Hayer reported on the terrorist activities of a Sikh fundamentalist group for fifteen years. He was partially paralyzed and confined to a wheelchair after an assassination attempt in 1988, but he persisted in his reporting until, on November 18, 1998, he was shot dead in his garage. In Oakland, California, on August 2, 2007, Chauncey Bailey, a veteran TV and print reporter, was gunned down after writing about a local business he connected to long-standing criminal activities. Both men lived in the communities where their journalism put them at risk, and their murders were probably instigated by the stories they had bravely pursued.

While journalists in the West generally do not fear that they will be killed in the line of duty, we have no reason to be complacent. Freedom of speech—and freedom from fear—can disintegrate relatively quickly when societies become stressed by declining economies or external threats. Ultimately what stands between us and the loss of our freedoms is the accountability of our officials. If they break the law, it is up to journalists to alert the public. Without that scrutiny, impunity takes hold. And in societies where impunity reigns, ordinary people eventually join the lawbreakers. The murdered journalists I've written about all witnessed that phenomenon, and died in the attempt to reverse it.

Since I began my research, Mexico and Sri Lanka have been elevated to the list of the world's most murderous countries for journalists. That list is always changing, but the motives of the murderers, and the ideals of the journalists who oppose them, remain the same. On January 8, 2009, three days before he was murdered, the Sri Lankan journalist Lasantha Wickramatunga predicted his fate and phrased his motives for continuing his reporting in an editorial published after his death: "People often ask me why I take such risks and tell me it is a matter of time before I am bumped off. Of course I know that: it is inevitable. But if we do not speak out now, there will be no one left to speak for those who cannot, whether they be ethnic minorities, the disadvantaged or the persecuted."

There are probably thousands of journalists at work today who are no less courageous than the fallen. Courage is not a quality we can assign only to those who have not survived their pursuit of journalism as a deed. I have met some of these men and women in the countries I visited. Except for good luck and quick reflexes, many of them would be dead too. They are living examples of the values for which their colleagues have died. They wake each morning knowing that at any moment they too could be killed for their work.

It is something to think about the next time you hear about journalists who have been murdered in faraway places. Often enough, they will have followed in the footsteps of colleagues who pressed on, knowing the fate that awaited them. They refused to bow to threats, penned their last exposé, and would have penned their next had not the expected assassin arrived to stop them.   ◈

This book is based on my interviews and research conducted from the spring of 2005 to mid-February 2009. Many of my sources are cited in the text. The dates of my interviews with these sources are given below. The names of other sources are also given below, along with the dates of interviews. A complete list of my interview sources can be found in the Acknowledgments, along with their special roles in helping with my research. I used numerous translators for my interviews and for reading the murdered journalists' work. I have supplied the names of my translators as well. Photos I took of my interview subjects and of translators in overseas countries are in my personal files. Almost all of the dialogue in this book comes from thousands of pages of notes and hundreds of hours of taped interviews. In some cases, I corrected grammar and made cuts to keep the dialogue readable or to protect a source. Source notes are matched to page numbers and sometimes include information that proved too lengthy to include as footnotes in the text. Some source notes in this book refer to my previously published work, particularly regarding the Philippines.

The epigraph to the book is from Vaclav Havel's *Letters to Olga: June 1970 to September 1982* (New York: Alfred A. Knopf, 1988), "Letter 95," p. 232.

INTRODUCTION: **THE PSYCHOLOGY OF SACRIFICE**

1–2: Efraín Varela was driving into Arauca with his brother-in-law Nicolas Valbuena when he was hauled from his car by paramilitaries and driven down the road. Varela's colleague at Radio Meridiano-70, Miguel Angel Rojas, was the first journalist to arrive at the murder scene. In an interview in Arauca on November 4, 2005, Angel told me Varela's cheek had been cut open and his tongue cut out; he'd also been shot numerous times. The police did not mention the torture in their reports, and Angel did not reveal it out of respect for the family, and also fear for his own safety. In 2007, a paramilitary was convicted for the murder, but the torture was not mentioned at the trial. I was accompanied to Arauca by Carlos Cortés Castillo, the director of Fundación para la Libertad de Prensa. My translators in Arauca were Cortés and Felipe Martinez. Martinez served as my translator for my interviews with Angel and Valbuena in Arauca's Hotel Monte Blanco.

Murder stats: The worldwide murder statistics are from the Committee to Protect Journalists (CPJ). The CPJ and Reporters sans frontières (RSF) have similar statistics for journalist murders. However, the country-by-country statistics of both NGOs are sometimes lower than those given by local press freedom groups who keep track of journalist murders in their individual countries. For countries with large numbers of killed journalists, the discrepancy can be substantial. See source note to p. 7 on the explanations offered for the differences in the tallies of journalists murdered for their work.

"between 2000 and 2003": Refers to the period I was working on *Paper Fan: The Hunt for Triad Gangster Steven Wong* (Toronto: Random House Canada, 2004; New York: Thunder's Mouth Press, 2004). I made frequent trips to the Philippines during that time and interviewed members of the Philippine Center for Investigative Journalism (PCIJ) and many other journalists, politicians, senior police and human rights workers. They are all listed in the sources to *Paper Fan*.

My references in *Paper Fan* to the appalling number of journalists being murdered in the Philippines can be found in that book on pp. 182, 351, 431–32, 459–60, 474 and 488.

2–3: In December 2004, I submitted to my publisher Random House Canada an idea for a book about journalists murdered in their home countries. The CPJ's report, "Marked for Death," was published on May 2, 2005. Random House Canada then accepted my book proposal. I spent the following months planning the first leg of my research. I was in frequent contact with the CPJ and their contacts in the countries that the CPJ listed as the most murderous for journalists. I flew to New York and, on October 17 and 18, 2005, I met with the CPJ staff responsible for the countries I would be visiting. They included CPJ Director Ann Cooper, for an overview; Carlos Lauría for Colombia; Abi Wright for the Philippines and Bangladesh; and Alex Lupis and Nina Ognianova for Russia. For Iraq, I interviewed the CPJ's Joel Campagna by phone in the summer of 2005. I left New York for Colombia, my first research locale, on October 19, 2005.

"those closest to them": A full list of my interview subjects and their relation to the victims can be found in the country-by-country section of the Acknowledgments. Most are also identified in the Source Notes and in the text.

4–5: My theory of the principle of organized crime was first stated in *Paper Fan*, pp. 295–96. I base that theory on my reporting of organized crime and my interviews with domestic and overseas criminal informants and politicians, as well as the experience of my contacts in domestic and overseas law enforcement agencies who handle informants within organized criminal structures.

5: My arrival date at Moscow's Sheremetyevo Airport, October 7, 2006, is stamped in my passport. I was in touch with representatives of the CPJ just before I left for Russia and as soon as I arrived, including Masha Yulikova and Alex Lupis in Moscow, and Nina Ognianova in New York. PEN Canada's Isobel Harry and David Cozac gave me Politkovskaya's private Yahoo e-mail address during an interview in Toronto on October 14, 2005.

CHAPTER ONE: **SMALL TOWN, BIG HELL**

7: The newsroom was in *La Nación*. The date of my first visit was October 21, 2005. Carlos Mora, the legal affairs reporter for *La Nación*, found back issues of the coverage of Bravo's murder for me and showed me uncropped file photos. "Asesinado periodista," *La Nación*, April 29, 2003. Also in the newsroom was Diógenes Cadena, who freelanced for *La Nación*. Bravo had only contributed freelance articles to *La Nacion*, but both Mora and Cadena had worked closely with him (see pp. 8–9). I also spoke with a number of other *La Nación* reporters in the newsroom who had known Bravo. I was accompanied by Carlos Cortés Castillo, the director of Fundación para la Libertad de Prensa, based in Bogotá, and my translator, Natalia Rey. Carlos Cortés also served as my translator in the *La Nación* interview. At the time, the threat of Westerners being kidnapped in Neiva by guerrillas was considered high by the Canadian embassy; Diógenes Cadena, a veteran war reporter, therefore accompanied me around Neiva as a guide and attended many of my interviews over the next several days.

Murder stats: The number of murdered Colombian journalists comes from the CPJ, which began keeping track of these murders in

1992; the number of murdered trade unionists comes from the International Confederation of Free Trade Unions, which dates its tally from 1985, and from oil union officials in Neiva.

As mentioned, different NGOs give different figures for the number of murdered journalists (as well as for murdered trade union members). For instance, in 2005 the Inter American Press Association's (IAPA) Rapid Response Unit in Colombia listed "54 cases of journalists murdered as a result of their work" between 1993 and the end of 2004; for roughly that same period, the CPJ gave the figure of thirty-six Colombian journalists murdered for their work. The explanation for the discrepancy is that the countries where the most journalists are being murdered are very violent generally and journalists are being murdered for reasons other than their work, which leaves the motive of the killers open to debate. In Colombia, the total number of journalists murdered in the above period was 105, and each NGO made its own assessment of which murders could be attributed to the journalist's work, which murders had motives yet to be determined and which murders were not related to the journalist's work. Thus, the determination of cause varies with each NGO, since the journalists were most often murdered with impunity. NGOs such as the CPJ and RSF generally have higher figures for "motive not yet determined" than do locally based NGOs such as the IAPA's Rapid Response Unit in Colombia.

While I was in Colombia, the CPJ published an article I found very useful in my research: Chip Mitchell, "Untold Stories: Threatened on all sides, Colombia's news media muzzle themselves," *Dangerous Assignments*, October 2005. I interviewed Chip Mitchell in Bogotá when his article was first published.

8: "Small Town, Big Hell": The phrase has been used by the press to describe several provincial capitals and towns in Colombia's war-torn regions. Neiva earned the sobriquet because of raids, murders and kidnappings by guerrillas and murders by paramilitaries in the period that preceded and followed the establishment of FARClandia.

Short summary of Bravo's career: Based on interviews in Neiva and Bogotá (interview subjects are given above and below for each phase of his career).

"shrouded by conquistadorean darkness": Bravo used this phrase in his early writing on economics, read aloud to me by his son Juan Carlos Bravo. Bravo often returned to the theme in issues of *Eco Impacto* and on his TV shows.

"Opitas Mafia": Almost all my interview subjects in Neiva referred to the Opitas Mafia by name, and Bravo frequently referred to it on his TV shows and in his journalism.

My translators for Bravo's written and TV work in Colombia were Natalia Rey and Carlos Cortés Castillo. Bravo's son Juan Carlos Bravo and Bravo's nephew Eduard Alexander Ortiz read out portions of Bravo's work and gave me samples of his magazines, Natalia Rey translating. When I returned home, my translator for Bravo's written work, and Spanish articles written about him, was Maria Solana Tristant.

9: "lady's man": Information on Bravo's number of wives and mistresses also comes from Bravo's family and other colleagues mentioned in this chapter, and his third wife (common-law), Ana Cristina Suarez.

9–10: "last death threat" and last days: Information on Bravo's last threat and the period of time leading up to his assassination also comes from other colleagues mentioned in this chapter and his common-law wife, Ana Cristina Suarez.

10–11: *Eco Impacto:* I was shown back issues of *Eco Impacto* by Bravo's son Juan Carlos Bravo, who contributed extensively to my research on Bravo's biography, politics and writings. I was also greatly helped by Bravo's nephew Eduard Alexander Ortiz and Bravo's first wife, Angela Ortiz Pulido. I interviewed Juan Carlos, Eduard Alexander Ortiz and Angela Ortiz Pulido on October 22, 23 and 24 in Neiva. My translators were Carlos Cortés Castillo and Natalia Rey.

Regalame: I interviewed Juan Carlos Cirdenas, head of the oil union's interunion affairs, on October 21, 2005, in the oil union headquarters (Union Sindical Obrera) in Neiva. Also present were other union officials, including Augusto Medina, subdirector of the union. My translator was Natalia Rey.

11: Bravo used some of his research from his thesis in his Bolívar Award–winning article, "Bonanza: The Rise and Fall of the Economy." Juan Carlos read me excerpts from the thesis and article.

"Flying into western Colombia": I flew in on October 19, 2005.

11–15: My summation of the history of Colombia is based on my general knowledge of the country and several texts, including Frank Safford and Marco Palacios, *Colombia: Fragmented Land, Divided Society* (New York: Oxford University Press, 2002); Steven Dudley, *Walking Ghosts: Murder and Guerrilla Politics in Colombia* (London:

Rutledge, 2004); and Robert T. Buckman, *Latin America 2003* (Harpers Ferry, 2004). Most of my interview subjects gave me invaluable insights into Colombian history.

14: "blowing up a downtown electronics store": "Atentado contra IBG," *Diario del Huila,* October 21, 2005.

15–26, overview: The narrative of Bravo's life from 1938 to 1985 is, in large part, taken from interviews with his son Juan Carlos Bravo, Bravo's first wife, Angela Ortiz Pulido, and Bravo's nephew Eduard Alexander Ortiz. Many of the details were supplied on October 22 in Neiva and then added to on October 23 and 24. The summary of and quotation from *Morir de Pie* come from Juan Carlos Bravo and Eduard Alexander Ortiz. Many other people mentioned in the text or in the Acknowledgments filled in details of what they knew of Bravo's years in Neiva from 1981 to 1985.

27–29: Bravo's cavalier attitude to the death threat is from Angela Ortiz Pulido.

My interview with Jaime Lozada Perdomo took place on October 22, 2005, in his condo in Edificio Mira Flores in Neiva. Lozada spoke some English and often switched back and forth between English and Spanish. My translators were Carlos Cortés Castillo and Natalia Rey.

29–35: Information on Bravo's life from the mid-1980s to mid-1990s comes from his family and colleagues cited in the text. Specific details of Bravo's writing on Huila's oil industry come from my interviews with Juan Carlos Cirdenas, head of the oil union's interunion affairs, on October 21, 2005, in the oil union headquarters (Union Sindical Obrera) in Neiva. Also present were other union officials, including Augusto Medina, subdirector of the union. My translator was Natalia Rey.

33–34: I interviewed Ana Cristina Suarez on October 22, 2005, at the Peter Pan ice cream parlor in Neiva, and again on October 23, 2005, at the house where she'd lived with Bravo. My translators were Carlos Cortés Castillo and Natalia Rey on October 22, and Natalia Rey on October 23.

34–35: I interviewed Irma Castaneda on October 23, 2005, at her home in Neiva. Natalia Rey was my translator.

35: Bernardo Jaramillo's diary entry was quoted in Dudley's *Walking Ghosts*, p. 134.

36–41: My narration of Bravo's life between the spring of 1995 and the 2000 mayoralty race is based on my interviews with his son, nephew, wives, and journalist and union colleagues, as listed above; back issues of *Eco Impacto*; and news articles from that period in *La Nación* and *Diario del Huila*.

40: I interviewed Roberto Castaño on October 22, 2005, at HJKK, the Neiva radio station where Castaño worked as a broadcaster.

41–42: Bravo's news conference was taped by Juan Carlos Bravo and Edward Alexander Ortiz on February 4, 2000. Bravo then went on to give interviews with individual reporters in the city.

42–43: I interviewed Germán Hernández several times between October 21 and 24, 2005. My translators were Carlos Cortés Castillo and Natalia Rey.

43: The tape of the TV debate was shown to me by Juan Carlos Bravo and Eduard Alexander Ortiz. Natalia Rey was my translator.
   "*testaferro*": Bravo's use of the epithet in the article that he published in *La Nación* was widely reported in Neiva, mentioned by all my interview subjects and recounted after his death in *Diario del Huila* and *Semana* magazine.

44–45: Details of the kidnapping and ransom of Jamie Lozada's family come from my interview with Lozada, October 22, 2005 (see source note, pp. 27–29).
   Lozada's wife, Gloria Polanco, was finally freed by the guerrillas on February 27, 2008.
   Bravo's TV eulogy of Gimbler Perdomo was shown to me by Juan Carlos Bravo.

45–48: Information on the hiring of "The Regretful Shooter" and his visit to Bravo's house comes from my interviews with Germán Hernández and Ana Cristina Suarez, as attributed in the text. My translators were Carlos Cortés Castillo and Natalia Rey.

48–49: At the same time that I researched the murder of Efraín Varela in Arauca, I researched the murder of his young colleague, Luis Alfonso Parada (see source note for pp. 1–2). My numerous sources for the murders of both are listed in the Arauca section of the Acknowledgments.

49: "last note": Bravo inscribed the note on the front page of his novel, *The Night of the Hate*. Juan Carlos Bravo gave me a photocopy of the inscribed page. It reads in full (in translation): "Fabio: It's been a long time since we've heard from each other. S.O.S: the person that carries this book is a great personal friend and confidant, William Trujillo. He is delivering some information that I cannot mention here. My security situation for exposing corruption is extremely grave. William will tell you all about it. I ask you for your help, he will give you the details. See you soon, if the killers allow it. A big hug, Guillermo Bravo." Translated by Maria Solana Tristant.

50–51: Bravo leaving the door open: Ana Cristina Suarez, interview October 22, 2005.

51–52: Neighbor Dianna La Rotta, interviewed on October 23, 2005, in Bravo's house, along with Ana Cristina Suarez. Natalia Rey was translator.
    On October 22, 2005, Juan Carlos Bravo and Eduard Alexander Ortiz showed me the TV program that Bravo was working on at the time of his death; Eduard Ortiz gave me his account of editing the last video and Bravo's last written words, while we watched the video. Natalia Rey was translator.

53: Details of the funeral supplied by Juan Carlos Bravo, Eduard Alexander Ortiz and other colleagues of Bravo listed above. During my interview on October 22, 2005, Juan Carlos and Eduard Alexander described being approached by Teófila Forero.

53–54: The *Semana* article is an account of Bravo's murder published a few days after the second anniversary of Bravo's death; it was simultaneously published in *Diario del Huila*, on a single page, 3A. There is no byline to the article but Germán Hernández was one of its main authors. *"La última cuartilla de un periodista asesinado,"* *Semana*, May 2, 2005, pp. 70–74.

55–56: My interview with Jaime Lozada Perdomo: October 22, 2005 (see note for pp. 27–29).

56–57: I was alerted by Carlos Cortés Castilloto to the circumstances of Lozada's assassination as soon as it happened. The incident was widely covered in the Colombian press.

CHAPTER TWO: **I GREW UP ON BULLETS**

59: "many rulers of poor countries": quotation taken from Asiatour.com, http://www.asiatour.com/philippines/e-03mani/ep-man17_h.htm, Metro Manila section.

59–60: History of the Philippines: I wrote extensively about Philippine history and the nation's three People Power revolutions in *Paper Fan*, chaps. 16, 24, 25, 26 and 27. References can be found in Sources in *Paper Fan*, pp. 461–64 and 472–83.

60–61: Esperat's letter to President Gloria Arroyo: Photocopies of the original letter were given to me in Manila by Esperat's colleague at the Department of Agriculture, Fermin Diaz, on January 26, 2006, and by her lawyer, Nena Santos, in Koronadal, Mindanao, on January 31, 2006. Marlene had sent copies to both of them. In the original, Esperat underlined the phrase that is italicized on p. 61, and boldfaced and capitalized certain words within the phrase. Her intensives are shown on pp. 90–91, where the letter is quoted at length.

61: I arrived in Manila on January 24, 2006.

62–68: With the exception of the tradition of *pasalubong-pabaon*, the historical and statistical analysis of corruption in the Philippines contained in these pages is a very condensed version of that contained in *Paper Fan*, chaps. 16, 24, 25, 26 and 27. References for the analysis can be found in Sources in *Paper Fan*, pp. 461–64 and 472–83.

The tradition of *pasalubong-pabaon* was explained to me by Joel Egco, a reporter for *The Manila Standard*, on February 8, 2006.

Three texts on Philippine corruption I would recommend are Sheila S. Coronel, ed., *Pork and other Perks: Corruption and Governance in the Philippines* (Manila: Philippine Center for Investigative Journalism, the Evelio B. Javier Foundation and the Institute for Popular Democracy, 1998); Sheila Coronel, ed., *Betrayals of the Public Trust: Investigative Reports on Corruption* (Manila: Philippine Center for Investigative Journalism, 2000); and Gemma Luz Carotan, *Brother Hood* (Manila: Philippine Center for Investigative Journalism, 1995).

68: I arrived in General Santos City, Mindanao, on January 30, 2006, accompanied by Nathan Lee, a staff member of the Manila-based Center for Media Freedom and Responsibility (CMFR), who had just published an article on Marlene Esperat: "Marlene Esperat: Mother, Journalist, Crusader," *PJR Reports*, January 2006. I accompanied Lee as he interviewed the spouses of murdered journalists living under a witness protection program in General Santos City, as well as several law enforcement officials. Lee returned to Manila, and on January 31, Salvador Ramos, a guard with the witness protection program, accompanied me to Koronadal, where I was met by Esperat's lawyer, Nena Santos, who accompanied me to most but not all of my interviews in Koronadal and Tacurong. Santos served as my translator in instances where my interview subjects did not speak English.

69: I first interviewed Marlene Esperat's parents, Luis Garcia and Pacencia Garcia, on February 1, 2006, at their home in Tacurong. Nena Santos translated. Also present and interviewed extensively was Marlene's brother, Charlie Garcia, who spoke English, and who helped translate for his parents.

69–73: The narration of Marlene Esperat's life from her birth in 1959 to the murder of her common-law husband, Severino Arcones, in 1989, is based in part on my interviews with her parents, Luis Garcia and Pacencia Garcia; her brother, Charlie Garcia; her sisters, Valmie Garcia Mariveles and Lilibeth Garcia Lacorte; her legal husband, George Esperat; her lawyer, Nena Santos; her twenty-three-year-old daughter by Arcones, Rynche Arcones; her best friend, Alma Vidal; her colleague Fermin Diaz; and her editor at the *Midland Review*, Juanito Laguna. Her young sons by George Esperat, James Derreck Garcia-Esperat and Kevin Jorge Garcia-Esperat, ages ten and fourteen at the time I interviewed them, also contributed what Marlene had told them of her early life. In addition, I consulted her 2001 detailed résumé, given me by Nena Santos; her letter to President Gloria Arroyo in February 2005; her interviews with the Philippine Center for Investigative Journalism; and published accounts in Philippine newspapers and press freedom groups in the Philippines and overseas that had reported on her murder, including the CPJ, RSF, the PCIJ and the CMFR.

73: "The murder changed her life": I first interviewed Valmie Mariveles on February 1, 2006, in Karonadal, and interviewed her several times in Karonadal over the next few days, including February 2, 3, 4, and 5.

73–75: In interviews with me, Marlene Esperat's family; lawyer, Nena Santos; and husband, George Esperat; summarized Marlene's first two years at the Department of Agriculture. The PCIJ, Santos and Esperat's sisters directed me to an account of those years, which includes an accounting of the Provido and Jardino cases, published by the PCIJ in "Arson and Murder Fail to Silence Whistleblowers," *iReport* (2000).

75: Quotations from Valmie Mariveles regarding Marlene's perspective on her courtship of, and marriage to, George Esperat are taken from my interview with Mariveles at her home in Karonadal on February 3, 2006. Marlene's sister Lilibeth Lacorte and Marlene's daughter Rynche Arcones then contributed to the discussion during a family dinner, corroborating and adding to Mariveles' account. Marlene's best friend, Alma Vidal, gave a similar account on February 1. Marlene's lawyer, Nena Santos, gave a similar account during numerous interviews between January 31 and February 5, 2006. The accounts remained consistent over a period of several interviews between February 1 and February 5.

I interviewed George Esperat on February 1, 2006, in Tacurong, where he informed me he was a onetime friend of Osmeña Montañer at the Department of Agriculture and that Montañer became godfather to his and Marlene's son Kevin Jorge.

77: During my interviews, Marlene Garcia-Esperat's family and her lawyer, Nena Santos, told me about George's inappropriate attention to Marlene's daughters from her previous marriage, Rynche and Janice Arcones. On February 3, 2006, in an interview with Marlene's daughter Rynche, and Marlene's sisters, Valmie Mariveles and Lilibeth Lacorte, they addressed the specific manner of the attention George paid the girls. The interview took place at the dinner table at Valmie Mariveles's house in Koronadal. All of the parties spoke in English.

"George isn't your father, your father was killed," I said. "What do you think of George?"

"We don't have a good relationship as a father and daughter," Rynche said.

"Why?" I asked

"He was attempting to touch us," Rynche said, referring to herself and her older sister, Janice.

"Both of them," Valmie Mariveles said

"Did Marlene know about that?" I asked.

"Yes," Rynche replied

"The word in English is 'abuse,'" I said.

"Yeah, yeah, yeah," Lilibeth Lacorte said.

"How old were you when he did that?" I asked Rynche.

"Grade six," Rynche said.

"So you were like ten or eleven," I said. "How old was Janice?"

"The same time," Rynche replied. [It happened at the same time]

"The same time?" I asked "When she was ten or eleven too?"

"No, thirteen, fourteen," Rynche said, referring to Janice's age at the time.

"I've actually heard that," I said. "I just wanted to confirm it."

"Every time, when Marlene was out of town, so we used to get the girls to stay with us, my mother's house," Lilibeth Lacorte said.

"Because of that, Marlene plans to separate from him [George] because of this, because he's a bad guy," Valmie Mariveles said.

(I re-confirmed this account in a phone interview with Lilibeth Lacorte on January 13, 2009.)

77–84: Sources for the period of Marlene Esperat's life from May 1996 through 2001 include her detailed résumé given me by Santos; all members of Marlene's family mentioned above; her lawyer, Nena Santos; her best friend, Alma Vidal; George Esperat; her colleague in Manila, Fermin Diaz; her future editor at the *Midland Review*, Juanito Laguna; and the lengthy interview she gave to the PCIJ's Luz Rimban in "Madam Witness," *iReport* (2001).

80: George Esperat's retirement from the Commission of Audit: On February 1, 2006, in Tacurong, Nena Santos told me about Marlene's concerns regarding George Esperat, and Marlene's view of why she asked George to retire.

81: George Esperat's explanation for his retirement from the Commission of Audit was offered to me in an interview on February 1, 2006, in Tacurong.

82: "she told Luz Rimban": Luz Rimban, "Madam Witness," *iReport* (2001).

84: "flurry of graft cases": These graft cases are listed in full in a document Nena Santos gave me, entitled "Marlene Garcia Esperat: List of Cases with the Office of the Ombudsman." They are summarized in the April 2005 report of RSF, entitled "Philippines: An End to Impunity," p. 3.

84: Information on the libel lawsuit comes from Nena Santos and an article published in the *Midland Review* (March 30–April 5, 2005 edition) just after Esperat's death. Esperat won the lawsuit, just before her murder. The lawyer who represented Osmeña Montañer and Estrella Sabay in the lawsuit was Tocod Ronda, who was later appointed by Justice Secretary Raul Gonzales as the prosecutor to review the murder case against Montañer and Sabay (see p. 97 in the text). Information on Tocod Ronda comes from Nena Santos and the Center for Media Freedom and Responsibility.

85: I followed the 2004 Philippine presidential election closely because of my previous work on the Philippines for my book *Paper Fan*. Senator Panfilo Lacson, one of the subjects of *Paper Fan*, was running for president as a third-party candidate.

Information on Esperat's election campaign comes from Esperat's family, particularly her father, Luis Garcia, and Nena Santos. Esperat's quotation comes from her post-election column, "Dare to Fail" ["*Nangahas Mabigo*"], in the *Midland Review*.

85–87: Excellent sources for the 2004 election campaign run by Gloria Macapagal-Arroyo are two editions of the Philippine Center for Investigative Journalism's *iReport* (September 2005); and a special edition, published shortly thereafter, on the election and the "Hello Garci" tapes scandal. There are some twenty investigative articles in both magazines that cover the period leading up to the election. In the special edition, see particularly: Yvonne T. Chua, "Working 'Miracles' in Mindanao," p. 22; Sheila S. Coronel, "Virgilio Garcillano: Master Operator," p. 18; and Yvonne T. Chua, "The Election: Who Really Won in 2004?," p. 12. In the September 2005 edition, see particularly: Luz Rimban, "Running on Taxpayers' Money," p. 12; and Yvonne T. Chua, "Jekyll-and-Hyde Campaign," p. 6. For Esperat's views on what was going on during this election period and afterward I relied on Fermin Diaz, Nena Santos, and Esperat's weekly articles in the *Midland Review*.

88–89: Esperat's epiphany: For Esperat's dramatic encounter with the woman in the Manila dorm, I relied on accounts of the incident she gave to her brother, Charlie Garcia; her colleague Fermin Diaz;

her best friend, Alma Vidal; her sisters, Valmie Mariveles and Lilibeth Lacorte; her lawyer, Nena Santos; and her daughter Rynche Arcones.

89–91: Esperat's letter to President Gloria Arroyo: photocopies of the original letter were given to me in Manila by Esperat's colleague at the Department of Agriculture, Fermin Diaz, on January 26, 2006, and her lawyer, Nena Santos, in Koronadal, Mindanao, on January 31, 2006. Marlene had sent copies to both of them. She also sent copies to the PCIJ and to Justice Secretary Raul Gonzalez. The bold-faced, underlined and italicized phrases on these pages match the original.

91–92: Esperat drew up the first draft to the DA-NFA Fertilizer Scam Summary on December 13, 2004. The summary of the scam begins with the date May 12, 2003.

Esperat's list of cases filed with the Office of the Ombudsman goes on for three pages. After Esperat's murder, Nena Santos sent the list to Secretary of Justice Raul Gonzales, the prosecution team in the Esperat case, the Director of the Philippine National Police, other high-ranking police officials in Mindanao, and RSF.

On February 1 and 2, 2006, Nena Santos explained to me the events surrounding George Esperat's move into Marlene's house, as well as Marlene's motivations for taking him back.

92: Rowie Barua: Prosecuting Attorney Leo Dacera arranged my meeting with Rowie Barua in the Department of Justice Building, Manila. The interview took place on February 7, 2006, in the presence of Arnold Arcano, the administrative chief of the Witness Protection Group, who translated. I first interviewed Dacera in General Santos City, Mindanao, on January 30, 2006.

92–95: I have relied on Rowie Barua's eyewitness account, as told to me in our interview on February 7, 2006, for the events that took place in the Cotabato office of the Department of Agriculture from January to March 2005. Barua later offered his testimony at the Cebu City Regional Court trial, which began on February 15, 2006.

I have also relied on the eyewitness accounts of Marlene's family to narrate the events leading up to the murder, as related to me in interviews. I have corroborated these accounts with the perspectives of other members of her family.

In my interviews with Marlene's sons on February 1 and February 3,

2006, James and Kevin told me about Randy Grecia playing chess with them.

In my February 1, 2006 interview with Marlene's brother, Charlie Garcia told me about Marlene's call to him on March 21, 2005, in which she informed him of her dream that led her to believe "God is trying to wake me up."

Information for Marlene's informing her bodyguard that he could take the evening of Maundy Thursday and Good Friday off comes from lawyer Nena Santos, Rynche Arcones and Charlie Garcia, as well as Marlene's sisters, Valmie Mariveles and Lilibeth Lacorte.

Rynche, Marlene's sisters and Nena Santos told me about the visit of Orfelina Segura, accompanied by her bodyguard, and Jerry Cabayag taking his water from the sari-sari store and leaving for Strum's Bar.

George Esperat told me about his preparation of bayan fish for the family's supper, Marlene rejecting it as too salty, and his preparation of sushi. Rynche, and Marlene's sisters, Valmie and Lilibeth, told me that George had had a drink of bourbon in the kitchen while he prepared supper.

James and Kevin Esperat offered me their eyewitness account of the shooting, and instructed me in the drawing of a diagram.

95–96: "The death from a bullet to the head of Marlene Esperat": From a press release issued by Reporters sans frontières, on June 23, 2005, to protest the manner in which the case was being handled by the authorities and courts.

"'the most murderous country' for journalists": Taken from the CPJ's report "Marked for Death," May 2, 2005. The number of murders per country were calculated from 2000 to the date of the report.

The following organizations signed the letter to President Arroyo: Canadian Journalists for Free Expression; Center for Media Freedom and Responsibility; Committee to Protect Journalists; International PEN; International Press Institute; Freedom Fund for Filipino Journalists; Reporters sans frontières; Southeast Asian Press Alliance; The Rory Peck Trust; World Press Freedom Committee.

96: Gloria Arroyo's news conference: "Get Esperat slay mastermind, GMA orders," Philippine Daily Inquirer, May 17, 2005.

97: "I helped many of them": iReport, special edition, fall 2005. This edition contains extensive coverage of the "Hello Garci" tapes scandal.

The September 2005 edition of *iReport* contains extensive coverage of the events leading up to the scandal.

"symphony of fraud": Sheila S. Coronel, "Virgilio Garcillano: Master Operator," *iReport*, special edition, fall 2005, p.19.

"Since everyone is tainted with guilt": Back cover to *iReport*, special edition, fall 2005.

98–99: The events following the revelation of the tapes were covered daily by the Philippine media.

99: "the real masterminds": "Esperat case: a miscarriage of justice," *Manila Standard*, September 26, 2005.

100: Arnold Arcano: As mentioned in the note to p. 92, the interview took place on February 7, 2006, in Manila's Department of Justice Building.

101: As of January 13, 2009, Montañer and Sabay still had not been arrested. On that day, I phoned Marlene Esperat's sister Lilibeth Lacorte, and she agreed that the pair had good cause to be confident they would remain as overseers of the Department of Agriculture in Cotabato City.

Arroyo's declaration of a state of emergency: The news was covered around the world. Here is an excerpt from the *International Herald Tribune*, February 25, 2006: "Seeing plot, Arroyo declares emergency: people-power rallies are held; military on 'double red alert.'" The front-page photo shows hundreds of troops turning back demonstrators at the entrance to Edsa Square. "Alleging a conspiracy by political opponents, Communists and rightists to remove her from power, President Gloria Macapagal-Arroyo of the Philippines declared emergency rule Friday and banned rallies marking the 20th anniversary of the fall of Ferdinand Marcos, the former Philippine dictator."

102: The conference I am referring to was the Global Investigative Journalism Conference, held in Toronto, May 24–27, 2007, at which I met Sheila Coronel and Luz Rimban, of the PCIJ.

CHAPTER THREE: JEWEL MOON AND THE HUMAN UNIVERSE

103–104: I arrived in Dhaka, Bangladesh, on February 15, 2006, and traveled to Khulna on February 19 with Mainul Islam Khan, joint director of the Bangladesh Center for Development, Journalism and Communication (BCDJC). Saleem Samad, a Bangladeshi journalist living in exile in Canada, put me in touch with Khan. The CPJ's Abi Wright put me in touch with Samad.

104: "the seven godfathers": Information on the seven godfathers comes from many of the Khulna journalists mentioned in the text. Dip Azad, now living in Dhaka, was particularly helpful. Fakre Alam, who lives in Jessore, was another helpful source. My translator for my interviews in Khulna, Jessore and Dhaka was Mainul Islam Khan, and my translator of written works was Nafida Adib Tuli, then an intern at the BCDJC.

104–105: As mentioned, the statistics regarding the number of journalists murdered for their work changes over time, not only because more journalists are murdered but because further analysis adds or deducts murders from the list. The CPJ, in its May 2005 report, "Marked for Death," listed Bangladesh as the fourth most murderous country, with nine journalists murdered since 2000, and their past files then showed fifteen journalists had been murdered for their work between 1992 and 2005. The figure of sixteen that I use is from the BCDJC.

Information on the deputy inspector general of the Khulna police weeping in public on the news of Saha's murder comes from Saha's brother Prodip Kumar Saha. The deputy inspector general's name was Abdul Khan. The nationwide reaction to Saha's death was covered extensively in the Bangladeshi press.

"the forty-nine-year-old Saha": Various press sources and NGOs give different ages for Saha at the time of his murder. His brother Prodip told me Saha's actual birth date was June 10, 1954, not June 10, 1956, the date found in most of Saha's documents. The explanation for the different dates is given on p. 117.

105–106: My summary of Saha's career is based on interviews I conducted in Khulna, Dhaka and Jessore, and on Saha's CV given to me by his wife, Nanda, and translated by Nafida Adib Tuli. Many of the sources for this overview are listed in the text as the events of Saha's life are recounted below, and all of the sources are listed in the Acknowledgments.

106: "no God to answer the prayers of the poor": Interview with Saha's wife, Nanda Saha, February 20, 2006, Mainul Khan translating.

Lecture in Jessore: The event, three days before Saha's murder, was recounted to me by journalist Fakre Alam in Jessore, on February 22, 2006.

106–107: A copy of the original photos of the decapitated Saha was given to me by Mainul Islam Khan. One of the photos appeared in the *Daily Star*, January 16, 2004.

Many journalists in Khulna described the assassination to me. Dip Azad was one of the first at the scene, and his account, given to me on February 24, 2006, in Dhaka, was most detailed.

I recorded the titles to the boxes containing research for the articles Saha was working on just before his murder. My visit to his house took place on February 20, 2006, Mainul Khan translating.

108: Background on *New Age* comes from many Bangladeshi journalists I interviewed, particularly Nayeemul Islam Khan, president of the BCDJC.

Overview of the period between 2001 and Saha's assassination comes from many Bangladeshi journalists and family members I interviewed. See source notes below for pp. 138–46.

"Two days before his death": Interview with Swapan Guha conducted in Khulna on February 20, 2006.

108–109: Interview with Nayeemul Islam Khan conducted on February 16, 2006, in Dhaka.

Humayun Kabir was murdered on June 27, 2004. Dip Azad's survival of a bomb attack is based on his own account, related to me on February 24, 2006. His assessment of the alliance between various forces in Bangladesh was given to me in Dhaka, on February 24, 2006, Mainul Islam Khan translating.

109: Save the Sundarbans conference: Saha's opening remarks given to me by Nanda Saha.

Almost all of the journalists I spoke to in Bangladesh stated that Saha was the subcontinent's expert on the Sundarbans. Summary of Saha's travels and work in the Sundarbans comes from interviews with his wife, Nanda, his brother Prodip, and many others. I interviewed Nanda and Prodip several times between February 20 and February 24, 2006. I also consulted Manik Saha's *Sundarban*

Anusandhan (Dhaka/Khulna: published in Bengali with support from the BCDJC, June 2002).

110: Historical overview of Bangladesh: There is a dearth of books in English devoted to Bangladesh history. Almost all of the journalists I interviewed in Bangladesh were well versed in that history, and some were historians, including Shahriar Kabir. I interviewed Kabir on February 17, 2006, in Dhaka. In the summer and fall of 2005, before I left for Bangladesh, Saleem Samad spent hours with me on the phone explaining Bangladesh's history and politics. Mainul Islam Khan was my history tutor for most of the period I spent in Bangladesh.

111: "June 10, 1954": See source note for pp. 104–105; see p. 117 in the text for explanation of why this is Saha's true birth date.
    Historical overview of Khulna: Several journalists in Khulna explained this history to me, as did Shahriar Kabir in Dhaka.

111–13: Krishnapada's history: Sources are Saha's brother Prodip, in Khulna; Saha's one-hundred-year-old aunt, Chapala, in the village of Suktagram; Saha's wife, Nanda, in Khulna; Saha's eldest daughter, Natasha, in Dhaka. To interview Aunt Chapala I visited the remote village of Suktagram with Prodip and Mainul Islam Khan on February 21, 2006. I interviewed Natasha on February 25, 2006.
    The history of Saha's mother, Chanchala, comes from the same sources.

113–15: Saha's youth to age ten: Sources are Saha's brother Prodip, in Khulna; Saha's one-hundred-year-old aunt, Chapala, in the village of Suktagram; Saha's wife, Nanda, in Khulna; and Saha's eldest daughter, Natasha, in Dhaka.

115–17: Saha's youth, ages ten to seventeen: Sources are Saha's brother Prodip, in Khulna; Saha's one-hundred-year-old aunt, Chapala, in the village of Suktagram; Saha's wife, Nanda, in Khulna; and Saha's eldest daughter, Natasha, in Dhaka.
    Early schooling: From Saha's CV given to me by his wife, Nanda Saha, and translated by Nafida Adib Tuli.

119–22: Saha's enlightened atheism, ethical humanism and intellectual awakening: Sources are Saha's brother in Khulna, Prodip; Saha's one-hundred-year-old aunt, Chapala, in the village of Suktagram;

Saha's wife, Nanda, in Khulna; and reflections by many of Saha's colleagues in Khulna, including Gouranga Nandy (interviewed on February 22, 2006 at *Daily Janakantha*), Syed M. Habib (interviewed February 20–23, 2006), Sk. Abu Hassan and Hare Krishna Ghosh (interviewed at the Press Club on February 20, 2006), Dip Azad, Swapan Guha, and members of the board of the Ratan Sen Public Library, including Mujibar Rahman and Sharif Atiquazzaman. I interviewed Rahman and Atiquazzaman at the library on February 22, 2006.

A transcript of the 1930 conversation between Albert Einstein and Rabindranath Tagore can be found in Amiya Chakravarly, ed., *A Tagore Reader* (New York, Macmillan, 1961) pp. 100–103, 110–13.

123: "Khulna's first modern godfathers": Sources are Dip Azad and Fakre Alam.

Saha's schooling during this period: Saha's cv given to me by his wife, Nanda Saha, and translated by Nafida Adib Tuli.

123–25: Saha and Ratan Sen: Sources for their meeting and friendship are members of the board of the Ratan Sen Public Library, including Mujibar Rahman and Sharif Atiquazzaman (interviewed at the library on February 22, 2006); Saha's wife, Nanda; daughter Natasha; and Saha's brother Prodip. Physical description of Sen based on a photo of him hanging in the library.

125–27: Saha's imprisonment and time in prison: Saha's wife, Nanda, brother Prodip, and members of the board of the Ratan Sen Public Library as listed above.

Saha's law degree and early law career: Saha's wife, Nanda, brother Prodip, and Saha's cv.

Saha hired by *Daily Sangbad:* Saha's wife, Nanda, brother Prodip, and *Sangbad* editor Monjural Ahsan Bulbul (interviewed in Dhaka on February 18, 2006).

128–29: The modern seven godfathers: Sources are Dip Azad in Dhaka, and other journalists in Khulna and Jessore, including Fakre Alam.

129–30: "Shrimp cultivation": "Commercial Shrimp Cultivation in Bangladesh and Human Rights," a presentation by Manik Saha delivered in Sydney, Australia.

131–32: Saha's trip to the Soviet Union: Sources are Saha's wife, Nanda, brother Prodip, daughter Natasha, and members of the board of the Ratan Sen Public Library as listed above.

132–33: Saha's break with the Communist Party of Bangladesh: Saha's wife, Nanda, brother Prodip, daughter Natasha, and members of the board of the Ratan Sen Public Library as listed above.

133: The assassination of Ratan Sen: Sources are members of the board of the Ratan Sen Public Library including Mujibar Rahman and Sharif Atiquazzaman (interviewed at the library on February 22, 2006); Saha's wife, Nanda; daughter Natasha; and Saha's brother Prodip; as well as numerous journalists, including Dip Azad, and published accounts in the *Daily Star* (see below). The head of the Khulna Communist Party of Bangladesh, Ashim Ananda Das, filed the formal criminal complaint with the court, asking that the police investigate the murder of Sen. Das did not name any suspects, but the police eventually charged fifteen people, including, as alleged mastermind, Shaharuzzaman Martuza. All were acquitted.

In 2000, the Communist Party of Bangladesh requested that the case be reopened and the Home Ministry ordered it reinvestigated. The case was reopened, but by 2006, all the evidence had "gone missing." The story of the missing evidence was reported on August 1, 2006, in the national newspaper the *Daily Star* (see below).

Over the years, public figures in opposition to Shaharuzzaman Martuza have stated in interviews that they base their opposition to him in part on the fact that he was charged with the murder of Ratan Sen (see below).

In June 2007, Martuza was arrested for holding two foreign passports and the police announced they were investigating him for allegations of extortion and corruption.

At this writing Martuza is still head of the Khulna Chamber of Commerce and Industry.

"Ratan Sen murder case still limps as documents missing: CPB pays tribute at rally "
By Staff Correspondent, Khulna
The Daily Star (August 1, 2006)
http://www.thedailystar.net/2006/08/01/d608010703108.htm

Documents of communist leader Ratan Sen murder case is missing from Khulna thana and Detective Branch of Khulna Metropolitan Police (KMP). As a result, reinvestigation of the case, ordered by home ministry in 2000, is uncertain. Ratan Sen, who was president of Khulna district unit of Communist Party of Bangladesh (CPB), was stabbed to death on July 31, 1992 in front of Khulna police superintendent's office. Khulna CPB leader Ashim Ananda Das lodged an FIR [first information report] with Khulna thana as complainant, without naming any accused. The case was later transferred to CID [Criminal Investigation Division] for investigation. CID submitted charge sheet accusing 15 persons including Shaharuzzaman Martuza, now president of Khulna Chamber of Commerce and Industry and a prominent member of a faction of Khulna city BNP [Bangladesh Nationalist Party] led by Ali Asgar Lobi MP and the city Mayor. All the charge sheeted accused were earlier acquitted by court due to lack of evidence and weak charge sheet. In 2000, the home ministry issued an order for reinvestigation of the case following a petition submitted on behalf of Khulna CPB. The Khulna thana Officer-in-Charge Abdul Hamid told this correspondent that he is not aware of the officer who investigated the case as the case docket is missing. August 14 is the date for hearing on progress of reinvestigation in the case in the court of Chief Metropolitan Magistrate. Meanwhile, Khulna CPB observed the 14th death anniversary of Ratan Sen yesterday through holding a rally in the morning and a public meeting at Shahid Maharaj square in the afternoon. Khulna CPB leaders yesterday submitted a memorandum to the state minister for home through the deputy commissioner demanding re-arrest of the chargesheeted accused.

"Intra-Party Feud in Khulna BNP Takes New Turn:
One faction to 'probe' corruption by rivals"
By Staff Correspondent, Khulna
The Daily Star (August 1, 2006)
http://www.thedailystar.net/2006/08/05/d60805070195.htm

Paragraph 12: "Mortuza has no right to retain even primary membership of BNP and the post of president of Khulna Chamber of Commerce and Industry as he is the principal charge sheeted accused in CPB leader Ratan Sen murder case, Nurul Islam told the meeting."

"KCCI president arrested for double passport"
By Staff Correspondent, Khulna
The Daily Star (June 30 2007)
http://www.thedailystar.net/2007/06/30/d70630011510.htm

Police yesterday arrested Khulna Chamber of Commerce and
Industry (KCCI) President Shaharuzzaman Martuza at his residence at Bhairab Strand road under Khulna Sadar Police
Station on charges of holding two international passports. The
law enforcers raided the house of the KCC president at 7:15pm
and arrested him. They also seized an international passport
from his possession. Officer-in-Charge (OC) Asaduzzaman of
Khulna Sadar Police Station said the KCCI president was arrested
under section 11(A) of the Passport Act, 1973 for keeping two
international passports in his possession.

Sub-Inspector (SI) Shiba Prashad of the police station lodged
an FIR (first information report) as complainant while SI Jamil
Hossain has been made investigation (IO) officer of the case.
Shaharuzzaman Martuza is also member-secretary of BNP
Khulna City Convening Committee (mayor faction). Police said
they are also investigating the allegations of extortion and cor-
ruption against the KCC president. Martuza went to Pakistan on
May 21 to attend an International Trade Fair held in Islamabad.
He returned to Khulna on May 28.

134: Saha's social activism: Sources are members of the board of the
Ratan Sen Public Library (see above); Saha's wife, Nanda, daughter
Natasha, and Saha's brother Prodip; as well as numerous journalists,
and Saha's CV.

135–36: Shahriar Kabir's narrative: I interviewed Kabir on February 17,
2006, in Dhaka.

137–38: Saha's career, threats and murders of his colleagues (1998–2000):
Sources are journalists Dip Azad, Monjural Bulbul and Gouranga
Nandy; members of the board of the Ratan Sen Public Library (see
above); Saha's wife, Nanda, and Saha's brother Prodip; and published
accounts of the journalists' murders in the BCDJC, CPJ and RSF files.

138–41: Press Club mural controversy, and the period September 11,
2001, to end of 2003: Sources are Mainul Islam Khan, Dip Azad, Saha's

wife, Nanda, Press Club members Sk. Abu Hassan and Hare Krishna Ghosh, Monjural Bulbul (for Saha's affiliation with Ekushey TV and the shutdown of the station) and Gouranga Nandy.

140: For arrest of Channel 4 TV crew: Sources are Mainul Islam Khan, Shariar Kabir and Saleem Samad (in Canada).

141–42: Saha as organizer and keynote speaker at antiterrorism conference: Sources are Saha's brother Prodip, wife, Nanda, and colleagues Dip Azad and Syed M. Habib.

143–45: Saha's affiliation with *New Age* and last trip to Dhaka: Sources are Nayeemul Islam Khan, Swapan Guha, Mainul Khan, Saha's wife, Nanda, Saha's brother Prodip and Dip Azad.

145–46: Saha's last day: Sources are quoted in the text. Nanda Saha gave me her account of Saha's last day in an interview on February 23, 2006, at her place of work, Mainul Khan translating.

146–48: Photo of Dip Azad and Press Club colleagues at scene of Saha's murder appeared in the *Daily Star*, January 16, 2004. Photo of them carrying Saha's decapitated body appeared in the *Daily Star*, January 16, 2004. Reaction of the nation to Saha's death is based on the sources cited above. Reactions of Khaleda Zia and Sheikh Hasina, from the files of the Khulna reporters who covered Saha's death, including Dip Azad, Gouranga Nandy and Syed Habib.

Funeral procession, stops along the way and cremation: Sources are numerous journalists in Khulna who took part, including Dip Azad; as well, Saha's family members cited above; Mainul Islam Khan; a report by Bangladesh's Human Rights Tribune; and press accounts from numerous sources, including the *Daily Star*. I visited Khulna's Rupsha cremation grounds on February 20, 2006, and interviewed the caretaker, Horipada Das, Mainul Khan translating.

148–50: I visited Suktagram and interviewed Saha's aunt Chapala on February 21, 2006. I was accompanied by Saha's brother Prodip, and Mainul Khan, who translated the interview.

CHAPTER FOUR: **ANNA HAD NO ROOF**

151–52: The article I was researching about Russian organized crime in Vancouver was published as "Bleak Russians" in *Vancouver* magazine (Winter 1995/1996, front page coverline, "Russian Mob"). I attended a dance at which several émigré Russian mobsters were partying, and heard about the murder of journalist Andrei Ulanov (though not by name) in Togliatti (see p. 237). For the article, I interviewed intelligence officers in the organized crime section of the Coordinated Law Enforcement Unit.

On the afternoon of October 6, 2006, I left Vancouver for Russia to research the lives of Valery Ivanov and Alexei Sidorov. The press freedom groups I'd spoken to in Moscow about the two journalists were the Glasnost Defense Foundation (Alexei Simonov) and the CPJ (Anne Cooper and Nina Ognianova in New York), Alex Lupis (on a fellowship in Moscow) and Masha Yulikova (a Moscow-based researcher for the CPJ).

Summary of Ivanov's and Sidorov's careers and murders: The full life stories of the two journalists, with sources, are given in Chapter Five, "The Boys from Car City."

"Krysha is at the core": From a speech Ivanov delivered to Togliatti City Council in fall 2001, recollected for me by Ivanov's fellow councilmember and political ally, Borislav Greenblat, on October 16, 2006, in the Togliatti City Council building, Lara Nuzhdina translating.

152–53: My description of the workings of krysha reflects a nearly universal understanding of the concept among the many journalists, lawyers, NGOs and unaffiliated civilians I interviewed in Moscow and Togliatti, as well as Russian crime experts in the West.

Quotation from Politkovskaya, "That is exactly how, during the Yeltsin years": Anna Politkovskaya, *Putin's Russia: Life in a Failing Democracy*, translated by Arch Tait (New York: Metropolitan Books, 2004), p. 127. This summative sentence appears at the bottom of the page; just above the sentence, Politkovskaya gives an example of the workings of krysha in Russia's organized crime–dominated liquor industry. "As Skvortsov's first deputy, Fedulev appointed a certain Andrey Taranov. In the Urals, he was believed to be the protector (or 'roof') within the police force of Olef Fleganov, the region's leading supplier of wines and spirits."

My arrival date at Moscow's Sheremetyevo Airport, October 7, 2006, is stamped in my passport. I was in touch with representatives of the

CPJ just before I left for Russia and as soon as I arrived, including Masha Yulikova and Alex Lupis in Moscow (then on a fellowship), and Nina Ognianova in New York. PEN Canada's Isobel Harry and David Cozac gave me Politkovskaya's private Yahoo e-mail address during an interview in Toronto on October 14, 2005. They told me Politkovskaya was a "must" interview, outlining the many threats she faced. At the time I arrived, Politkovskaya was one of many Russian journalists and NGOs I'd arranged to interview; I had no idea how significant a part she would play in this book until I learned she had been murdered that day.

154: This summary of Politkovskaya's career reflects her published works and what I knew of her career when I'd landed, plus my interviews with her colleagues and son, Ilya, in the following weeks. On October 15, 2006, a week after her murder, I read her English PEN article, published in *The Washington Post* under the headline "Her Own Death Foretold," p. B1. The quotation is taken from the *Post*, and can be referenced in English PEN's anthology, edited by Lucy Popescu and Carole Seymour-Jones, *Writers Under Siege: Voices of Freedom From Around the World*, Politkovskaya's article translated by Arch Tait (New York: New York University Press, 2007), p. 222.

"forty-eight dangerous trips to Chechnya": The number of trips comes from Politkovskaya's human rights colleague Svetlana Gannushkina, interviewed at her Moscow Civil Assistance office on October 25, 2006, Svetlana Tougan-Boronovskaya translating.

"that Putin's vertical system of authority": Politkovskaya, *Putin's Russia*, p. 249.

155: "whose government she'd previously claimed had threatened her with death": Politkovskaya made the claim in the essay she'd written for English PEN, first published after her death in the *Washington Post*, October 15, 2006, under the headline "Her Own Death Foretold." That version of her essay, still available for purchase on the *Post*'s website, states that women in a Chechen crowd "reminded me that Kadyrov has publicly vowed to murder me. He said during a meeting of his government that he had had enough, and that Politkovskaya was a condemned woman. I was told about it by members of the government." Eight paragraphs later in the *Post* version, she rhetorically asks the question: "Why has Ramzan vowed to kill me?" In Popescu and Seymour-Jones, *Writers Under Siege*, pp. 219–20, the first quotation reads: "That reminded me that Kadyrov's government has publicly vowed to murder me. It was actually said at a meeting that his government had had enough, and that I was a condemned woman. I was told about it by members of the government." Seven paragraphs later in *Writers Under Siege*, p. 220, her essay reads, "Why has Kadyrov's government vowed to kill me?" There is an intervening paragraph on the *Post*'s website that is not in the *Writers Under Siege* version. For the original *Washington Post* version of the essay, see: http://pqasb.pqarchiver.com/washingtonpost/access/1146082791.html ?dids=1146082791:1146082791&FMT=FT&FMTS=ABS:FT&fmac=61d 56d90e65329oc91acdddc7a7623bc&date=Oct+15%2C+2006&author=& desc=Her+Own+Death%2C+Foretold&pf=1

"I am conducting an investigation about torture": Radio Free Europe/Radio Liberty's Russia Service conducted the interview with Politkovskaya on October 5, 2006; it was published in English on their website, www.rferl.org, on October 9, 2006.

156: "what is shown on television": Popescu and Seymour-Jones, *Writers Under Siege*, p. 222.

"80 percent": From interviews with the CPJ's Alex Lupis and Nina Ognianova on October 18, 2005, CPJ headquarters, New York. The figure is also used in Ognianova's article on *Novaya Gazeta*, "Anya's Papers," *Dangerous Assignments*, May 2007.

157: "to let her know I'd arrived": I called the CPJ's Moscow researcher, Masha Yulikova, and Alex Lupis, the CPJ's former program coordinator for Europe and Central Asia, who was in Moscow on a fellowship.

158–60: The interview with Alexei Simonov (the first of several with him) took place on October 9, 2006, at the Glasnost Defense Foundation. I'd been communicating with Simonov since fall 2005, and had arranged this interview with him before I left for Russia. He spoke fluent English.

"The funeral and burial": I attended Politkovskaya's funeral with Masha Yulikova as my guide and translator (see pp. 169–70).

160: "Poisoned by Putin," by Anna Politkovskaya, *The Guardian*, September 9, 2004.

"colleagues urged": The colleagues I interviewed are cited below. Among them are Vyacheslav Izmailov and Galina Mursalieva.

I visited Politkovskaya's house on October 25, 2006, sixteen days after my first interview with Simonov.

"I will be next": Politkovskaya said this to Galina Mursalieva at the funeral of Yuri Shchekochikhin (see p. 205). My interview with

Mursalieva took place on October 25, 2006, at the Pyramid Café, Victoria Mashkova translating. See pp. 198–200.

162–63: The article in the *New York Times*, published the day after the first anniversary of Politkovskaya's assassination, summarized the way the assassination had been viewed internationally, both immediately after the assassination and in the intervening year. "The killing was one in a string of murders of journalists in Russia. It drew international condemnation and demands for a vigorous investigation. In the year since, it has been framed as a challenge to Mr. Putin's legacy—an example of the criminality, corruption and culture of impunity beneath the surface of the partial recovery of Russia's economy and of the Kremlin's confidence that have accompanied Mr. Putin's rule." the *New York Times*, October 8, 2007.

My interview with Vyacheslav Izmailov took place on October 19, 2006, in the cafeteria of *Novaya Gazeta*, Svetlana Tougan-Boronovskaya translating. Izmailov is quoted throughout this chapter. For the full context of the quotation on this page, see pp. 182–84.

I interviewed Oleg Panfilov several times between October 11 and October 24, 2006. This quotation is taken from my interview with him on October 11, at the Center for Journalism in Extreme Situations (CJES), Masha Yulikova translating.

I interviewed Vitaly Yaroshevsky on October 26, 2006, in his office at *Novaya Gazeta*, Svetlana Tougan-Boronovskaya translating.

Politkovskaya's impatient comments about liberals who had enormous respect for her are taken from the book she was preparing for publication at the time of her death and reflect the views she had shared with the people I interviewed for this chapter, as well as her articles critical of the left, quoted elsewhere in the chapter. See Anna Politkovskaya, *A Russian Diary*, translated by Arch Tait (London, England: Harvill Seeker, 2007): "sweetened up" by the Kremlin (p. 20); "tuck[ing] their tails between their legs" (p. 18); "playing games" (p. 81); "sordid compromises" (p. 173); "never straying beyond the bounds of what was permissible" (p. 83).

My interview with Galina Mursalieva took place on October 25, 2006, at the Pyramid Café, Victoria Mashkova translating.

162–68: My interview with Svetlana Gannushkina took place at her Moscow Civil Assistance office on October 25, 2006, Svetlana Tougan-Boronovskaya translating.

164–65: "machinery of racially based state retribution" to "regardless of age": Politkovskaya, *Putin's Russia*, p. 211.

166: "Taunton boarding school": I interviewed Politkovskaya's son, Ilya, in the office of *Novaya Gazeta* on October 19, 2006, Svetlana Tougan-Boronovskaya translating.

   In interviews with two Russian newspapers after his wife's death, Sasha Politkovsky discussed his drinking habits. See pp. 177–78 in the text and source notes below for pp. 175–76 and p. 178 on his October 11, 2006, interview in *Moskovski Komsomolets* and his October 12, 2006, interview in *Komsomolskaya Pravda*.

168: "worth a life": This interview was rebroadcast on PBS *Frontline* on March 30, 2007, part of a fourteen-minute tribute to murdered journalists called "Requiem: Reporting in a Dangerous World."

169–70: On October 10, 2006, I attended Politkovskaya's funeral with Masha Yulikova as my guide and translator. Yulikova no longer works for the CPJ.

170–71: "People call the newspaper": Anna Politkovskaya, *A Small Corner of Hell: Dispatches from Chechnya*, translated by Alexander Burray and Tatiana Tulchinsky (Chicago: University of Chicago Press, 2003), pp. 26–27.

171–72: For background on Anna's parents I have relied on my interviews with her son, Ilya, and Alexei Simonov and Oleg Panfilov. I interviewed Politkovskaya's son in the office of *Novaya Gazeta* on October 19, 2006, Svetlana Tougan-Boronovskaya translating.

172: Politkovskaya's maiden name, Mazepa, was frequently (and jocularly) mentioned to me in my interviews. These include my interviews with Alexei Simonov and Oleg Panfilov.

173: I first learned of Politkovskaya's interest in Marina Ivanova Tsvetaeva, and about her college thesis on the poet, from Politkovskaya's son, Ilya.

174–75: "In life, you strive": Anna Politkovskaya, *A Small Corner of Hell*, pp. 76–77.

175–76: Alexander "Sasha" Politkovsky gave two newspaper interviews shortly after his ex-wife's murder. They covered his personal life and his marriage to Anna. The first was published on October 11, 2006, in *Moskovski Komsomolets*; the second was published on October 12, 2006, in *Komsomolskaya Pravda*. During my time in Moscow, Oleg Panfilov tried to arrange an interview for me with Politkovsky, but Politkovsky told Panfilov he would be giving no more interviews for the time being. The two newspaper interviews were translated for me by Michael Dubman and Janie Dubman.

Girlfriends' opinions of Anna as a devil in a skirt, Sasha as the old man, the wedding, Sasha's attire, Anna's parents' reaction, Anna learning to cook, the entire household hanging on her while Sasha pursued journalism, colossal arguments, laughter afterwards and life as "a strangely striped creature" are from the *Moskovski Komsomolets* interview. (There are also references to some of these events in the *Komsomolskaya Pravda* interview.)

"Every journalist got free tickets": Politkovskaya's interview with the *Guardian:* "Dispatches from a savage war," October 15, 2004.

177: Anna's "professional life was difficult": Sasha Politkovsky interview with *Moskovski Komsomolets*, October 11, 2006.

178: Paul Klebnikov: The 1996 *Forbes* article was called *Godfather of the Kremlin*. Klebnikov was murdered on April 9, 2004. For more on Klebnikov's murder, see pp. 266–67.

"My bastard colleagues": Sasha Politkovsky interview with *Moskovski Komsomolets*, October 11, 2006. To describe the events in Sasha Politkovsky's life from the mid-1990s to the early-2000s, I relied on Sasha's version in his two newspaper interviews and on background interviews with Moscow journalists who knew about Sasha's hard times. Bar buddies: Sasha Politkovsky interview with *Moskovski Komsomolets*, October 11, 2006.

Information on Politkovskaya's articles about minorities comes from Svetlana Gannushkina and Vyacheslav Izmailov, Svetlana Tougan-Boronovskaya translating.

178–80: Politkovskaya meeting Vyacheslav Izmailov and his history: My interview with Vyacheslav Izmailov took place on October 19, 2006, in the cafeteria of *Novaya Gazeta*, Svetlana Tougan-Boronovskaya translating.

183: "nervous breakdown": Sasha Politkovsky's interview in *Komsomolskaya Pravda*, October 12, 2006, translated for me by Michael Dubman.

184: "first day of work coincided with that of Galina Mursalieva": My interview with Mursalieva took place on October 25, 2006, at the Pyramid Café, Victoria Mashkova translating.

185: "The present catastrophe": Politkovskaya's articles were published in *Novaya Gazeta* and later translated and collected in her first book, *A Dirty War: A Russian Reporter in Chechnya*, translated by John Crawfoot (London, England: The Harville Press, 2001), p. 33.

186: "Fifteen thousand Chechens": Politkovskaya, *A Dirty War*, p. 325 (Appendix).

186–87: Ryazan: For an excellent account of this incident, see David Satter, *Darkness at Dawn: The Rise of the Russian Criminal State* (New Haven: Yale University Press, 2003), pp. 24–33.

See Politkovskaya's article in *Novaya Gazeta*, October 7, 1999, republished in *A Dirty War*. At the end of the article (p. 56), Politkovskaya makes her first comparison between Nazi Germany's treatment of Jews and Russia's treatment of Chechens, comparing the apartment house bombings in Moscow, Volgodonsk and Buinaksk to "the burning of the Reichstag," the event Hitler used as an excuse to consolidate his power.

"corner the bandits in the shithouse": Putin is quoted in an epigraph on p. 58 of Politkovskaya, *A Dirty War*.

"Where are the human rights activists?": Politkovskaya, *A Dirty War*, pp. 49–50.

187–88: "We are the people caught in the bombing" to "resemble a deathbed": Politkovskaya, *A Small Corner of Hell*, p. 32.

188: "What can you Russians do right": Politkovskaya, *A Dirty War*, p. 76.

188–90: This account of the old folks' home in Grozny was given to me by Vyacheslav Izmailov. My interview with Izmailov took place on October 19, 2006, in the cafeteria of *Novaya Gazeta*, Svetlana Tougan-Boronovskaya translating.

191: "Not even my newspaper": Politkovskaya, A Small Corner of Hell, p. 42.

"Even close friends": Politkovskaya, A Small Corner of Hell, p. 42.

Her displays of emotion were described to me by her colleagues Vyacheslav Izmailov and Galina Mursalieva.

"Only the very strong": From a dispatch she wrote on July 24, 2000, translated and republished in Politkovskaya, A Dirty War, p. 202. (NOTE: The book's translation of the last line of this quotation in A Dirty War reads "hordes of thin, homeless puppies.")

191–92: "No journalists come here" and Politkovskaya's descriptions of Shali: Politkovskaya, A Small Corner of Hell, p. 42.

"bacchanalia of indifference": Politkovskaya, A Russian Diary, p. 272.

192–93: Politkovskaya's interview with Ahmad Kadyrov: Politkovskaya, "The Ordinary Man Does Not Need Freedom: Chechnya's New Leader," A Dirty War, pp. 192–201.

193–96: Izmailov's account of Politkovskaya being held prisoner in Khatuni is taken from my interview with him on October 19, 2006, in the cafeteria of Novaya Gazeta, Svetlana Tougan-Boronovskaya translating. Politkovskaya's account of the incident is given in A Small Corner of Hell; her account occasionally switches back and forth in time, pp. 47–53.

Politkovskaya's conversation with Colonel Romanov: Politkovskaya, A Small Corner of Hell, p. 50.

"Two minutes later, she was put under arrest": Politkovskaya, A Small Corner of Hell, p. 51.

Her torture: Politkovskaya, A Small Corner of Hell, pp. 52–53.

198–200: My interview with Galena Mursalieva took place on October 25, 2006, at the Pyramid Café, Victoria Mashkova translating.

198: The reaction of the United Group of Forces in Chechnya to Politkovskaya's article was reported in a chronology of threats to Politkovskaya in the newspaper Kommersant on October 9, 2006. I confirmed the UGF's reaction with Izmailov.

199: "When these people find out": Politkovskaya, A Small Corner of Hell, p. 44.

200: "Disappearing People": A summary of Politkovskaya's article and "Cadet" Lapin's response was offered in the newspaper *Kommersant* on October 9, 2006. I confirmed the incident with Izmailov and other colleagues at *Novaya Gazeta*.

201: Politkovskaya's move to Vienna and return: Oleg Panfilov explained to me the circumstances surrounding this move, on October 24, 2006, Svetlana Tougan-Boronovskaya translating.

201: "I wanted to stay alive!": *The Guardian*, October 15, 2004.

201: "hiding from the FSB": The incident was reported in a chronology of threats to Politkovskaya in the newspaper *Kommersant* on October 9, 2006. I confirmed the incident, and her reporting of it, with Izmailov.

202: "'They won't let me speak!'": From my interview with Galena Mursalieva on October 25, 2006, at the Pyramid Café, Victoria Mashkova translating.

202: "This spring I have been in Amsterdam": Politkovskaya, *A Small Corner of Hell*, pp. 28–29.

202–203: *Nord-Ost* hostage-taking; Politkovskaya lecturing in Santa Monica, California: Politkovskaya, *A Small Corner of Hell*, p. 220 (she calls Santa Monica "an ocean suburb of Los Angeles," and describes her lecture at "the local university" as being about life in Russia and the second Chechen war).

Her phone conversation with her son: Politkovskaya *A Small Corner of Hell*, p. 221. In at least one of her accounts to journalists, she recounted that on her arrival at the theater the Federal Security Service of the Russian Federation (FSB) agent drew his gun.

"To be quite frank": quoted in Peter Baker and Susan Glasser, *Kremlin Rising: Vladimir Putin's Russia and the End of Revolution* (New York: Scribner, 2005), p. 167.

The figure of 129 dead from the gas comes from *Novaya Gazeta* http://en.novayagazeta.ru/data/2008/49/03.html. Some accounts differ on the number of dead.

"'murderous' rescue operation": Politkovskaya, *Putin's Russia*, p. 187.

"chosen by the president personally": Politkovskaya, *Putin's Russia*, p. 187.

"the interests of society must come first": Politkovskaya, *Putin's Russia*, p. 187.

204: "Let us look at the ethnic purging": Politkovskaya, *Putin's Russia*, p. 188.

"What sort of a nation are we, the Russian people?": Politkovskaya, *Putin's Russia*, p 224.

"A depraved society wants comfort": Politkovskaya, *Putin's Russia*, p. 202.

"Stick it up your ass," and "Your dollars come from the CIA," quoted by Peter Baker and Susan Glasser, *Kremlin Rising*, p. 178.

204–205: "Politkovskaya returned to Grozny": An account of this visit can be found in an article by Natalya Estemirova, published in the *International Herald Tribune* on October 5, 2007. The article was titled "Anna Politkovskaya." Vyacheslav Izmailov also gave me an account of this visit, as Politkovskaya related it to him.

205: "I will be the next": My interview with Mursalieva took place on October 25, 2006, at the Pyramid Café, Victoria Mashkova translating.

205–206: The Presidential Human Rights Forum took place on December 10, 2003. Alexei Simonov and Svetlana Gannushkina gave me their personal accounts of Politkovskaya's criticism of their attendance at the forum, as well as her criticism of the attendance of other liberals. Her withering opinion of the forum can be found in Politkovskaya, *A Russian Diary*, pp.16–20; the excerpts I used are on p. 20. She was preparing the book for publication when she was killed.

206–207: "the deranged Ramzan Kadyrov": Politkovskaya, *A Russian Diary*, p. 145. Her account of her interview with Ramzan Kadyrov can be found in *A Russian Diary*, pp. 144–53.

"They hold people prisoner": Politkovskaya, *A Russian Diary*, pp. 145–46.

"his foot": Politkovskaya, *A Russian Diary*, p. 147.

"You personally are the enemy": Politkovskaya, *A Russian Diary*, p. 150.

"You are an enemy of the Chechen people": Politkovskaya, *A Russian Diary*, p. 152.

"I get into the vehicle": Politkovskaya, *A Russian Diary*, p. 153.

207–209: Beslan hostage-taking: "We've taken you hostage": Baker and Glass, *Kremlin Rising*, p. 18.

Politkovskaya's poisoning and her version of the Beslan hostage-taking can be found in her article "Poisoned by Putin," *The Guardian*, October 9, 2004. Her quotations used in this section are from this article.

The stomach pain she endured is recounted in Baker and Glass, *Kremlin Rising*, p. 25.

In "Poisoned by Putin," Politkovskaya states she was taken to the hospital in Rostov after the poisoning, and she implies that she watched the events in Beslan from the Rostov hospital. In an interview for the documentary film *A Letter to Anna*, however, her editor Dmitry Muratov implies she was taken to Moscow.

"our principal task in the current situation": Putin's quotation from Baker and Glass, *Kremlin Rising*, p. 25.

210: "*Novaya Gazeta* had a stringer": From my interview with Vyacheslav Izmailov, October 19, 2006, in the cafeteria of *Novaya Gazeta*, Svetlana Tougan-Boronovskaya translating.

"That fall she brought a human arm": Oleg Panfilov related this incident to me in our interview on October 11, 2006, Masha Yulikova translating.

"Putin has, by chance": Politkovskaya, *Putin's Russia*, pp. 243–45.

"To this day": Politkovskaya's interview in *The Guardian*, "Dispatches from a savage war," October 15, 2004.

211: "poisoned by FSB agents": *Kommersant*, September 2, 2004.

"*Novaya Gazeta* wants to stay out of trouble": Politkovskaya, *A Russian Diary*, p. 263.

"In her articles": My interview with Vitaly Yaroshevsky took place on October 26, 2006, in his office at *Novaya Gazeta*, Svetlana Tougan-Boronovskaya translating.

"There was a bitter exchange between them": Natalya Estemirova, in her article "Anna Politkovskaya," published in the *International Herald Tribune* on October 5, 2007. On November 27, 2007, Lapin was convicted again on the same charges and sentenced to ten and a half years.

212–13: August 2006 trip to Chechnya. "A few days ago, on August 5": Politkovskaya's essay in Popescu and Seymour-Jones, *Writers Under Siege*, p. 218. For the version of this quotation first published in the *Washington Post* on October 15, 2006, see source note to p. 155.

"The 'people in Chechnya'": Popescu and Seymour-Jones, *Writers Under Siege*, p. 220.

"pariah": Popescu and Seymour-Jones, *Writers Under Siege*, p. 217.

"Of course I don't like": Popescu and Seymour-Jones, *Writers Under Siege*, p. 222.

213: Politkovskaya's "Vindictive Collusion" was published in *Novaya Gazeta on* September 28, 2006.

"We Declare You a Terrorist" was published as a fragment in *Novaya Gazeta* on October 12, 2006, and reprinted in translation that day in the *International Herald Tribune*.

"one criminal case": Radio Liberty interview, October 5, 2006.

"She looked very tired": My interview with Izmailov took place on October 19, 2006, in the cafeteria of *Novaya Gazeta*, Svetlana Tougan-Boronovskaya translating.

213–14: "I got a call from the editor": My interview with Mursalieva took place on October 25, 2006, at the Pyramid Café, Victoria Mashkova translating.

214: "Only if those responsible": Ramzan Kadyrov quoted in "Kadyrov hails detention of suspects in Politkovskaya murder case," Interfax, August 29, 2007.

215: "working on behalf of the FSB": "Editor Links FSB to Politkovskaya Death," *The Moscow Times*, December 8, 2008.

"A defendant and a key witness in the Anna Politkovskaya murder trial worked on behalf of the Federal Security Service, one of the slain reporter's editors testified in court Friday. Sergei Sokolov, deputy editor of *Novaya Gazeta*, where Politkovskaya wrote critical reports about federal abuses in Chechnya, said the FSB was tailing the journalist before she was killed in October 2006. 'It has become known to me that Dzhabrail Makhmudov was an agent,' he told the packed courtroom. Three men are on trial on charges of participating in Politkovskaya's murder—Chechen brothers Dzhabrail and Ibragim Makhmudov and Moscow police officer Sergei Khadzhikurbanov."

215: "New legislation": "Bill Expands Definition of Treason," the *New York Times*, December 18, 2008.

"New legislation backed by Prime Minister Vladimir V. Putin would allow Russian authorities to label any government critic a traitor.

The bill, which is expected to pass in Parliament, would expand the definition of treason to include damaging Russia's constitutional order, sovereignty or territorial integrity. That, critics said, would essentially let the authorities interpret any act against the state as treason, a crime punishable by up to 20 years in prison. A group of human-rights advocates issued a statement on Wednesday saying that the legislation 'returns the Russian justice system to the times of the 1920–1950s.'"

CHAPTER FIVE: **THE BOYS FROM CAR CITY**

217–19: This summary is based on my numerous interviews in Togliatti and Moscow (cited in the sources), as well as many documents and back issues of the *Togliatti Observer*, translated from the Russian for me by Elena and Michael Dubman and by Lara Nuzhdina. Additional summary information comes from the Russian edition of Ruslan Gorevoy's *Murders of Journalists in Togliatti*, translated for me by Peter Bolatski (Moscow: The Glasnost Defense Foundation, 2005); my interview with Gorevoy; Satter's *Darkness at Dawn*, which has an excellent short section on organized crime in Togliatti (pp. 127–31)— although Satter does not mention the *Observer*'s coverage of the city, nor does Satter mention Ivanov and Sidorov; the BBC's *The Russian Newspaper Murders* (2004), reported and directed by Paul Jenkins; and information procured for me from the Togliatti Chamber of Commerce by my translator in Togliatti, Lara Nuzhdina, and her colleague Tanya. I was first briefed on Togliatti by Ann Cooper, then the executive director of the CPJ, on August 25, 2005. I was given more background information by the CPJ's Alex Lupis and Nina Ognianova on October 18, 2005, and over the next year prior to my visit to Russia.

218: "Another Record Day!": This was a running joke in Togliatti related to me by Alexei Sidorov's father, Vladimir.

219–20: I arrived at the Samara airport on October 12, 2006, two days after Politkovskaya's funeral. My translator and guide in Moscow, Masha Yulikov, had arranged for me to be met at the airport by Alexei Mironov, the *Togliatti's Observer's* new editor-in-chief. He was accompanied by my translator, Lara Nuzhdina, and her colleague Tanya.

220–21: My first visit to the *Observer* took place on October 13, 2006. Mironov and Nuzhdina picked me up at my hotel. I interviewed Mironov numerous times over the next several days, Lara Nuzhdina translating.

221–22: My first interview with Oleg Novikov took place on October 13, 2006, Lara Nuzhdina translating. Novikov related the affidavit to me that day, and I later procured a copy of it from the Glasnost Defense Foundation's lawyer, Karen Nersisyan; Elena Dubman translated it for me. Novikov swore the affidavit in Togliatti on January 29, 2004, before Investigator C. A. Korepin.

222: My first interview with Rimma Mikareva took place on October 13, 2006, Lara Nuzhdina translating.

223: "The police chief": Col. Sergei Korpilov.
   Ivanov's childhood novel related to me by Ivanov's sister, Stella Ivanova, and by Ivanov's wife, Elena, on October 14, 2006, in Togliatti's Sicilian Pizzeria, Lara Nuzhdina and her colleague Tanya translating. Ivanov's six-page memoir was first written in the summer of 2000 as part of his campaign for a seat on city council, and republished in the *Togliatti Observer* on May 4, 2002, just after his murder, with the headline: "Memoir of an Editor." The quotations from this memoir are taken from the May 4, 2002, issue of the *Togliatti Observer*. The memoir was translated for me by Elena and Michael Dubman.

223: Ivanov's gravestone poem translated for me by Lara Nuzhdina.

224–26: Early years of Ivanov's life: Based on my interviews with his sister, Stella, and wife, Elena (Lara Nuzhdina and her colleague Tanya translating), as well as his newspaper memoir, translated for me by Elena and Michael Dubman.

226–28: Early years of Sidorov's life: Based on my interviews with Sidorov's father, Vladimir, and mother, Tatanya, conducted on several occasions in Togliatti between October 13 and October 17, 2006.

228–30: Ivanov's and Sidorov's lives from the autumn of 1989 to 1992: Based on my interviews with Ivanov's sister, Stella, and wife, Elena, and Sidorov's father, Vladimir, and mother, Tatanya (Lara Nuzhdina and her colleague Tanya translating).

230–34: The First Gang War: Sources are interviews with *Togliatti Observer* journalists mentioned in this chapter; Ivanov's newspaper memoir; Gorevoy's *Murders of Journalists in Togliatti*; and Satter's *Darkness at Dawn*. Sources for Ivanov's and Sidorov's individual reactions to the First Gang War are Ivanov's sister, Stella, and wife, Elena, and Sidorov's father, Vladimir, and mother, Tatanya.

"The Blood-Colored Car," and Ivanov's research for it, was summarized in Ivanov's newspaper memoir.

Ivanov's reasons for quitting *Everything and Everybody* are stated in his newspaper memoir. Other details were given to me by Stella Ivanova.

234: Quotations from Vladimir Voronov are from Gorevoy, *Murders of Journalists in Togliatti*. I interviewed Ruslan Gorevoy on October 18, 2006, in Moscow. Peter Bolatski translated Gorevoy's book for me by reading the entire book aloud in English into a tape recorder in my presence, and I then transcribed the tapes.

235: Sidorov's reasons for leaving *Everything and Everybody* are from my interviews with his parents. The account of his personal life up to the end of 1994 is also from his parents.

"Togliatti's Second Gang War": Interviews with Oleg Novikov, and the Glasnost Defense Foundation's lawyer, Karen Nersisyan (in Moscow on October 20, 2006, Svetlana Tougan-Boronovskaya translating); Ivanov's memoir; Gorevoy's *Murders of Journalists in Togliatti*; and Satter's *Darkness at Dawn*.

235–36: Ivanov's court reporting and reaction are from Ivanov's "Memoir of an Editor," *Togliatti Observer*, May 4, 2002.

236: Ivanov meeting Sidorov in February 1995: The incident was related to me by Vladimir Sidorov on October 15, 2006.

236–37: Ivanov's search for financing: Sources are Ivanov's "Memoir of an Editor," *Togliatti Observer*, May 4, 2002; Vladimir Sidorov; and the people I quote in the text who commented on the financial means he came up with to fund the paper.

Murder of Andrei Ulanov: Interviews with the *Observer*'s journalists who recollected the murder and its possible motives, and Gorevoy's *Murders of Journalists in Togliatti*.

"We could earn the necessary funds ourselves": From "Memoir of an Editor," *Togliatti Observer*, May 4, 2002.

237–38: Ivanov's business ventures: Sources are my interviews with the *Observer*'s journalists; Karen Nersisyan in Moscow; Ivanov's sister, Stella, and wife, Elena; Vladimir Sidorov; Ruslan Gorevoy in Moscow and Gorevoy's *Murders of Journalists in Togliatti*. Voronov's quotation is taken from *Murders of Journalists in Togliatti*.

238–39: Bureau of Investigations and Analysis: Ivanov's "Memoir of an Editor," *Togliatti Observer*, May 4, 2002; and Vladimir Sidorov.

239: "There was a coup in the city": Ivanov's "Memoir of an Editor," *Togliatti Observer*, May 4, 2002.

239–40: Break-in at the BIA/*Observer*: Ivanov's "Memoir of an Editor," *Togliatti Observer*, May 4, 2002; Stella Ivanova; and Vladimir Sidorov.
    Quoting Pushkin to Alexei Sidorov: Vladimir Sidorov. Ivanov also quotes Pushkin in the section of his newspaper memoir dealing with the 1996 election, but not in the context of uttering the quotation to Sidorov in the wake of the break-in.
    "To secure the paper": "Memoir of an Editor," *Togliatti Observer*, May 4, 2002.

240: "Our edition went off like a bomb": "Memoir of an Editor," *Togliatti Observer*, May 4, 2002.

241: "just after the murder of a Togliatti reporter": The reporter was Nikolai Lapin: Gorevoy's *Murders of Journalists in Togliatti*.
    "We connected the criminal underworld": "Memoir of an Editor," *Togliatti Observer*, May 4, 2002.
    "I said to him, 'Why state their names'": Vladimir Sidorov, October 15, 2006.

242: "You see, my son": Ivanov's mother, Tatanya, October 15, 2006.
    "Nobody believed the paper was independent!": "Memoir of an Editor," *Togliatti Observer*, May 4, 2002.

242–43: "in mid-1997 the *Observer*": Summary of back issues of the *Observer* offered to me by Alexei Mironov, Rimma Mikareva, Oleg Novikov and Vladimir Sidorov in Togliatti, and Karen Nersisyan and Ruslan Gorevoy in Moscow, as well as Gorevoy's *Murders of Journalists in Togliatti*.
    Operation Cyclone was well documented by Ivanov and Sidorov in the *Observer* throughout fall 1997. The operation is summarized in Satter's *Darkness at Dawn*, p. 130.

243: Shekinsky gang: Oleg Novikov first told me the story of the Shekinsky gang on October 13, 2006.

244–45: FSB investigation and the fires in Samara and Togliatti: Ivanov's "Memoir of an Editor," *Togliatti Observer*, May 4, 2002, and back-issues of the *Observer* in the winter and spring of 1999. See also Satter's *Darkness at Dawn*, pp. 127–28, 130–31.

245: "We ran a counter-investigation": Ivanov's "Memoir of an Editor," *Togliatti Observer*, May 4, 2002.

"Ruzlyaev's seized assets": Sources are Oleg Novikov; Novikov's affidavit of January 29, 2004; Vladimir Sidorov; and Nersisyan in Moscow.

Ada Trade House scandal: Ivanov's "Memoir of an Editor," *Togliatti Observer*, May 4, 2002.

"Billions of rubles": Ivanov's "Memoir of an Editor," *Togliatti Observer*, May 4, 2002.

246: Voronov's claims: Gorevoy's *Murders of Journalists in Togliatti*, and interview with Gorevoy in Moscow, October 18, 2006.

247: "Two hundred members of the Samara Union of Journalists": The reaction to Gorevoy's book was still very emotional when I conducted my interviews in Togliatti.

247–48: Oleg Panfilov: My interview on his views of Ivanov and Sidorov took place on October 24, 2006, at the CJES office, Svetlana Tougan-Boronovskaya translating.

"the overwhelming number of sources I spoke with in Samara": I am referring to Samara State.

"Ivanov was in politics": My interview with Karen Nersisyan took place in Moscow on October 20, 2006, Svetlana Tougan-Boronovskaya translating.

248–50: Borislav Greenblat and Sergei Andreev: I interviewed them on October 16, 2006, in the Togliatti City Council building, Lara Nuzhdina translating.

Gasoline contracts: Ivanov's memoir, first published in the *Togliatti Observer* in the summer of 2000, ends before he won a seat on city council. Information on the gasoline contracts comes from Greenblat and Andreev, Vladimir Sidorov, Stella Ivanova, journalists at the

Observer, and "Black Gold," published in the *Togliatti Observer* in December 2001.

250: "Cold War": *Togliatti Observer,* March 1, 2002.

251–53: The meeting between Ivanov and Sirotenko: My sources were Novikov and Greenblat.

"maybe Sirotenko just wanted to see his name in print again": Greenblat had actually attended grade school with Sirotenko, and knew his manner of thinking.

The 2004 election for mayor was held in March of that year.

"Many people suspected he was working on an article": My interview with Nersisyan took place in Moscow on October 20, 2006, Svetlana Tougan-Boronovskaya translating.

253–54: "in conjunction with Oleg Novikov and Sidorov": Sources are Novikov, Nersisyan, and Sidorov's father, Vladimir.

"I was the last": My interview with Greenblat, Togliatti City Council building, October 16, 2006, Lara Nuzhdina translating.

255: "He phoned to tell us": Sidorov's mother, Tatanya, October 15, 2006, Lara Nuzhdina and her colleague Tanya translating.

256: Amounts of reward are from Gorevoy's *Murders of Journalists in Togliatti.*

"Nikolai Utkin did not interrupt his vacation": Almost everyone I interviewed in Togliatti recollected this. It is also stated in Gorevoy's *Murders of Journalists in Togliatti.*

Between Ivanov's murder and August 2007, Utkin was arrested three times and charged with crimes relating to his office, the most recent arrest occurring on August 16, 2007, on charges of extortion and abuse of power, in a case that dated back to 2001. See "Togliatti Mayor Suspected of Extorting 4-Storey House," *Kommersant* August 17, 2007:

> "Court sanctions to charge Togliatti's mayor with abuse of power. A regional court in Samara on Thursday ruled [that it would] charge Togliatti Mayor Nicola Utkin with abuse of power. Prosecutors believe that the mayor extorted a four-storey building from a local construction firm. Mr. Utkin's defense says that prosecutors 'dug out a six-year-old story' because 'all previous cases are crumbling down.' Abuse of power [is] the third criminal charge against Mr. Utkin."

I visited the cemetery with Vladimir Sidorov on October 15, 2006 (see source note to p. 268).

257: "He was bereft": Vladimir Sidorov, October 13, 2006.

"Sidorov had been psychologically dependent": Nersisyan, October 20, 2006.

"They were quietly forming a monopoly": Greenblat, October 16, 2006.

258–59: "It was his favorite movie": Vladimir Sidorov showed me the video of *The Patriot* that his son had played.

"They can't kill us all": The quotation is used as an epigraph to Gorevoy's *Murders of Journalists in Togliatti*.

Media-Samara: The takeover bid is related in Gorevoy's *Murders of Journalists in Togliatti*. I confirmed the information with journalists at the *Observer*.

"regionally popular Internet magazine": The website was volga.ru, although the domain name has since been taken over by a commercial company.

260: Spetsroi: Gorevoy's *Murders of Journalists in Togliatti*, confirmed by my interviews at the *Observer*.

"King of the Mountain": Gorevoy's *Murders of Journalists in Togliatti*, confirmed by my interviews at the *Observer* and with Greenblat and Andreev.

"Our public buildings": Recollected for me by Greenblat in our interview.

261: Sidorov's "main goal" and "secondary goal": Nersisyan in our interview.

261–63: The narrative of the gang lawyers Fedulov and Kazeev, Sidorov's motives in pursuing the story and Sidorov's request that Oleg Novikov prepare a draft of their research on Ruzlyaev's wealth, are based on my interview with Novikov; his affidavit, sworn in Togliatti on January 29, 2004, before Investigator C. A. Korepin; and my interview with Karen Nersisyan.

263: "October 9, Sidorov called Novikov into his office": From my interview with Novikov.

"they should be prepared to publish the article Wednesday, October 15, the day after the Fedulov verdict": From my interviews with Nersisyan, and Novikov's affidavit.

Sidorov's good mood: "The Last Day of the Editor in Chief," *Togliatti Observer*, October 11, 2003. "[He] discussed plans for the next week and everybody noticed that Alexei was very happy and in a good mood. He radiated energy and infected all others with his energy. . . . He said: 'I'm confident for the future of the paper. I'm happy. Everything will be okay.'" (Translated for me by Elena Dubman.)

"He was beholding": From my interview with Nersisyan.

"About 9 p.m., Sidorov received a call from his wife, Olga": From my interview with Nersisyan.

264–65: Sidorov's last hour and murder were recounted to me by Nersisyan and Sidorov's father, Vladimir. The manner of Sidorov's murder was extensively documented in the BBC's *The Russian Newspaper Murders* (2004), reported and directed by Paul Jenkins and aired on the series *Storyville*. One room of Vladimir Sidorov's Togliatti apartment is filled floor to ceiling with the legal filings in his son's case, detailing the murder.

266: "a BBC crew": The BBC's *The Russian Newspaper Murders* (2004), reported and directed by Paul Jenkins. Jenkins's reporting was the first major international exposé of the Maininger affair. On October 26, 2006, I spoke with Jenkins by phone in Moscow, where he was looking into the murder of Politkovskaya.

266–67: Paul Klebnikov and Togliatti: Sources are my interview with Nersisyan and Nersisyan's interview with the *Observer*. See "The Deadline," *Togliatti Observer*, October 11, 2005 (translated for me by Elena and Michael Dubman).

267–68: "A few days later a woman named Svetlana Okruzhko": The Okruzhko affair is revealed here for the first time. My reporting is based on my interviews with Vladimir Sidorov, Nersisyan and Simonov, and on Okruzhko's affidavit given me by Nersisyan and translated by Elena Dubman. Okruzhko wrote her seven-page affidavit longhand on October 15, 2003.

268: My visit to the cemetery with Vladimir Sidorov took place on October 15, 2006, Lara Nuzhdina translating.

269–71: My interviews with Colonel Sergei Korpilov and Marina Novikova took place in Alexei Mironov's office in the *Togliatti Observer* on October 16, 2006, Lara Nuzhdina translating.

271–72: Mironov accompanied me to Togliatti's Central Square for the human rights rally in honor of Anna Politkovskaya.

CHAPTER SIX: **SOLID KHALID**

273–74: This summary of Hassan is based on the following: My research in Iraq in fall 2008; my interviews with Iraqi and Western *New York Times* reporters in Baghdad and elsewhere; interviews I conducted with Hassan's fiancée in Baghdad; interviews I had conducted for me with Hassan's mother and father and uncles; and reports and files of the *New York Times*. All sources are cited below. Hassan's gravestone's Arabic inscription is from photos in my files of his gravestone. Hassan's birth date is on the gravestone: January 12, 1984. The Iran-Iraq War began in September 1980.

"after he'd been kidnapped": For an account of Hassan's kidnapping and bravery award, see pp. 292–94, and accompanying source notes.

274: "weighed three hundred pounds": Jeffrey Gettleman in his July 13, 2007, online reminiscence for the *Times,* and my interviews with Hassan's Iraqi colleagues and others who knew him.

"At least 130 Die as Blast Levels Baghdad Market," the *New York Times,* February 4, 2007 (Khalid W. Hassan was a contributing reporter).

"God willing, we'll see each other soon": see p. 298 in the text and accompanying source note.

John Burns's news story: "In A Baghdad Killing, Questions That Haunt Iraq," the *New York Times,* July 13, 2007.

"eight of Hassan's Western colleagues": Jeffrey Gettleman, Dexter Filkins, Paul von Zielbauer, Damien Cave, Edward Wong, Diana Oliva Cave, Michael Luo and Marc Santora.

275: In his original online posting, Filkins wrote: "had taken to America and its gadgets and its liberties like no other foreigner I had ever met." He later polished this line for the republication of his reminiscence of

Hassan, and included it in his book *The Forever War*. I have used his polished version: "had taken to America and its gadgets and its liberties like no other son of the Muslim world I had ever met." Dexter Filkins, *The Forever War* (New York: Alfred A. Knopf, 2008), p. 338.

"We just want the same things": From *New York Times* reporter Damien Cave's online reminiscence.

"A little over a year after Hassan's death": I met Filkins at a reading of *The Forever War* on September 21, 2008, and spoke to him about Hassan. Filkins put me in touch with Alissa J. Rubin, deputy bureau chief of the *New York Times* in Baghdad, and some of Hassan's colleagues living in the United States and Canada. One of the Iraqis was Ali Adeeb, former manager of the Iraqi staff, who put me in touch with Khalid al-Ansary in Baghdad. In total, the former-*Times* Iraqi staff I interviewed in the United States and Canada were: Yusra al Hakeem, Zaineb Obeid, Ehab Ahmed, Abdul Razzaq al-Saiedi and Ali Adeeb. The former-*Times* Iraqi staff I interviewed in Iraq were Khalid al-Ansary and Wisam Habeeb. I also interviewed Fouad al-Sheikhly in the Baghdad bureau (who was then on staff), and Anwar J. Ali in the Baghdad bureau, who helped me search the back files of the *Times* for Hassan's stories. I also spoke extensively about Hassan with Jane Scott Long, the manager of the *Times* Baghdad bureau, on October 8 and October 13, 2008. Although my publisher and I tried, I did not succeed in getting an interview with John Burns. Jane Scott Long is Burns's wife, and I received Burns's early view of Hassan from her and from Burns's news article on Hassan's murder. I spoke by phone with Alissa J. Rubin on October 4, 2008, and in Baghdad at the *Times* bureau on November 5, 2008.

276: "His area was filled with very radical insurgents": I interviewed Abdul Razzaq by phone on October 10, 2008.

"Khalid will be a different case for you": I interviewed Ali Adeeb by phone on October 13 and October 18, 2008.

"I landed at Baghdad International Airport": I first landed on October 30, 2008, and was deported. The Iraqi consul in Amman who helped me get into Iraq on my second attempt was Mohamad Al-Shaboot. Ranya Kadri, a freelance fixer for the *Times* in Amman, was also of enormous help.

276–77: "After a ride in an amor-plated sedan": the *Times*' security staff picked me up at the airport on November 1, 2008, and took me to the Hamra Hotel.

"touring his city in a two-ton Beemer": My security team worked for the firm Pilgrims, which defended the Hamra Hotel (and me on my outings). It was headed by Pete Scott. Khaldoon Khalid, an eyewitness to Hassan's murder, and one of my bodyguards, worked for Pilgrims. See pp. 312 and 315 and accompanying notes.

278–79: "Two former colleagues of Khalid Hassan": I had numerous interviews with Wisam Habeeb and Khalid al-Ansary between November 2 and November 8, 2008, including this one on November 5, 2008. Later that night I spoke with Hassan's fiancée, Nida Al Salmani, who confirmed what Habeeb told me Khalid had said to her on the nights before he was murdered.

279–86: "January 12, 1984": Hassan's birth date is from his gravestone.
Summary of Hassan's heritage and youth up until September 11, 2001, is from my interviews with his fiancée, Nida Al Salmani, and his Iraqi colleagues, including Wisam Habeeb and the interviews he conducted on my behalf with Hassan's uncles, mother and father. (Waleed Hassan was out of touch when I was in Baghdad, and Wisam placed the call to Larnaca, Cyprus, where Samira Hassan lived in exile.) As stated on p. 302, because he drove Hassan to and from work for almost a year, Habeeb was probably closer to Hassan than anyone else outside his family. Other important interviews were with Ahab Ahmed, Khalid al-Ansary and Zaineb Obeid. Al-Ansary viewed Hassan as a younger brother. Zaineb Obeid became closer to Hassan than some others at the *Times* because of her sympathy for him and because he would meet her after she left the *Times* to sell her his electronic equipment. Ahab Ahmed spent many hours with Hassan driving back and forth to Basra. Nevertheless, all the people I interviewed who knew Hassan, Western and Iraqi, contributed details to this chronological portrait of Hassan and his family up to 2001.
The history of Iraq in this section is taken from my general knowledge of the country gleaned from the many books and articles about Iraq published after the 2003 invasion. Volumes that I consulted for Hassan's pre-invasion perspective include the high-minded travel guide by Karen Dabroska, *Iraq: The Bradt Travel Guide* (London, England: Bradt Travel Guides, Ltd, 2002) — one of the only books with a street map; Tony Horwitz's *Baghdad Without a Map* (New York: Plume, 1991), pp. 103–31, 267–85; Albert Hourani's *A History of the Arab Peoples* (Cambridge, MA: Belknap Press of Harvard University Press, 1991); and Nizar Tawfiq Qabbani's *Arabian Love Poems* (Boulder, CO: Lynne

Rienner Publishers, 1998) and *On Entering the Sea: The Erotic and Other Poetry of Nizar Qabbani* (Northampton, MA: Interlink Publishing Group, 1996). Horwitz (p. 108) identifies the Western joke about Saddam and the number of billboards of him as being from the 1980s; the joke (as I heard in Baghdad) was continually updated by Western journalists through the 1990s to reflect the growth of the Iraqi population.

286–88: "Iraqi Olympic Committee": I was first told about Hassan's employment at Uday Hussein's *Babil* newspaper by Abdul Razzaq and Ali Adeeb. Zaineb Obeid gave me the personal details of Hassan's reaction to Uday in an interview on November 21, 2006. I pursued the subject of *Babil* with Hassan's colleagues when I was in Baghdad.

288–89: "We were all really happy": From an interview with Khalid al-Ansary in the Hamra Hotel, November 2, 2006.

289: "He discovered himself there": From an interview with Zaineb Obeid on November 21, 2006. Several other sources confirmed Hassan's experiences at CBS.
    Hassan's "CBS" e-mail address: I have several e-mails which were forwarded to me that still carried this address at the end of his life.

289–90: Hassan's perusal of pornographic websites at CBS and the reason he was fired: This was first told to me by highly placed off-the-record sources. Almost everybody I spoke with knew of Hassan's penchant for perusing porn websites, and quite a few knew of his fascination with older women websites. For the trouble that his perusal of porn sites caused him at the *Times*, see pp. 295 and 300–301. Al Adeeb offers his perspective on pp. 300–301.
    "hired by the bureau chief, Susan Sachs": Abdul Razzaq in our interview on October 10, 2006.
    "six hours of electricity": There are several (and varying) estimates of electricity in Baghdad during this period. The U.S. State Department estimates that in May 2003 there were four to six hours of intermittent electricity per twenty-four-hour period. Figures for June 2003 to February 1, 2004, are not available. For February 2004, the figure was up to 13.4 hours of intermittent electricity per day, but by January 2006, it was down to four hours per day. The Brookings Insitution, "Iraq Index: Tracking Variables of Reconstruction & Security in Post-Saddam Iraq" (Oct. 1, 2007), http://www.brookings.edu/fp/saban/iraq/index.pdf, p. 40. Most Iraqis I spoke to told me electricity was so unreliable that

they essentially lived without it until they got a generator (or illegally tapped into someone else's). In November 2008, when I was in Baghdad, the electricity would fail on average every hour during peak use periods. (The Hamra Hotel had a private generator, which the neighborhood had tapped into.)

291: "We usually hid our press credentials": Interview with Abdul Razzaq, October 10, 2008.

"I'll never forget the day": Gettleman in his July 13, 2007, online *Times* reminiscence.

"fifteen hundred dollars a month": By the time of his murder, Hassan was earning $1,650 a month.

292: Hassan's shopping spree: Sources include Zaineb Obeid, who worked with Hassan during this period, and Wisam Habeeb, to whom Hassan explained the period when he first began accumulating his possessions. Most of Hassan's colleagues confirmed these accounts.

292–94: Hassan's kidnapping near Fallujah. I have relied on two accounts of this episode: Hassan's account as told to Ehab Ahmed just after Hassan's release, and related to me in interviews on November 24 and November 25, 2008; and Lynsey Addario's account, "Kidnap," published online by her as an independent blog in May 2004. Ahmed told me about the bravery award given to Hassan by the *Times* afterward. He also told me about John Burns's kidnapping and release in Najaf that day. Burns always played down his own kidnapping in interviews, but it is mentioned in "The *Times*' Man In Baghdad Swears Off Tea," *New York Observer*, June 17, 2004, which also alludes to the kidnapping of Gettleman, Addario and Hassan at the same time. The *Observer* dates the kidnappings "last month," which would seem to place them sometime in May 2004, although Addario places her own kidnapping in April and Ahmed is certain Burns was kidnapped the same day.

294: "in Burns's view": At the time of his death, Hassan was the longest-serving employee at the Baghdad bureau, Western or Iraqi. As reflected in his news account of the murder and my interviews with Burns's wife, Jane Scott Long (manager of the bureau), Burns was always impressed with Hassan's performance in the field. As mentioned, although I made attempts, I did not get to interview Burns; it seems fair to say, however, that given Hassan's troubles at the bureau (see pp. 295 and

300–301), Burns was sufficiently impressed with Hassan to consider Hassan's position at the *Times* "cemented."

"Khalid returned to Fallujah": "The Reach of War: The Military; Strike Aimed at Terrorists Kills 17 in Fallujah," the *New York Times*, June 20, 2004. Byline: "By Edward Wong and Somni Sengupta: Khalid W. Hassan contributed reporting from Fallujah for this article."

295–97: Hassan's troubles at the bureau, as recounted here, were well known to almost all of his Iraqi and Western colleagues that I interviewed, both in Iraq and elsewhere. The dates for my interviews with Obeid and Ahmed, quoted here, are the same as above.

297: Steven Vincent's opinion piece in the *Times*: "Switched Off in Basra," July 31, 2005.

298: The account of this trip to Basra after Vincent's murder was given to me by Ahab Ahmed, on November 24 and 25, 2008, in Vancouver.

"exemplified what an Iraqi stringer must be": "The Twilight World of the Iraqi News Stringer," by James Glanz, the *New York Times*, September 25, 2005.

298–99: Accounts of Fakher Haider's last visit to the *Times*' Baghdad bureau were given to me by Khalid al-Ansary on November 2, 2008, in Baghdad; Ahab Ahmed gave me his account on November 24, 2008, from his home in Canada; and Fouad al-Sheikhly gave me an account at the *Times* bureau in Baghdad, on November 5, 2008. I also spoke about Haider with Jane Scott Long.

299: Palestine and Sheraton Hotel bombings: I have relied on Dexter Filkins's account of the bombing in *The Forever War*, p. 170; news accounts of the bombing; and my own visit to the *Times* bureau on November 5, 2008.

"It was during this period": Hassan related the incident of the threat, his move to another apartment and his unconcern (as expressed to his mother) to Nidaa Al-Salmani when he met her a year and a half later. He also discussed it with several of his colleagues, including Abdul Razzaq, Ahab Ahmed and Khalid al-Ansary.

300: "In November 2005": Yusra al-Hakeem told me the incident concerning Khalid's advances to her in my interview with her on October 10, 2008.

300–301: "I don't know how to define the word *mature*": Ali Adeeb's views on Hassan and the events described here are from my interview with Adeeb on October 13, 2008. Adeeb's ability to defuse confrontations are from my interviews with Khalid al-Ansary and other of his colleagues.

301: Hassan's articles for the *Times:* "3 Truck Bombs Kill at Least 62 in Iraqi Town," September 30, 2005; "24 hurt as Bombs Shatter New Year's Calm in Baghdad and Kirkuk," January 2, 2006; "4 Schoolchildren Are Killed as Baghdad Violence Surges," February 16, 2006.

301–303: Wisam Habeeb and his relationship to Hassan: I first interviewed Habeeb on November 2, 2008, when he related his biography and discussed Hassan at length. I interviewed Habeeb about Hassan every day until I left Iraq on November 8.

304: Sadriya Market bombing: "At Least 130 Die as Blast Levels Baghdad Market," the *New York Times*, February 4, 2007.

305: "when he sold his DVD player to Zaineb": By then Zaineb Obeid was working at Knight-Ridder, which was located in the Hamra Hotel. Hassan used to meet with Zaineb in the cafeteria of the hotel, where he would sell her his three-week-old gadgets for a 20 percent markdown and then trade up to a new product.

305–306: Hassan and Al-Salmani: I interviewed Al-Salmani on November 5, 2008. She lived and worked in Sunni-controlled Mansour, and was too frightened of being seen with a Westerner to meet me in person, so we spoke over the phone. In the first part of our conversation she spoke in English; in the second part she spoke in Arabic, with Wisam Habeeb translating. She later e-mailed me the photo of herself and Khalid that was featured on their engagement announcement. As mentioned in the text, Hassan constantly talked about Al-Salmani to Habeeb as the relationship unfolded. Habeeb also knew Hassan's uncles. (Coincidentally, Habeeb had met Al-Salmani in 1989, and had even contemplated proposing to her. "The world is a village," he told me.)

307–309: Hassan's trip to Karbala. I relied on three sources to describe this trip: The reminiscence of *Times* reporter Diana Oliva Cave, published online after Hassan's death; my interview with Al-Salmani; and Habeeb.

309: Marc Santora: The bombing of Hassan's house was mentioned by several Western *Times* reporters in their online reminiscences, including Santora's description of Hassan's cavalier reaction to it. Hassan told Al-Salmani how he had tried to reassure his mother and sisters that night.

Shoqaq Al Saydia: My security team and I were stopped at a military roadblock before we could get to Hassan's block. My bodyguard Khaldoon, who lived in the neighborhood, proceeded on his own and took pictures of the house for me, giving me the rental complex's name. He even managed to talk his way into Hassan's old apartment and photographed the interior for me.

309–310: Nidaa Al-Salmani offered me her description of Hassan's meeting with her cousin Osama. She described the engagement party to me, and most of Hassan's colleagues that I interviewed told me how Hassan had described it to them. Abdul Razzaq told me his reaction to the engagement pictures, in our interview on October 10, 2008.

Wisam described to me his visit with Samira Hassan in our interview on November 2, 2008.

311: "I will consider you dead": Both Al-Salmani and Habeeb gave almost identical versions of what Hassan told them Samira had said to him.

Hassan's reaction to his mother's opposition, and Al-Salmani's reaction to Hassan, are both from my interview with Al-Salmani.

My interview with Yusra al-Hakeem took place on October 10, 2008. Hassan phoning Al-Salmani and their reconciliation are from my interview with Al-Salmani.

"Sectarian Attacks Kill Dozens in Baghdad," the *New York Times*, June 28, 2007. Hassan worked on the story with five of his Iraqi colleagues and two of his Western colleagues.

"By general consent, Saydia is one of the worst areas of Baghdad, if not the worst": "At Street Level, Unmet Goals in Iraq," the *New York Times*, September 9, 2007—a neighborhood-by-neighborhood analysis of the entire city, which had taken some time to prepare, according to Khalid al-Ansary, who had helped prepare it. The section on Saydia, from which this quotation comes, was called "Saydia: Thousands Flee Active Battle Zone."

312–13: Khaldoon Khalid, as mentioned above, worked for Pilgrims, and was one of my four bodyguards, as well as my driver.

Wisam Habeeb told me the story of his encounter with the boy in the alley and his emergency move to the Babylon Hotel, in an interview on November 5, 2008. In the same interview he told me Hassan's reaction to the news that al-Qaeda was in the neighborhood.

313: "Khalid's last story for the *Times*": "Iraq Hangs Insurgent Who Killed Shiite Leader in Bombing of Shrine in 2003," July 7, 2007.

Hassan's visit to Al-Salmani: Her interview with me on November 5, 2008.

314: Khalid al-Ansary's murdered colleague was named Luay Hameed. He worked for Reuters.

Hassan's last visit with Al-Salmani, and last phone calls, are from my interview with Al-Salmani.

I drove most of the route Hassan took from Saydia to the *Times* compound.

315: Hassan's last text message in Arabic: From my interview with Ali Adeeb.

Khaldoon's eyewitness report of Hassan's murder was told to me on November 5, 2008, at the murder site. Pilgrims security firm operations manager Pete Scott, Khaldoon and I were parked opposite Baya Benzene at the time. The account of Hassan's initial wound is from John Burns, "In A Baghdad Killing, Questions That Haunt Iraq," the *New York Times*, July 13, 2007.

316–17: The post-mortem events, from Habeeb receiving the news of Hassan's murder to his burial, are as Habeeb described them to me.

Quotation from John Burns, "In A Baghdad Killing, Questions That Haunt Iraq," the *New York Times*, July 13, 2007.

Ehab Ahmed: My interview with him on November 25, 2008.

In September 2007, Wisam Habeeb returned to Baghdad, where he and his friend Khalid al-Ansary remain working as journalists.

CONCLUSION: JOURNALISM AS AN ACT OF COURAGE

322: Lasantha Wickramatunga. "And Then They Came For Me," *The Sunday Leader*, January 11, 2009.

Words cannot express my gratitude to the local journalists and press freedom advocates in the most dangerous places for journalists. I could not have researched the lives of their fallen colleagues without their selfless help. They introduced me to most of the people I interviewed for this book. I am also deeply grateful to those who opened their homes and hearts to discuss the life and work of a murdered love one, colleague or friend.

This project would have taken me twice as long without the advice and published research of the Committee to Protect Journalists (CPJ) in New York, as well as the research of other international organizations such as Reporters sans frontières (RSF) and the Canadian Journalists for Free Expression (CJFE). These organizations treat every journalist's murder as a case that *must* be solved, lest the killers feel free to murder again.

Below, find a list of the people to whom I am indebted for granting me interviews or aiding my research. Those who deserve special mention for the assistance they gave me in their countries are cited at the beginning of each country section. The country sections are divided into the areas where I interviewed people about the journalists whose lives I have recounted, as well their own experiences in their countries.

I thank the following people for giving me their time in interviews and for helping me conduct my research:

COLOMBIA

Carlos Cortés Castillo, director of La Fundación para la Libertad de Prensa (FLIP), served as my guide, protector, teacher and translator in Colombia in 2005. He helped me arrange most of my interviews and accompanied me around Bogotá, Neiva and Arauca. Without Carlos, I never would have been able to write my portrait of Guillermo Bravo Vega.

BOGOTÁ: Julian Ochoa, a Simón Bolivar laureate, was shot in the neck for his journalism and survived to tell me his story; Elena Luz Daz was captured and traumatized by FARC guerrillas while reporting on their activities, and told me of her ordeal; Angelica Rubiano, a radio broadcaster, fled Bravo's home province for her life; Constanza Viera, a Bogotá journalist, gave me valuable insights about Bravo; Marta Chinchilla, a psychologist who counsels wounded or traumatized journalists, explained the mental state of journalists after an attack; Diana Calderón Fernandez was the director of the Inter American Press Association's Rapid Response Unit in Colombia, investigating the murders of journalists; Enrique Santos Calderon is the editor-in-chief of *El Tiempo*; Maria Teresa Ronderos was the head of FLIP; Lisandro Falla, a photographer in Bogotá, introduced me to Appeals Court Justice Hernandez Valenzuela, who gave me his views on the Colombian justice system; Jesus Abad Colorado is among the bravest (and most award-winning) of Colombian photojournalists (interviewed in Vancouver); Beatrice Diego Solano was an *El Tiempo* correspondent in the Sucre Department, whom I met in Bogotá; Ignacio Gomez is a threatened investigative journalist; Chip Mitchell is an American journalist who was living in Bogotá when I interviewed him, and who has written incisively for the CPJ about threatened journalists in the country; Joel Simon, whom I first met in Bogotá, was then the assistant director of the CPJ, and is now its executive director; Royal Canadian Mounted Police liaison officer Darrel Gyorfi, attached to the Canadian embassy in Bogotá, gave me an assessment of threats to journalists and his view of Colombia; RCMP Staff Sgt. Mike Hiller (Vancouver) arranged my interview with Gyorfi; Canadian embassy consul David Smart and press attaché Stewart Wheeler also gave me their views of Colombia and the murder of journalists there.

NEIVA: The testimonies of people I interviewed in Bravo's home-town are related at length in the text. Without their help I never would have been able to document Bravo's life. They include the following members of his family: his son Juan Carlos Bravo; nephew Eduard Alexander Ortiz; first wife, Angela Ortiz Pulido; and third wife, Ana Cristina Suárez. His colleagues and acquaintances were also invaluable to my research. They include his fellow journalists Carlos Mora, Diógenes Cadena, German Hernandez and Roberto Castano; his union colleagues Juan Carlos Cirdenas and Augusto Medina; his researcher and assistant, Irma Castaneda; and his neighbor Dianna La Rotta. Ex-governor Jaime Lozada Perdomo was gracious enough to grant me an interview; as mentioned in the text, he was murdered by guerrillas six weeks later.

ARAUCA: I spent several days in the town researching the lives and murders of Efraín Varela Noriega and his colleague at Radio Meridiano-70, Luis Alfonso Parada. At the time of my research, Arauca's journalists were terrorized by paramilitaries, who controlled the town, and by FARC guerrillas, who had it completely surrounded — the same situation Varela and Alfonso had faced before their murders. I regret that I could not include Varela's and Alfonso's full biographies in this book, but their careers and reporting paralleled my other Colombian subject, Guillermo Bravo Vega. Thank you to the following family members for granting me interviews: Varela's brother-in-law Nicolas Valbuena Cameo, widowed wife, Evelyn, and daughter Mabel; Jose Domingo Alfonso, grandfather of Alfonso; Alfonso's aunt Bertha de Capucho; cousin Victor Hugo Alfonso and uncle Oscar Alfonso. The radio colleagues of Varela and Alfonso I interviewed were: Miguel Angel Rojas, Danilo Sarmiento, Narda Guerrero and Jose Gutierrez. Other colleagues and friends I interviewed in Arauca were: Carmen Rosa Pabon, Garrick Munoz Tello, Carlos Diaz, Octavio Perez (from Tame), Rafael Colina Coiran and Eduardo Marquez, of the International Federation of Journalists.

For my trip to Colombia, I received advice from the following NGO staff in the United States and Canada: Joan MacNeil, the Canadian Journalists for Free Expression; Carlos Lauria, Americas program coordinator at the CPJ; and Isobel Harry and David Cozac, PEN Canada. In addition to Carlos Cortés Castillo, my translators in Colombia were Natalia Rey and Felipe Martinez. In Vancouver, my translator of written works was Maria Solana Tristant. I thank them all.

PHILIPPINES

A person who played a major part in research for this chapter was Nena Santos, Marlene Esperat's lawyer and the private prosecutor in the ongoing case against the accused masterminds of Esperat's murder. In 2006, Santos gave me her time as my guide and translator in Mindanao, and arranged the majority of my interviews there.

The staff and research of two organizations were of enormous help to me in the Philippines: The Committee for Media Freedom and Responsibility (CMFR)—Rachel Khan, deputy director, and Nathan Lee, staff writer for the CMFR; and the Philippine Center for Investigative Journalism (PCIJ)—Sheila Coronel, director, and Luz Rimban, an investigative journalist with the PCIJ.

MANILA: Fermin Diaz, Esperat's longtime colleague at the Department of Agriculture, was of great help to me. Others I interviewed in Manila were: Sgt. Rowie Barua, who took orders from the accused masterminds of Marlene's murder; Arnold Arcano, the chief of the Witness Protection Program who accompanied Barua to our interview, and who offered me his own perspectives; Joel Egco, the journalist who founded ARMED (Association of Responsible Media); Francisco "Kiko" Calado and Mei Magsino, both journalists under threat; Mary Ong, a former undercover agent with the Philippine National Police who gave me her perspective on official corruption in the country; and Lt. Commander Leon Batan, who gave me his perspective of Philippine corruption, based on his experiences as a naval officer.

MINDANAO: I never would have been able to document Marlene Esperat's life without the help of many people in Tacurong and Koronadal. They include her father, Luis Garcia; mother, Pacencia Danes Garcia; brother, Charlie Garcia; sisters, Valmie Garcia Mariveles and Lilibeth Garcia Lacorte; daughter Rynche Garcia Arcones; sons James Derreck Garcia Esperat and Kevin Jorge Garcia Esperat; husband, George Esperat; best friend, Alma Vidal; and Esperat's editor at the *Midland Review*, Juanito Laguna. Thanks also to Ida Hernandez, who hosted a dinner at which I met several sources, including Felix Barrientos, Nena Santos's partner who offered his insights into Philippine corruption; and Jes Bascon, a government auditor. I am also grateful to the interviews or assistance granted me by Joseph T. Jubelag, editor-in-chief of the *Mindanao Bulletin*; Edilberto Jamora, a prosecutor in General Santos City; and Leo Dacera, the government prosecutor in the Esperat case, who arranged my interview with Barua. Thanks also to Valmie's husband, Felipe Mariveles, for his good-humored perceptions of the Philippines. I am grateful to Salvador "Bodong" Ramos, who served as an officer with the Witness Protection Program and who protected me in General Santos City and accompanied me to Koronadal and into the countryside.

In General Santos City I interviewed the widowed wives of two murdered journalists: Grace Binoya, widow of Elpido "Ely" Binoya, murdered June 17, 2004; and Violetta Morales, widow of Rolando Morales, murdered July 5, 2005.

I additionally thank all of those I interviewed for my previous book, *Paper Fan*, which documented crime and impunity in the Philippines. Special thanks to Dante Jimenez, founding chairman of Volunteers Against Crime and Corruption, and Leonard de Vera, former spokesman of the Philippine Bar Association.

At the CPJ in New York, Abi Wright's cooperation and research was of great assistance to me. At the time, she served as the CPJ's Asia program coordinator.

My translators in Mindanao were Nathan Lee and Salvador "Bodong" Ramos (General Santos City), and Nena Santos (Tacurong and Koronadal).

BANGLADESH

Mainul Islam Khan is one of the heroic figures I was privileged to meet during my research in his country. He is the joint director of the Bangladesh Center for Development, Journalism and Communication (BCDJC), and he arranged almost all my interviews. He accompanied me around Dhaka and Khulna and served as my guide, protector, translator and teacher while I researched the life and murder of Manik Saha.

Another hero of Bangladeshi journalism is Saleem Samad. Arrested and tortured for his work, he lives in exile in Canada. His tireless help in the summer and fall of 2005 helped pave the way for my trip to Bangladesh in early 2006.

DHAKA: I can't thank Dip Azad enough for his insights into Saha and facts about Saha's life as a journalist in Khulna. Others who gave me insightful interviews were Nayeemul Islam Khan, president of the BCDJC and editor of *Daily Amader Shomoy*; Muhammad Nurul Hassan, joint director of the BCDJC; Dr. M. A. Hannan Feroz, vice chancellor of the Stamford University of Bangladesh and an editor at *Daily Amader Shomoy*; Tipul Sultan, a journalist badly beaten for his exposés; Shawkat Milton, a fearless journalist who worked in Biasol province, just east of Khulna, and knew Manik Saha; Shahriar Kabir, head of the Forum for a Secular Bangladesh; and Monjural Ahsan Bulbul, Saha's former editor at *Daily Sangbad*.

KHULNA: I would not have been able to document Manik Saha's life without the help of many people in Khulna. They include his wife, Nanda Saha; daughters Portia and Natasha (the latter interviewed in Dhaka); brother Prodip Kumar Saha; and Manik's century-old aunt Chapala (in Suktagram). Colleagues I interviewed who gave generously of their time were: Syed M. Habib, Swapan Guha, Gouranga Nandy, Sk. Abu Hassan, Hare Krishna Ghosh, Fakre Alam (in Jessore), Mujibar Rahman and Sharif Atiquazzaman. Colleagues not mentioned in the text were: Md. Zahidul Islam, photojournalist with the *Daily Samakal*; and Amal Saha (no relation to Manik Saha), senior staff reporter at the *Daily Janakantha*. Thanks also to K. Zahedul

Islam, manager of the BRAC Prawn Hatchery in Khulna, who explained the cultivation of prawns to me.

Nafida Adib Tuli, an intern with the BCDJC, freely gave of her time to serve as my translator of written materials about and by Saha, for which I am grateful.

At the CPJ in New York, Abi Wright's cooperation and research was of great assistance to me.

RUSSIA

MOSCOW: Ask Russian journalists about the struggle for press freedom in their country and two names will be mentioned first: Alexei Simonov, head of the Glasnost Defense Foundation, and Oleg Panfilov, head of the Center for Journalism in Extreme Situations. Both men gave generously of their time and views regarding the lives and murders of Anna Politkovskaya, Valery Ivanov and Alexei Sidorov. Simonov and Panfilov were particularly helpful in reflecting on Politkovskaya's fiercely independent and self-sacrificing personality.

Without the help of Politkovskaya's colleagues in 2006, I never would have been able to write my chapter about her. I am also very grateful to Ilya Politkovsky for allowing me to interview him so shortly after the murder of his mother. Anna's colleagues at *Novaya Gazeta* who helped me greatly in interviews were: Vyacheslav Izmailov, Galina Mursalieva and Vitaly Yaroshevsky. At the NGO Civil Assistance, where Anna came to realize her calling in life, I interviewed her long-time colleague in human rights, Svetlana Gannushkina, who gave freely of her time in the midst of a crisis, for which I am most grateful.

For perspectives on all three murder cases in my two Russia chapters, I also interviewed: Masha Yulikova, researcher for the CPJ, who was there to help me with my research when I arrived on the day of Anna's death, then arranged my trip to Togliatti, accompanied me to events and interviews in Moscow and served as my translator in some Moscow interviews; Alex Lupis, the former program chair for Eastern Europe at the CPJ (on a fellowship in Moscow when I arrived); and Masha Lipman, a political commentator and member of the Carnegie Moscow Center of the Carnegie Endowment for International Peace.

Ruslan Gorevoy offered me his insights into Ivanov and Sidorov and his research into the murders of six journalists in Togliatti. Karen Nersisyan is the expert on the murders of Ivanov and Sidorov, and he gave me long interviews and many documents which hitherto had not been published, and without which I could not have offered many details in the chapter about the two Togliatti journalists.

TOGLIATTI: Ivanov's and Sidorov's families gave me great cooperation, for which I am indebted. They include: Ivanov's wife, Elena, sister, Stella, and daughter, Maria; and Sidorov's mother, Tatanya, and father, Vladimir, who also drove me around the city to locations connected to his beloved son. Without the help of the journalists' colleagues at the *Togliatti Observer* I never would have been able to write the chapter. The colleagues of Ivanov and Sidorov that I interviewed at the *Observer* include: the current editor Alexei Mironov, who went out of his way to pick me up at the airport, arrange a translator and take me around the city; and Rimma Mikareva, Oleg Novikov and Marina Novikova (who was working for *The Square of Freedom* at the time of our interview). Borislav Greenblat and Sergei Andreev, who served with Ivanov on Togliatti's city council, were exceptionally helpful in their interviews at the council building. I thank Col. Sergei Korpilov, the police chief of Sidorov's district when he was murdered, for agreeing to be interviewed, and for Novikova and Mironov for help in arranging that interview.

My translators in Moscow were: Masha Yulikova, Svetlana Tougan-Boronovskaya and Victoria Mashkova. In Togliatti, my translators were: Lara Nuzhdina and her associate Tanya. Elena Dubman, Michael Dubman, Janie Dubman and Peter Bolatski translated written works and books for me in Vancouver. Much of that translation involved them reading entire books and articles aloud into a tape recorder in my presence, a tedious process they endured and for which I am grateful.

Paul Jenkins, the director and writer of the BBC's groundbreaking *The Russian Newspaper Murders* (2004), was kind enough to send me a tape of his documentary, and to phone me in Moscow after I arrived.

At the CPJ in New York, I received a lot of valuable advice during my 2005 and 2006 interviews with then-CPJ executive director Ann Cooper, Nina Ognianova (now program coordinator of Europe and Central Asia) and Alex Lupis (first in New York when he was program coordinator of Europe and Central Asia, then in Moscow in 2006 when he was on a fellowship). Isobel Harry and David Cozac, PEN Canada, gave me Anna Politkovskaya's personal e-mail address, and advice about the country.

IRAQ

I owe the chapter "Solid Khalid" to two of Khalid W. Hassan's Baghdad colleagues at the *New York Times*, Khalid al-Ansary and Wisam Habeeb, fearless journalists with golden hearts and vast intelligence who gave me time whenever I needed it, and acted as if my project were their own. They visited me at the Hamra Hotel on my first day in

Baghdad, and many days thereafter—in Habeeb's case, almost every day. Habeeb arranged my interview with Hassan's fiancée, Nida Al-Salmani, and on my behalf interviewed Hassan's parents, Samira and Waleed, plus Hassan's uncles when a direct interview or phone call proved impossible. I am extremely grateful to Nida Al-Salmani for her long interview that gave me information about Hassan's private reflections on his origins, family, youth and career that I could have not accrued otherwise. I thank Samira Hassan, Waleed Hassan and Khalid Hassan's uncles for cooperating in my research.

Wisam Habeeb also instructed my security team on how to follow the route that took me along Hassan's daily commute from Saydia to the *Times*, and explained the significance of Hassan's burial place.

At the *Times* Baghdad bureau, Fouad al-Sheikhly and Anwar J. Ali were of great help to me, the former in reflecting on Hassan's life and his career at the *Times*, the latter in helping me search back-files for Hassan's articles.

Hassan's Iraqi colleagues living in North America helped my research greatly, and gave generously of their time in interviews. I thank Yusra Al Hakeem, Abdul Razzaq Al-Saiedi, Ali Adeeb, Zaineb Obeid and Ehab Ahmed. I am very grateful to Ali Adeeb for putting me in touch with Khalid al-Ansary.

I am most grateful to the *Times* correspondent Dexter Filkins for giving me the e-mail addresses of three of Hassan's colleagues living in the United States and Canada, and the e-mail address of the deputy bureau chief of the *Times* in Baghdad, Alissa J. Rubin. Rubin graciously put me in touch with Ranya Kadri in Jordan, who arranged for me to pick up my Iraqi visa in Amman. Kadri also helped me get back into Iraq after my deportation by securing the aid of Iraqi consul Mohamad Al-Shaboot. Rubin arranged for the *Times'* security team to pick me up at the Baghdad airport and bring me to the Hamra Hotel. In addition, Rubin gave me her time at the bureau, even though she was exhausted after coming off an embed. I also thank Sudarsan Raghavan, bureau chief of the *Washington Post*, who reserved a room for me at the Hamra Hotel before I arrived.

One other senior member of the Western staff of the *Times* gave me a lot of time on the phone, even though she was on vacation in Europe. I thank Jane Scott Long, manager of the *Times* bureau in Baghdad, for her perspectives on Hassan.

I would not have been able to travel Baghdad's streets were it not for my security team from the company Pilgrims, which also protected the Hamra Hotel. Pete Scott was the operations manager who accompanied me everywhere outside the hotel. One of the gunners he assigned as my bodyguard and driver was Khaldoon Khalid, who proved invaluable to this chapter. As mentioned in the text, Khaldoon lived in Saydia, near Hassan, and was a witness to his murder. He gained access to Hassan's last apartment for me and took pictures of the interior. He was my protector, a willing interview subject, as well as an assistant to my research.

Thank you to Lt. Col. Eric Jordan, U.S. Army, for giving me the names of military contacts in Iraq in 2005. My thanks also to journalist Julian Sher for setting aside time to give me a backgrounder in 2007 after his trip to Iraq.

From the CPJ I received helpful advice during my 2008 interviews with researcher Mariwan Hama, deputy director Rob Mahoney and (in 2005) Joel Campagna, then program director for the Middle East and North Africa.

An author who takes years to research and write a book better have a publisher and editor who understands the high hurdles of his project. From the outset, Anne Collins, the publisher of Random House Canada and my editor for seventeen years, understood the challenges that this book presented—even as she recognized that I had to deny those challenges to myself when I began. I often wonder what I have done to deserve Anne. As she has always done for me, she recognized how this book should be told, and guided it to its present form over a long period of research and writing.

Throughout that long period, my wife, Leslie, never lost faith that the lives of the people I was writing about were precious, and that they deserved the time I spent overseas assembling the information that allowed me to chronicle their stories. She understood that the tales of murdered journalists were not "all the same"—that each of their lives, while similar in their displays of heroism in the face of certain death, was a testament to their unique motivations. With her deep and profound humanism, Leslie embodies the spirit of kindness reflected in the life of Manik Saha.

Thanks also to the staff at Random House Canada who have worked long and hard to get this book through production: Craig Pyette, who helped with some of the editing; Deirdre Molina, managing editor; and Stephanie Fysh, copy editor.

Thank you to Dr. Marketa Goetz-Stankiewicz for suggesting the Havel quote that serves as the epigraph to this book, and to my friend Dr. Josef Skala for introducing me to Goetz-Stankiewicz.

Thanks to my friend and lawyer (but mostly my friend), Arthur Evrensel, who has never failed to show me warmth and enthusiasm when I most needed it.

I am deeply grateful to the Canada Council for the Arts for awarding me a grant to help me research and write this book.

To the murdered journalists themselves it is impossible for me to express my thanks. But I know they still live in their work, and in the hearts of all those who knew, loved and admired them. They live in my heart as well.

Page 7

Undated and uncredited photo of GUILLERMO BRAVO VEGA, published in *Le Semana,* and at www.impunidad.com.

Page 59

Photo of MARLENE GARCIA-ESPERAT and her children: (from left) James, Rynche, Kevin, Marlene and Janice. Courtesy of the Garcia-Esperat family.

Page 103

MANIK CHANDRA SAHA. Courtesy of Nanda Saha.

Page 151

ANNA POLITKOVSKAYA. Reuters/file, and multiple websites.

Page 217

From left, VALERY IVANOV and ALEXEI SIDOROV. Uncredited photo. Image may be subject to copyright; appears on multiple websites.

Page 273

KHALID W. HASSAN. Courtesy of Khalid al-Ansary.

—

*Every effort has been made to contact the copyright holder. In case of inadvertent errors or omissions please contact the publisher.

Terry Gould is a Brooklyn-born investigative journalist who focuses on organized crime and social issues. He has won forty-seven awards and honors for his reporting. His most recent non-fiction book, *Paper Fan: The Hunt for Triad Gangster Steven Wong*, took him through the organized crime circles of six countries and gave him unique insight into the way impunity works: many of the police supposedly chasing Wong were actually in league with Wong and his criminal allies. Gould has spent four years investigating the lives and work of the murdered journalists he profiles in the pages of this book. Gould himself has been nominated by Canadian Journalists for Free Expression for the Tara Singh Hayer award for bravery in journalism. Gould lives in Vancouver.